STUDY GUIDE
to accompany | **Economics**

STUDY GUIDE
to accompany Lipsey, Purvis, Sparks, Steiner:

|Economics
Fourth Edition

prepared by **Douglas A. L. Auld**
University of Guelph

E. Kenneth Grant
University of Guelph

with the assistance of **Dascomb R. Forbush**
Clarkson College of Technology

HARPER & ROW, PUBLISHERS, New York
Cambridge, Philadelphia, San Francisco,
London, Mexico City, São Paulo, Sydney
1817

Study Guide to accompany Lipsey, Purvis, Sparks, Steiner: ECONOMICS, Fourth Edition

Copyright ©︎ 1982 by Harper & Row, Publishers, Inc.

ISBN: 0-06-044053-8

Contents

To the Student

In light of the substantive changes found in the fourth edition of Lipsey, Purvis, Sparks, and Steiner, we decided on a fundamental change in the format of the Study Guide. The underlying philosophy of this edition is that its content basically examines the student's understanding of the concepts and analytical techniques stressed in each chapter of the textbook. Our own teaching experience has led us to believe that students have the greatest difficulty when it comes to understanding technical information and applying theoretical concepts to particular situations. Consequently, we have expanded considerably the number of multiple-choice questions and exercises in each chapter. The exercises tend to be technical and numerical in nature. We feel that policy issues and specific applications of theory to "real-world" examples are primarily the responsibility of the textbook. You will find excellent discussions of these issues in the body of the text as well as in the "boxes" in each text chapter.

Each chapter in the Study Guide corresponds to a text chapter and is divided into three basic sections. The Key Concepts and Definitions section serves as a reminder of the important terms and concepts found in the text. You should learn these not by memorizing them but by understanding them through reviewing their meaning in the context of the textbook itself.

The Multiple-Choice Questions examine your comprehension of various definitions, analytical concepts, and techniques. When you answer these questions, avoid the temptation to leap at the first answer that seems plausible. For each question there is one best answer, and you should be able to explain why any other answer is not as satisfactory as the one you have chosen.

Probably the greatest reinforcement to learning economics is found in the Exercise section. You are usually asked to demonstrate numerically and/or graphically the sense of what has been expressed verbally. In addition, you are often asked to explain your method of analysis and your results. The ability to solve problems and to communicate and interpret results are often considered important goals in an introductory course in economics.

Do not be discouraged if you have difficulties with certain questions. Some are quite challenging for a beginning student, and a full appreciation of the points involved can be achieved only after you have participated in lectures and carefully read the text.

The answers found in the back of the guide are limited in detail. They are provided as a way to check your comprehension of the material involved in the chapter.

ACKNOWLEDGMENTS

We would like to express our gratitude to our colleagues at the University of Guelph, and at other Canadian universities and colleges, who assisted with the preparation of the fourth edition through comments and criticisms on the third edition: Jack W. Guthrie, Camosun College; D. B. Kennedy, Red River Community College; D. S. Spafford, University of Saskatchewan; and Farrokh R. Zandi, Carleton University. Bruce Wilkinson of the University of Alberta reviewed the final manuscript. We would particularly like to thank our research assistant, Tom Heslip, who continually pressed upon us the need to devise questions which were clearly stated and directly related to the materials in the text.

Douglas Auld
E. Kenneth Grant

STUDY GUIDE
to accompany |Economics

Part One

The Nature
of Economics

The Economic Problem | 1

1. The important economic issues of the 1970s involve the stability of the economy, energy, productivity and growth, pollution, and the role of government.
2. Productivity is defined as the growth in output per person employed.
3. The main economic issues facing a society are the result of trying to use scarce resources to satisfy unlimited human wants.
4. Factors of production are combined and the process of production results in goods and services. The act of using these commodities is consumption.
5. Scarcity often means an individual or society has to make a choice. In choosing one alternative over another, the production of one commodity must be foregone, and this foregone production is the opportunity cost of the choice that is made.
6. A production-possibility curve depicts what can be produced with given resource endowments. What combination of outputs will occur depends on the economic institutions that prevail in a society. Different combinations of output imply alternative allocation of resources.
7. A point on the production-possibility curve indicates that resources are fully employed; inside the boundary implies unemployment or an inefficient use of resources.
8. An outward shift in the production-possibility curve reflects an increase in resources or the introduction of technical innovation.
9. The concave shape of the production-possiblity boundary implies that opportunity cost increases the more the production of one commodity increases.
10. The major problems of economics fall into the following categories: (a) what commoditites are being produced and in what quantities (b) how are they produced (c) who consumes what quantities of commodities (d) are resources fully employed (e) what is the value of money (f) is the economy a productive one?
11. An understanding of economics can lead to identification of conflicts involving the goals of public policy and the formulation of policy to achieve a public policy goal.

1

MUTLTIPLE-CHOICE QUESTIONS

1. The fundamental problem of economics is
   (a) too many people
   (b) finding jobs for all
   (c) the scarcity of resources relative to wants
   (d) constantly rising prices

2. Scarcity is a problem that
   (a) proper use of resources could eliminate
   (b) will probably exist as long as resources are limited
   (c) the twentieth century has solved
   (d) is confined to poor countries

3. The productivity slowdown in the late 1970s may be attributed to
   (a) increased participation rate
   (b) changes in the composition of output
   (c) a reduction in the share of ouput going to equipment
   (d) all of the above

4. Drawing a production-possibility boundary for education and medical care will help us to
   (a) estimate how much it is necessary to spend on education
   (b) estimate the amount of unemployment that is likely to result from a given federal expenditure on medical care
   (c) illustrate the cost of education in terms of the expenditure on medical care that will have to be foregone
   (d) show the relative desires of the public for these two commodities

5. Opportunity cost
   (a) is measured by how much of one commodity you have to forgo in order to get some stated amount of another commodity
   (b) measures how many different opportunities you have to spend your money
   (c) measures opportunities in terms of their relative prices
   (d) is the same as money cost

6. If tutition plus other costs of going to college come to $4,000 per year, and you could have earned $10,000 per year working instead, the opportunity cost of your college year is
   (a) $10,000
   (b) $ 4,000
   (c) $14,000
   (d) $ 6,000

7. If a commodity can be produced without sacrificing the production of anything else,
   (a) its opportunity cost is zero
   (b) the economy is on its production-possibility boundary
   (c) the opportunity-cost concept is irrelevant and meaningless
   (d) its opportunity cost equals its money cost

8. Points to the left of the current production-possiblity boundary
   (a) are currently unobtainable and are expected to remain so
   (b) will be obtainable if there is economic growth
   (c) will result if some factors of production are unemployed or used inefficiently
   (d) have lower opportunity costs

2

9. A country's production-possibility boundary shows
   (a) what percentage of its resources is currently unemployed
   (b) what choices in production and consumption are currently open to it
   (c) what it is actually producing
   (d) the available methods of production

10. A shift outward in the production-possiblity boundary
    (a) would result if more of one product and less of another were chosen
    (b) could reflect higher prices for goods
    (c) could reflect increased unemployment
    (d) could result from the increased productivity of resources

11. The question of what goods and services are produced, and how much of them, is covered by the general term
    (a) resource allocation
    (b) macroeconomics
    (c) consumption
    (d) scarcity

12. The causes of general unemployment and inflation are topics studied in
    (a) resource allocation
    (b) macroeconomics
    (c) opportunity costs
    (d) production possibilities

13. Even government policy measures have "opportunity costs," which means
    (a) higher taxes will be necessary
    (b) moving toward one goal may require moving away from another goal
    (c) government action is usually inefficient
    (d) government action provides new opportunities

EXERCISES

1. Chapter 1 gives a six-way classification of economic problems. List them here in the order presented, numbering them from 1 to 6. Then, after each of the topics listed below, place the appropriate number indicating in which classification it belongs.
   (1) _____
   (2) _____
   (3) _____
   (4) _____

   (5) _____

   (6) _____

   (a) A blight hits the corn crop; harvest is 15 percent below previous year. (   )
   (b) Farmers are seeking a different kind of corn seed to plant in order to avoid blight, but it is more expensive. (   )
   (c) Inflation rose in most nations in 1981. (   )
   (d) Statistics indicate that the distribution of income has become somewhat less unequal in recent years in Canada. (   )
   (e) The standard of living in Canada, measured by real GNP per capita, has risen steadily over the last century. (   )
   (f) The cost of living rose at about 4 percent per year during the latter part of the 1960s. (   )

3

(g) Neither the government nor private business was willing in the mid-1950s to go ahead with building the Avro Arrow jet fighter. (   )

(h) Whether our future power needs will be met by nuclear energy or by fossil-fuel plants depends not only on technology but also on the relative availability of uranium and petroleum. (   )

2. The following data show what combinations of corn and beef can be produced annually from a given piece of land.

Corn (bushels)	Beef (pounds)
10,000	0
8,000	900
6,000	1,200
4,000	1,400
2,000	1,450
0	1,500

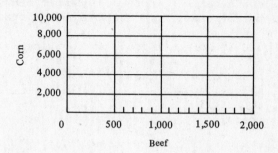

(a) On the graph above, draw the production-possiblity boundary for this piece of land.

(b) Can this acreage produce 5,000 bushels of corn and 500 pounds of beef?

(c) Can this acreage produce 8,000 bushels of corn and 1,200 pounds of beef?

(d) What is the opportunity cost of expanding beef production from 900 to 1,200 pounds per annum?

(e) What would the production of 5,000 bushels of corn and 500 pounds of beef suggest about the use of this acreage?

3. The production-possibility boundary below indicates the output of fossil fuels and manufactured goods that is possible with given technology and full employment. On the diagram, indicate a position or change in position implied by the following statements.

(a) New technology that enhances the output of manufactured goods only.
(b) Government incentives that channel resources into fossil-fuel production.
(c) Generalized unemployment in the economy.

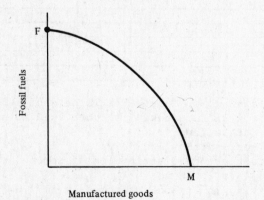

Economics as a Social Science | 2

1. Statements or questions concerning <u>positive</u> issues may be settled by empirical investigation while those of a <u>normative</u> nature involve a strong element of value judgment.

2. By appealing to evidence related to specific questions, the scientific approach can be used to answer positive questions.

3. The difficulty in predicting individual human behavior does not preclude a scientific approach to economics if groups of individuals are the subject of investigation.

4. <u>The "law' of large numbers</u> asserts that random movements in individual observations or actions tend to offset one another. It is based on the <u>normal curve of error</u>, which allows us to predict with considerable accuracy how a large group will make its errors.

5. Theory is important to the scientific investigation of economic phenomena. An <u>economic theory</u> consists of a set of definitions of the variables to be used in the analysis, assumptions related to the conditions in which the theory is to apply, and a set of testable <u>hypotheses</u> emanating from these definitions and assumptions.

6. A hypothesis is a general statement as to how variables are related while a function is a formal, mathematical expression of the relationship.

7. Theories are used to construct testable hypotheses of a conditional nature; for example, if one (or more) event occurs, <u>then</u> certain consequences follow. Statistical analysis is then employed to determine the significance of the prediction.

8. There are basically two categories of variables used in theoretical analysis: <u>endogenous</u> variables which are explained within the theory and <u>exogenous</u> variables which influence endogenous variables but whose value/size is determined outside the framework of the theory.

9. It is convenient to measure both endogenous and exogenous variables in terms of <u>flows</u> (which have a time dimension) and <u>stocks</u> (which have no time dimension).

APPENDIX TO CHAPTER 2

A.1. A hypothesis about the relationship of two variables X and Y can be expressed as a general function as X = f(Y).
A.2. A precise function expressing the relationship between X and Y could be X = 2Y.
A.3. In formulating a relationship between variables, it is important to recognize the existence of error by including an error term in functional relationships.

MULTIPLE-CHOICE QUESTIONS

1. Positive statements are concerned with what is or what exists; normative statements are concerned with
   (a) what was
   (b) what is the normal situation
   (c) what is likely to occur
   (d) what ought to be

2. The statement, "Rising prices have affected the poor more than the rich," can be resolved by
   (a) asking both rich and poor what they feel about inflation
   (b) appealing to facts and statistical evidence
   (c) devising the appropriate normative statement
   (d) appealing to economic theory

3. Which of the following is a normative statement?
   (a) Unemployment has increased while inflation has decreased.
   (b) Unemployment is a greater burden on society than inflation.
   (c) If unemployment is increased, inflation will decrease.
   (d) High unemployment and inflation cannot exist at the same time.

4. A physical or biological science that has much the same problem as economics in testing theories is
   (a) chemistry
   (b) astronomy
   (c) microbiology
   (d) organic chemistry

5. The law of large numbers asserts that
   (a) physical and social sciences are the same
   (b) experiments must always be based on large numbers of observations
   (c) random changes in a large number of items offset each other to some extent
   (d) accurate individual measurement is not necessary to the scientific approach

6. Which of the following statements is most appropriate for economic theories?
   (a) The most reliable test of a theory is the realism of its assumptions.
   (b) The best kind of theory is worded so that it can pass any test to which it could be put.
   (c) The most important thing about the scientific approach is that it uses mathematics heavily.
   (d) We expect our theories to hold only with some margin of error.

7. A theory may contain all but one of the following:
   (a) an unorganized collection of facts about the real world
   (b) a set of definitions of the terms used
   (c) a set of assumptions defining the conditions under which the theory will be operative
   (d) one or more hypotheses about how the world behaves

8. The term "empirically testable" means that a theory
   (a) is a priori obvious and therefore needs no testing
   (b) is capable of being shown to be a probable explanation of a given event
   (c) is proved to be true
   (d) is not testable, really

9. A general functional relationship between two variables X and Y
   (a) allows us to precisely predict X given Y
   (b) can be expressed by X = f(Y)
   (c) must include an error term
   (d) only exists if X and Y are independent of other variables

10. In economic theory, an exogenous variable
   (a) is one that can be predicted with accuracy
   (b) has no influence on the theory
   (c) is not determined by other variables in the theoretical framework
   (d) is always constant

11. Which of the following is not a flow concept in economics?
   (a) national income
   (b) the rate of inflation
   (c) the number of machines used today to produce automobiles
   (d) personal savings rate

12. Given the following sets of relationships among variables, X = f(Y, Z),
    Y = g(Q, W), the endogenous variables are
   (a) X and Y
   (b) X and Z
   (c) X and Q
   (d) Q and W

APPENDIX TO CHAPTER 2

A.1. If X were to increase by one unit for every three-unit increase in Y, we would
     write this relationship as
   (a) X = 3Y
   (b) X = 1/3(Y)
   (c) X - 3 = Y
   (d) X + Y = 3

   Given the following data and assuming X = f(Y), answer multiple-choice questions
   A.2. and A.3. below.

X	Y
4	0
10	3
12	4
16	6
20	8

A.2. The relationship between X and Y can be described as
   (a) X is a decreasing function of Y
   (b) X is an increasing function of Y
   (c) X and Y vary inversely with each other
   (d) X does not depend on Y

A.3. The precise relationship between X and Y is
      (a) X = 4 + Y
      (b) X = Y - 4
      (c) X = 4 + 2Y
      (d) X = 4 - 2Y

EXERCISES

1. The following information is made available to you.

Annual Change in Housing Starts in Province X	Annual Change in the Average Mortgage Rate (%)
-10,000	+1.2
-10,000	+1.5
+ 8,000	-1.0
- 5,000	+0.5
+13,000	-2.0
+10,000	-1.1

   (a) What can you say about the relationship, in general, between the change in
        housing starts and the change in the mortgage interest rate?

   (b) Would these data enable you to test the hypothesis "For every 1 percent change
        in the mortgage interest rate, there is always an opposite change of 10,000 in
        building starts"?

2. Variables used in economic theory are frequently classified as exogenous or
    endogenous. Another important distinction between variables is whether they are a
    stock or flow variable.

    Complete the statements below.
    (a) The demand for steak (Q_d) will vary as the price of steak (P) changes.
         Q_d is thus an _____ variable and a _____ variable.
    (b) The money supply (MS) at the end of March was $50B, and the rate of inflation
         (P) for March was 7.5 percent.
         The MS is a _____ variable while P is a _____ variable.
    (c) Consumer spending (C) is influenced by after-tax income (Y_d) and the
         interest rate (r). In this case r is an _____ variable, Y_d
         an _____ variable, and C an _____ variable.
    (d) Indicate whether the following are flow variables (F) or stock variables (S).
         (i)   annual gross national product   _____
         (ii)   the total value of factories in Canada _____
         (iii) monthly per capita milk consumption   _____
         (iv)   the quarterly output of automobiles   _____

8

EXERCISES FOR APPENDIX

A.1. Given the data below, answer questions A.1(a) to A.1(c).

X=f(Y)		X=g(Z)			
X	Y	X	Z	Z	H
1	1	20	0	2	0
4	2	19	2	4	0
9	3	18	4	6	0
16	4	17	6	8	0
25	5	16	8	10	0

A.1.(a) Write out the precise functional relationship between X and Y.

A.1.(b) Write out the precise functional relationship between X and Z. How would you describe this relationship?

A.1.(c) How would you describe the relationship between Z and H?

A.2. Given that $X = 10 - 3Y^2$, complete the table below.

X	Y
	0
	1
	2
	3
	4
	5

9

The Role of Statistical Analysis

3

KEY CONCEPTS AND DEFINITIONS

1. An <u>index number</u> measures the percentage change in some broad average since some <u>base period</u> (the point in time from which the change is measured). One of the most familiar <u>price indices</u> is the <u>Consumer Price Index</u> (CPI), which covers the price of commodities commonly purchased by households.

2. A price index number of a given year tells the ratio of the cost of purchasing a bundle of commodities in that year to the cost of purchasing <u>the same bundle</u> in the base year multiplied by 100.

3. A <u>quantity index</u>, such as the Index of Real Domestic Product in Manufacturing, measures average changes in quantities of commodities where each quantity is weighted by its value in the base year.

4. Statistical analysis is used to test the hypothesis that certain things are related and, when they are, to estimate the numerical values of the function that describes the relation. The twofold role of statistical analysis is <u>measurement</u> (obtaining a <u>random sample</u>) of the variables and the <u>analysis of the data</u>, including testing.

5. Analysis of the data can be as simple as the use of a <u>scatter diagram</u>, which plots the relation between two variables, or as sophisticated as <u>regression analysis</u>, which provides quantitative measures of what the relationship is and how closely it holds.

6. The measure of how closely the relationship holds is called the <u>coefficient of determination</u>. It indicates the proportion of the variance in the dependent variable (the variable which one is trying to explain) that can be explained by associating it with the variations in the independent variables (those that determine the value of the dependent variable).

7. In general, a hypothesis can never be proved or refuted conclusively, no matter how many observations are made. Nonetheless, since decisions have to be made, it is necessary to accept some hypotheses (to act as if they were proven) and reject some hypotheses (to act as if they were refuted).

MULTIPLE-CHOICE QUESTIONS

1. If an output index increases from 140 in year t to 144.2 in year t + 1, then
   (a) output has risen by 4.2 percent from one year to the next
   (b) output has risen by 3.0 percent from t to t + 1
   (c) output in year t + 1 is 4.2 percent higher than in the base year
   (d) output in year t is 140 percent higher than in the base year

2. A price index typically involves
   (a) a fixed bundle of goods
   (b) a fixed set of prices
   (c) a fixed value of goods
   (d) two different base years

3. If the price of food items increases by 15 percent, the Consumer Price Index will
   (a) increase by more than 15 percent
   (b) increase by exactly 15 percent
   (c) increase by less than 15 percent
   (d) remain constant because families reduce their consumption of food as a proportion of their budget

4. If the price of energy rises, the increase in the CPI will underestimate the increase in the cost of living for a family that spends
   (a) proportionately more than the overall fixed weight of energy-related products in the CPI
   (b) proportionately less than the overall fixed weight of energy-related products in the CPI
   (c) the same proportion as the fixed weight of energy-related products in the CPI
   (d) nothing on energy-related products

5. In order to ascertain the national support for the NDP, the best sample to choose would be the views of
   (a) union members
   (b) a constituency that strongly voted NDP in the last election
   (c) potential voters across the country who were chosen on a random basis
   (d) members of local NDP associations distributed throughout the country

6. Suppose a scatter diagram indicates that imports are on average directly related to national income over time. If in one year imports fall when national income increases, the observation
   (a) disproves the direct relationship between the two variables
   (b) suggests that other factors influence the quantity of imports
   (c) proves an inverse relationship between the two variables
   (d) suggests that a measurement error has necessarily been made

7. Suppose that a regression analysis of beef consumption and income level indicates that the coefficient of determination is 0.60. This means that
   (a) for every $1 increase in income, households on average will spend 60 cents on beef
   (b) beef consumption is approximately 60 percent of a household income
   (c) 60 percent of the variation in beef consumption is associated with variations in household incomes
   (d) 40 percent of the unexplained variance is due to measurement error

8. Which of the following equations is consistent with the hypothesis that beef consumption (Q) is directly related to income (Y), inversely related to the price of beef (P), and directly related to the price of pork (K)?
   (a) $Q = 25YP/K$
   (b) $Q = 25 - 1.85P + .08Y + .6K$
   (c) $Q = 25 + .08Y + 1.85P + .6K$
   (d) $Q = 25 - .6K - 1.85P + .08Y$

9. Suppose that a regression analysis suggests that imports (M) and national income (Y) are given by the expression $M = 100 + .15Y$. This means that
   (a) imports are inversely related to national income
   (b) when national income is zero, imports are zero
   (c) imports are 15 percent of national income
   (d) ceteris paribus for every $1 decrease in national income, imports will fall by 15 cents

10. Past evidence indicates that married women reduce their involvement in the labor force when the income of their husband increases. This means that
   (a) the inverse relationship between the two variables has been proven
   (b) the direct relationship between the two variables has been proven
   (c) the inverse relationship between the two can be treated as if it were proven until new evidence suggests otherwise
   (d) married women, regardless of changing attitudes in the future, will reduce their involvement in the labor market as the income of their spouse increases

EXERCISES

1. Construction of a Price Index
   Suppose that the government's data collection agency has determined that on average consumers spend in the following proportions:

Shelter	30%
Food	25
Transportation	15
Clothing	10
Entertainment	10
Other	10

   The average prices of these consumer items for two years are

	Base Year	Next Year
Shelter	$3,000	$3,300
Food	2,500	2,500
Transportation	5,000	5,000
Clothing	100	110
Entertainment	60	60
Other	300	330

   (a) Compute the average price level in the base year and in the next year. You must assume the proportions do not change.

12

(b)   The price index for the base year, by definition, is 1.00 or 100. Compute the
price index for the next year.

(c)   You may have noticed that the price of shelter, clothing, and other goods
increased by 10 percent each. Does your answer in part (b) indicate a 10
percent increase in the price index from the base year? Why or why not?

(d)   Suppose that a group of households in this country consume the products listed
above according to the following proportions:
Shelter 40 percent; Food 30 percent; Transportation 5 percent; Clothing 15
percent; Entertainment 0 percent; Other 10 percent.
Does the increase in the overall price index [in part (b)] underestimate or
overestimate the cost of living increase for this particular group of
households?

(e)   If the oil-producing countries substantially increased the prices of home fuel
oil and gasoline, what commodity prices would be most seriously affected? If
the oil price increase was a permanent one, what might happen to overall
consumer spending proportions?

2.   The Calculation of a Quantity Index
There are two industries in an economy. The output and value of output for each
industry are shown for three years. Prices are assumed constant.

	Output			Value of Output (millions of dollars)		
	Base Year = 1979	1980	1981	1979	1980	1981
Industry A	4,000 tons	6,000 tons	8,000 tons	$ 10	15	
Industry B	20,000 yards	21,000 yards	25,000 yards	6	___	7.5
Total				16	___	___
Index value (1979 = 100)				100	___	171.9

(a)   Calculate the "quantity relative" for 1980 for each industry. Do the same for
1981.

(b)   Calculate the value of industry B's output in 1980. Then calculate the total
value of output in 1980. In 1981.

13

(c)   Calculate the index for total output in 1980. By what percent did output
      increase from the base year?

(d)   By what percent did output change in 1981 from the base year? Between 1980
      and 1981?

3.   The Relationship Between Consumption (C) and Disposable Income (Y_d)
     Statistic Canada collected information concerning the expenditure of households on
     all goods and services and levels of household after-tax income, which is referred
     to as disposable income, over the period 1950-1970. These data are called
     time-series data. The agency then adjusted both Y_d and C in two ways; it divided
     each by the total Canadian population in each year to obtain per capita consumption
     and disposable income, and then it adjusted these figures for changes in prices in
     order to obtain real per capita, or constant dollar per capita, consumption and
     disposable income. The data are recorded below:

Year	C Real Per Capita Consumption	Y_d Real Per Capita Disposable Income
1950	$1,142	$1,216
1951	1,126	1,255
1952	1,168	1,303
1953	1,217	1,333
1954	1,224	1,300
1955	1,294	1,292
1956	1,358	1,360
1957	1,365	1,446
1958	1,375	1,462
1959	1,418	1,479
1960	_____	1,496
1961	1,422	1,475
1962	1,457	1,557
1963	1,500	1,600
1964	1,561	1,644
1965	1,626	1,737
1966	1,680	1,818
1967	1,729	1,864
1968	1,786	1,914
1969	1,841	1,974
1970	1,858	1,994

(a)   To ensure that you understand the definition of real per capita consumption,
      you are asked to compute its value for 1960 and fill in the missing value in
      the table. You are told that total consumption expenditure in 1960 (in 1960
      dollars) was $25,479 million. The population was 17.87 million, and the price
      index was 99.36 (1961 = 100) in 1960. Calculate per capita consumption. Then
      divide this number by .9936 in order to compute real per capita consumption.
      Were prices lower or higher than the base year according to the information
      you have been given?

14

(b) Plot the scatter diagram between the two variables.

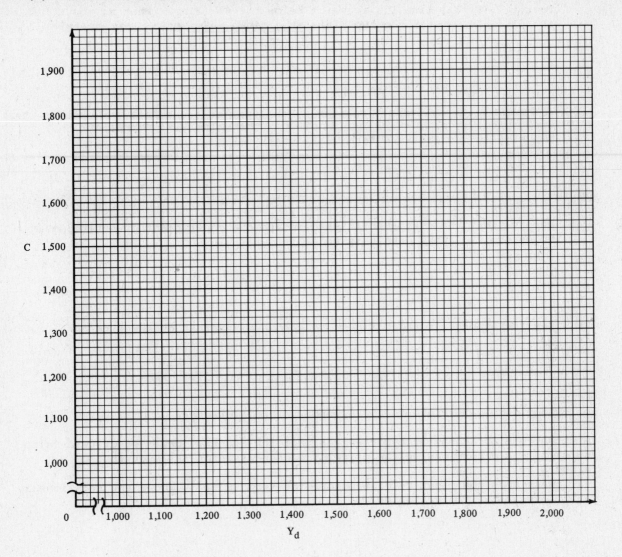

(c) Do the data suggest a direct or an inverse relationship between C and Y_d?

(d) What was the increase in consumption between 1950 and 1960?   Call this value ΔC, where the symbol Δ stands for "change in." Find ΔY_d between 1950 and 1960. Calculate the value $\Delta C/\Delta Y_d$. What is the meaning of this value? Calculate the value $\Delta C/\Delta Y_d$ for the period 1960 to 1970.

(e) Draw a 45° line in the graph starting at the coordinate (1,000, 1,000). Does the (C, Y_d) line lie above or below the 45° line? What do you think the distance between the two lines <u>at a given level</u> of Y_d represents?

(f) A statistician conducts a regression analysis of these data and obtains the expression C = 5.16 + .93 Y_d. What does the value 0.93 represent? Why is the sign in front of the term .93Y_d positive?

(g) Suppose that the statistician also obtained a coefficient of determination value of .99. What does this mean?

(h) Has the hypothesis that disposable income determines consumption been proven?

The following exercises relate to the appendix of this chapter.

4. Suppose that an economist hypothesizes that the quantity demanded of television sets (Q_d) is determined by the price of each television (P) such that Q_d = 8,000 - 4P.
(a) What does the negative sign before the term 4P imply about the relationship between the two variables?

(b) Calculate the values of Q_d when P = 500, P = 1,000, P = 2,000, and P = 0.

(c) Plot the relation between P and Q_d on the graph on the opposite page. Indicate the intercept values on both axes.

(d) Calculate the change in Q_d when the price increases from 500 to 1,000. Calculate the value $\Delta Q_d / \Delta P$. What does this value represent?

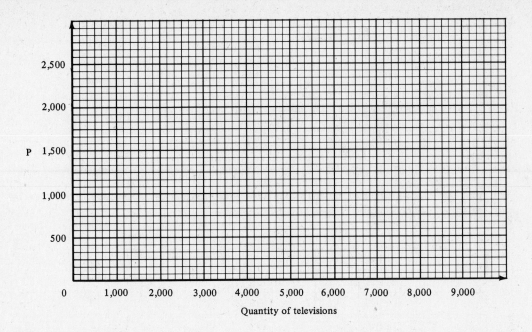

Quantity of televisions

(e) Calculate the value $\Delta Q_d/\Delta P$ when the price increases from 1,000 to 2,000. When the price increases from 500 to 2,000. What have you concluded about the value $\Delta Q_d/\Delta P$?

(f) Suppose that the economist has additional evidence that the relationship in subsequent time periods has changed to $Q_d = 9,000 - 4P$. Plot the new relationship and indicate the intercept values on each axis. What do you notice has happened to the relation between the two variables?

5. Joe Businessman ascertains that the quantity of his firm's output (Q) is related to the amount of labor (N) employed by the expression $Q = 10N^2 - .1N^3$. This is called a <u>production function</u>. The first two columns of the schedule below show the relation between N and Q.

N	Q	AP
0	0	--
10	900.0	90.0
15	1,912.5	127.5
20	3,200.0	160.0
25	4,687.5	187.5
30	———	———
35	7,962.5	227.5
40	9,600.0	240.0
45	11,137.5	247.5
50	———	———
55	13,612.5	247.5
60	14,400.0	———

17

(a) Fill in the missing values in the Q column.

(b) The average product (AP) of Joe's firm is Q/N, or in this case AP = $10N - .1N^2$. Fill in the missing values in the AP column.

(c) Plot the AP curve on the diagram below and join the points. You should check your diagram with Figure 3A-8 in the text.

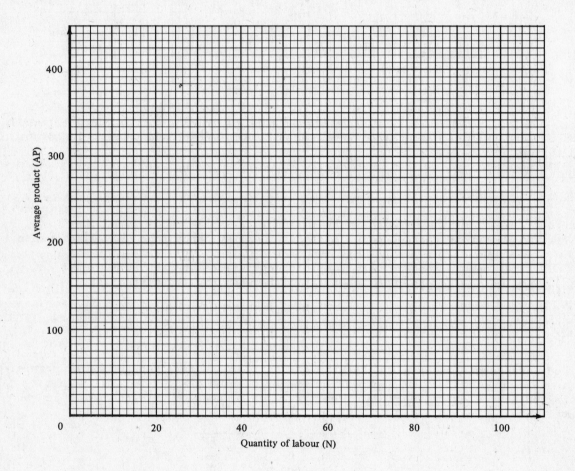

(d) The slope of the AP curve is (<u>positive/negative</u>) between N values of 10 to 50 and is (<u>positive/negative</u>) thereafter. Average product reaches its maximum value at N equals _____.

18

6. Finding Solutions to Equations

Suppose there are buyers and sellers of hogs. Buyers and sellers are influenced by the price of hogs. Sellers are willing to supply more hogs if the price/hog increases. Buyers will purchase more hogs if the price/hog falls. The specific relationships are given as follows:

[A] Buyers: $q = 1,000 - 2P$

[B] Sellers: $q = 400 + 4P$

where q = quantity of hogs
       P = price per hog

(a) If P = 50, what quantity of hogs are suppliers willing to sell? What quantity are buyers willing to buy? Calculate these values for P = 100 and P = 150.

(b) If buyers want more hogs than are supplied, the price of hogs will rise. If suppliers offer more hogs than buyers wish, the price will fall. An equilibrium is said to exist when buyers and sellers are simultaneously satisfied at a given price. Equilibrium values are determined by equating equation [A] with equation [B] and solving for P. Use this value and solve for q.

(c) Suppose equation [B] was replaced by $q = 400 + .5P$. Calculate the new equilibrium values of P and q.

An Overview of the Economy | 4

<u>KEY CONCEPTS AND DEFINITIONS</u>

1. <u>Specialization of labour</u> involves individuals having different jobs. This requires that there be trade among individuals or groups in order for them to acquire all the goods they require. This exchange is done through a <u>market economy</u>.
2. Although one good can be traded for units of another, <u>money</u> facilitates the trade by establishing a common unit for exchange.
3. <u>The division of labour</u> is a high degree of the specialization of labour where one person performs only a specialized task in producing a particular good.
4. In producing goods, the <u>factors of production</u> are used in various patterns. This is the <u>allocation of resources</u>.
5. The <u>household</u> is the unit making decisions about the purchase of goods and the sale of the labour services. Its activity is assumed to be largely governed by attempts to maximize satisfaction or utility.
6. A <u>firm</u> employs factors of production to produce and sell goods and/or services.
7. <u>Central authorities</u> are either governments or agencies and other organizations under the direct control of government.
8. <u>Product and factor markets</u> are areas where buyers and sellers negotiate to buy and sell a well-defined product or factor of production, and the interrelated activities of these markets are referred to as an <u>economy</u>.
9. <u>Free-market economies</u> are characterized by households and firms exercising virtually all the control over the allocation of resources. In contrast, in a <u>command economy</u> this is carried out largely by central authorities.
10. An economy consists of a <u>market sector</u> and a <u>nonmarket sector</u>, the former involving the direct sale or purchase of commodities. An economy may also be characterized as having a <u>private</u> and <u>public sector</u>, the latter referring to all production activities of the central authorities.
11. Exchanges in the market sector work through the price system, which reflects changes in preferences and costs and allocates resources accordingly.
12. The flow of goods to individuals and factors of production to firms is part of the <u>real flow</u> in the economy. Payment for goods or factors is part of the <u>money flow</u>.

13. Not all countries are characterized by a high degree of free enterprise. In a number of countries, ownership of large important sectors of the economy is in the hands of the central authorities. Most economies are, however, mixed economies.

14. In a planned economy, it is the central authorities who have a major say in the allocation of resources.

MULTIPLE-CHOICE QUESTIONS

1. The division of labour is a concept that refers to
   (a) allocating labour to different parts of the economy
   (b) the market economy's use of labour
   (c) specialization of labour within a given production process
   (d) only a barter economy

2. In order to move from a barter economy to one in which trade is greatly facilitated,
   (a) there must be many goods produced
   (b) buyers and sellers must be prepared to use money
   (c) everyone must be highly specialized
   (d) there can be no surpluses of products in any one person's hands

3. The allocation of resources in a market economy is
   (a) determined by central authorities or other government agencies
   (b) possible only in a barter economy
   (c) determined by producers who purchase factors of production
   (d) a result of decisions made by producers and consumers in various markets

4. Households, as economic units, can be described by all but one of the following:
   (a) consistency in decision making
   (b) maximization of utility
   (c) owners of factors of production
   (d) purchasers of scarce factors of production

5. A firm can be described by all but one of the following:
   (a) profit maximization
   (b) suppliers of most public goods
   (c) consistency in decision making
   (d) principal users of factors of production

6. The difference between a free-market economy and a command economy is
   (a) that large economies tend to be command economies and small ones tend be free-maket economies
   (b) in terms of who makes the major decisions that influence resource allocation
   (c) that the free-market economy is a barter economy while the command economy is not
   (d) that the command economy is always in balance while surpluses and scarcities are trademarks of free-market economies

7. Which of the following is not a market sector activity?
   (a) the sale of automobiles
   (b) a fee-for-use public swimming pool
   (c) baby-sitting services through an agency
   (d) traffic control officers

8. A change in consumers' preferences toward chicken and away from pork may be
    predicted to lead to
    (a) a rise in the price of chicken
    (b) a fall in the production of pork
    (c) a fall in the incomes of owners of land particularly well suited for raising
         pigs but not chickens
    (d) all of the above

9. A fall in the price of peas could result from
    (a) a shift in producers' preferences, with an increased willingness to grow
         string beans and a decreased willingness to grow peas
    (b) decreases in the amount of land available for growing vegetables through the
         expansion of shrubs
    (c) a shift in consumers' preferences, with an increased willingness to eat string
         beans and a decreased willingness to eat peas
    (d) an unusually small crop of peas because of adverse weather conditions

10. With respect to just who owns the resources in an economy, which one of the
    following statements does not reflect the points in this chapter?
    (a) All economies are neither completely free-market nor command.
    (b) There is, in the world, a wide spectrum with respect to the degree of
         free-market and command activity.
    (c) The command economy cannot achieve production goals that market economies can.
    (d) The degree of free-market and command elements in an economy has changed over
         time for a number of countries.

EXERCISES

1. In the circular flow diagram below, indicate which of the following are represented
    by the boxes on the diagram. (Place the appropriate Roman numeral in the box.)
    I.   Household expenditure on food
    II.   Household expenditure on shelter
    III.   Household purchase of stocks and bonds
    IV.   Production of food for household consumption
    V.   Wages paid to employees in food sector
    VI.   Wages paid to employees in shelter sector
    VII.   Volunteer social services work
    VIII. Hours worked in food and shelter sectors of economy

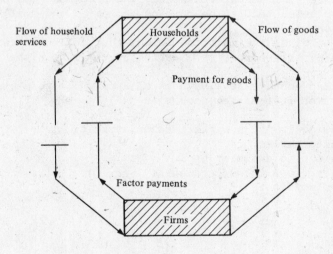

2. Indicate by placing the Roman numeral of the statement in the right column how this statement has affected the market in the left column.

    (a) price of beef falls _____
    (b) housing prices in Moncton decline _____
    (c) production of propane barbecues increases _____
    (d) there is a shortage of loggers to cut firewood _____
    (e) the price of coffee increases significantly _____

    I.   oil prices increase fourfold
    II. tastes change in favour of eating outdoors
    III. beef producers have large excess stocks
    IV. people move out of Moncton
    V.   South America experiences heavy frosts and cold weather in late summer

3. Given the list of economic activities below, indicate whether they are attributable to the market economy (M), nonmarket economy (NM), private sector (R), or public sector (P). Any given activity may have more than one attribution.

    (a) the provision of national defence _____
    (b) repairs to the home by the owner _____
    (c) the sale of fresh produce at a market _____
    (d) government operated toll bridge _____
    (e) cable television service _____
    (f) volunteer work for the local United Way _____

4. Complete the blanks in the paragraph below using only the words "increase," "decrease," and "stay the same."

    Following early damaging frost and cold weather in Manitoba, the price of corn will immmediately _____ due to the _____ in local supply. This will encourage the _____ in supply from other provinces, resulting in a _____ in the price. If squash is considered a reasonable substitute for corn, the demand for squash will _____. Instead of selling squash to other markets, the local supply will increase, which will result in a price that will _____. If the high price of corn persuades corn growers to plant more corn next year, and given no disastrous weather, next year's supply will _____ and the price will _____ compared to this year.

Part Two

A General View
of the
Price System

| Demand, Supply, and Price | **5** |

KEY CONCEPTS AND DEFINITIONS

1. For any commodity, the <u>quantity demanded</u> is the <u>desired</u> amount of purchase at a given price while the <u>quantity bought or exchanged</u> refers to the <u>actual</u> purchase.
2. For a given good, the amount of quantity demanded depends upon the price of that good, income, preferences, population, the price of other commodities, and the distribution of income.
3. If all factors influencing quantity demanded are held constant, with the exception of price, it is a basic hypothesis that quantity demanded will vary inversely with the price of that commodity.
4. A <u>demand schedule</u> is a numerical tabulation of how the quantity demanded varies with the price of the product being demanded, all other influences assumed constant.
5. The <u>demand curve</u> is a graphical representation of the demand schedule.
6. The demand curve will shift in the event that one or more factors (other than price) that influence the quantity demanded are changed.
7. Changes in the price of goods that are <u>substitutes</u> for or <u>complements</u> to a given commodity will cause the demand curve of that given commodity to shift.
8. Movements along the demand curve are <u>changes in the quantity demanded</u> while shifts in the demand curve are referred to as <u>changes in demand</u>.
9. The <u>concept of supply</u> can be expressed by asking what quantities of goods and services are firms willing to produce and offer for sale.
10. A <u>supply schedule</u> is a numerical tabulation showing what quantities a firm (firms) is (are) willing to produce and offer for sale at various prices. A <u>supply curve</u> is a graphical representation of a supply schedule.
11. Several factors influence the quantity supplied. If all factors other than price are held constant, it is a basic hypothesis that quantity supplied will vary directly with price.
12. Changes in the cost of factors of production will cause the supply curve to shift, all other factors held constant.
13. A movement along a supply curve is a <u>change in the quantity supplied</u> while a shift in the curve is a <u>change in supply</u>.

14. Excess demand exists when at a given price the quantity demanded exceeds the quantity supplied. Excess supply is a reverse situation.
15. Prices tend to respond upward to excess demand and downward when there is excess supply. Such situations are often referred to as states of disequilibrium.
16. When the quantity demanded equals the quantity supplied, that price is the equilibrium price.
17. The method used to analyze how price and output respond to disequilibrium situations is known as comparative statics.
18. Relative price change refers to how the price of one commodity changes relative to another commodity.

MULTIPLE-CHOICE QUESTIONS

1. A survey shows that if car prices are, on average, $7,500, consumers want to purchase 2 million cars. Statistics for last year indicate that consumers bought 1.8 million cars.
   (a) The survey records quantity exchanged and the statistics record intended demand.
   (b) The survey records quantity demanded and the statistics record quantity exchanged.
   (c) The difference between the survey and the statistical report shows that a disequilibrium exists.
   (d) The survey and statistics both show what output is actually produced eventually.

2. A large increase in the price of coffee will ceteris paribus
   (a) cause a rightward shift in the demand curve for tea
   (b) cause a leftward shift in the demand curve for coffee
   (c) cause a downward movement along the demand curve for tea
   (d) cause both the demand curve for coffee and tea to shift right

3. A significant decline in the cost of home building materials will likely
   (a) cause the price of homes to rise
   (b) cause the demand curve for serviced building lots to shift right
   (c) cause the demand curve for serviced building lots to shift left
   (d) cause a movement along the demand curve for serviced building lots

4. An increase in the quantity demanded refers to
   (a) rightward shifts in the demand curve only
   (b) a movement down the demand curve
   (c) what consumers actually purchased at those prices
   (d) a rise in household income

Use the table below to answer questions 5 and 6.

(1) (Case A) Quantity Offered for Sale	(2) Price	(3) (Case B) Quantity Offered for Sale
0	0	0
10	1	12
12	2	14
15	3	17
20	4	22
30	5	32

25

5. Columns (1) and (2) refer to
   (a) the supply curve
   (b) the revenue schedule for the firm
   (c) the supply schedule
   (d) a series of equilibrium price and output levels

6. If, given column (2), column (1) was replaced by column (3)
   (a) the corresponding graph would show a supply curve shift to the right
   (b) there would no longer exist a supply schedule
   (c) the corresponding graph would refute the basic hypothesis about supply
   (d) any firm would now be able to sell more

7. The supply curve of houses would probably shift to the left if
   (a) construction workers' wages increased
   (b) cheaper methods of prefabrication were developed
   (c) the demand for houses showed a marked increase
   (c) the cost of building materials declined

8. If the cost of fertilizer falls significantly
   (a) the supply curve for corn will shift to the left
   (b) there will be a movement up the supply schedule for corn
   (c) the supply curve for corn will shift to the right
   (d) the price of corn will rise

Use the diagram below to answer questions 9 to 11.

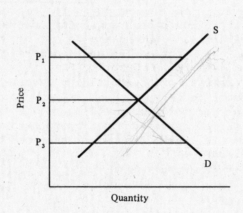

9. In the figure above, at price P_1
   (a) quantity exchanged will exceed quantity supplied
   (b) the price will likely rise because demand is higher
   (c) there exists a disequilibrium
   (d) quantity demanded equals quantity supplied

10. At price P_3
    (a) there will be a tendency for the price to rise
    (b) there is excess supply
    (c) equilibrium can be restored only if the supply curve shifts
    (d) quantity exchanged equals quantity demanded

11. If the price is P_2 and the supply curve shifts to the right and at the same time incomes fall,
    (a) price will remain constant
    (b) output will rise, price being constant
    (c) price will fall <u>but</u> output at the new equilibrium may not change
    (d) at the new equilibrium, quantity demanded will not equal the original demand

12. In the market for compact cars, a fall in gasoline prices and increased costs for safety and antipollution equipment will most likely
    (a) result in a decline in quantity of compact cars sold
    (b) cause prices of compact cars to fall
    (c) result in a movement along both the supply and demand schedules for compact cars
    (d) cause the output of compact cars to rise

13. Today the price of strawberries is $.80 a quart and of raspberries, $1.00. Tomorrow strawberries will be $.60 and raspberries $.75.
    (a) The relative price of raspberries is $.75.
    (b) The relative price of raspberries has fallen.
    (c) Relative prices have not changed.
    (d) Relative prices are now higher.

<u>EXERCISES</u>

1. The demand and supply schedules for good X are hypothesized to be as follows:

(1) Price per Unit	(2) Quantity Demanded (Units per Time Period)	(3) Quantity Supplied (Units per Time Period)	(4) Excess Demand (+) Excess Supply (−) (Units per Time Period)
$1.00	1	25	−24
.90	3	21	−18
.80	5	19	−14
.70	8	15	−7
.60	12	12	0
.50	18	9	+9
.40	26	6	+20

(a) Using the grid on the following page, plot the demand and supply curves. Indicate the equilibrium level of price and quantity of X by P_x and Q_x.
(b) Fill in column (4) for values of excess demand and excess supply. What is the value of excess demand (supply) at equilibrium? _____
(c) Indicate and explain the likely direction of change in the price of X if excess demand exists. Do the same for excess supply.

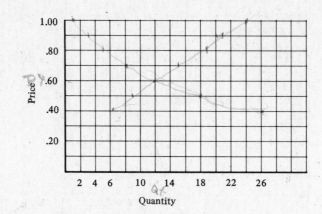

2. <u>The hypothesis of demand and supply:</u> Fill in the table below. Draw new curves on the graphs to aid you. Show the initial effects predicted by the hypotheses of the indicated events on the markets. For changes in demand and supply D and S (meaning shifts in the curve), equilibrium price P, and quantity Q, use + or - to show increase or decrease; for no change, use 0. If the effect cannot be deduced from the information, use U.

	Market	Event	D	S	P	Q
(a)	Canadian wine	Early frost destroys a large percentage of the grape crop in British Columbia.	0	−	+	−
(b)	Copper wire	The Bell Telephone Co. greatly increases orders for wire to satisfy transmission needs.	+	0	+	+
(c)	Pine antique furniture	"Antique hunting" becomes popular and Canadians attempt to furnish their homes with antique pine chairs and tables.	+	0	+	+
(d)	Auto tires	Incomes and population rise as synthetic rubber, cheaper than natural rubber, is invented.	+	+	U	+

28

Market	Event	D	S	P	Q

(e) Cigarettes — A new law requires this notice on each pack: "Warning: The Department of National Health and Welfare advises that danger to health increases with amount smoked."

(f) Automobile fuel — Middle East oil producers decrease the total amount of crude oil going to North America.

(g) Heating gas — The National Energy Plan announces an $800 subsidy to homeowners to connect to gas heating.

3. The graph below describes a hypothetical market for beer in Nova Scotia.

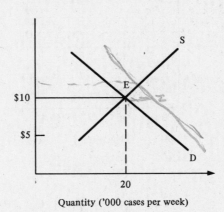

Quantity ('000 cases per week)

(a) In a prolonged heat spell, which curve would shift and in what direction? What would happen to the equilibrium price in output?

29

(b) Assume there is a constraint imposed on production such that 20,000 cases per
     week is the maximum. If demand shifts to the right, indicate this shift on
     the graph by D' and the initial excess demand by EZ. How is this excess
     demand eliminated?

(c) Suppose the Provincial Legislature decided to impose a tax of $1 per case on
     beer producers. What would happen to the supply schedule, equilibrium price,
     and output?

4. The demand for firewood (Q_d) and supply (Q_s) are given by

$$Q_d = 300 - 1.5P$$

$$Q_d = 1.0P$$

where P is price per unit.

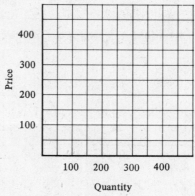

(b) What is the equilibrium price and output?

(c) If the demand schedule became $Q_d = 300 - .75P$, which way has the demand
     curve shifted? What happens to quantity exchanged and price? (Calculate the
     new values. Show the new demand schedule as D'.)

30

Elasticity of Demand and Supply | 6

1. Price elasticity refers to how the quantity demanded or supplied responds to a price change.
2. The elasticity of demand is a measure of the responsiveness of quantity demanded to price change.
3. In measuring the elasticity of demand, use of the average price and quantity rather than the new or old price and quantity is common. This is referred to as the arc elasticity.
4. Demand is inelastic when the percentage change in quantity is less than the percentage change in price. If the percentage change in quantity is greater than the percentage change in price, demand is elastic.
5. The elasticity of demand can also be measured in terms of whether or not a price change increases total revenue, decreases total revenue, or leaves it unchanged.
6. The degree of demand elasticity depends to a considerable extent on how the commodity is defined.
7. Quantity demanded may change if income changes, and this responsiveness is known as the income elasticity of demand. The responsiveness of the quantity demanded to income changes determines whether or not the good is a normal good or an inferior good.
8. The cross elasticity of demand refers to how the quantity of one commodity, let us say X, responds to a change in the price of another, let us say Y.
9. The elasticity of supply parallels that of demand. The greater the responsiveness of firms to offer more for sale as price rises, the higher the elasticity.

31

1. To say that the demand for a commodity is <u>elastic</u> means
    (a)   that the demand curve slopes downward to the right
    (b)   that more is sold at a lower price
    (c)   that a rise in price will increase total revenue
    (d)   that the change in quantity sold is proportionally greater than the change in price ✓

2. When the demand is elastic
    (a)   a fall in price is more than offset by an increase in quantity sold, so that total revenue rises ✓
    (b)   the good is probably a necessity
    (c)   a rise in price will increase total revenue, even though less is sold
    (d)   buyers are not much influenced by prices of competing products

Questions 3 through 5 refer to the figures below.

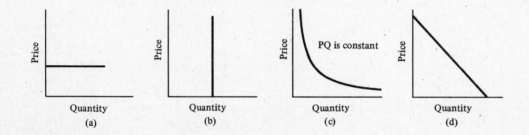

3. The demand curve with an elasticity of 0 is
    (a)   a
    (b)   b
    (c)   c
    (d)   d

4. The demand curve with an elasticity of 1 is
    (a)   a
    (b)   b
    (c)   c
    (d)   d

5. The demand curve with an elasticity of infinity is
    (a)   a
    (b)   b
    (c)   c
    (d)   d

Questions 6 and 7 refer to the schedule below. (Consult Key Concepts for the precise calculation of elasticity.)

Price/Unit	Quantity Offered for Sale
$10	400
8	350
6	300
4	200
2	50

6. The supply curve implied by the schedule is
   (a) elastic
   (b) inelastic
   (c) of zero elasticity
   (d) variable, depending on initial price chosen ✓

7. As price rises from $6 to $10 per unit, the supply response is
   (a) elastic
   (b) of unit elasticity
   (c) of zero elasticity
   (d) inelastic ✓

8. A demand curve is completely inelastic if
   (a) a rise in price causes a fall in quantity demanded
   (b) a fall in price causes a rise in sellers' total receipts
   (c) the commodity in question is highly perishable, like fresh strawberries
   (d) a change in price does not change quantity demanded

9. If a 100 percent rise in the membership fee of a club caused the number of members to decline from 600 to 450,
   (a) demand was inelastic ✓
   (b) demand was infinitely elastic
   (c) demand was elastic
   (d) the price rise caused a shift in demand for membership, so it is impossible to say

10. Which of the following would you expect to have the highest income elasticity?
    (a) spaghetti
    (b) bus rides
    (c) TV computer games
    (d) baby carriages

11. Inferior commodities
    (a) have zero income elasticities of demand
    (b) have negative cross-elasticities of demand
    (c) have negative elasticities of supply
    (d) have negative income elasticities of demand ✓

12. Margarine and butter probably have
    (a) the same income elasticities of demand
    (b) very low price elasticities of demand
    (c) negative cross-elasticities of demand with respect to each other
    (d) positive cross-elasticities of demand with respect to each other ✓

13. If price elasticity of demand for a product is .5, this means that
    (a) a change in price changes demand by 50 percent
    (b) a 1 percent increase in quantity sold is associated with a .5 percent fall in price
    (c) a 1 percent increase in quantity sold is associated with a 2 percent fall in price ✓
    (d) a .5 percent change in price will cause a .5 percent change in quantity sold

14. If, when incomes rise by 5 percent, the quantity sold of a commodity rises by 10 percent, income elasticity is
    (a) -2
    (b) 2 ✓
    (c) -(1/2)
    (d) 1/2

33

15. If, when income rises from $10,000 to $12,000, expenditure on food rises from $1,000 to $1,100 and on entertainment from $500 to $600,
    (a) food expenditure is income elastic and entertainment expenditure is income inelastic
    (b) food expenditure is income inelastic and entertainment expenditure is income elastic ✓
    (c) both commodities have the same income elasticity
    (d) the income elasticity of entertainment is one-half that of food

EXERCISES

1. (a) The table below provides data on price, income, and quantity consumed. Complete the table as required. (Consult Key Concepts for the precise calculations of elasticities.)

Income	Price of X	Quantity of X Demanded	Price of Y	Quantity of Y Demanded	Price Elasticity of Demand for X	Price Elasticity of Demand for Y	Income Elasticity of Demand for X	Income Elasticity of Demand for Y	Cross Elasticity of Demand for X
$10,000	$25	10	$10	40					
10,000	28	9	10	40	____				
10,000	28	8	15	35		____			____
11,000	28	9	15	36			____	____	
11,500	30	7	14	34					

   (b) As the quantity of X demanded falls from 9 to 7, why is it that we cannot "legitimately" calculate the price elasticity of demand for X?

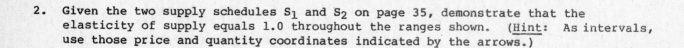

2. Given the two supply schedules S_1 and S_2 on page 35, demonstrate that the elasticity of supply equals 1.0 throughout the ranges shown. (Hint: As intervals, use those price and quantity coordinates indicated by the arrows.)

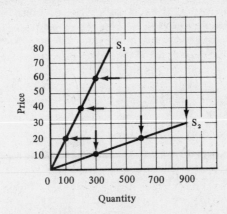

3. (a) Given the demand schedule below, D_1, demonstrate that as one moves down the demand schedule the elasticity of demand goes from being elastic to becoming inelastic. (Hint: Again, use the reference points indicated by the arrows.)

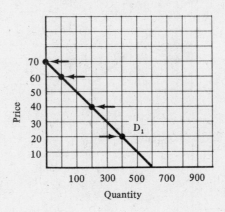

(b) What is the elasticity of demand for D_1 when the price falls from $40 to $30? What is happening to total revenue as the price falls further?

4. The six diagrams below represent different situations with regard to the elasticity of demand and supply at the equilibrium price P_E. Complete the statements below by indicating which diagram responds to the statement. (E_s refers to elasticity of supply and E_d refers to elasticity of demand. If you have not worked through the Appendix to text Chapter 6, refer to Footnote 4 before proceeding.)

(a) E_d is greater than one and E_s is unity   _____

(b) E_d is unity and E_s is infinity   _____

(c) E_d is unity and E_s is unity   _____

(d) E_d is greater than one and E_s is zero   _____

(e) E_d is zero and E_s is unity   _____

(f) E_d is infinity and E_s is unity   _____

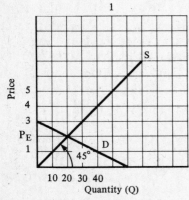

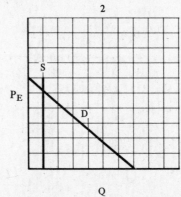

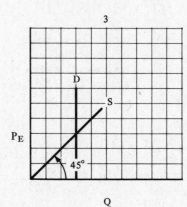

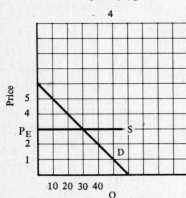

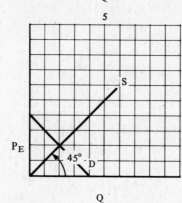

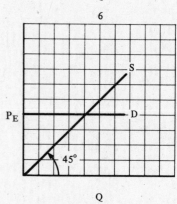

5. In the diagram on the opposite page, there are two demand schedules, D_1 and D_2.
   (a) What is the equation of each?

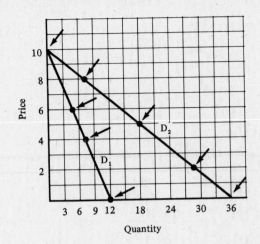

(b) Calculate (roughly) the price elasticity of demand for each demand curve using the ranges indicated by the arrows and moving down the demand schedule. Is there any relationship between the slope of the curve, measured by $\Delta P/\Delta Q$, and elasticity?

Supply and Demand in Action I: Price Controls and Agricultural Problems

KEY CONCEPTS AND DEFINITIONS

1. Comparative statics is an approach that allows us to predict how a market responds to changes in demand or supply when there are controls on prices or output levels.
2. A nonequilibrium or disequilibrium price occurs when controls prevent price and output from being what true costs (supply) and preferences (demand) would dictate.
3. A disequilibrium price will result in unsold goods or unfulfilled demand.
4. Through legislation, government can establish a price ceiling for one or more products/services. If this price is below the equilibrium market price, a situation of excess demand will result.
5. A price floor can be established by government that states the minimum price at which a good can be sold. If the price floor is above the free-market equilibrium, there will be excess supply.
6. Rationing is a system whereby the government decides the maximum amount of a commodity that can be purchased, regardless of individual preferences.
7. A black market exists when goods, purchased at the controlled price, can be resold (illegally) above that price, due to the excess demand created by the price ceiling.
8. Rent control is a legislated price ceiling which requires that landlords not charge rent beyond a certain level or not increase the rent by more than a certain percentage.
9. Comparative statics suggests that rent control will result in housing shortages, seller's preferences or tenure laws, and the emergence of black markets.
10. The housing market is characterized by an inelastic short-run supply and elastic long-run supply.
11. Rent controls will curb short-run windfall profits, but in the long run, new residential construction will not be forthcoming, causing a shortage.
12. The effect on agricultural prices of unplanned changes in output depends to a considerable extent on the elasticity of demand for farm products.

13. Government can maintain the price of a commodity at an equilibrium level by purchasing excess supply and selling its own holdings of the commodity when there is excess demand. Unless the amount bought and sold is in inverse proportion to changes in the farmers' output, farm income will not be stabilized.

14. Marketing board quotas are used to limit supply and keep prices higher than would be the case without a quota. For those that are allowed to produce, the marketing board can alter profit levels.

MULTIPLE-CHOICE QUESTIONS

1. At a disequilibrium price
   (a) profits of sellers are eliminated
   (b) changes in demand must be matched by changes in supply
   (c) there are always unsold goods
   (d) the quantity bought and sold is determined by the lesser of quantity demanded or quantity supplied

2. Price ceilings below the equilibrium price and price floors above the equilibrium price
   (a) lead to production controls
   (b) lead to rationing
   (c) lead to a drop in quality
   (d) lead to a reduction in quantity exchanged

3. Allocation by sellers' preferences refers to
   (a) giving people what they want
   (b) government franchises to certain firms to sell goods
   (c) businesses selling only to regular customers
   (d) quotas on output

4. In a free-market economy, the rationing of scarce goods is done by
   (a) the price mechanism
   (b) the government
   (c) business
   (d) consumers

Questions 5 and 6 refer to the figure below, which shows the demand for and supply of labour in the restaurant waiter/waitress industry.

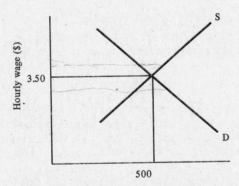

39

5. If a minimum wage was legislated at $4.00 per hour,
    (a) all those employed at $3.50 per hour would get a raise
    (b) fewer people would be willing to work in the industry
    (c) there would be unemployment in the industry
    (d) employers would tend to give "under the table" bonuses to attract labour

6. If a minimum wage was legislated at $3.00 per hour,
    (a) all those employed at $3.50 per hour would get the same; new workers would earn $3.00 per hour
    (b) employers would tend to give "under the table" bonuses to attract labour
    (c) total employment would rise above 500
    (d) the wage cost to the industry would be constant

Questions 7 through 10 refer to the figure below.

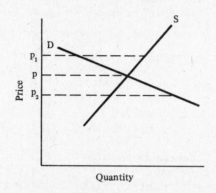

7. If p_1 is a minimum price,
    (a) it will have no effect on equilibrium output
    (b) it will lead to shortages and probably to black-market activity
    (c) it will lead to surpluses and possibly to undercutting of the minimum price
    (d) it would represent a response to Nader's Raiders

8. If p_2 is a minimum price,
    (a) it will have no effect on equilibrium output
    (b) it will lead to shortages and probably to black-market activity
    (c) it will lead to surpluses and possibly to undercutting of the minimum price
    (d) it would represent a response to Nader's Raiders

9. If p_1 is a maximum price,
    (a) it will have no effect on equilibrium output
    (b) it will lead to shortages and probably to black-market activity
    (c) it will lead to surpluses and possibly to undercutting of the minimum price
    (d) it would represent a response to Nader's Raiders

10. If p_2 is a maximum price,
    (a) it will have no effect on equilibrium output
    (b) it will lead to shortages and probably to black-market activity
    (c) it will lead to surpluses and possibly to undercutting of the minimum price
    (d) it would represent a response to Nader's Raiders

11. Rent controls are likely to produce all but one of the following effects:
    (a) rental housing shortage in the long run
    (b) the development of a "black market"
    (c) rental housing unit increases in the short run
    (d) resource allocation away from rental housing industry

12. The rental housing market is characterized by
    (a) long- and short-run supply elasticities of equal magnitude
    (b) inelastic demand
    (c) short-run inelastic supply and long-run elastic supply
    (d) short-run elastic supply and long-run inelastic supply

Question 13 refers to the figure below in which the demand for rental housing decreases from D_0 to D_1 when rents are fixed. (SR and LR refer to short-run and long-run.)

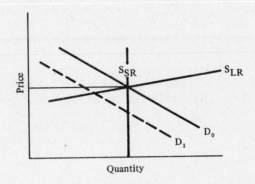

13. In the situation described
    (a) rents will fall
    (b) those still renting will be paying more than if there were no controls
    (c) the amount of rental housing will not be affected
    (d) rents will rise

14. The main reason for agricultural price supports is to
    (a) stabilize farm incomes
    (b) make certain there are always extra stocks of goods on hand
    (c) give the government control over agriculture
    (d) reduce competition

15. Price changes tend to be large given unexpected changes in agricultural output because
    (a) the demand for agricultural output is elastic
    (b) the demand for agricultural output is inelastic
    (c) the long-run and short-run supplies are the same
    (d) buyers' incomes change when output changes

16. Most farm receipts vary inversely with output levels
    (a) whenever buyers' preferences change
    (b) because most farm products have inelastic demands
    (c) because lower outputs means higher total costs
    (d) as long as supply is elastic

17. A price completely stabilized by a government buying surpluses and selling its stocks when there are shortages means that
    (a) poor farmers will benefit the most
    (b) there will be no storage costs
    (c) farmers' revenues will be proportional to output
    (d) all farms will have satisfactory incomes

41

18. Agricultural output in Canada has increased substantially since World War II mainly because
    (a) many people are going back to farming
    (b) productivity and yields have risen
    (c) rising demand has kept prices steadily increasing
    (d) there has been good growing weather

19. Assigning quotas to producers of agricultural goods
    (a) places a burden on new producers who wish to enter the industry
    (b) ensures an equitable distribution of farm income
    (c) maintains stable prices for food products
    (d) guarantees a fixed income to farmers

20. If markets are highly regulated and controlled,
    (a) costs can be lowered below those in unregulated markets
    (b) the signals required for the allocation of resources will not operate
    (c) relative prices will still change to reallocate resources
    (d) the distribution of income will be unchanged from that observed in an unregulated market

APPENDIX TO CHAPTER 7

A.1. Dynamic analysis
    (a) allows us to predict accurately a price change from one period to the next
    (b) is only applicable if the demand or supply schedule is fixed
    (c) allows us to predict price, not quantity change, over time
    (d) is the study of how a market behaves in disequilibrium situations
A.2. If, in the operation of a free market, there emerges a situation where the desire to expand output exceeds what has actually been produced, it is referred to as
    (a) unsold inventories
    (b) a supply lag
    (c) unintended inventories
    (d) a demand shift
A.3. If, in a given free market, the price at any point in time always induces a change in supply or demand, and hence price change,
    (a) we are possibly observing an unstable equilibrium
    (b) we must analyze such a market using comparative statics
    (c) the market cannot be regulated
    (d) all of the above

EXERCISES

1. Given the two market situations described below, reply to the following questions.

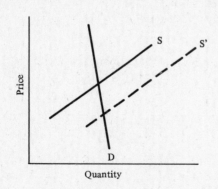 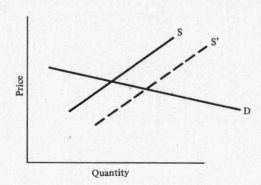

42

(a)   If S and D denote the original supply and demand schedules, indicate, by

vertical hatching ⦀ , the total receipts in both markets.

(b)   If the supply schedule shifts to S' in both A and B, indicate the new

receipts by horizontal hatching ▤ .

(c)   Which market shows the largest loss in total receipts? What is the nature of
the demand schedule in that market?

(d)   Suppose there was a price floor equal to the original equilibrium price
(before the shift in supply) and the government was committed to purchasing
unsold stocks at this price. Given the shift in supply in both A and B, would
there be any difference in the quantity of produce the government would have
to purchase in the two cases? Explain.

2.   Using the basic supply and demand framework below, demonstrate that, given a fixed
quota in both markets A and B, the cost to the consumer when demand shifts to the
right by the same amount in both markets varies with the elasticity of demand.
(The quota is the equilibrium quantity determined by the original supply and
demand schedule.)

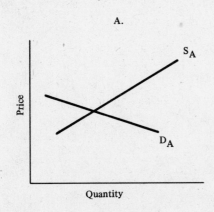

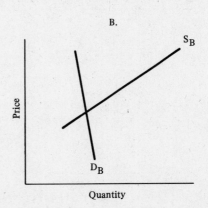

3. The graph below illustrates a short-run situation in the rental housing market. The subscripts for the demand and supply schedules represent subsequent periods of time all within the short run.

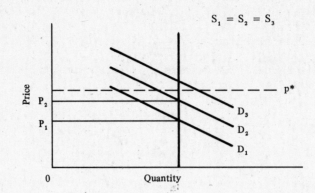

(a) From period one to period two (the short run), demand shifts from D_1 to D_2 and price rises. What would you expect to happen to the stock of rental housing in the long run? Why?

(b) Demand increases again, in the short run, to D_3 and rent controls are established, setting the price at p^*. Indicate the short-run supply necessary to clear the market.

44

(c) In the diagram below, the long-run supply S_{LR} has been added and demand stabilizes at D_3. Rental controls remain in force.

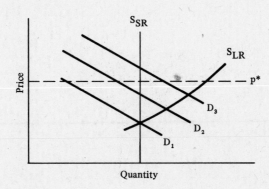

(i)   What will be the long-run quantity of rental housing demand? What will producers want to supply?

(ii) If rent controls are removed, what happens to price and quantity?

4. The diagram on the following page illustrates the rental housing market at a point in time. The government decides that the current "average" rent of $300 per month is socially desirable and fixes rents at that price. Subsequently, the costs of supplying rental housing (fuel, maintenance, etc.) rise by $50 per month.
(a) Draw the short- and new long-run supply schedule (S_{SR} and S_{LR}').
(b) What happens in the long run (with controls) to the quantity of rental housing supplied? (Label it Q_{LR}'.)

(c) Indicate the price of rental housing (P_E) and quantity supplied (Q_E) if there were no controls.

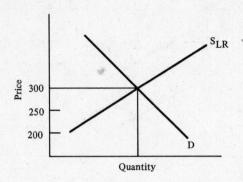

5. Given the agricultural market described in the figure below,

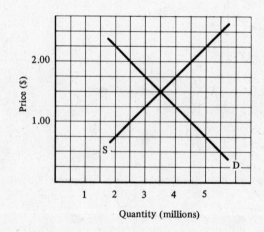

(a) What is the total revenue to producers? _____
(b) A price floor of $2 is set and any excess produce is purchased by the government. What is the producers' revenue now? _____
(c) What change in quantity demanded will occur? _____
(d) How many units of output will the government buy? _____
(e) What will be the cost to consumers in terms of the taxes needed to purchase excess output? _____

6. You are advising the Minister of Agriculture on whether to establish a quota, equal to current quantity produced and sold, or a price floor, equal to 50 percent above the current price. The Minister wants to maximize farm income but is not prepared to purchase any excess produce. You have calculated that the demand is likely to shift as shown by D' on the following page. What do you advise the Minister? Explain your answer.

46

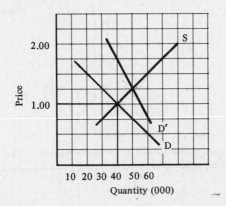

Price

2.00

1.00

S

D'

D

10 20 30 40 50 60

Quantity (000)

EXERCISE TO APPENDIX A.1.

The market described below is characterized by a short-run supply (S) and long-run supply (S_L). Given that demand shifts from D_0 to D_1, indicate the dynamic path of adjustment given there is a conventional supply lag. (Label your prices p_1, p_2, p_3, . . ., and carry it out for four time periods.)

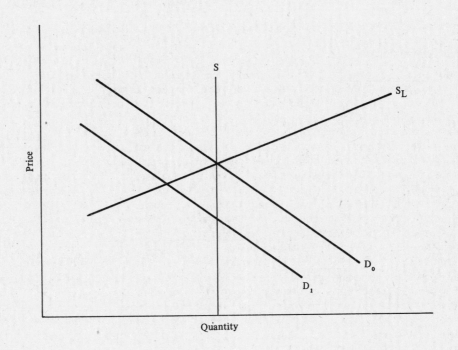

S

S_L

Price

D_0

D_1

Quantity

47

Supply and Demand in Action II: International Trade and Exchange Rates

8

1. <u>International trade</u> allows a country to expand its consumption set. By selling goods and services to the rest of the world (<u>exports</u>) and buying goods and services from the rest of the world (<u>imports</u>), consumption possibilities and production possibilities can differ.

2. <u>Autarky</u> is a situation of no trade. It reflects a <u>closed economy</u>. In an open economy, where there is trade, the ratio at which goods can be exchanged in the international market is the <u>terms of trade</u>. The benefits in terms of increased consumption possibilities derived from going to an open economy are the <u>gains from trade</u>.

3. To have trade between two countries, it must be possible to exchange one country's currency for another. The amount of one currency required to buy a unit of another currency is the <u>exchange rate</u>.

4. The <u>balance of trade</u> is said to be in a <u>surplus</u> when a country's exports exceed its imports. A <u>trade deficit</u> occurs when imports exceed exports. If exports exceed imports, a country will experience a currency <u>appreciation</u>, while a trade deficit would lead to a currency <u>depreciation</u>.

5. The demand for a foreign currency requires that a country such as Canada be prepared to sell its domestic currency. Foreign currency is supplied to the foreign exchange market whenever a foreign country wishes to purchase our domestic Canadian currency.

6. The exchange rate is determined by the intersection of the supply and demand schedules in the foreign exchange market. A shift in either schedule will change the exchange rate. A shift in both schedules may or may not alter the exchange rate depending on the magnitude and the direction of the shifts.

7. In using a <u>pegged</u> or <u>fixed exchange rate</u>, a country's monetary authorities do not allow the value of the exchange rate to respond to changes in the supply and demand for foreign exchange at the fixed rate, and purchase foreign exchange whenever there is an excess supply at the fixed exchange rate.

MULTIPLE-CHOICE QUESTIONS

1. The two-good consumption possibility set can be expanded through trade
    (a) if domestic and world prices are the same
    (b) if a country cannot use all of both goods it produces
    (c) if a country produces more than it needs of at least one good
    (d) only when the point on the possiblity set can be changed

2. Nations through trade
    (a) may consume at levels beyond their production-possibilities frontiers
    (b) will be limited in their consumption to points on the production-possibilities frontiers
    (c) will not alter their previous production patterns
    (d) are more likely to be confined to choices inside their production-possibilities frontiers

3. By altering its production mix away from what is desired by consumers, the consumption set can be increased if
    (a) the surplus production of one good can be traded for a quantity of the other good that exceeds what was given up in order to specialize
    (b) the terms of trade are variable
    (c) more of both goods can be consumed
    (d) the difference between the desired consumption and actual production of one good is the same for both goods

4. Exports and imports arise from
    (a) the unwillingness of some countries to produce certain goods
    (b) the exploitation of a country's comparative advantage
    (c) balanced trade in both countries
    (d) none of the above

5. For a traded commodity, the market price
    (a) is determined by domestic supply and domestic demand
    (b) is determined by world supply and world demand
    (c) will always be below that which would prevail without trade
    (d) does not reflect equilibrium

6. The rate at which the Canadian dollar exchanges for the U.S. dollar is referred to as
    (a) the terms of trade
    (b) the adjusted world price
    (c) the exchange rate
    (d) all of the above

7. If, at a given world price for a commodity, domestic demand exceeds supply
    (a) that commodity will be imported
    (b) that commodity will be exported
    (c) the price will decline
    (d) there is no autarky price

49

8. If the exchange rate between Canadian dollars and U.S. dollars is Can. $1.00 = U.S. $0.85,
   (a) the volume of trade will be in the ratio 1.00 to .85
   (b) Canadian dollars will buy more goods in the U.S. if prices are the same in both countries
   (c) an American could purchase $1.18 Can. for one U.S. dollar on the foreign exchange market
   (d) Canada will always have an excess of imports over exports as far as trade with the United States is concerned

9. The appreciation of the Canadian dollar on the foreign exchange market
   (a) causes the Canadian price of imports to rise
   (b) causes the Canadian price of imports to fall
   (c) causes the balance of trade to change in the direction of a surplus or smaller deficit
   (d) results in domestic inflation

10. In the exchange market between dollars and pounds sterling, a demander of dollars is also
    (a) a supplier of dollars
    (b) a supplier of pounds
    (c) a demander of pounds
    (d) all of the above

11. If the Canadian dollar depreciates against the British pound, and if the British demand for Canadian goods is price elastic,
    (a) more dollars will be required by British importers
    (b) the British will be supplying more pounds to the foreign exchange market
    (c) Canadian imports from Britain will rise
    (d) the value of the pound has increased

12. If, in a foreign exchange market where the exchange rate is floating, there is a greater quantity of a currency demanded than is being supplied at a given value for that currency,
    (a) the demand schedule must shift
    (b) the supply schedule must shift
    (c) the value of the currency on the exchange market will rise
    (d) the trade balance will move into a surplus

13. When the price of domestically produced goods and services falls, relative to prices elsewhere in the world, and given a floating exchange rate,
    (a) the domestic currency will appreciate in the foreign exchange market
    (b) exports from the domestic country will decline
    (c) the domestic currency will depreciate on the foreign exchange market
    (d) the domestic country will experience a balance of trade deficit

14. Under a system of pegged or fixed exchange rates, a government that has fixed its currency has two choices if, at the fixed rate, there is an excess demand for its currency:
    (a) devaluation or increasing the demand for its currency
    (b) revaluation or decreasing the demand for foreign currency
    (c) revaluation or increasing the supply of its currency
    (d) devaluation or lowering the exchange rate

15. In place of a formal fixed exchange rate, governments and their central banks could slow down the appreciation of the exchange rate in all but one of the following ways. Which one is it?
    (a) remove tariffs on imported goods
    (b) lower domestic short-term interest rates
    (c) tighten up restrictions on foreign currency purchases
    (d) sell Canadian dollars in the exchange market

EXERCISES

1. Suppose that the rate at which wool and lumber could be exchanged in international markets was 2:1. Initially, production and consumption are at R, with W_0 and L_0 being the amounts of wool and lumber produced and consumed.

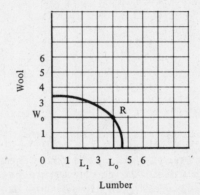

   (a) If, in autarky, only L_1 of lumber was desired, what change in the production of wool would be required? Indicate the new point on the graph.
   (b) Exploiting the opportunity of trade, what consumption point could this country reach while not altering its production mix at that point? Indicate the exports and imports on the graph.

2. You are given the following export and import data for Canada and Australia.

Commodity	Canadian Exports to Australia		Canadian Imports from Australia	
	Quantity	Price	Quantity	Price
Lumber	100,000 bd. ft	Can. $500 per 1,000 bd. ft		
Tractors	130	Can. $10,000 per tractor		
Aluminum			10,000 tons	A. $50 per ton
Wool			100,000 lb	A. $4 per lb

The exchange rate is A. $1.00 = Can. $1.30.

51

(a) What is the value of Canada's balance of trade in terms of Canadian dollars? In this example, does Canada have a trade surplus or deficit? Why?

(b) If the exchange rate became A. $1.00 = Can. $1.50 what would happen to the balance of trade given that the same quantities of goods were bought and sold?

(c) A change in the exchange rate will cause the amount of exports and imports to change if demand is elastic. If the exchange rate moves from A. $1.00 = Can. $1.30 to A. $1.00 = Can. $1.50, is this, from Canada's viewpoint, appreciation or depreciation of the exchange rate? What would you expect to happen to the volume of Canada's exports and imports?

3. Suppose that the exchange rate has been £1 = $2.50 for some time. A British importer has been purchasing 100 tons of Canadian-produced newsprint each month at $300 per ton. The exchange rate suddenly becomes £1 = $2.75.
   (a) Has the Canadian dollar appreciated or depreciated? _____
   (b) How has the U.K. price of newsprint (in pounds) changed? _____
   (c) If the demand for newsprint is elastic, how will the change in the exchange rate affect the demand for dollars? Why?

(d) If the price elasticity of demand is -1.2, by how much will Canadian exports of newsprint change (direction and magnitude of volume per month)? In making your calculation, use the formula for the arc elasticity.

4. On the accompanying diagrams, illustrate what is taking place in the foreign exchange market and indicate the outcome of the events described.

(a) Canadians take more interest in British history and culture and increase their holiday trips to Britain. At the same time, the British increase their investment in Canada. The new price of the dollar will be (i) above (ii) below (iii) cannot say, relative to P_1.

(b) Canadian exports to Britain increase and, at the same time, there is much less interest on the part of Canadians to invest in Britain. The new price of the dollar will be (i) above (ii) below (iii) cannot say, relative to P_1.

(c) There is a rapid rise in the Canadian domestic price of wheat and newsprint (both exports) and, at the same time, a change in taste by Canadians for more British automobiles. The new price of the dollar will be (i) above (ii) below (iii) cannot say, relative to P_1.

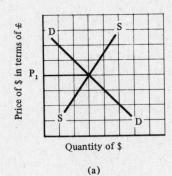

(a)

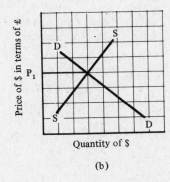

(b)

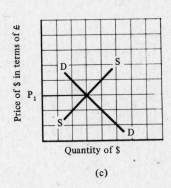

(c)

5. (a) Assume that the Bank of England is trying to maintain a fixed rate of about
        £1 = $2.65. Given the demand and supply curves in the diagram below, will the
        Bank have to buy or sell pounds to maintain this price? About how much?

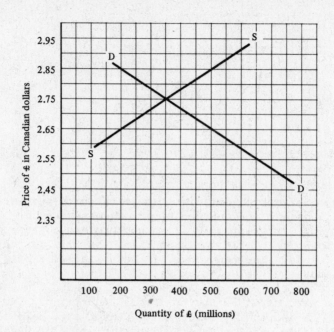

Quantity of £ (millions)

    (b) If the Bank is trying to maintain a fixed exchange rate of about £1 = $2.85,
        will it be prepared to buy or sell pounds to maintain this price? About how
        much?

6. Described on the next page are a series of hypothetical events that could confront
    the central bank while it is trying to maintain a fixed exchange rate of U.S.
    $1.00 = Can. $1.15. Assume in each case that the free market price is initially
    equal to the fixed rate. On each of the accompanying diagrams, illustrate how the
    event described would affect the Canadian dollar (if it were free to adjust) and
    what the Bank of Canada must do to ensure that the fixed rate is maintained. (Show
    the new supply and demand schedules if they change.)

54

(a)   The demand for Canadian exports by the United States results in a "free" market value for the Canadian dollar of .89.

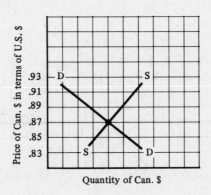

(b)   A strong desire on the part of Canadians to travel in the United States results in a "free" market value of the dollar equal to .85.

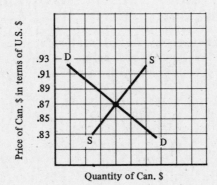

(c)   An inflow of foreign capital into Canada and a decline in the purchase by Canadians of U.S. goods result in a "free" market value of the dollar equal to .91.

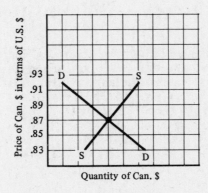

7. Suppose Jane Doe, a member of the foreign exchange department of a large Canadian bank, is responsible for checking the cross-rates of Canadian dollars, pounds, and Italian lire each day. If disorderly or inconsistent rates should arise, she is to report this to the manager. On a particular day she obtains the following information:

One Unit of This Currency	Exchanges for Stated Number of Units of This Currency		
	Can. Dollar	Lira	Pound
Can. dollar	1	600	0.417
Lira	0.00167	1	0.000833
Pound	2.40	1,200	1

The first row indicates that 1 Can. dollar trades for 600 lire and .417 pounds sterling.

(a) Is the pound price of dollars (.417) consistent with the dollar price of pounds? _____

(b) Is the lira price of dollars (600) consistent with the dollar price of lire? _____

(c) Is the pound price of lire consistent with the lira price of pounds? _____

(d) Is the cross-rate of pounds to lire in terms of dollars consistent with the pound price of the lire? Hint: Divide .417 by 600 and compare with the pound price of lire in the second row _____

(e) Would this bank make profits by using $1,000 to buy lire then purchasing pounds with the lire, and then purchasing dollars with the pounds? How much?

8. Imagine it has been established that the demand and supply schedules for the Canadian dollar can be represented by

$$Q_d = 1.5 - 1.0P \qquad (1)$$

$$Q_s = -.25 + 1.0P \qquad (2)$$

where Q_d is the quantity demanded, Q_s the quantity supplied (in millions of dollars), and P the price of the Canadian dollar in terms of U.S. currency.

(a) What is the equilibrium value of the Canadian dollar? What is the quantity of dollars exchanged?

(b) (i) If the demand schedule became $Q_d = 1.75 - 1.0P$, would this represent an increased or decreased demand for Canadian goods by Americans?

(ii) Would the exchange rate appreciate or depreciate? By how much?

(c) If the supply schedule was $Q_s = 2 + .001P$, would the exchange rate be highly responsive or unresponsive to shifts in the demand schedule?

9. Between the early fall of 1976 and the early spring of 1977, the Canadian dollar depreciated significantly, as the table below indicates. For many retired Canadians who planned to spend the winter in the United States, the uncertainty of the dollar had an impact on their financial planning. The following example parallels the situation many people faced at that time.

Recently retired Alias Smith wanted to spend six months in Florida starting October 1, 1976. Financing this stay required some planning. He could:
(i) liquidate his $4,667 Canadian savings certificate which earned 5 percent on a semiannual basis and purchase U.S. dollars immediately
(ii) buy U.S. dollars at the beginning of each month from his pension, which was automatically deposited into his chequing account in Canada.
He chose (ii), instructing the bank manager to convert the pension into U.S. $800 at the beginning of each month and transfer the funds south.

Month	Monthly Average Price of U.S. Dollars (in Terms of Canadian Dollars)
October 1976	.9722
November 1976	1.0364
December 1976	1.0088
January 1977	1.0180
February 1977	1.0457
March 1977	1.0539

(a) What was Smith's total cost in Canadian dollars of obtaining U.S. $4,800 through the option he chose? _____

(b) What would the cost to Smith have been in Canadian dollars if option (i) had been chosen? _____

57

Part Three
Demand

| Household Consumption Behaviour | 9 |

KEY CONCEPTS AND DEFINITIONS

1. The market demand schedule is simply the horizontal addition of all individual demand schedules.

2. Marginal utility is the additional satisfaction a person receives as a consequence of consuming a little more of some good or service. In choosing between alternative increases in consumption, the concept of marginal utility is important.

3. If, as additional units of a good are consumed by a household, the marginal utility derived from each additional unit becomes smaller and smaller, the household is said to experience diminishing marginal utility.

4. A basic assumption of household consumption behavior is that whatever the activities of the household, it seeks to maximize total utility. For a given dollar outlay, this means that spending will be allocated to ensure that the utility of the last dollar spent on each item is equal.

5. The formal condition for household utility maximization where two goods (X and Y) are being purchased is the following: $MU_X/P_X = MU_Y/P_Y$ which, when rearranged, becomes $MU_X/MU_Y = P_X/P_Y$.

6. The household demand schedule for any commodity will be an inverse relationship between price and quantity demanded, given that the household (a) maximizes total utility and (b) there is diminishing marginal utility for each good.

7. The elasticity of demand, which relates changes in quantity demanded to changes in price, depends on the marginal utility of the good in the range of the price change.

8. A budget line indicates the quantities of two goods that a household can purchase with a given income and fixed prices. Parallel shifts in the budget line result from changes in the household's income. Changes in the slope of the budget line result from changes in the relative prices of the goods.

9. An indifference curve shows different combinations of two goods that give the same level of total utility to the household. The slope of an indifference curve at any point on the curve is the marginal rate of substitution, or the rate at which one good can be substituted for another without changing total utility.

10. Household consumption equilibrium occurs at the point where the slope of the indifference curve (marginal rate of substitution) is tangent to the budget line.

1. Marginal utility is defined as
    (a) total utility divided by the amount of a good consumed
    (b) What a consumer would pay for one more unit of a good
    (c) the change in satisfaction due to a change in the amount of a good consumed
    (d) a good that gives no more satisfaction if more is consumed

2. If a commodity gives less satisfaction for each additional unit consumed, that commodity
    (a) will not be purchased
    (b) displays diminishing marginal utility
    (c) has zero marginal utility
    (d) has a zero price

3   Disutility occurs when
    (a) the consumption of an additional unit of a commodity reduces total utility
    (b) utility is increasing at a decreasing rate
    (c) a commodity is no longer needed
    (d) none of the above

4. The hypothesis of diminishing marginal utility states that
    (a) the less of a commodity one is consuming, the less the utility obtained by an increase in its consumption
    (b) the more of a commodity one is consuming, the more the utility obtained by an increase in its consumption
    (c) the more of a commodity one is consuming, the less the utility obtained by an increase in its consumption
    (d) marginal utility cannot be measured, but total utility can

5. According to utility theory, for a consumer who is maximizing total satisfaction, MU_a/MU_b
    (a) equals P_a/P_b
    (b) equals P_b/P_a
    (c) will not necessarily be related to relative prices
    (d) equals TU_a/TU_b

6. The "paradox of value" is that
    (a) people are irrational in consumption choices
    (b) the total utilities yielded by commodities do not necessarily have a relationship to their market values
    (c) value has no relationship to utility schedules
    (d) free goods are goods that are essential to life

7. Elasticity of demand
    (a) varies inversely with total utility
    (b) varies inversely with marginal utility
    (c) is less, the greater the substitution effect
    (d) is greater when marginal utility declines slowly rather than rapidly

8. Consumer surplus derived from the consumption of a commodity
    (a) is the difference between the total value derived from that consumption and the total payment made to acquire the commodity
    (b) will always be less than the total amount paid for the commodity
    (c) is the extra amount received by the consumer because some units of the commodity are free
    (d) none of the above

9. The slope of the budget line with product Y on the vertical axis and product X on the horizontal axis is
    (a) $-(P_Y/P_X)$
    (b) $-(X/Y)$
    (c) $-(Y/X)$
    (d) $-(P_X/P_Y)$

10. A change in household income will always shift the budget line parallel to itself if
    (a) money prices stay constant
    (b) relative prices stay constant with money prices changing by the same percentage as income
    (c) real income stays constant
    (d) prices change in the same direction

11. Halving all absolute prices, ceteris paribus, has the effect of
    (a) halving real income
    (b) halving money income
    (c) changing relative prices
    (d) doubling real income

12. A change in one absolute price, with all other things remaining constant, will
    (a) shift the budget line parallel to itself
    (b) change money income
    (c) cause the budget line to change its slope
    (d) have no effect on real income

13. An indifference curve includes
    (a) constant quantities of one good with varying quantities of another
    (b) the prices and quantities of two goods that can be purchased for a given sum of money
    (c) all combinations of two goods that will give the same level of satisfaction to the household
    (d) combinations of goods whose marginal utilities are equal

14. Where the budget line is tangent to an indifference curve
    (a) equal amounts of goods give equal satisfaction
    (b) the ratio of prices of the goods must equal the marginal rate of substitution
    (c) the prices of the goods are equal
    (d) the household has revealed a preference for that combination of goods

15. Indifference curve theory assumes that
    (a) buyers can measure satisfaction
    (b) buyers can identify preferred combinations of goods without necessarily being able to measure their satisfaction
    (c) buyers always behave consistently
    (d) all buyers have the same preference patterns

16. If the relative prices of X and Y were 2:1, and an individual was consuming X and Y such that MU_X/MU_Y was 3:2, then to achieve maximum utility,
    (a) the individual must consume more of X and less of Y
    (b) the price of X must rise
    (c) the individual must consume less of X and more of Y
    (d) the individual's income must rise

17. When the price of commodity X triples, all other prices and income remaining constant, then for an individual consuming X,
    (a) the quantity of X consumed must fall to one-third its previous level
    (b) the quantity of X consumed must fall until the marginal utility of X has tripled
    (c) the individual must increase his/her consumption of X
    (d) the consumption of all other commodities must fall

18. If an individual is prepared to pay $3 for the first unit of a commodity, $2 for the second unit, and $1 for the third unit, and the market price is $1 per unit,
    (a) consumer surplus is $3
    (b) the demand schedule for the commodity is negatively sloped
    (c) the individual will purchase three units of the commodity
    (d) all of the above

19. With commodity X on the vertical axis and commodity Y on the horizontal axis, a change in the slope of the budget line from - 3/2 to - 7/2, given indifference curve analysis, will
    (a) cause the consumption of X to rise relative to Y
    (b) signal a decline in the price of Y relative to the price of X
    (c) cause a parallel shift in the budget line
    (d) reduce total utility

20. If the slope at a point on the indifference curve of an individual consuming X and Y is -1.0,
    (a) the budget line must have a slope of -1.0
    (b) utility is maximized if the budget line has a slope of + 1.0
    (c) the marginal rate of substitution is -1.0
    (d) the ratio of the marginal utilities is unequal

EXERCISES

1. The table below relates total utility and the number of milkshakes consumed per weekend.

Number of Milkshakes	Total Utility
0	0
1	50
2	90
3	120
4	130
5	130
6	120

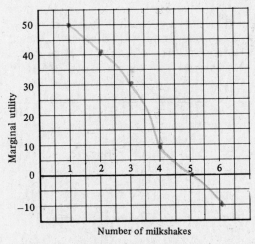

Number of milkshakes

    (a) In the diagram at the right, plot the marginal utility schedule.
    (b) At what point does the consumer experience disutility? (e.g., after how many milkshakes per weekend?)

61

2. Suppose a consumer spends recreation time and income on two leisure activities: tennis and fishing. The consumer has the basic equipment to pursue both activities. The costs associated with these activities are court fees (for tennis) and the expense (gasoline, etc.) of travel (for fishing).

   The marginal utility schedules for hours spent on these activities are shown below.

Number of Hours per Week Spent on ⟶	Marginal Utility Schedule	
	Fishing	Tennis
1	20	20
2	18	19
3	16	18
4	14	17
5	12	16
6	10	15
7	8	14
8	6	13

(a) If the cost per hour of each activity was the same and the consumer spent 5 hours per week on recreation activity, how many hours would be spent on each activity in order to maximize total utility?

(b) Suppose the cost of tennis increased 19 percent. What change in the "mix" of tennis and fishing would be required to maximize utility? Explain, using marginal utility to price ratios, why this is the case. (Consider the initial cost of both activities in (a) to be $1 per hour.)

3. Goods X and Y display diminishing marginal utility. Given specific relative marginal utilities representing particular consumption bundles of X and Y, and the absolute prices shown below, what rearrangement in consumption is necessary to achieve utility maximization? (Complete the last column of the table below.)

Case	Relative Marginal Utilities (MU_x/MU_y)	Price of		Change: Increase (▲) or Decrease (▼) in Consumption of	
		X	Y	X	Y
1	4/3	$ 3.00	$6.00		
2	3/1	3.00	1.50		
3	2/3	1.00	1.00		
4	9/2	12.00	2.00		

4. The marginal utility schedules for three commodities A, B, and C are given on the following page. For each of these commodities, how responsive will the change in quantity be to a rise in price? (I.e., will the elasticity of demand be high, low, or close to zero?) Why?

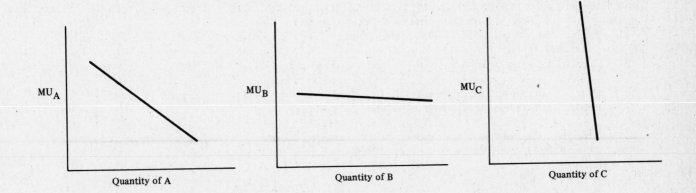

MU_A   Quantity of A   MU_B   Quantity of B   MU_C   Quantity of C

Commodity A:

Commodity B:

Commodity C:

5. Suppose an individual was prepared to pay for the first and subsequent large bottles of cola per week according to the following schedule.

Bottles of Cola per Week	Amount the Individual Is Prepared to Pay for Each Bottle
1st	$1.50
2nd	1.20
3rd	.90
4th	.60
5th	.50
6th	.40

(a) If the market price of large cola is $.50 per bottle, how many bottles per week will the individual consume? (Assume no budget constraint.)

(b) What is the total consumer surplus enjoyed by this individual?

(c) If the market price rises to $.90 per bottle, what effect does this have on demand and consumer surplus?

6. Assume that a household has a recreation budget of $800 per annum to be spent on two recreational activities: skiing (at $20 per unit of skiing) and movie-going (at $16 per unit of movie-going). These units might, for example, be defined in terms of half days of skiing and a 90-minute movie.

(a) Using the graph below, draw the budget line for recreation expenditure for this household.

(b) Can this household consume 30 units of skiing and 15 units of movie-going?

(c) If this household consumed 20 units of skiing, how many units of movie-going could it consume and keep within its budget?

(d) Suppose, because of an increase in family income, this household decides to allocate $1,200 to recreation. Draw in the new budget line.

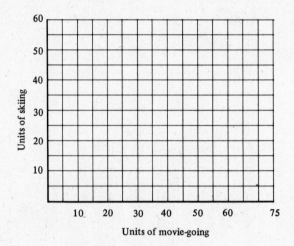

Units of movie-going

7. Referring to the household recreation budget of $1,200 in Exercise 6, part (d), suppose now that the price of skiing has increased to $30 per unit.

(a) Draw the new budget line on the graph below.

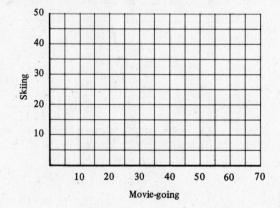

Movie-going

(b) If the family consumed 20 units of skiing, approximately how much movie-going is possible given the budget constraint?

64

(c) In addition to the increase in the price of skiing, suppose the price of movie-going increases to $24 per unit. With a budget of $1,200, draw in the new budget line. How does it compare with the budget line in Exercise 6, part (a)? Why?

8. (a) If all household income of $10,000 is spent on two goods, A and B, draw on the graph below the three budget lines possible for the pairs of prices shown below. Label the budget lines I, II, and III.

Commodity	Price per Unit		
	I	II	III
A	$100	200	80
B	50	150	100

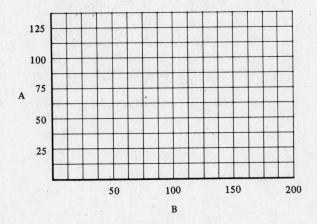

(b) What is the slope of each budget line?
   I:
   II:
   III:
(c) For budget line I, write the algebraic equation.

(d) If the price of A relative to B is said to be 3:1, what is the opportunity cost of one unit of B?

9. If the following combinations of apples and oranges give equal satisfaction, an individual is said to be indifferent to each combination.

Apples	Oranges
30	10
24	12
19	15
15	19
12	24
10	35

(a) Plot the indifference curve on the graph below.

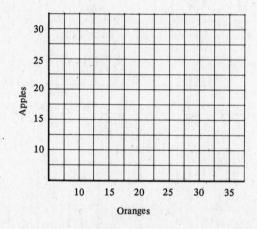

(b) Suppose that at the moment an individual is consuming 19 oranges and 15 apples per month. Would a combination of 15 oranges and 20 apples be preferred? Why?

(c) What (approximately) is the marginal rate of substitution at the point on the indifference curve where 15 apples are consumed? (Hint: draw a line tangent to the indifference curve at this point and extend the tangent to both axes.)

10. Below you will find information on two indifference curves that are part of an individual's indifference map.

INDIFFERENCE CURVES

I		II	
Food	Shelter	Food	Shelter
50	10	54	13
35	15	39	18
30	18	34	21
25	25	29	28
21	37	25	40
18	46	22	49

(a) Draw these indifference curves on the graph below.

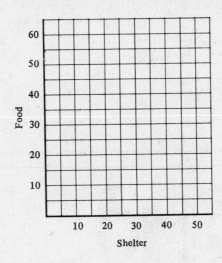

(b) If the household budget is $1,000 and food and shelter per unit cost $20 and $22.22, respectively, draw in the budget line on the graph.

(c) Given (a) and (b) above, what combination of food and shelter will maximize household utility? Explain.

11. Between 1969 and 1974, average after-tax family income and expenditure on specific goods changed as shown below.

	1969	1974	Percent Change in Prices in Same Period
Nominal After-Tax Family Income	$7,761	$12,043	
Family Expenditure on			
Food	1,605	2,442	48.3
Clothing	727	988	21.9
Transportation	1,111	1,708	25.3
Alcohol/Tobacco	341	482	15.1
All Goods and Services			31.3

(a) What was the percentage change in <u>real</u> after-tax income between 1969 and 1974?

(b) What were the percentage increases in <u>real</u> expenditure on the following items?
Food:
Clothing:
Transportation:
Alcohol/Tobacco:

(c) During this five-year period, what change occurred in the relative prices of food and clothing? Of alcohol/tobacco and transportation? (Assuming that relative prices were 1:1 in 1969, what were they by 1974?)

Demand Theory in Action | 10

1. Individually, goods that are <u>substitutes</u> one for another display a price elastic demand; but as a group, the demand is likely to be inelastic.
2. <u>Income elasticities</u> tend to vary according to the nature of the commodity. <u>Luxury goods</u> are income elastic; <u>necessities</u> are income inelastic. In fact, the more basic the good, the lower the income elasticity.
3. The change in the quantity consumed for a given commodity can be explained by several factors. The income elasticity, price elasticity, and <u>cross elasticity</u> are ways of measuring the influence of income, price, and substitutes on the change in a commodity. To measure how the quantity demanded responds to a price change, careful statistical analysis is required.
4. Not all households behave at all times according to the laws of demand theory, and thus perfect prediction is not possible. But the theory, supported by <u>statistical analysis</u>, is useful because it clearly tells us what is most likely to happen.
5. Some interesting deviations from basic demand theory involve <u>Giffen goods</u>, and <u>conspicuous consumption goods</u>. A positive relationship between price and quantity changes for certain groups of individuals cannot be generalized for the market as a whole.
6. Income elasticities are known not to change quickly, nor do they exhibit for the most part bizarre behavior. <u>Predictions</u> about certain commodities for income changes are thus possible and very useful.

MULTIPLE-CHOICE QUESTIONS

1. The price elasticity of demand refers to
   (a) how the demand for a commodity changes when the price of that commodity changes, <u>ceteris paribus</u>
   (b) the response of price to a supply change
   (c) how the quantity demanded of a commodity responds to a change in a substitute
   (d) how rapidly price changes when demand changes

2. Where there are close substitutes available,
   (a) we would expect the commodities as a group to have high elasticity
   (b) each commodity in the group would be unrelated to the elasticity of substitutes
   (c) we could expect the elasticity of one commodity to be higher than that for the group
   (d) the elasticities of all commodities are equal

3. Demand studies have indicated that the price elasticities of demand for most foodstuffs
   (a) are less than 1
   (b) are greater than 1
   (c) are of unitary elasticity
   (d) have no general tendency that has been noted

4. For the "average" household, we would expect the income elasticity of demand for children's clothing
   (a) to be very high
   (b) to be relatively low
   (c) to be equal to unity
   (d) to be negative

5. Which of the following is not an important use of demand theory?
   (a) to study the aggregate behavior of households
   (b) to make statements about the probable response of households to changes in prices and incomes
   (c) to assist in establishing appropriate statistical tests of consumer behavior
   (d) to make statements about what each household will do

6. Which one of the following variables, which cannot be measured directly, could be easily misused as an alibi whenever it appeared that the theory of demand had been refuted?
   (a) income
   (b) supply
   (c) tastes
   (d) price

7. A series of observations in which the lower the price, the lower the quantity sold, could represent all but which one of the following:
   (a) an unchanged supply with a changing demand
   (b) a conventional demand with a changing supply
   (c) the demand for a "Giffen" good with a changing supply
   (d) a changing supply and a changing demand

8. To demonstrate that elasticities are not stable, it is necessary to
   (a) give at least three or four good reasons why they should not be stable
   (b) show that two elasticities of demand for the same commodity are not exactly the same
   (c) demonstrate their instability by logical, deductive reasoning
   (d) investigate the matter by measuring elasticities over time

9. The category of expenditures classed as meals purchased at restaurants
   (a) has been observed to have low income elasticities
   (b) has been observed to have high income elasticities
   (c) has been observed to have negative income elasticities
   (d) shows no consistent relationship with income

1. Given the information in the table below, what can be said about the value of the
    price and income elasticities of commodity X in the three periods Year 1 to Year 2,
    Year 2 to Year 3, and Year 3 to Year 4? (Hint: Pay particular attention to the
    years when price does not change or income does not change.)

Period	Per Household Annual Real Disposable Income	Per Household Real Consumption of X (annual)	Price for Unit of X
1	$15,000	$2,000	$100
2	16,000	2,100	100
3	16,000	2,150	95
4	17,000	2,150	105

(i)   Year 1 to Year 2:

(ii)   Year 2 to Year 3:

(iii)   Year 3 to Year 4:

2. The graph on the left below gives hypothetical data on annual gasoline consumption
    per household and prices for 1960-1973. The graph on the right provides
    "observations" for 1974-1980. A straight line has been "fitted" to the data. (See
    the references to scatter diagrams and correlation in Chapter 3 of the Study Guide.)

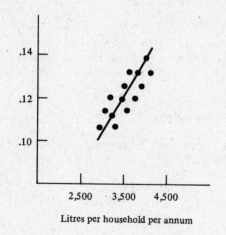

Litres per household per annum

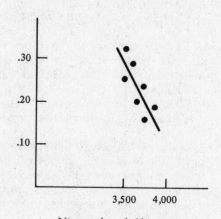

Litres per household per annum

70

(a) Do these "fitted" lines represent demand schedules for the two periods? Explain your answer.

(b) What assumptions would you have to make about household income and tastes for the 1974-1980 period in order to state that the graph on the right does represent a demand schedule?

3. By mid-1977, Canadian lumber prices had risen substantially compared to earlier in the year. It was stated at the time that the price rise was due to increased U.S. demand for housing and virtually fixed short-run supplies.
   (a) Illustrate on the graph below what occurred in the short run. What is the elasticity of supply in this instance?

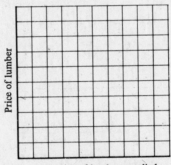

Quantity of lumber supplied
and demanded

(b) If builders in Canada were expecting housing demand to rise soon, and they believed supplies would continue to be restricted, what action would they take? What impact would this have on the market?

4. <u>Real Per Capita Consumption and Real Per Capita Income</u>
The table below shows per capita real consumption of three commodities or commodity groups, along with data on real per capita income for selected years.

	Categories of Spending (per capita in real terms)			
Year	Food and Nonalcoholic Beverages	Alcohol	Automobiles	Real Per Capita Disposable Income
1960	$338	$64	$71	$2,009
1963	330	69	94	2,132
1967	351	82	126	2,446
1971	391	98	132	2,779
1975	424	119	177	3,532
1979	434	126	183	3,805

<u>Source:</u> Statistics Canada, <u>National Income & Expenditures Accounts.</u>

(a) Graph the relationship between real per capita income and per capita consumption for each commodity.

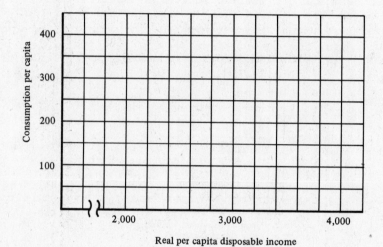

Real per capita disposable income

(b) If we assume that consumption was equal to demand, calculate the income elasticity of demand for each commodity over the 1960-1979 period.

(c) Does the income elasticity for these products confirm the theory suggested in the textbook?

72

5. Per Capita Consumption

The table below shows annual per capita consumption data on pork and eggs, along with the price change for each good in the years noted.

PER CAPITA CONSUMPTION AND PRICE CHANGE

Years	Pork (lb.)	Price Change (%)	Years	Eggs (doz.)	Price Change (%)
1964	51.8		1963	32.1	
1965	47.9	+ 11.4	1964	32.0	- 13.7
1970	58.7		1966	30.7	
1971	68.3	- 16.9	1967	31.2	- 15.6
1974	59.4		1972	30.8	
1975	50.9	+ 28.0	1973	29.2	+ 44.4

Source: Handbook of Food Expenditure, Price and Consumption, Agriculture Canada, 1977.

Note: The years were deliberately selected to ensure a substantial change in the price of the commodity.

(a) Assume that the change in per capita income from one year to the next has a negligible impact on per capita spending of selected food items and that the short-run response is to price fluctuations. Calculate the price elasticity of demand for each commodity for the pairs of years given. (In calculating percentage change in quantity, use both absolute quantities in the denominator. See the discussion of arc elasticity in Chapter 6.)

(b) What do these elasticities suggest about the importance of the two products in family consumption patterns?

(c) Do these elasticities confirm demand theory?

Part Four

Production and Cost

The Firm, Production, and Cost | 11

1. The legal structure of a business in Canada (i.e., partnership, corporation) establishes responsibility for liability of owners/managers with respect to debt and affects the ability of the business to raise funds for capital expenditure.
2. The major factors of production in the firm are land, labour, and capital.
3. The combination of inputs or factors of production in a manner that produces the most output with a minimum of inputs is said to be a technologically efficient method of production.
4. An economically efficient use of inputs refers to one that minimizes factor costs and hence depends on technological efficiency and the price of factors.
5. Opportunity cost is a concept used to measure the benefit foregone by not doing something in its best alternative use.
6. Interest is the payment made to borrow money or the payment received when money is loaned.
7. Physical assets of a firm such as building and machinery wear out eventually in the process of being used to produce an output. The annual wear and tear on assets is called depreciation, and the monetary value of that wear and tear is a depreciation cost chargeable to the firm.
8. Economic profits on goods sold are defined as the difference between revenues received from the sale of the goods less the opportunity cost of all resources used to make the goods.

APPENDIX A-11

A.1. A balance sheet provides a picture of the financial state of a firm at a moment in time. An income statement is a summary of the flow of income into disbursements from the firm during a period of time.
A.2 The accountant and economist may have different views on the balance sheet and income statement of a firm because of differences in their treatment of costs.

MULTIPLE-CHOICE QUESTIONS

1. Which statement is correct?
    (a) All technologically efficient methods are economically efficient.
    (b) All economically efficient methods are technologically efficient.
    (c) Some economically efficient methods are not technologically efficient.
    (d) Both (a) and (b) are true because economically efficient and technologically efficient methods must coincide.

2. Which of the following groups of claimants would be the last to have their claims honored in a bankruptcy?
    (a) bondholders
    (b) commercial creditors
    (c) common stockholders
    (d) employees owed back wages

3. Limited liability for the claims against a firm is an advantage for
    (a) single proprietors
    (b) corporate shareholders
    (c) paid employees
    (d) general partners in a partnership

4. Which of the following is not an advantage of the corporate form of business organization?
    (a) limited liability
    (b) separate legal existence
    (c) close identification of owners with management
    (d) relative ease of obtaining capital funds

5. The difference between economic profits and normal profits is that
    (a) normal profits are smaller
    (b) normal profits are necessarily larger for all firms
    (c) normal profits are part of opportunity cost, whereas economic profits are returns in excess of opportunity costs
    (d) normal profits take into account monopoly power; economic profits do not

6. If you give up a full-time job to go to the university, the major cost is
    (a) tuition and fees
    (b) room and board
    (c) the income you could have received from employment
    (d) social and miscellaneous expenses

7. We can be certain of the usefulness of opportunity-cost concepts when our purpose is
    (a) to help a firm make the best decision it can to achieve maximum profits
    (b) to predict the responses of the firm to a change in conditions
    (c) to describe the firm's actual behavior
    (d) to predict the money costs of a firm's activities

8. The major role of economic profits, as seen in this chapter, is
    (a) to provide income for shareholders
    (b) to provide income for entrepreneurs
    (c) to act as a signal to firms concerning the desirability of devoting resources to a particular activity
    (d) to encourage labour to reform the system

75

9. "Profits are necessary for the survival of Canadian business." This chapter
   (a) disagrees with this viewpoint entirely
   (b) accepts this viewpoint but defines the necessary profits as costs
   (c) accepts this viewpoint without qualification or clarification
   (d) does not consider the subject

10. Inputs to productive processes
    (a) can be the outputs of other firms
    (b) are solely land and labour
    (c) can be clearly distinguished from factors of production
    (d) consist primarily of capital equipment in a capitalistic society

11. Economic theory frequently assumes that firms try to maximize profits
    (a) because firms always maximize profits
    (b) because firms ought to maximize profits to be fair to their stockholders
    (c) because use of this simple assumption has frequently led to accurate
        predictions
    (d) because economists wish thus to criticize the greed of firms

12. Depreciation is defined as the loss of value of an asset associated with its use in
    production, and thus it
    (a) is clearly a cash cost
    (b) is a function only of wear and tear in use
    (c) is not an economic cost if the asset has no market value or alternative use
    (d) does not apply to used equipment

EXERCISES

1. Assume that there are two methods of making 100 widgets per month with capital and
   labour as shown below.

	Method A	Method B
Capital	10 units	5 units
Labour	100 units	200 units

   The cost of these factors of production are $5 per unit of labour and $20 per unit
   of capital.
   (a) Can you distinguish which method (A or B) is the most technologically
       efficient? Explain.

   (b) Can you distinguish the most economically efficient method? Explain.

(c)   If labour cost dropped to $1 per unit, would this change your answer to (b)?
Why?

2.   Arrange the following items and use the information below to obtain (a) net profit
before income taxes, (b) economic profit before taxes, and (c) economic profit
after income taxes.
1.   Revenue from sale of goods = $5 million
2.   Tax rate = 50 percent of net profit before tax
3.   Depreciation = $500,000
4.   Salaries, cost of raw materials = $3 million
5.   Return to capital and risk-taking = $500,000

(a)   Net profit before income tax _____
(b)   Economic profit before tax _____
(c)   Economic profit after tax   _____

3.   Assume that there are two basic methods of producing vegetables for sale from a
garden plot, and that the grower can sell all output at a given price. One method
involves hand tools and labour; the other, power tools and labour. The following
information gives an idea of the production processes involved. (Output from the
garden is proportional to the size of the lot.)

| Garden size | Man-Hours to Produce Output | |
(square feet)	Hand Tools	Power Tools
200	50	20
500	125	50
1000	250	100
2000	500	200

Note: (1) The hand tools are depreciated at $10 per
year; (2) the power tools are depreciated at $300 per
year; (3) labour cost is $4 per hour.

77

(a) At what garden size is it economically efficient to use power tools?

(b) If the price of labour declined to $2 per hour, would this affect the answer in (a)? How?

4. (This is a true story: only the numbers have been changed to protect the business.) In the early 1970s, an enterprising student decided to enter the paper and glass recycling business. He left the university, where he had been studying economics, and set about establishing a business, using his meagre savings, to collect and deliver used paper and glass to paper mills and glass-using firms. His (hypothetical) monthly costs and revenues were:

Costs		Revenue	
Rent for old warehouse	$250	12 tons of paper at $50 per ton	$600
Depreciation of truck	100	1000 pounds of glass at $.40 per pound	400
Labour (other than his own)	300		
Miscellaneous	100		

Shortly after being in business, large provincewide companies in the scrap business entered the recycling business. The buyers of used paper and glass were flooded with material, and the price of used paper plummeted to $30 per ton. Large companies simply intensified the use of capital in the recycling business to cut costs.

Our young entrepreneur sought to increase the capital intensity of his firm and upgrade the quality of his capital but was unable to find anyone who would lend him the money to do so at less than an exorbitant rate of interest. He closed his business and returned to complete his degree in economics.

(a) Why did this business feel the need to enter truck depreciation as a cost?

(b) What was the level of monthly accounting profits for the business before the price declined? What is inappropriate about using this figure as a profit figure?

(c) Given that the owner of the business worked 40 hours per week, do you think there were any "excess profits" in the firm?

(d) What was the opportunity cost of going back to the university?

Production and Cost in the Short Run | 12

KEY CONCEPTS AND DEFINITIONS

1. If we consider a time horizon where a firm's fixed factors, such as a building, cannot be varied, the firm is operating in the short run. Those factors of production that can be varied in such a time horizon are called variable factors.

2. For the purpose of analyzing the firm in the short run, it is important that at least one important factor is fixed.

3. A long-run time horizon is said to exist when all factors are variable, but the technology of production is unchanged. If the latter is also allowed to change, the time horizon is said to be the very long run.

4. The relationship between factors of production and outputs is the production function.

5. Total product is the physical volume of output produced in a given period of time while average product is total product divided by the variable factor. The point at which average product is a maximum is the point of diminishing average productivity.

6. For a given production process, an important concept is marginal productivity: the change in total product or output that occurs when one more unit of a variable factor is used in the production process.

7. The hypothesis of eventually diminishing returns, or the law of diminishing returns, describes the phenomenon that if more and more of a variable factor is applied to a fixed factor of production, the addition that this variable factor makes to total output starts to fall.

8. The law of diminishing average returns implies that if additional units of a variable factor are applied to a given quantity of fixed factors, the average product of the variable factor will eventually decrease.

9. A firm must pay for both its fixed and variable factors of production. A fixed cost is one that does not vary with the level of output. Variable costs do change with output levels. A firm that wished to cut production by 10 percent would still have to pay rent for land, but its energy costs would decline.

10. Average total cost, or average cost, is total cost divided by the units of output. Average fixed costs and average variable costs are computed in a similar manner.

79

11. If output is increased, costs will usually increase. The increase in total cost due to producing one more unit of output is called the marginal cost.
12. The law of diminishing returns showed that average product increased and then began to decrease as more labour (variable factor) was used. Each unit of labour, however, added the same amount of cost. Thus, average variable cost fell and then started to increase.
13. Average total cost is the sum of average variable cost and average fixed cost. It will decline as output is expanded initially, but at some time the rising average variable cost will cause average total cost to rise.
14. Excess capacity refers to a firm that is producing at an output level below the minimum average total cost.
15. If the quantity of a fixed factor is changed in the production process, the short-run average total cost curve will change as well.

MULTIPLE-CHOICE QUESTIONS

1. Decision making for the firm in the short run involves
   (a) having access to only a few additional fixed factors
   (b) being able to vary only some factors
   (c) no additional variables or fixed factors
   (d) no opportunity to change prices

2. Which of the following is an example of a production decision in the short run?
   (a) A contractor buys two additional cement mixers and hires two new drivers for them.
   (b) A contractor decides to work his crew overtime to finish a job.
   (c) A railroad decides to eliminate all passenger service.
   (d) A paper company takes only three weeks to install antipollution equipment.

3. Long-run decisions
   (a) do not affect short-run decisions
   (b) can consider all factors variable
   (c) are not very important because the long run is a succession of short runs
   (d) are taken with fewer alternatives open than in the case of short-run decisions

4. In the very long-run planning horizon
   (a) only technology is allowed to change
   (b) the ratio of variable to fixed factors is given
   (c) all factors can vary as well as the production technology
   (d) firms cannot reduce their output

5. The production function relates
   (a) cost to input
   (b) cost to output
   (c) wages to profits
   (d) inputs to outputs

Use the table on the opposite page, which describes a hypothetical firm, to respond to questions 6 through 8.

6. The firm is
   (a) operating in the long run
   (b) operating in the short run
   (c) experiencing constant average product
   (d) altering its technology to increase its output

80

Variable Factor	Fixed Factor	Output
0	20	0
1	20	50
2	20	120
3	20	220
4	20	300
5	20	360
6	20	410
7	20	450
8	20	470
9	20	480

7. For the firm,
   (a) average product is rising for all levels of output
   (b) marginal product is constant
   (c) the point of diminishing average productivity occurs when output increases from four to five
   (d) average product falls when output goes from two to three

8. For the firm,
   (a) the marginal product is defined as the change in total product divided by the amount of the variable factor
   (b) the point of diminishing marginal productivity occurs when output goes from 50 to 120
   (c) the point of diminishing marginal productivity occurs when output goes from 230 to 300
   (d) marginal product becomes negative at output level of 360

9. The hypothesis of eventually diminishing returns applies to production functions
   (a) having at least one fixed factor
   (b) in the long run only
   (c) in the very long run preferably
   (d) in which inputs are applied in fixed proportions

10. Average total cost is
   (a) total fixed cost plus total variable cost divided by the number of units produced
   (b) total fixed cost minus total variable cost
   (c) total cost divided by the number of units of the fixed factor
   (d) always constant if fixed cost is constant

11. Which of the following necessarily declines continuously as output increases?
   (a) marginal cost
   (b) average fixed cost
   (c) average variable cost
   (d) total fixed cost

12. When average cost is declining,
   (a) marginal cost must be declining
   (b) marginal cost must be above average cost
   (c) marginal cost must be below average cost
   (d) marginal cost must be rising

13. Diminishing average productivity
   (a) occurs over all ranges of ouput
   (b) is due to low-skilled workers
   (c) only occurs in the long run
   (d) implies that average variable costs will eventually rise

81

14. Plant capacity is
    (a) the output at which unit costs are a minimum
    (b) the maximum output possible for a firm
    (c) where unit costs are a maximum
    (d) where marginal cost begins to rise

EXERCISES

1. (a) The relationship between a variable input and output for a firm is shown in
         the first and second columns in the table below. Calculate the average and
         marginal productivity.

Variable Input	Output	Average Product	Marginal Product
1	20		
2	60	_____	_____
3	120	_____	_____
4	200	_____	_____
5	270	_____	_____
6	324	_____	_____
7	364	_____	_____
8	384	_____	_____
9	396	_____	_____
10	404	_____	_____

    (b) Graph the average and marginal product. (Remember to plot marginal product at
         the interval.)

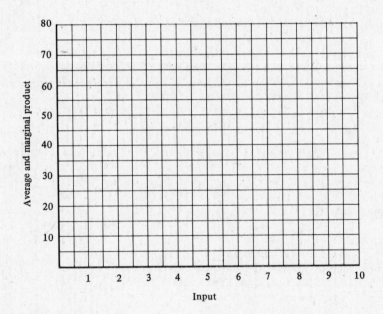

(c) The cost structure for the same firm is shown in the first and second columns
in the table below. Complete the columns in the table.

Output	Fixed Cost	Total Variable Cost	Total Cost	Average Fixed Cost	Average Variable Cost	Average Total Cost	Marginal Cost
20	168	80					
60	168	160					
120	168	240					
200	168	320					
270	168	400					
324	168	480					
364	168	560					
384	168	640					
396	168	720					
404	168	800					

(d)   Graph approximately the average total cost curve and the marginal cost curve.

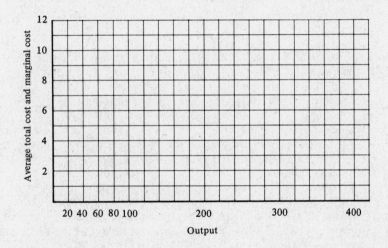

2. The marginal cost schedule of a firm producing good X is shown in the graph below.
(Assume that fixed costs = zero.)
(a) Complete the table below. Note that the marginal cost from the graph applies
to output level at the next highest whole number (e.g., MC of $3.50 applies to
output of 1 unit).

Output	Total Cost	Average Total Cost
1		
2		
3		
4		
5		
6		

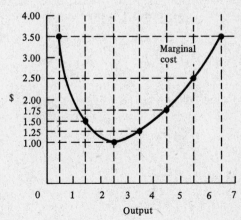

83

(b) Plot the average total cost schedule (approximately) on the graph below.

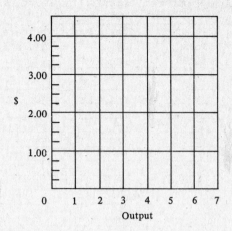

(c) What is the capacity level of output?

3. Suppose the following costs apply to a single flight from Toronto to Vancouver on a Boeing 707 with 180 seats.

Depreciation	$2,400
Fuel	6,000
Salary for crew	7,000
Administration salaries	4,000
Sales and publicity	2,000
Office rent	4,000
Interest on debt	6,000

(a) What are the average fixed costs (AFC) and average variable costs (AVC) for this flight? (Assume that fuel and crew salary are variable costs.)

(b) In establishing fares, the government regulatory agency sets the price per seat at the level that allows the airline to cover AFC when operating at 50 percent of capacity. What will be the regular fare per person on this run?

(c) Given this price, what is the marginal cost to the airline of carrying the ninety-first passenger on the flight?

(d)   Should the airline agree to supply a charter flight for a group that offers to guarantee the sale of 140 tickets at $120 per seat?   Explain.

4.   A producer of a particular commodity finds that he has a total-cost curve that can be described by the equation: TC = $50 + $3Q + $Q^2.
   (a)   Complete the columns below.   [Hint: (3Q + Q^2) is obviously variable costs, and $50 is the fixed cost.]

Q	FC	VC	TC	MC	AFC	AVC	ATC
0							
1							
2							
3							
4							
5							
6							
7							
8							
9							
10							
... 20							

(b)   At what output are total costs per unit (ATC) at a minimum?

(c)   What is the marginal cost at this output?

(d)   If, as shown above, there were only variable costs and no fixed costs, would MC be affected?

(e)   By examining the table above, explain why ATC decreases to a minimum value and then starts to rise.

5. Given the cost curves of a hypothetical firm shown below, answer the following questions.
    (a) The capacity of the firm occurs at an output of _____.
    (b) The effect of eventually diminishing average productivity occurs after an output level of _____ (approximately).
    (c) ATC = MC at an output level of _____.

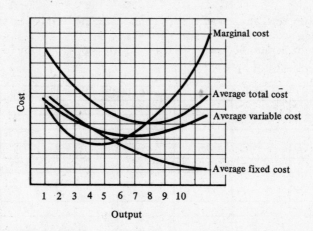

Production, Substitution, and Productivity Increases: Cost in the Long and Very Long Run

13

KEY CONCEPTS AND DEFINITIONS

1. In the long run, all factors are variable.
2. For two factors of production, the cost-minimizing use of these factors calls for a mix of factors such that the ratio of their marginal productivities equals the ratio of their prices.
3. It follows from 2 above that if relative prices of factors are altered, the method of production will change since factor inputs will have to be altered. Relatively more of the cheaper and less of the expensive factor will be used. This is known as the principle of substitution.
4. Relative factor prices reflect to a considerable extent the relative scarcity of factors and thus automatically encourage the use of plentiful factors and conservation of scarce ones.
5. Increasing returns, where output expands faster than inputs as the scale of production is increased, is synonymous with decreasing costs where the long-run average-cost curve is falling as the scale of the plant is increased.
6. The long-run cost curve is horizontal when there are constant returns.
7. When expansion of output is less in proportion to expansion of inputs, the long-run cost curve is increasing, reflecting decreasing returns or increasing costs.
8. The long-run average-cost curve is sometimes referred to as the envelope curve, as it encloses a family of short-run cost curves.
9. Shifts in the short-run average total cost curves are due to such things as changes in factor prices or technology.
10. An isoquant shows how two factors are combined to produce a given output. The rate at which one factor is substituted for another to maintain a constant output is the marginal rate of substitution, and it is equal to the ratios of the marginal products of the two factors.
11. The convexity of an isoquant is implied by assuming that both factors of product are subject to the law of diminishing returns.
12. A series of isoquants, each for a given level of output, is known as an isoquant map.

13. Given factor prices and a fixed sum of money, an <u>isocost line</u> shows what amount of each of two factors can be used that will exhaust the fixed sum of money. The slope of that line will equal the relative prices of the two factors of production.

14. Cost minimization occurs at the tangency between an isoquant and isocost line, or where the ratio of the marginal products equals the ratio of the factor prices.

15. The notion of <u>productivity</u>, or output per unit of input, is an important factor in gauging technical change over time.

16. Long-run productivity increases stem from changes in factor proportions, new techniques of production, and improvements in factor input quality.

17. An <u>invention</u> is the discovery of a new technique, while <u>innovation</u> refers to the application of the invention.

MULTIPLE-CHOICE QUESTIONS

1. For cost minimization where both capital and labour inputs can vary,
   (a) both factors are used until their marginal productivity is zero
   (b) the factors are used such that the marginal productivity per dollar expended on each factor is equalized
   (c) the factors are used such that the ratio of the amounts of the factors used equals the ratio of their marginal productivities
   (d) marginal productivity varies indirectly with price

2. If for a given combination of labour and capital, the ratio of their marginal productivities is 2:1, then for cost minimization
   (a) the ratio of their prices must be 2:1
   (b) two units of labour are combined with one unit of capital
   (c) the ratio of their prices must be 1/2
   (d) there is more capital being used than labour

3. If the marginal product of capital is six times that of labour, and the price of capital is three times that of labour,
   (a) capital will be substituted for labour
   (b) labour will be substituted for capital
   (c) the price of capital will fall, or labour will rise
   (d) twice as much capital as labour will be employed

4. A rise in labour cost relative to capital costs in an industry, <u>ceteris paribus</u>, will
   (a) lead to replacement of some workers by machines where possible
   (b) cause the industry to be unprofitable
   (c) necessarily increase long-run costs
   (d) tend to be offset by rising labour productivity

5. The long-run average cost curve
   (a) shows total ouput related to total input
   (b) assumes constant factor proportions throughout
   (c) reflects the least-cost production method for each output level
   (d) rises because of the "law" of diminishing returns

6. Constant long-run average costs for a firm mean that
   (a) there are greater advantages to small- rather than large-scale plants
   (b) an unlimited amount will be produced
   (c) any scale of production is as cheap per unit as any other
   (d) no addition of factors is taking place

7. Decreasing average costs for a firm as it expands plant size and output
   (a) result from decreasing returns to scale
   (b) results usually from the effects of increased mechanization and specialization
   (c) result from the increased complexity and confusion of rapid expansion
   (d) are a very rare case caused by exogenous events

8. The long-run average cost curve is determined by
   (a) long-run demand
   (b) long-run supply
   (c) population growth and inflation
   (d) technology and input prices

9. Long-run decreasing returns may be the result of
   (a) rising factor prices
   (b) replication
   (c) "spreading the overhead"
   (d) management problems

10. A firm facing long-run increasing returns should expand by
    (a) substituting labour for capital
    (b) replication
    (c) building smaller plants
    (d) building larger plants

11. The short-run average cost (SRAC) cannot fall below the long-run average cost (LRAC)
    (a) because factor prices are fixed
    (b) unless marginal productivities change
    (c) because the LRAC defines the lowest attainable costs
    (d) unless relative prices are changed

12. The family of SRAC curves will shift down for all but one of the following:
    (a) lower prices for labour and capital
    (b) lower costs of energy inputs
    (c) improved technology
    (d) lower demand and reduced product prices

13. In terms of combining factors of production, the marginal rate of substitution
    (a) measures relative prices as output changes over time
    (b) refers to the equivalence between the ratio of marginal productivities and prices
    (c) is always positive
    (d) measures the rate one factor is substituted for another with output held constant

14. If the marginal rate of substitution is -2 at a point on an isoquant involving two factors,
    (a) the ratio of factor prices is +1/2
    (b) the ratio of marginal productivities is -1/2
    (c) the ratio of marginal productivities is -2
    (d) one factor of production has negative marginal productivity

15. An isocost line for two factors C and L (their respective prices are P_C and P_L) could have which of the following equations?
    (a) LC = $100

    (b) $100 = P_C + P_L

    (c) $100 = $P_L L + P_C C$

    (d) $100 = $P_L P_C$

16. If two factors C and L are graphed in the same unit scale with C on the vertical axis, and an isocost line has a slope = -2, then
    (a) $P_L = 2P_C$

    (b) $P_C/P_L = 2$

    (c) $C = 2L$

    (d) $L = 2C$

17. At the point of tangency of this isocost line with an isoquant,
    (a) the desired factor combination has 2C for each L
    (b) the marginal product of labour is twice that of capital
    (c) the desired factor combination has 2L for each C
    (d) the marginal product of capital is twice that of labour

18. If firms are profit maximizers, we should not expect to find a competitive firm expanding its scale if it faces
    (a) increasing returns to scale
    (b) decreasing returns to scale
    (c) constant returns to scale
    (d) pecuniary returns to cost

EXERCISES

1. The table below shows six methods of producing 100 widgets per month using capital and labour.

Method	Units of Capital	Units of Labour	△Capital	△Labour	Rate of Substitution
A	10	80			
B	15	58	_____	_____	_____
C	25	40	_____	_____	_____
D	40	24	_____	_____	_____
E	58	15	_____	_____	_____
F	80	9	_____	_____	_____

(a) Complete the last three columns.
(b) On the graph below, plot the isoquant indicated by the data above.

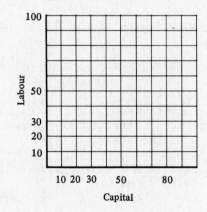

2. Suppose the input-output data for a firm are as shown in the table below.

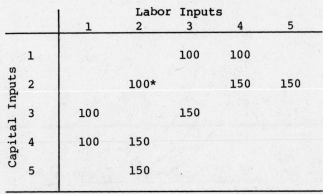

		Labor Inputs			
	1	2	3	4	5
1			100	100	
2		100*		150	150
3	100		150		
4	100	150			
5		150			

*Units of output.

(a) Draw the isoquant map for the two levels of output.

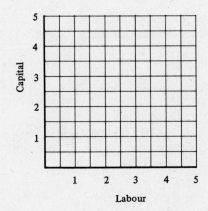

(b) Suppose that the firm was producing 100 units of output, and the isocost line had a slope of approximately -.40. How much capital and labour is the firm using?

(c) If the relative prices of capital and labour were altered to become 1:1, would this alter the nature of the production process for this firm? Explain.

3. The diagram below illustrates how various levels of output can be produced by different combinations of capital and labour.

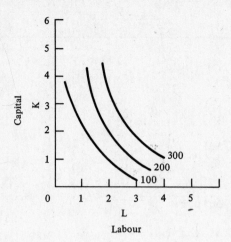

(a) If the ratio of the price of capital to that of labour was K/L = 1/1, how many units of capital and labour will the firm use to produce 100 units of output?

(b) If the price of capital per unit was to become one-half the original price, and the firm wished to produce 200 units of output, approximately how much capital and labour would it employ?

4. At the beginning of some time period, it is observed that a firm producing 10,000 bottles of wine per month uses the following inputs of capital (K) and labour (L) per month:

$$K = \quad 50 \text{ units}$$
$$L = 1000 \text{ units}$$

The price of capital per unit is $20, and for labour the price is $4.

As the firm increases its output over time, the following changes in the use of capital and labour are observed:

Output per Month	K	L
20,000	100	1800
40,000	180	3000
60,000	250	4000
80,000	400	7200
100,000	600	10000

(a) Calculate and graph the long-run average cost curve.

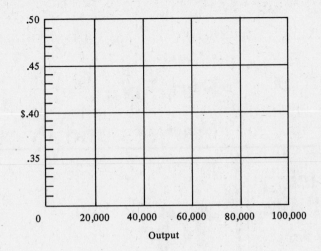

(b) At what output level do increasing returns come to an end?

(c) What happens to the ratio of capital to labour inputs as output expands?

Part Five

Markets and Pricing

<table>
<tr><td>Pricing
in Competitive
Markets</td><td>14</td></tr>
</table>

KEY CONCEPTS AND DEFINITIONS

1. An industry is a collection of firms selling a well-defined product or closely related set of products.
2. A market describes the exchange between households and firms of a well-defined product.
3. If the average revenue received from producing a certain output level does not at least equal the average variable cost at that level of output, the firm should not produce that output.
4. Marginal revenue is the addition to total revenue that occurs when one more unit of output is sold. If it is an advantage to produce at all, output should be expanded up to the level of output where marginal revenue equals marginal cost to maximize profits.
5. Under perfect competition, no firm can by itself influence the market price of the commodity that the firm produces.
6. Perfect competition describes a market in which each firm is a price taker; that is, no one firm can influence the market price of the commodity it produces. Such an industry is marked by freedom of entry and exit.
7. A firm that is a price taker therefore has an average revenue schedule on price that is fixed. Thus the demand schedule can be assumed a straight horizontal line equal to the price.
8. With a given or fixed price, marginal revenue will also be constant and equal to average revenue.
9. For the competitive firm, short-run equilibrium is achieved by adjusting output until the marginal cost equals the marginal revenue, which is also the demand schedule to the firm. Thus the short-run supply curve for the firm is the marginal cost curve or at least that portion above average variable cost.
10. A firm will expand output if price equals or exceeds average variable cost. The marginal cost curve above the average variable cost thus becomes the firm's supply schedule.
11. By adding the supply schedules (curves) of each firm horizontally, we obtain the industry supply schedule (curve).

12. If a perfectly competitive industry generates profits, the ability of firms to enter the industry in response to profits will force prices down until profits are once again zero. If losses occur, some firms will leave the industry and the price will be forced up to a level sufficient to cover total costs.

13. Technological expansion and development leads to industries in which the average variable cost exceeds the average total cost of a new plant.

14. In a declining industry, falling price does not warrant the introduction of new capital.

15. Resource utilization is _efficient_ when it is impossible to recombine resources to make one household better off without making at least one other household worse off. This is known as _Pareto efficiency_ or _Pareto optimality_.

16. Productive efficiency calls for all firms in a perfectly competitive industry to be profit maximizers; _allocative efficiency_ refers to resource allocations among industries that are Pareto optimal.

17. Perfect competition where price equals marginal cost ensures allocative efficiency.

APPENDIX TO CHAPTER 14

A.1. The long-run supply curve is a locus of long-run equilibrium following demand-induced adjustments.

A.2. A _rising cost industry_ or _rising supply price_ is characterized by a positively sloped long-run supply, while a negatively sloped long-run supply is referred to as a _falling cost industry_.

MULTIPLE-CHOICE QUESTIONS

1. A large number of independent plants producing steel products would be referred to as
   (a) a consortium
   (b) an industry ✓
   (c) a co-op
   (d) a market

2. Which is _not_ a required characteristic of a perfectly competitive industry?
   (a) consumers have no reason to prefer one firm's product to another
   (b) there are enough firms so none can influence market price
   (c) any firm can enter or leave the industry
   (d) industry demand is highly elastic ✓

3. If the market price is below average variable cost for a firm,
   (a) the firm must change technology
   (b) the firm must cease production
   (c) fixed costs are not covered
   (d) the firm should consider altering its level of output ✓

4. Marginal revenue
   (a) refers to a firm about to go bankrupt
   (b) is the additional output necessary to lower price
   (c) is the additional revenue when output expands by one unit ✓
   (d) is the ratio of average revenue to total revenue

5. One of the following is <u>not</u> a necessary condition for profit maximization:
   (a) price must exceed average variable cost
   (b) marginal cost must equal marginal revenue
   (c) the elasticity of demand must equal unity
   (d) marginal cost must cut marginal revenue from below

6. A perfectly competitive firm does not try to sell more of its product by lowering its price below the market price because
   (a) this would be considered unethical price chiseling
   (b) its competitors will not permit it
   (c) its demand curve is inelastic, so total revenue will decline
   (d) it can sell all it wants to at the market price

7. If the market demand for wheat has an elasticity of .25
   (a) an individual wheat farmer can increase his revenue by reducing output
   (b) nothing can be said about the elasticity of demand for a wheat farmer
   (c) revenue from wheat sales will rise with an increase of industry production
   (d) each wheat farmer, nevertheless, faces a highly elastic demand ✓

Questions 8 through 10 refer to the diagram below.

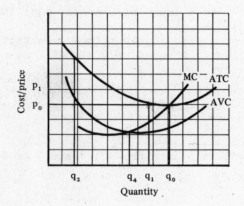

8. At output q_2, given price p_0, the firm (in a perfectly competitive industry)
   (a) should reduce output by one-half
   (b) should raise its price
   (c) is worse off than if it produced nothing ✓
   (d) must expand output to q_4 to maximize profits

9. At q_1, the firm
   (a) is maximizing profit
   (b) is producing where the cost of additional output exceeds the additional revenue generated
   (c) is in long-run equilibrium
   (d) should expand output to q_0 to maximize profits

10. If the market price of the product produced by this firm was to rise from p_0 to p_1,
   (a) existing firms would increase output to a point where price = ATC
   (b) new firms would enter the industry causing the price to return to p_0, <u>ceteris paribus</u>
   (c) existing firms would enjoy, in the long run, windfall profits
   (d) there would be a permanent disequilibrium in the industry

11. In perfect competition, the supply curve of the firm is
   (a) the marginal cost schedule above average variable cost
   (b) the marginal cost schedule above average total cost
   (c) the marginal cost schedule above average fixed cost
   (d) the marginal cost schedule

12. Long-run profits are incompatible with a perfectly competitive industry because
   (a) new firms will enter the industry and eliminate them
   (b) corporate income taxes eliminate such excess profits
   (c) competitive industries are too inefficient to be profitable
   (d) increasing long-run costs eliminate profits

13. The conditions for long-run competitive equilibrium include all but one of the following for all firms:
   (a) P = AVC
   (b) P = MC
   (c) P = AVC + AFC
   (d) P = LRATC

14. Capital stock is likely to become obsolete whenever
   (a) shifts in demand cause a rise in price
   (b) an industry is characterized as an expanding industry
   (c) technology remains unchanged in the long run
   (d) the average total cost of new capital is less than existing variable costs of the firm

15. A Pareto-efficient use of resources means that
   (a) changes in resource utilization will cause costs to rise
   (b) using resources in a different manner can only be done at the expense of making at least one household worse off
   (c) at least one firm is producing at a minimum long-run average cost
   (d) the allocation of resources among industries is fixed in the long run

16. Perfect competition
   (a) ensures allocative efficiency because firms can exit the industry if demand declines
   (b) ensures allocative efficiency since price will equal marginal cost in every industry
   (c) only guarantees productive efficiency in the short run
   (d) requires that at least one firm produces at minimum average total cost

APPENDIX

A.1. Long-run equilibrium in perfect competition occurs when
   (a) plant size cannot be changed to achieve a lower average total cost
   (b) short-run average cost is above marginal cost
   (c) there is no entry or exit of firms
   (d) price declines as output expands

A.2. An increasing cost industry can be characterized by all but one of the following:
   (a) rapid growth causing input prices to rise due to demand
   (b) an increase in the number of firms in the industry
   (c) higher costs of inputs due to exogenous factors
   (d) a rising long-run marginal cost curve

A.3. A decreasing cost industry may lead to
  (a) excessive demand for ouput and eventually higher prices
  (b) domination of the market by one or a few firms
  (c) inefficiency in resource allocation even if the industry remains perfectly competitive
  (d) all of the above

EXERCISES

1. The diagram below illustrates a firm that produces in a perfectly competitive market. Complete the questions below with reference to the diagram.

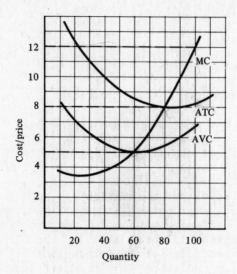

Note: MC = marginal cost
       AVC = average variable cost
       ATC = average total cost

If the market price is ⟶	$ 12	$ 8	$ 5
(a) equilibrium output will be	100	80	60
At this output			
(b) total revenue is	1200	640	300
(c) total cost is	825	640	510
(d) total profit is (+) or (−)	375	−	-210
(e) profit per unit of output is	3.75	0.50	-3.50

2. The basic cost schedules for a firm producing in a perfectly competitive market are shown below.

Output/Month	Fixed Cost	Variable Cost (VC)	Total Cost (TC)	AVC	ATC	MC
0	20	—	20	0	0	15
1	20	15	35	15	35	9
2	20	24	44	12	22	6
3	20	30	50	10	16.66	18
4	20	48	68	12	17	27
5	20	75	95	15	19	45
6	20	120	140	20	23.33	

98

(a) If the firm is producing an output where ATC is a minimum and the market price is $8.00, should the firm continue production or go out of business? Why? (Complete the table.)

(b) If market price was $16.67, should the firm adjust its output from that suggested in (a)? Explain.

(c) If market price rose to $20.00, what would the firm experience? How would the industry respond?

3. At present output levels, a competitive firm finds itself with the following:

           Output: 5,000 units
           Market price: $1.00
           Fixed costs: $2,000
           Variable costs: $2,500
           Marginal cost: $1.25 and rising

(a) Is it maximizing profits? Why?

(b) Should it produce more, produce less, or stay the same?

4. The diagram below illustrates the cost position of firms operating in a perfectly competitive market immediately following the introduction of a cost-saving innovation.

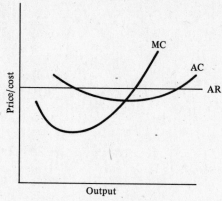

(a) What initial advantage are the firms enjoying?

(b) Can this advantage remain? Justify your answer by noting what will be taking place in the market as a whole.

5. The supply (S) and demand (D) schedules for an industry are shown below in the figure on the left. The cost schedule for one firm in this industry is shown in the figure on the right.

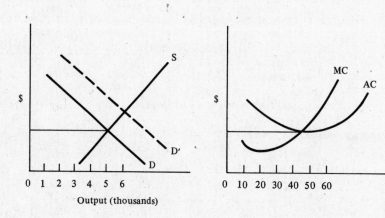

(a) Does the above information suggest that the industry is a perfectly competitive one? Give your reasons.

100

(b) If the market demand schedule were to shift to D', what is the initial impact on the price of output in this industry and on the profits of the firm?

(c) What change in the diagrams would be necessary to bring the firm back into a position of "normal" profits?

6. In the table below are basic data on three firms that we are assuming comprise a perfectly competitive market. Complete the table. Then on the graph, plot at the intervals of output the short-run supply curve for each firm and a portion of the industry supply schedule. Note that the industry supply schedule will be a "rough" approximation given the format of the data. (In drawing the industry schedule, use the graphs for each firm, not the schedules.)

| | Firm A | | | Firm B | | | Firm C | |
Output	Total Cost	Marginal Cost	Output	Total Cost	Marginal Cost	Output	Total Cost	Marginal Cost
30	120		25	80		36	150	
		___			___			___
40	160		30	82.5		40	166	
		___			___			___
50	210		35	95		44	186	
		___			___			___
60	280		40	135		48	214	
		___			___			___
70	380		45	195		52	254	
		___			___			___
80	520		50	285		56	310	

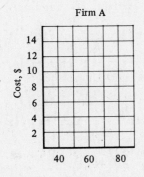

Firm A

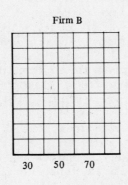

Firm B

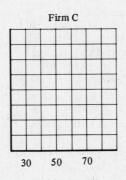

Firm C

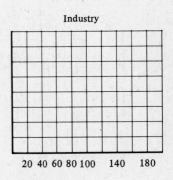

Industry

Pricing
in Monopoly
Markets

15

KEY CONCEPTS AND DEFINITIONS

1. By definition, a monopoly is a single-seller market. Hence, the demand curve or average-revenue curve for the monopolist is identical with the market-demand curve.

2. The marginal revenue for the monopolist is always below the average revenue provided market demand is not infinitely elastic.

3. Since an inelastic portion of a demand schedule coincides with negative marginal revenue, the monopolist will set his price in the elastic portion of the demand schedule.

4. The monopolist, like the firm in perfect competition, will, if it is maximizing profit, produce where marginal cost equals marginal revenue. The price that corresponds to the given demand schedule is usually higher than average cost.

5. A situation of monopoly will only exist if there are barriers to entry.

6. The potential inefficiency that exists in monopoly is that there is no tendency for the monopolist to produce at minimum average cost.

7. The level of output of a monopolist is not allocatively nor Pareto efficient since price exceeds marginal cost.

8. In actual fact, no firm is totally insulated from other products all the time, and this fact limits monopoly power. A measure of monopoly power is the degree to which one firm's decision on output-price affects the demand curve of other producers.

9. Collusion is a procedure whereby a few firms agree to set a common price or fix market shares.

10. A concentration ratio shows the fraction of total sales controlled by the largest four or eight sellers. Such a ratio measures only the potential for monopoly power.

11. Conscious parallel action or tacit collusion refers to parallel behavior by firms in the absence of formal collusion.

12. When different buyers pay different prices for the same commodity, or when a single buyer pays different prices for different units of the commodity, price discrimination exists.

13. To be able to discriminate, a producer must be able to prevent the resale of his product and control the supply available to different buyers.
14. On the part of buyers, price discrimination is only possible if different groups of buyers have different degrees of willingness to pay.
15. Given the potential to price discriminate, such action will always generate more total revenue than a single monopoly price and will, in general, result in greater output.

MULTIPLE-CHOICE QUESTIONS

Questions 1 through 4 refer to the diagram below.

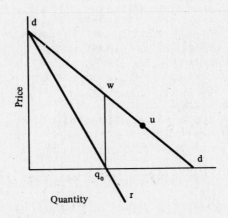

1. The curve labelled dd is
    (a) the monopolist's average fixed cost curve
    (b) the monopolist's average revenue curve
    (c) where marginal cost = marginal revenue
    (d) is an elastic demand curve of unity

2. The curve labelled dr is the monopolist's
    (a) demand schedule
    (b) total revenue curve
    (c) marginal revenue curve
    (d) long-run supply curve for a decreasing cost industry

3. If a monopolist sets his price at u, then it follows
    (a) that he is maximizing profits
    (b) that demand is elastic at u
    (c) that he should raise price and reduce output
    (d) that the marginal cost schedule goes through u

4. Profit maximization for a monopolist will occur when
    (a) output is equal to or less than q_0 ✓
    (b) price equals w
    (c) price is halfway between d and w
    (d) output is to the right of q_0

5. If profits are to be maximized by a firm, whether a monopolist or a competitor,
    (a) output should be increased whenever marginal cost is below average cost
    (b) output should be increased whenever marginal revenue is less than marginal cost
    (c) output should be set where unit costs are at a minimum
    (d) output should be increased whenever marginal revenue exceeds marginal cost

6. A monopolist has a downward-sloping demand curve
   (a) because it has an inelastic demand
   (b) because, typically, it sells only to a few large buyers
   (c) because it is the same as the industry
   (d) because consumers prefer that product

7. Barriers to entry, which sustain monopoly, may be due to all but one of the following:
   (a) patent laws
   (b) economies of scale
   (c) long-run constant costs
   (d) franchises

8. The monopoly firm is unlikely to be Pareto-optimal because
   (a) the demand schedule for the firm is not horizontal
   (b) the short- and long-run costs are identical
   (c) price exceeds marginal cost
   (d) marginal revenue and average revenue do not coincide

9. Concentration ratios have been found
   (a) to have considerable correlation with profit rates
   (b) to have little usefulness where there are more than two firms
   (c) to have little relevance in measuring the degree of monopoly power in an industry
   (d) to be very low in the great majority of manufacturing industries

10. A producer with monopoly power may choose a price that is not a long-run profit-maximizing price because
   (a) the cost curve is unknown
   (b) marginal cost does not equal marginal revenue
   (c) the firm's demand curve may shift due to price changes that cause other firms to alter their prices
   (d) the firm's cost curve is responsive to price changes brought about by other firms

11. Price discrimination is possible only
   (a) in the case of perfect monopoly
   (b) if it is possible to keep it a secret
   (c) if it is possible to conspire with competitors
   (d) if it is possible to separate the buyers or units that can be sold at different prices

Questions 12 through 14 refer to the diagram below.

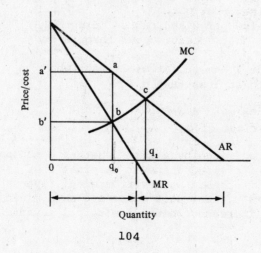

12. The degree of allocative inefficiency of a monopoly is shown by
    (a) the area abc
    (b) the area a'b'ba
    (c) the distance q_0a
    (d) the area $0b'bq_0$

13. The profit-maximizing monopolist will establish price and output at
    (a) a' and q_1
    (b) b' and q_0
    (c) a' and q_0
    (d) c and q_1

14. Profit-maximizing monopoly profits per unit of output are shown by
    (a) ab
    (b) ca_1/aq_0
    (c) $0q_0/a'b'$
    (d) none of the above

15. Price discrimination is equivalent to perfect competition when
    (a) both situations result in price equal to average cost
    (b) the price of the last unit of output sold equals marginal cost
    (c) price or average revenue equals marginal revenue
    (d) there are no monopoly profits

EXERCISES

1. In the diagram below, the basic cost and revenue schedules of a hypothetical monopoly firm are given.

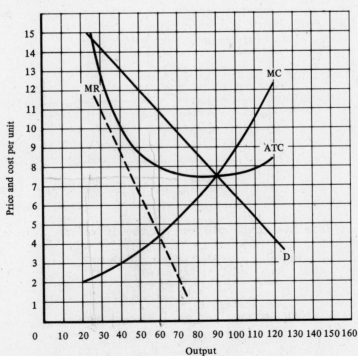

(a) What is the output where the firm's profits will be at a maximum? _____
(b) What will be the price at this output? _____

(c) What will be the total revenue (at this output)? _____

(d) What will be the total costs? _____

(e) What will be the total profit? _____

(f) Within what <u>range</u> of output and price will the firm also make at least <u>some</u> profit, though not maximum? _____

(g) What price would limit the monopolist to competitive profits? _____

2. The data below relate to a pure monopolist and the product that he produces.

Output	Total Cost	Price	Quantity Demanded				
0	$20	$20	0				
1	24	18	1				
2	27	16	2				
3	32	14	3				
4	39	12	4				
5	48	10	5				
6	59	8	6				

(a) What additional cost and revenue information do you need before you can calculate the profit-maximizing output and price for the monopolist?

(b) Calculate these additional schedules, record them in the columns next to the given data, and plot them (approximately) below.

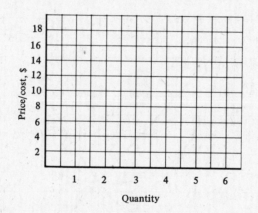

<u>Note</u>: All marginal data are to be plotted in the interval.

(c) What is the approximate profit-maximizing output?

(d) At what price will the monopolist sell his product?

(e) What are the monopolist's (approximate) profits?

106

3. The diagram below shows the basic cost and revenue schedules for a monopolist.

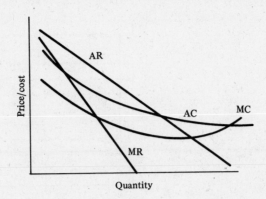

(a) Illustrate on the diagram the price the profit-maximizing monopolist will set and the quantity sold. (Label these P_M and Q_M.)

(b) Indicate by vertical hatching,▯▯▯▯▯▯▯, monopoly profits.

(c) Suppose the monopolist, to be allocatively efficient, set price or AR = marginal cost. Label the price P_E and the output Q_E. Would this output be sustainable in the long run? Explain with reference to the cost the monopolist faces.

4. Two demand curves for the same product are shown below in diagrams A and B. These schedules represent buyers that can be separated. The basic cost schedule for the monopolist producing this product is shown in diagram C.

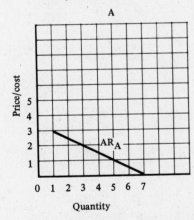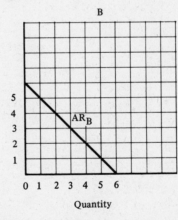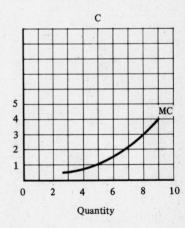

(a) Graph the aggregate demand curve (AR curve) in diagram C.

(b) If the monopolist price-discriminates in a "perfect" manner, he will sell an output corresponding to MC = MR for the total market, but set his price in each of the two markets such that the MR of last unit sold in each market is the same. (Refer to pages 284 and 285 in the text.) Illustrate in the diagrams above:

(i) total output sold Q_{A+B}

(ii) output sold in market A and B (Q_A and Q_B)

(iii) the price charged in each market (P_A and P_B).

5. Some of the basic cost data for a monopolist are given in the following table.

Output	Total Cost
0	40
5	50
10	65
15	90
20	130
25	190
30	275

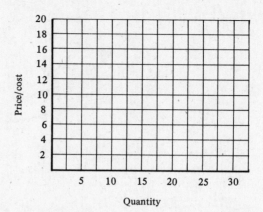

The demand or average curve schedule is given by $Q_d = 20 - 1.0AR$, where Q_d is quantity demanded and AR is average revenue or price.

(a) Graph the average cost, marginal cost, average and marginal revenue schedules. (Note: Because the scales for the axes are not the same, the slope of the AR curve will not appear to be that which is given in the equation. Also, consult Chapter 14 for discussion of relationship between average and marginal revenue.)

(b) What approximately is the profit-making monopolist's profits? Show this by shading the area in the diagram you have completed.

(c) If the government imposed a tax equal to $4.00 per unit of output, would the monopolist change his price and output? Why and in what way?

Industrial Organization and Theories of Imperfect Competition

16

KEY CONCEPTS AND DEFINITIONS

1. The Canadian economy is not characterized by monopoly and perfect competition, but it can perhaps be more appropriately described as industries with a large number of relatively small firms and industries with a few relatively large firms.

2. Between perfect competition and monopoly, there are a number of industrial organization structures that have some of the characteristics of both extremes. Oligopoly, where a few large firms dominate the industry and where there are significant barriers to entry, and monopolistic competition, which is characterized by product differentiation and relative ease of entry, are two such structures.

3. Product differentiation between firms in the same industry gives individual firms market power such that their demand schedules are not perfectly elastic, as in perfect competitions. They are said to produce a differentiated product, in contrast to the production of a homogeneous product as in perfect competition.

4. The excess capacity theorem states that under monopolistic competition, productive efficiency is not reached because firms do not produce at minimum average cost.

5. An administered price is a characteristic of oligopoly since it is set by the seller after consideration of costs, demand, and the prices of rival products.

6. In a duopoly there are only two firms in the industry and price/output behavior by one firm is based on what the other firm is doing, assuming it will not alter its behaviour.

7. An industry characterized by oligopoly, or competition among the few, suggests that collusion among the firms to form a monopoly would maximize profits. Preventing this collusion, however, is the desire of each firm to maximize its share of total industry profits.

8. One important barrier to entry in oligopoly is the minimum efficient scale (MES), the smallest size for a firm that allows for the gain from economies of scale.

9. A limit price allows existing members of an oligopoly to earn profits, but potential entrants will suffer losses.

10. Members of an oligopoly can create barriers to entry by predatory pricing, pre-emptive expansion, advertising, and brand proliferation.

11. The existence of a <u>kinked demand curve</u> in an industry suggests that there is price flexibility whereby a price increase by one firm would result in a drastic reduction in sales, and a price reduction would produce little increase in output.

<u>MULTIPLE-CHOICE QUESTIONS</u>

1. The Canadian economy is characterized by
    (a) government-controlled single-firm industries in the manufacturing and service sector
    (b) perfect competition in all but one or two industries
    (c) monopoly in the key sector of manufacturing and perfect competition in agriculture
    (d) industries having many small firms and industries having a few large and dominant firms

2. Product differentiation refers to
    (a) the fact that consumers have a wide choice of goods to buy
    (b) a situation whereby firms have some control or power over their price and output decisions due to the subtle uniqueness of their product
    (c) an industry that produces more than one commodity
    (d) the degree by which a firm can change its output from one product to another

3. A differentiated product can be defined as
    (a) belonging to a general group to be called a product but having sufficiently different characteristics such that a producer of a differentiated product has some power over price
    (b) a product that is different from others such that the seller has monopoly control over its price
    (c) a product within a group where all characteristics of the product are the same, except price
    (d) one that, within a group, is different from all others in the group but has the same price

4. The excess capacity theorem refers to
    (a) a lack of aggregate demand leading to less than full use of resources
    (b) monopolistic competition and output pricing at less than minimum average cost
    (c) less than full employment in some industries
    (d) a pricing situation where the slope of the demand curve does not equal the slope of the long-run average total cost curve

5. An important prediction of monopolistic competition is that the equilibrium output of the firm occurs at an output
    (a) where price exceeds average cost
    (b) less than the one at which average cost is at a minimum
    (c) less than the one at which average cost equals average revenue
    (d) less than the one at which marginal cost equals marginal revenue

6. According to the theory, temporary profits of a monopolistic competitor are eliminated primarily by
    (a) production where average costs are above the minimum
    (b) nonprice competition
    (c) entry of new firms
    (d) price reductions to meet new competition

7. An oligopoly is characterized by
   (a) a single dominant firm in the industry
   (b) a formal agreement among firms on how much to produce and at what price
   (c) a few firms facing downward sloping demand curves that they cannot consider to be their own
   (d) an industry of less than four firms

8. A major difference between oligopoly and monopolistic competition is
   (a) the number of firms in the industry
   (b) the ability to sustain long-run profits
   (c) the degree of difficulty of entry into the industry
   (c) all of the above

9. A decision-making process referred to as conjectural variations
   (a) guarantees a constant price across all firms in an oligopoly
   (b) applies only to duopoly
   (c) involves consideration of how rivals will respond to price change
   (d) is used only in monopolistic competition

10. In an oligopolistic industry, joint profit-maximizing by setting prices through tacit agreement is
    (a) more likely the fewer the number of firms
    (b) more likely the less similar the products
    (c) more likely when prices are falling than when they are rising
    (d) invariably illegal under the anti-combines law

11. All but one of the following characterizes oligopolistic behaviour:
    (a) Joint profit maximization is likely to be enhanced, the smaller the number of firms.
    (b) In the long run, entry will eliminate profits.
    (c) The more similar the product, the more likely there will be joint profit maximization.
    (d) If barriers to entry are high, there is a greater tendency for joint profit maximization.

12. Minimum efficient scale (MES) is related to
    (a) the long-run average cost of an oligopolist
    (b) the marginal cost curve
    (c) the size of the industry
    (c) the price necessary to earn a profit

13. The "limit price" just below which an oligopolist might set his price to prevent new firms from entering is determined by
    (a) the oligopolist's lowest unit cost
    (b) the lowest price at which the oligopolist can still make a profit
    (c) the lowest price at which a new entrant could cover costs
    (d) the price that can be set where marginal revenue equals marginal cost

14. All but one of the following are barriers to entry created by the firms in an oligopoly.
    (a) predatory pricing
    (b) pre-emptive expansion
    (c) advertising
    (d) minimum required capital stock

15. Brand image advertising is most likely to be found in an oligopoly
    (a) when the demand curve is inelastic
    (b) where natural barriers to entry are weak
    (c) where the product being sold is almost identical for each firm
    (d) where prices cannot be quickly changed

16. If firms in an oligopoly did not alter price when marginal cost increased, we might conclude
    (a) that there was tacit collusion about price in the short run
    (b) that the products were very similar and rivalry was intense
    (c) that the firms faced a kinked demand schedule
    (d) all of the above

APPENDIX

Answer A.1. and A.2. referring to the diagram below:

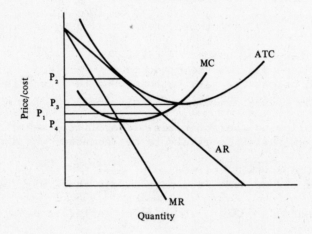

A.1. The firm in monopolistic competition will set its price equal to
    (a) P_1
    (b) P_2
    (c) P_3
    (d) P_4
A.2. The equilibrium situation described by the combination P_2 and ATC is
    (a) equivalent to perfect competition since profit is eliminated
    (b) a long-run equilibrium in monopolistic competition
    (c) unstable; new firms will enter the industry and existing firms lose out
    (d) Pareto efficient

EXERCISES

1. The figure on the following page describes a firm operating in a monopolistically competitive industry.
    (a) What price will the firm set? _____
    (b) What total profit will this firm receive? _____
    (c) Given that entry is relatively easy, is this a long-run equilibrium situation? Explain.

112

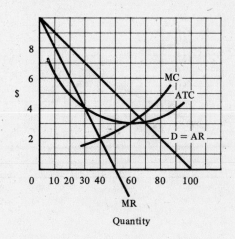

(d) If this and other firms in the household-soap industry undertook a single, large-scale advertising campaign, what curve in the figure would be affected the most? Explain.

(e) If new firms were attracted to this industry, what curves in the figure would be affected the most? Why? What would be the main consequence for this firm?

2. One of the columns below lists characteristics of an industry; the other column lists behaviour. Match the two columns by placing the number from the right column in the blank space after each description in the left column.

Characteristic of Industry	Behaviour
(a) very few firms and very similar products ___3___	1. duopoly behaviour
(b) large number of firms, ease of entry, and differentiated product ___4___	2. price change not highly responsive to MC changes
(c) a contracting oligopoly ___5___	3. joint profit-maximization behaviour
(d) high barriers of entry and few firms ___3___	4. long-run monopoly profits equal to zero
(e) two-firm oligopoly ___1___	5. little tendency to joint profit maximization
(f) oligopolists experiencing kinked demand curves ___2___	

113

3. The diagram below illustrates two kinked demand curves.

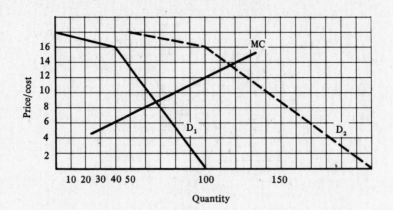

(a) Draw the MR (marginal revenue curves) and label them MR_1 and MR_2.
(b) Given the marginal cost curve above, the price when demand is D_1 will
     be _____ ; when it is D_2, the price will be _____ .
(c) If the marginal cost became slightly lower, then for D_1, price
     would _____ ; for D_2, it would _____ .
(d) If the marginal cost became slightly higher, then for D_1, price
     would _____ ; for D_2, it would _____ .
(e) Demand schedules of the type shown above are likely to be associated with what
     type of market structure? _____

114

Price Theory in Action | 17

KEY CONCEPTS AND DEFINITIONS

1. A <u>cartel</u> is a producers' organization that, in limiting output, raises prices above their competitive level. In a <u>producers' association</u>, each firm agrees to restrict output.
2. Unless they can be enforced, <u>quotas</u> will be violated, since it pays for any single member to do so believing that others will not.
3. If a cartel is successful, the excess profits earned by member firms will attract new entrants and reduce profits.
4. Limiting competition may have short-run gains that are not likely to remain in the long run.
5. The OPEC cartel and its aftereffects clearly demonstrate the importance of time in moving from one equilibrium to another and underscore the many adjustments that markets have to make.
6. In monitoring adjustments to price and ouput changes in a market, it is important to distinguish between long- and short-run elasticities.

MULTIPLE-CHOICE QUESTIONS

1. A cartel is likely to succeed in raising and maintaining price above its competitive level if
   (a) it can prevent cheating
   (b) entry is difficult
   (c) most producers support the cartel
   (d) all of the above ✓

2. If one firm violates the conditions of a cartel and lowers prices,
   (a) that firm will experience an elasticity of demand that is different from other firms
   (b) the violator will gain at the expense of others ✓
   (c) the cartel-induced price will fall to the original competitive level for all firms
   (d) the violator will lose revenue by cutting price

3. A producers' association raises the price of its product by 20 percent and quantity
   sold is reduced by 12 percent. If the original price was $5 and an average 200
   units were sold by each firm,
   (a) each firm experiences a 12 percent decline in revenue
   (b) the elasticity of demand is, in the range, 1.67
   (c) revenue for the average firm increases by 5.6 percent
   (d) the elasticity of demand is zero

4. Prior to the emergence of OPEC, the North American gasoline market
   (a) was characterized by a slow and steadily rising supply price
   (b) responded to increases in demand by generating significant price increases
   (c) experienced an elasticity of supply that was close to zero
   (d) was characterized by a cartel that set price above supply price

5. Which of the following markets are not likely to be affected in the long run by the
   OPEC embargo?
   (a) the automobile market
   (b) the housing market
   (c) the market for plastics and other synthetics
   (d) none of the above

6. When there is a sudden rise in the price of a product, we can expect a rapid
   increase in price initially followed by a price reduction
   (a) if governments hold the price down
   (b) when the short-run elasticity of demand is greater than the long-run elasticity
   (c) when the supply shock is permanent
   (d) when government imposes quantity controls

7. The degree of substitution away from a higher-priced commodity
   (a) is only possible if all demand curves are elastic
   (b) will be directly related to the time period from the initial price rise
   (c) will depend on the constancy of income
   (d) is only a short-run phenomenon

EXERCISES

1. The short-run (SR) and long-run (LR) demand curves are described by the equations
   below.

   $$Q_d = 14 - 2P \quad (LR) \quad \text{and} \quad Q_d = 6.5 - .5P \quad (SR)$$

   The supply schedule is given by P = 5.

   (a) What is the current equilibrium price and quantity sold for this market?

   (b) If the supply schedule becomes P = 6, what will be the short-run price and
       quantity sold? What will happen in the long run to price and quantity sold?
       Explain.

116

2. The table below gives some information about conditions in a monopolistically
    competitive market. Using this information, complete the table.

	Elasticity of Demand	Initial Price of Output	Initial Quantity Sold (units/mo)	Change in Price (%)	Change in Revenue ($)	Change in Output Sold (%)
(a)	-1.2	$2.50	250	+15%	_____	_____
(b)	_____	$1.50	1,500	+20%	_____	-25%
(c)	-1.8	$5.00	500	_____	_____	+10%

3. The diagram below shows a hypothetical market situation for the supply and demand
of water in a community that obtains its water from another political jurisdiction.

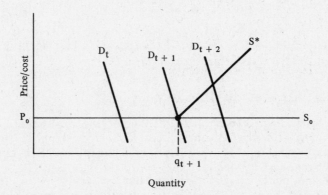

For years, water has been available at constant marginal cost reflecting
transportation expenses, as shown by S_0. As population has grown, the <u>short-run</u>
community demand has shifted to the right, as shown by D_t, D_{t+1}. When quantity
used is at q_{t+1}, the jurisdiction supplying the water limits the availability, as
indicated by S*. Demand continues to increase to D_{t+2}, but local authorities
keep the price at P_0.
(a) Indicate the short-run excess demand this situation will produce.
(b) What price would "clear" the market (no excess demand)? _____
(c) Population stabilizes in the community, and after a while water use declines
     and the market price falls. Explain what is likely taking place in terms of
     long-run equilibrium.

Monopoly Versus Competition | 18

1. A change in marginal cost will induce less response in price and output under monopoly than in competition.
2. Costs remaining the same, the monopolization of a competitive industry will lead to less output and higher prices.
3. There may be cost advantages to having only a one-firm industry, or natural monopoly, or a more oligopolistic structure. This is likely to occur when the minimum efficient size is large.
4. Economies of scope are said to exist when large firms, as contrasted to large plants, can achieve lower costs compared to highly competitive structure.
5. There are incentives to innovate in both monopolistic and competitive structures. These incentives, however, are likely to differ.
6. Patent laws confer a temporary monopoly to lengthen the period of earning supernormal profits due to innovation.
7. Competition policy is concerned with a wide variety of issues such as mergers, price discrimination, collusion, and resale price maintenance.
8. Recent changes in Canadian competition policy give the Restrictive Trade Practice Commission the power to control problems resulting from refusal to supply, exclusive dealing market restriction, tied sales, and misleading advertising.
9. Public utilities often have the features of a natural monopoly and public-utility regulation involves giving a company the right to exclusive production and sale of a service or commodity in exchange for a degree of government regulation.
10. In deciding what a public utility can charge, the regulators must consider what is a fair rate of return based on a measure of the capital stock known as the rate base.

MULTIPLE-CHOICE QUESTIONS

1. In a monopoly, price and output response to marginal cost changes will be less than in competition
   (a) because the monopolist is guided by the average revenue schedule, which is more elastic than marginal revenue
   (b) because monopoly firms tend to be large and adjustment to cost changes is slow
   (c) because monopolist is guided by marginal revenue, which is less elastic than the demand curve to which competition must respond
   (d) because the monopolist will not change price in the elastic portion of the average revenue curve

2. Assuming that cost curves would be the same in an industry under either monopoly or competition, a monopolist will produce in equilibrium at a point where, compared with the competitive equilibrium,
   (a) output is larger but price is higher
   (b) output is less but price is higher
   (c) output is less but price is the same
   (d) output is the same but price is higher

3. A natural monopoly
   (a) occurs only in the resources industry
   (b) evolves over time through merger practice
   (c) exists where the size of the market calls for only one firm in terms of the shape of the long-run average cost
   (d) does not, in contrast to other monopolies, require public intervention

4. If large firms are able to achieve lower costs in contrast to large plants, this suggests
   (a) that conditions are present for the emergence of a natural monopoly
   (b) that there are economies of scope
   (c) that there are economies of scale
   (d) that the MES is small

5. With regard to innovation and industrial structure, it is generally regarded that
   (a) monopolistic profits create the means for innovation, while competition requires that firms be innovative
   (b) competition will always be more conducive to innovation because of the need to lower costs
   (c) monopolists, because they have excess profits, have no need to innovate
   (d) innovation takes place in all industrial structures for the same reasons

6. A patent law
   (a) guarantees exclusive use of an innovation in perpetuity
   (b) covers only innovations that occur in competitive industries
   (c) is generally regarded as the most important factor in stimulating innovation
   (d) lengthens the time a firm can reap excess profits by attempting to grant exclusive use of an innovation for a period of time

7. If a manufacturer attempts to force a retailer to sell its produce at a fixed price, it is
   (a) engaged in exclusive dealing
   (b) resale price maintenance
   (c) tied orders
   (d) a fair business practice

8. The lack of combines enforcement in Canada has generally been attributed to
   (a) the government's reluctance to be concerned by competition policy
   (b) the limitations of criminal legislation to deal with economic issues
   (c) the absence of activity that reduces competition
   (d) the multinational character of large firms in Canada

9. The most significant feature of the 1975 Stage I amendments to competition law in Canada was
   (a) increasing the staff of the RTPC
   (b) allowing economic evidence as admissable in court cases
   (c) giving the RTPC power to order the cessation of certain activities
   (d) the transfer of certain matters dealing with competition policy to civil courts

10. The usual argument in favour of accepting a "natural" monopoly, if it is regulated, is that
    (a) regulation guarantees fair, low prices
    (b) more than one company would be obviously wasteful
    (c) it gives the same results as public ownership
    (d) regulation keeps it out of politics

11. From the public's standpoint, a "fair rate of return" on utility investment
    (a) should mean approximately the current rate on alternatives of similar risk
    (b) should be determined by historical costs
    (c) can always be earned, provided prices are set high enough
    (d) means what the stockholders think is fair

EXERCISES

1. The diagram below describes a hypothetical firm.

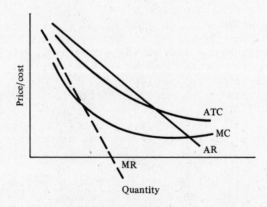

   (a) What type of industrial structure or organization is illustrated by the diagram?

   (b) Pareto-efficiency requires that a certain condition involving price and marginal cost be met. If this firm was "forced" to set price in a Pareto-efficient manner, what price would it charge and what output would be produced? (Illustrate on the diagram.)

(c) Suppose a regulatory authority required that price = average cost for this form. What would it produce and at what price?

2.

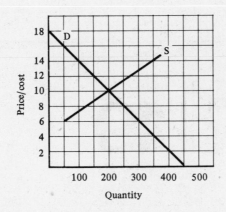

Quantity

(a) In the market described above, if there are many buyers and sellers, the price will be _____ and quantity exchanged will be _____ .
(b) If there is a profit-maximizing monopolist in this market, price will be _____ and output will be _____ .
(c) In the case of the monopolist, by how much will price be in excess of minimum average total cost, assuming that the cost curves are the same in (a) and (b)? _____

3. The diagrams below illustrate a perfectly competitive situation and a monopoly situation in a market. If costs were to rise by one dollar per unit of output, illustrate that the price would rise by less and output would fall by less in the case of monopoly.

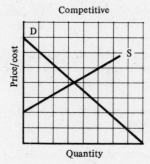

Competitive

Quantity

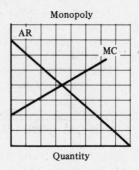

Monopoly

Quantity

Who Runs the Firm and for What Ends? | 19

1. The operation of the market system depends upon firms responding to consumers' desires. There are competing hypotheses claiming that firms manipulate demand and create needs in society.

2. If the theory of ultimate corporate power is valid, the "economic system is characterized by large dominant firms," firm-controlled demand, co-opted government policy, and activities that contravene society's wishes.

3. While some facts support some allegations of corporate control, other evidence clearly demonstrates the power of the consumer over the corporation, regardless of advertising and firm size.

4. Consumerism is a social force that contends that there is a fundamental conflict between the objectives of a firm and those of the public at large. If such conflict exists, then corporate behaviour ought to be altered by legislation, not exhortation.

5. Traditional profit-maximizing theory is not affected by the issue of ownership diversification. Other theories involving minority control, intercorporate control, and the separation of ownership from control contend that the issue is important.

6. Sales-maximization objectives are based on the notion that once a specified level of profit has been reached, it is more important to be big, not more profitable.

7. There are those who hold the view that firms do not maximize anything due to ignorance of the cost and revenue curves, due to particular ways of establishing price, and due to how the firm is organized.

8. Full-cost pricing is when price equals average cost at capacity output plus a mark-up, which may be per unit or a percent of average cost.

MULTIPLE-CHOICE QUESTIONS

1. If, as a matter of general practice, firms manipulated demand, we should observe all but one of the following:
    (a) highly effective barriers to entry
    (b) new products lasting a short time only
    (c) little change in observed tastes over time
    (d) no shortages of any commodities at any time

2. Which of the following does not offer support to Galbraith's hypothesis of the "new industrial state"?
    (a) large advertising budget for large corporations
    (b) interlocking directorships among large corporations
    (c) the adoption of new products without massive advertising
    (d) price competition

3. One thing generally agreed upon even by opponents of Galbraith is that
    (a) advertising is essential to ensure the existence of corporations
    (b) advertising shifts demands among products in monopolistically competitive structure
    (c) advertising results in movements along demand schedules
    (d) advertising must be limited to only informing consumers

4. Which statement best describes Galbraith's "new industrial state"?
    (a) The federal government now has a great deal of control over Canadian corporations.
    (b) Corporations are very responsive to the desires, needs, and best interests of the buying public.
    (c) Because of the power of unions and shareholders, industrial management has little real control.
    (d) The size and influence of large corporations give them too much power over government, consumers, markets, and other institutions.

5. Consumerism is chiefly concerned with
    (a) the variety of goods available to consumers
    (b) alternative theories of the consumption function
    (c) the extent to which actual consumer goods produced are not what society really wants
    (d) the conflict between the goals of a firm and those of society

6. The sales-maximizing hypothesis implies that
    (a) a firm will sell as many units as it can at a fixed price
    (b) firms have no interest in profits, only in growth
    (c) a firm will sell additional units by reducing price to the point where elasticity of demand is zero
    (d) a firm would reduce price so long as a minimum satisfactory level of profits was achieved

7. In Canada, the hypothesis of intercorporate control groups
    (a) is completely refuted by the evidence
    (b) exists particularly with respect to the links between chartered banks and corporations
    (c) cannot hold true due to the degree of foreign ownership
    (d) is verified for only the resource sector of the economy

8. If we find that one firm is content merely to make some level of satisfactory profits,
   (a) there is no specific prediction we can make about its equilibrium price and output
   (b) it is obviously a monopoly
   (c) it completely refutes our theory based on profit-maximizing assumptions
   (d) it will not long survive competition and change

9. The full-cost pricing hypothesis
   (a) predicts market behaviour and results better than the profit-maximizing hypothesis
   (b) means that the firm can never maximize profits
   (c) holds that the firm's pricing adjustments respond only to change in costs
   (d) implies that firms will always be able to cover all their costs

EXERCISES

1. Two nonprofit maximization theories of corporate behavior are (i) sales maximization and (ii) full cost pricing (where the markup is zero). Indicate on the graph the pricing and output decisions for firms with these objectives using the points labelled on the AR schedule. How do the results compare with profit-maximization results?

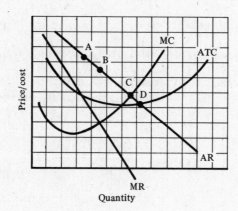

2. The cost/revenue structure and initial price and output of three firms are given on the next page. Indicate the change in price and output in response to tax changes that would need to be made in order that the firm meet the objectives outlined. You need not indicate the precise change in price; rather, indicate how price changes in response to the tax per unit or total tax. The initial position chosen is P_E in each case.

124

	Policy Change	Profit Maximizer	Sales Maximizer (min. profit, net of tax = $4000)	Full Cost Pricing (markup = 0)
1.	Per unit tax equal to $.50 per unit of output			
2.	Excess profits tax equal to 50% of "monopoly" profits			

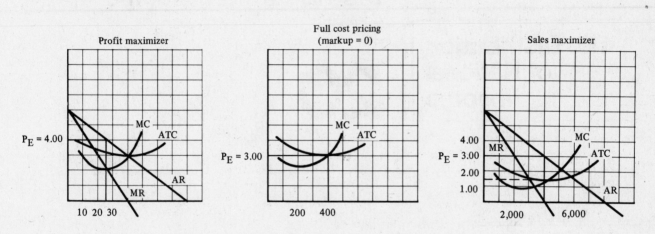

Profit maximizer

Full cost pricing (markup = 0)

Sales maximizer

Part Six

Factor Pricing and the Distribution of Income

| The Distribution of National Income | 20 |

KEY CONCEPTS AND DEFINITIONS

1. The _functional distribution of income_ refers to the distribution of total national income among the major factors of production--labour, capital, and land. It focuses on sources of income.

2. The _size distribution of income_ is the distribution of income between different households without reference to the social class to which they belong.

3. The inequality of income is depicted by the _Lorenz curve_, which shows how much of total income is accounted for by given proportions of the nation's families.

4. The income of a factor of production has two elements: (a) the price paid per unit of the factor and (b) the quantity of the factor used. In competitive factor markets price is determined by the demand for and supply of the factor.

5. The demand for a factor is said to be a _derived demand_ because a firm requires factors, not for their own sake, but in order to produce goods and services that the firm sells. The total demand for a factor is the sum of the derived demands for it in each productive activity.

6. The _demand curve_ for a factor of production shows how the quantity demanded of that factor will vary as its price varies, the price of all other factors held constant.

7. As the price of the factor falls, the quantity demanded may rise for two reasons: (a) The reduction in the factor price will decrease the cost of production and thus increase the output of commodities, thereby increasing the quantity demanded of the factor. This effect will be larger the _more elastic_ the demand for the goods that the factor helps to make is and the _more important_ the factor is in the _total costs_ of producing the goods. (b) The factor price decrease will lead to the _substitution_ of the now cheaper factor. This effect will be larger the easier it is to substitute one factor for another in production.

8. In equilibrium, a profit-maximizing firm will hire units of any variable until the last unit hired adds as much to costs as it does to revenue. The addition to revenue of an additional unit of the variable factor is called the _marginal-revenue product_. In a competitive factor market, the addition to cost is the price per unit of the factor. Algebraically, this is given as $\underline{w} = \underline{MRP}$.

9. In turn, the MRP is defined by the expression, MRP = MPP x MR, where MPP stands for the marginal physical product and MR is the marginal revenue. MPP is defined as the physical increase in output that an additional unit of the variable factor makes possible.

10. The total supplies of most factors of production are variable over time. The total supply of labour depends on the size of the population, the proportion of the population willing to work (the participation rate), and the number of hours each individual is willing to work.

11. The hypothesis of equal net advantage is a theory of the supply of factors to particular uses. Owners of factors will choose the use that produces the greatest net advantage, allowing both for monetary and nonmonetary advantages of a particular employment.

12. If a factor of production moves easily between uses in response to small changes in incentives, it is said to be highly mobile. Dynamic differentials, temporary factor price differences, serve as signals of disequilibria and induce factor mobility that eventually removes the differentials.

13. Equilibrium differentials are differentials in factor prices that may persist over time. They are related to differences in the factors themselves (differing land fertility, differences in the cost of acquiring skills, and differences in nonmonetary employment advantages).

14. The amount that a factor must earn in its present use to prevent it from transferring to another use is called its transfer price; any excess that it earns over this amount is called its economic rent. If the supply of a factor is completely inelastic, all of its earnings are rents; if its supply is elastic, all earnings are transfer earnings.

MULTIPLE-CHOICE QUESTIONS

1. The theory of factor prices in competitive markets says that
    (a) factors are paid what they are worth
    (b) factor prices are determined by supply and demand
    (c) factor prices depend on their cost of production
    (d) factors are not paid what they are worth

2. Which of the following statements is not true about the demand for a factor of production?
    (a) It is more elastic the more elastic is the demand for the final product.
    (b) It is more elastic in cases where technology dictates its use in fixed proportions with other factors.
    (c) It is less elastic the smaller a part it is of the total cost of the product.
    (d) The quantity demanded varies inversely with its price.

3. The marginal-revenue product of a factor is
    (a) marginal revenue minus marginal cost
    (b) marginal physical product times the units of factors used
    (c) marginal revenue minus factor price
    (d) marginal physical product times marginal revenue

4. The marginal-revenue product of a factor is
    (a) the amount added to revenue by the last hired unit of a factor
    (b) total output divided by units of factors, multiplied by price
    (c) less under competition than under monopoly, ceteris paribus
    (d) always equal to its price

5. The quantity demanded of a factor, _ceteris paribus_, will vary inversely
   (a) with income
   (b) with the price of the factor
   (c) with the prices of other factors
   (d) with changes in demand for the product √

6. Empirical evidence indicates that, historically, as real wage rates have risen in North America,
   (a) workers have shown a willingness to work longer hours
   (b) business has shown no actual tendency to substitute capital for labour
   (c) the average work week has declined
   (d) the supply of effort has sloped upward to the right

7. If a firm is a price taker in factor markets, it means that
   (a) it is also a price taker in product markets
   (b) it can set the price it pays for factors
   (c) it pays the market rate for whatever quantities of factors it wishes
   (d) it is maximizing profits

8. Economic rent is
   (a) the income of a landlord
   (b) earned only by factors in completely inelastic supply
   (c) the excess of income over transfer earnings
   (d) usually taxable under the income tax, whereas transfer earnings are not

9. A dynamic differential in factor earnings
   (a) can exist in equilibrium
   (b) will be more quickly eliminated if factor supply is inelastic rather than elastic
   (c) will tend to cause movements of factors
   (d) is greater the greater is the mobility of the factor

10. The need for the physical presence of the owner of the labour factor (the worker)
    (a) is comparable to that of owners of capital and land
    (b) is not economically significant
    (c) makes nonmonetary factors much more important for it than for other factors
    (d) has not been fully demonstrated

11. Which of the following will not shift the supply curve of labour?
    (a) an increase in the population
    (b) an increase in the proportion of people going to college
    (c) an increase in the wage level
    (d) increased preferences for leisure activities

12. The marginal-revenue product of labour declines more rapidly for a monopoly firm than a competitive firm because
    (a) workers are apt to be less productive when they work for a monopoly
    (b) the industry demand for the product is less elastic
    (c) the monopoly deliberately curtails output
    (d) with the monopoly firm, marginal revenue declines; with the competitive firm, it does not

13. The division of income among the three basic factors of production is called the
    (a) functional distribution of income
    (b) Lorenz distribution of income
    (c) size distribution of income
    (d) average productivity of income

128

14. Economic rents will <u>not</u> exist if the supply curve of a factor is
    (a) perfectly inelastic
    (b) upward sloping
    (c) perfectly elastic
    (d) flatter than the demand curve for labour

15. Data concerning the inequality of income among Canadian families indicate that the Lorenz curve for Canada is
    (a) above the diagonal line
    (b) below the diagonal line
    (c) equal to the diagonal line
    (d) none of the above

Questions 16 through 22 refer to the diagram below. You may assume competitive conditions.

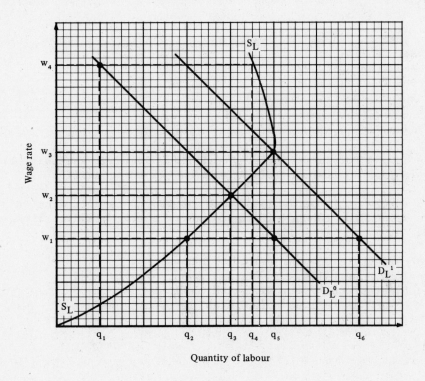

Quantity of labour

16. If the wage rate is w_1 and the demand curve for labour is D_L^0, the quantity of labour demanded is
    (a) q_2
    (b) q_5
    (c) q_3
    (d) q_6

17. The quantity of labour supplied with a wage rate of w_1 is
    (a) q_2
    (b) q_5
    (c) q_6
    (d) q_4

129

18. With D_L^0 as the demand curve of labour and a wage of w_1, an
    (a) excess supply of labour of (q_5-q_2) exists, and hence the wage rate will fall
    (b) excess supply of labour of (q_5-q_2) exists, and hence the wage rate will rise
    (c) excess demand for labour of (q_5-q_2) exists, and hence the wage rate will fall
    (d) excess demand for labour of (q_5-q_2) exists, and hence the wage rate will rise

19. With D_L^0 as the demand curve for labour, the equilibrium values of the wage rate and the quantity of labour are
    (a) w_3 and q_4
    (b) w_2 and q_4
    (c) w_2 and q_3
    (d) w_3 and q_3

20. If the wage rate increases from w_3 to w_4, the quantity of labour supplied
    (a) increases from q_3 to q_4
    (b) decreases from q_5 to q_4
    (c) increases from q_4 to q_5
    (d) is less than quantity demanded

21. If the demand-for-labour curve shifted from D_L^0 to D_L^1, then at a wage rate of w_2 an
    (a) excess demand for labour exists, and hence the wage rate will rise to w_3
    (b) excess demand for labour exists, and the wage rate will remain permanently at w_2
    (c) excess supply of labour exists, and the wage rate will rise to w_3
    (d) excess demand for labour exists but workers will withdraw labour services from the market

22. Both demand curves are downward sloping because
    (a) marginal revenue falls and output rises
    (b) the marginal productivity of labour falls as more labour is employed
    (c) both MPP_L and MR fall as more labour is used
    (d) both MPP_L and the marginal cost of labour fall as more labour is used

EXERCISES

1. Suppose a firm can vary its number of employees and output as shown in the table on the following page.
    (a) Fill in the missing values for APP and MPP.
    (b) Fill in the missing values for ARP and MRP for Case A. For MRP values in Case B.
    (c) Compare the ARP and MRP schedules for Case A. What is the portion of the MRP curve that is the demand curve for labour? You may wish to refer to the **Appendix to text Chapter 20** if you are in doubt.

Number of Workers	Units of Output per Day	APP	MPP	Case A				Case B	
				AR	MR	ARP	MRP	MR	MRP
0	0	–				–			
1	40	40.0	40	$2	$2	$80.0	$ 80	$1.85	$74.0
2	90	45.0	50	2	2	90.0	100	1.80	90.0
3	130	43.3	40	2	2	86.6	80	1.75	70.0
4	148	37.0	18	2	2	74.0	36	1.70	30.6
5	164	32.8	16	2	2	65.6	32	1.65	26.4
6	178	29.7	14	2	2	59.4	28	1.60	22.4
7	190	27.1	12	2	2	54.2	24	1.55	18.6
8	200	25.0	___	2	2	50.0	___	1.50	15.0
9	208	23.1	___	2	2	46.2	___	1.45	___
10	214	___	___	2	2	___	___	1.40	___
11	216	___	___	2	2	___	___	1.35	___
12	216	18.0	0	2	2	36.0	0	1.30	0
13	214	16.5	___	2	2	33.0	___	1.25	___

(d)   Why does the MRP decline in Case A?   Case B?

(e)   If the market wage rate that this firm must pay is $20 per day, how many workers will the firm hire to maximize profits?   Case A _____.
Case B _____.   Explain.

(f)   If the wage rate rises to $28 per day, how many workers will the firm hire?
Case A _____.   Case B _____.   Calculate the (arc) elasticity for the demand for labour given this wage increase for Case A.

(g)   In Case A, if the market price of the product rises to $3 and the wage is $28 per day, how many workers will be hired? _____.   Explain.

131

2. Economic Rents and Transfer Earnings
   Suppose there is a labour market for a specific type of worker. The demand for labour is given by the expression W = 380 - 4L. (W is the wage rate and L is the quantity of labour.) There are two possible labour supply curves. Case A: W = 20 + 2L. Case B: L = 60.
   (a) Draw the labour demand curve and the two labour supply curves in the diagram below.

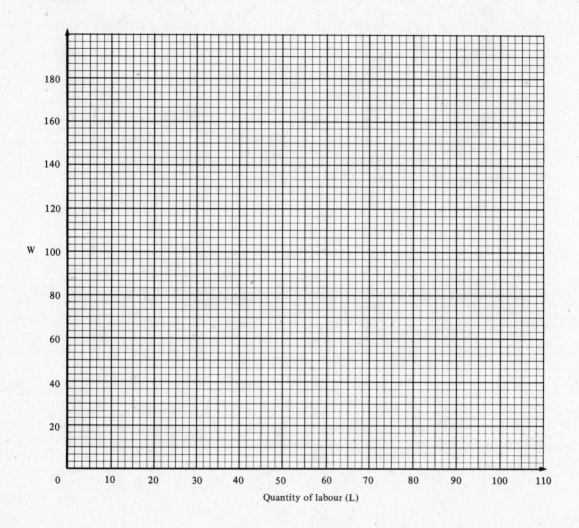

Quantity of labour (L)

(b) What are the equilibrium values of W and L for both cases?

(c) Illustrate in the diagram the amount of economic rents for Case A. For Case B. What transfer earnings is the sixtieth worker receiving in Case A?

   Suppose the government is considering two options designed to increase the supply of workers in this market. Assume that only the supply curve W = 20 + 2L applies.
   Option 1: Increase the demand for labour from W = 380 - 4L to W = 440 - 4L and keep the labour supply curve constant.
   Option 2: Increase the supply curve from W = 20 + 2L to W = -10 + 2L and the demand curve from W = 380 - 4L to W = 440 - 4L.

132

(d) If Option 1 is adopted, what are the new equilibrium values of W and L? What is the total magnitude of the economic rents earned by those workers who were in this market before the policy change?

(e) If Option 2 is adopted, what are the new equilibrium values of W and L? Have economic rents been created for those workers who were in this market before the policy change?

3. Suppose there are three adult persons in a hypothetical economy. Each individual has his own preferences for working and consuming leisure time. We have portrayed the labour supply curve of each person below. The labour supply curve depicts the number of hours per time period that the individual is willing to offer to the labour market at various wage rates.

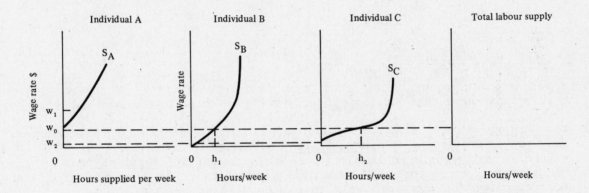

At wage rate w_0, A is not prepared to offer any hours per week, B is prepared to offer Oh_1 hours per week, and C is willing to offer Oh_2 hours per week. Therefore, we can say that the total number of hours offered to the labour market is $Oh_1 + Oh_2$. Furthermore, two of the three members of the population are willing to participate in the labour market. We say that the participation rate is two-thirds.

(a) Plot the total number of hours supplied per week at a wage rate of w_0. At w_1.

(b) Taking a higher wage rate of w_1, determine the effect of the higher wage on hours supplied to the labour market. Has the number of hours increased? Why?

(c) What are your predictions regarding the magnitude of the participation rate at a wage rate of w_2?

Labour Markets and the Determination of Wages | 21

1. A wage-setting labour union entering a competitive market can raise wages but only at the expense of reducing employment and creating a pool of unemployed workers.

2. A <u>monopsony</u> means a single purchaser of labour. Even when a few firms exist, they may form an <u>employer's association</u> in order to act as a single unit. Whenever the supply curve of labour is upward sloping, the <u>marginal cost of labour</u> exceeds the <u>average cost</u>. The marginal cost exceeds the wage paid (the average cost) because the increased wage rate necessary to attract another worker must be paid to everyone already employed.

3. The profit-maximizing monopsonist will hire until the <u>MC</u> of labour is equal to <u>MRP</u>. Monopsonistic conditions in the factor market will result in a lower level of employment and a lower wage rate than would exist under competitive conditions.

4. A wage-setting labour union entering a monopsonistic market may increase both employment and wages. If, however, it sets the wage above the competitive level, unemployment will be created.

5. A <u>union</u> is an association of workers that speaks for workers in negotiations with their employers. Unions are subdivided into <u>craft unions</u> (workers with a common set of skills) and <u>industrial unions</u> (organized along industry lines).

6. In general, individual union members belong to a local union. The local union belongs to a national or an international union. A <u>federation</u> is a loose organization of unions; in Canada the principal federation is the <u>Canadian Labour Congress</u> (CLC).

7. Three kinds of bargaining arrangements are (a) the <u>open shop</u>, where, although a union represents its membership, union membership is not a condition for having a job in the firm; (b) the <u>closed shop</u>, where only workers who are already union members may be employed; and (c) the <u>union shop</u>, where the employer is free to hire whom he chooses, but where all new employees must join the recognized union within a specified period.

8. Unions must decide on their goals. One conflict in goals is between raising wages by restricting supply, thus reducing the union's employed membership, and preserving employment for its membership. Other trade-offs are wage and job security, and wage and fringe benefits.

9. Minimum wage laws, enacted largely through provincial legislation, may have the same effects as a wage-setting union. In a competitive labour market, minimum wages set above competitive equilibrium wages are likely to have adverse employment effects. This result is reinforced by certain ripple effects. Minimum wages may cause firms to substitute workers who are not covered by wage legislation for workers who are; some firms may be driven out of business because of higher labour costs; and workers covered by minimum wages may avoid training programs, thereby reducing their long-term employment prospects.

10. However, a minimum wage imposed in a monopsonistic labour market may have the result of increasing both wages and employment as long as the wage is not above the competitive wage.

11. Discrimination in the labour market, by changing labour supply, can decrease the wages and incomes of a group that is discriminated against. In addition, labour-market discrimination may have adverse employment effects.

MULTIPLE-CHOICE QUESTIONS

1. If a group of workers or members of an occupation are able to reduce their numbers and prevent others from entering in an otherwise competitive market,
   (a) it will still be necessary for them to bargain for any wage increases
   (b) the antitrust laws may be used against them
   (c) their wages will rise, ceteris paribus
   (d) the individual members will benefit only if the demand curve for their services is inelastic

2. The Canadian Union of Public Employees is an example of
   (a) a federation in Canada
   (b) an international union
   (c) a national union
   (d) a member of the Confederation of National Trade Unions

3. Pension rights for workers may help employers keep total costs down because
   (a) they are a form of incentive pay
   (b) many workers choose not to accept them
   (c) employers have ways of avoiding providing them
   (d) they may reduce labour turnover

4. An arrangement in which workers must join the union upon employment is called
   (a) a union shop
   (b) a closed shop
   (c) an open shop
   (d) a jurisdictional shop

5. Where the supply curve of labour is upward sloping, the marginal cost curve of labour to the monopsonist
   (a) is the supply curve of labour
   (b) lies above the supply curve of labour
   (c) lies below and parallel to the supply curve of labour
   (d) lies above and parallel to the supply curve of labour

135

6. An employer may find that discrimination in employment against equally competent, skilled minority groups is more profitable than nondiscrimination
   (a) because he has to pay nonminority groups more
   (b) if the majority of his workers and customers are prejudiced against minority groups
   (c) because nonminority groups are better workers
   (d) if he is the only employer practising discrimination in a market of unprejudiced customers

7. A monopsonistic labour market without a union will generate
   (a) lower wages and employment compared with a competitive labour market
   (b) higher wages but lower employment compared with a competitive labour market
   (c) lower wages but higher employment compared with a competitive labour market
   (d) identical wage and employment values compared with a competitive labour market

8. A jurisdictional dispute in a labour market refers to
   (a) the legal rights of workers in a company
   (b) whether municipalities or provinces have control over union behaviour
   (c) which union shall have the right to organize a particular group of workers
   (d) the type of worker who is allowed to join the union

9. A lockout is an action taken by a
   (a) union
   (b) firm
   (c) mediator in order to force a union and a firm to negotiate a wage settlement
   (d) provincial legislature

10. Which of the following is not a requirement of a successful union?
   (a) difficulty of substituting other factors for union members
   (b) labour costs that are a relatively small contribution to total costs
   (c) relatively inelastic demand curve for labour
   (d) relatively elastic demand curve for labour

11. In Canada, minimum-wage legislation is principally a responsibility of the
   (a) municipal governments
   (b) federal government
   (c) provincial governments
   (d) Canadian Labour Congress

12. Extensive evidence supports the notion that much of the incidence of unemployment caused by minimum-wage legislation is borne by
   (a) teenagers
   (b) skilled workers
   (c) member of craft unions
   (d) workers who have undertaken training programs

Questions 13 through 19 refer to the diagram on the following page. The labour market is assumed to be characterized by lowly skilled workers.

13. If perfect competition existed in this market, the values for the wage rate and the quantity of employment would be
   (a) W_4 and L_1
   (b) W_1 and L_1
   (c) W_3 and L_2
   (d) W_2 and L_3

136

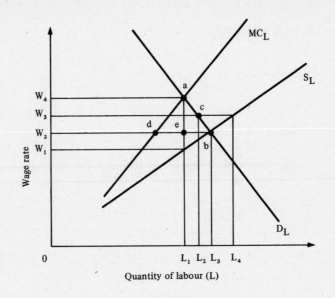

14. Under conditions of a monopsonistic labour market, a firm would hire
    (a) OL_3 workers

    (b) OL_1 workers

    (c) OL_2 workers

    (d) OL_4 workers

15. Under conditions of a monopsonistic labour market, a firm would pay wages of
    (a) W_4

    (b) W_1

    (c) W_3

    (d) W_2

16. If a minimum wage of W_2 is imposed in this market, the supply curve of labour becomes
    (a) $MC_L - S_L$

    (b) W_2bS_L

    (c) acb

    (d) W_2daMC_L

17. In this case a minimum wage of W_2 would generate employment of
    (a) W_2d

    (b) OL_1

    (c) OL_3

    (d) OL_4

18. If a minimum wage of W_3 is imposed in this market, the firm would hire
    (a) OL_2

    (b) more than OL_3 since the marginal cost of labour has fallen

    (c) OL_4 because the demand for labour shifts to the right

    (d) OL_1

137

19. With a minimum wage of W_3, total unemployment is
    (a) $L_3 - L_2$
    (b) $L_4 - L_2$
    (c) $L_4 - L_3$
    (d) $L_4 - L_1$

EXERCISES

1. Columns 1 and 2 represent the supply-of-labour relationship for a monopsonist buyer. Fill in the values for total cost in Column 3 and then calculate the marginal-cost values in Column 4. This exercise should demonstrate to you that the marginal cost of labour lies above the supply curve of labour in a nonparallel fashion.

(1) Quantity of Labour	(2) Wage Rate	(3) Total Cost	(4) Marginal Cost
8	$10.00	$80.00	—
9	10.50	_____	_____
10	11.00	_____	_____
11	11.50	_____	_____
12	12.00	_____	_____
13	12.50	_____	_____
14	13.00	_____	_____

2. Referring to the diagram below, which represents the labour market in an industry, answer the following questions.

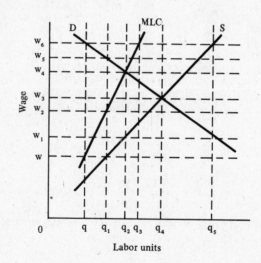

(a) If a completely competitive market prevailed, the equilibrium wage would be _____, and the amount of employment would be _____.

(b) If a wage-setting union enters this market and sets the wage at w_6, the amount of employment would be _____, and the amount of surplus labour unemployed would be _____. How would the labour-supply curve look?

138

(c) Assume that this market consists of a single large firm hiring labour in a labour market. If the firm hired q_1 workers, it would have to pay all workers the wage _____, but the marginal-labour cost of the last man hired would be _____. Because the marginal-revenue product of the last man hired is equal to the amount _____, there is an incentive for the firm to continue hiring to the amount _____, at which the wage will be _____, the marginal-labour cost will be _____, and the marginal-revenue product will be _____. Compare this with the result in (a).

(d) Suppose a union now organizes and sets a wage at w_3. The amount of employment will be _____.

(e) Draw a new labour-supply curve showing what happens when a union organizes this labour market but, instead of setting a high wage, excludes half the workers by a combination of stiff apprenticeship rules, high union dues, nepotism, and racial discrimination.

3. There are two competitive labour markets in the economy of Sask. Market X requires workers with skills only applicable to that market, while market Z requires skills common to all workers in Sask. The demand curves are $W = 360 - 3L$ and $W = 240 - 2L$ for X and Z, respectively. The supply curve of labour is $W = 40 + 2L$ (<u>without discrimination</u>) in each of the markets.

(a) What is the current wage differential between the two markets? What are the employment levels in each market?

(b) Does this differential likely represent a dynamic differential or an equilibrium differential? Explain.

(c) Suppose that a group of workers in X convinces employers to discriminate against workers in X who have green eyes. Employers in X reluctantly agree and fire green-eyed workers. These workers are forced to move to labour market Z, where no discrimination against them exists and where they have skills common to the workers already there. The supply curve in X becomes $W = 60 + 2L$ and in Z it becomes $W = 24 + 2L$. What is the new wage differential, assuming that all of the green-eyed workers from X are absorbed in Z and both markets adjust to the new supplies of labour?

(d) Workers in Z do not welcome this inflow of workers from X. Although they are
not able to discriminate against green-eyed workers, they do want to protect
their wages and incomes. Workers in Z realize that the migrants from X are
not able to use their skills obtained in X, but, nevertheless, employers in Z
will treat these migrant workers equally with the workers already in Z. Since
they must be competitive with migrants from X, workers in Z are likely to see
their wages fall unless something is done. Therefore, the workers in Z
successfully convince the government of Sask to impose a minimum wage of $140
for both labour markets. How will market X be affected? What will happen in
market Z?

Interest and the Return on Capital | 22

KEY CONCEPTS AND DEFINITIONS

1. Capital is all manmade aids to production. When production with capital is more efficient than production without, capital is said to be <u>productive</u>. The difference between the two flows of output (one with capital and one without) is a measure of the <u>productivity of capital</u>, or the <u>efficiency of capital</u>.

2. The amount of revenue available to the owners of the firm's capital is the excess of the firm's revenue over the amount payable to factors of production other than capital, and after allowance for the taxes the firm will have to pay. This excess is called the <u>gross return to capital</u>.

3. Economists divide the gross return into four components:
   (a) <u>depreciation</u> (the decrease in the value of capital through use);
   (b) a <u>pure return</u> (the amount that capital could earn in a riskless investment);
   (c) a <u>risk premium</u> (a return for risk-taking); and
   (d) <u>economic profits</u> (the residual after all other deductions have been made from the gross return).

4. The <u>net return</u> is the gross return minus (a) above, which is equal to items (b) plus (c) plus (d). The <u>opportunity cost of capital</u> is the sum of items (a), (b), and (c). In equilibrium the gross return must equal the opportunity costs, and hence economic profits (d) must be zero. If (d) is positive, capital should be expanded.

5. The <u>capital stock</u> refers to the total quantity of the physical units of capital. The monetary return is the product of the marginal productivity of capital and the value of output at its market price. The ratio of the monetary return to the market value of capital is called the <u>marginal efficiency of capital</u> (MEC).

6. The schedule that relates the rate of return on each additional dollar of capital stock to the size of the capital stock is called the <u>marginal-efficiency-of-capital schedule</u>.

7. If the population is fixed and technology is constant, adding more capital increases the ratio of capital to labour. This increase is known as <u>capital deepening</u>.

8. Increasing the quantity of capital without affecting the capital-labour ratio (or the ratio with respect to other factors) is called capital widening.

9. Capital deepening decreases the marginal efficiency of capital because capital is assumed to be subject to diminishing returns. The MEC schedule is therefore downward sloping.

10. Capital is valued because it promises an expected stream of future income to its owners. However, future incomes cannot be compared exactly with current incomes because of positive opportunity costs (usually considered to be the market rate of interest). The present value of income must be calculated. The PV refers to the value now of a payment or payments to be made in the future.

11. Present value depends directly on the income expected in the future and inversely on the rate of interest. The PV of a single payment of X after t years is given by the expression $x/(1+i)^t$.

12. A profit-maximizing firm will invest in an asset whenever the PV of expected income (or the capitalized value of the asset) exceeds the current purchase price of the asset. Alternatively, we can say that a firm will invest in an asset if the MEC exceeds the interest rate that correctly reflects the opportunity cost of the asset to the firm.

13. For the economy as a whole, competition among borrowers and lenders of funds for new investment will cause the rate of interest to move toward the MEC.

14. The accumulation of capital tends to lower the interest rate and the MEC. The growth of technical knowledge tends to raise both rates.

15. The return on physical assets (assuming no risk) is called the pure rate of interest. However, there are other factors that influence interest rates, and when their influence is added to the pure interest rate, the market rate of interest is determined. These factors include (a) other demands for money to borrow, (b) government policy, (c) bank administration of interest rates, (d) expectations about future business conditions, and (e) the rate of inflation.

16. Under conditions of inflation, it is necessary to distinguish between the money and the real rate of interest. The real rate of interest is the difference between the money rate of interest and the rate of change of the price level (inflation rate).

17. At any moment in time there is a whole structure of interest rates. Individual rates depend on the riskiness, the asset's duration, the liquidity, and the various costs of administering the loan.

18. Firms have three main sources for obtaining funds for investment: selling shares in the firm (equity); borrowing from financial institutions or by issuing bonds (debt); and reinvesting their own profits.

19. Securities (stock) markets allow firms to raise new funds from the sale of newly issued securities and allow holders of existing securities to sell their securities to other persons.

20. The stockholders are the owners of the company, and hence they share in its profits. Because stocks, unlike bonds, carry no promise to pay anything, they contain added elements of uncertainty, particularly with respect to the firm's expected earnings.

21. The value of a stock is largely determined by the expected income stream of the firm. The ratio of price to earnings, the price-earnings ratio, varies among companies because buyers have very different expectations of future earnings per dollar of present earnings.

MULTIPLE-CHOICE QUESTIONS

1. When a firm uses its own funds instead of borrowing for investment purposes,
   (a) its economic costs are lower because it does not have to pay interest
   (b) it should impute an interest rate to get a true picture of cost
   (c) it means it cannot get a loan at the bank
   (d) it does not have to worry about the rate of return on the investment

2. Capital earns income because
   (a) it is productive
   (b) it is expensive
   (c) it is always cheaper to substitute capital for labour
   (d) it is technically more efficient

3. The marginal efficiency of capital is defined as
   (a) the monetary return on the marginal dollar's worth of capital
   (b) the monetary return on the marginal dollar's worth of investment
   (c) the monetary return on the most efficient capital unit
   (d) the monetary return on the most inefficient capital unit

4. The present value of x dollars a year from now equals
   (a) xi
   (b) x(1 + i)
   (c) x/(1 + i)
   (d) (1 + i)/x

5. The higher the rate of interest, <u>ceteris paribus</u>,
   (a) the more investment opportunities will be profitable
   (b) the higher the necessary rate of return on any investment
   (c) the lower the amount of borrowing by the federal government
   (d) the greater the demand for investment funds

6. The marginal-efficiency-of-capital schedule relates the
   (a) rate of return on each additional dollar of capital stock to the level of investment
   (b) rate of return on each additional dollar of investment to the size of the capital stock
   (c) rate of return of each additional dollar of investment to the level of investment expenditure
   (d) rate of return on each additional dollar of capital stock to the size of the capital stock

7. The value of an income-earning asset
   (a) is the sum of all its income payments
   (b) is the discounted present value of its expected income stream
   (c) is measured by its reproduction cost
   (d) rises as interest rates rise

8. Capital deepening occurs
   (a) whenever investment takes place
   (b) when a firm doubles output by replicating its existing facilities
   (c) when capital accumulation increases the proportion of capital to other factors
   (d) when a firm must go more deeply in debt

9. If you borrow $300 and pay it back in 12 equal monthly installments of $28, the true rate of interest is about
   (a) 12 percent
   (b) 6 percent
   (c) 24 percent
   (d) 10 percent

10. The MEC shifts to the right
    (a) as capital is accumulated
    (b) as the interest rate drops
    (c) as technical knowledge increases
    (d) as households save more

143

11. The advantage for shareholders of cumulative preferred stock over common stock is that
    (a) the dividends will be higher than those on common stock
    (b) the opportunity for capital gains is greater
    (c) the payment of dividends is certain
    (d) preferred dividends (including arrears) will be paid before common dividends

12. The present value of $200 received two years hence with an annual rate of interest of 14 percent is
    (a) $153.89
    (b) $175.40
    (c) $200
    (d) $256

13. The PV of a given sum will be smaller the
    (a) nearer is the payment date
    (b) higher the rate of interest
    (c) higher the given sum
    (d) all of the above

14. The current capitalized value of a farm that yearly earns $40,000 in gross returns from agricultural crops in perpetuity is approximately equal to $276,000 when the current interest rate is
    (a) 6.9 percent
    (b) 14.5 percent
    (c) 13.2 percent
    (d) 16.8 percent

15. Irma has an opportunity to buy for $4,800 a particular asset that yields $800 in gross returns into the indefinite future. She insists that all her assets make a 16 percent rate of return. In this case Irma should
    (a) not buy the asset because the purchase price is less than the capitalized income stream
    (b) buy this asset because its rate of return is exactly equal to 16 percent
    (c) buy this asset because its rate of return is greater than 16 percent
    (d) not buy this asset because its rate of return is lower than 16 percent

16. If the money rate of interest is 17.2 percent and the expected rate of inflation is 14 percent, the real rate of interest is
    (a) 31.2 percent
    (b) 3.2 percent
    (c) 8.1 percent
    (d) 2.3 percent

17. A bond issued by Acme Drilling Inc. may have a higher interest rate than that issued by Software Computer Ltd. because
    (a) Acme is considered to have less chance of defaulting payments than Software
    (b) Software's bond has a higher term (duration) than Acme's bond
    (c) Acme's bond has a higher term than Software's bond
    (d) although the two bonds have identical terms and Acme is no more risky than Software, the price of Acme's bond is higher than Software's bond

18. A shareholder who holds a common stock
    (a) does not have voting rights in the firm
    (b) must be paid dividends by the firm
    (c) may receive profits before a shareholder who holds a preferred stock
    (d) receives company profits after profits have been paid to preferred-stock shareholders

19. The price of a firm's stock will increase if traders on the stock market expect
    (a) the firm to pay higher dividends in the future
    (b) the firm to have higher earnings in the future
    (c) to make capital gains from selling this stock in the future
    (d) all of the above

EXERCISES

1. As a practice exercise, fill in the following blanks using the present value (PV) table, Table 22-1, on page 146.

	This many $	in t years	has this PV	at i rate of interest
(a)	10	5	_____	6%
(b)	100	50	$60.80	_____
(c)	1,000	_____	3.00	12
(d)	_____	6	4.56	14

2. More practice, this time with the annuity table, Table 22-2, page 147.

	This many $	received each year for t years	has this PV	at i rate of interest
(a)	10	5	_____	6%
(b)	100	50	$3,919.60	_____
(c)	1,000	_____	8,304.00	12
(d)	_____	6	38.89	14

3. Present-Value Calculations
   (a) Dad leaves the firm. Business executive R.P. Squarehold, after a vigorous discussion with his son and daughter, is considering whether he should turn over the business to them. He is 50 years old and has $100,000 and adequate pension rights at age 60. Would a 6-percent 10-year annuity yield him the $13,500 a year he feels would make early retirement feasible? (Note that such an annuity would provide equal yearly payments, pay 6 percent on the declining balance, and exhaust his capital at the end of 10 years.)

   (b) To invest or not to invest? The Royal City Machine Shop is analyzing a proposal to purchase labour-saving equipment estimated to reduce costs by $14,000 a year. It calculates that the equipment will last for 10 years and has a salvage value of $10,000 at the end of 10 years. The equipment costs $75,000, and Royal City's shareholders will accept nothing lower than a 14-percent-per-year rate of return. Should Royal City purchase this machine?

145

Table 22-1   Present Value of \$1.00

$$PV = \left(\frac{1}{1+i}\right)^t$$

Years hence (t)	1%	2%	4%	6%	8%	10%	12%	14%	15%	16%	18%	20%	22%	24%	25%	26%	28%	30%	35%	40%	45%	50%
1	0.990	0.980	0.962	0.943	0.926	0.909	0.893	0.877	0.870	0.862	0.847	0.833	0.820	0.806	0.800	0.794	0.781	0.769	0.741	0.714	0.690	0.667
2	0.980	0.961	0.925	0.890	0.857	0.826	0.797	0.769	0.756	0.743	0.718	0.694	0.672	0.650	0.640	0.630	0.610	0.592	0.549	0.510	0.476	0.444
3	0.971	0.942	0.889	0.840	0.794	0.751	0.712	0.675	0.658	0.641	0.609	0.579	0.551	0.524	0.512	0.500	0.477	0.455	0.406	0.364	0.328	0.296
4	0.961	0.924	0.855	0.792	0.735	0.683	0.636	0.592	0.572	0.552	0.516	0.482	0.451	0.423	0.410	0.397	0.373	0.350	0.301	0.260	0.226	0.198
5	0.951	0.906	0.822	0.747	0.681	0.621	0.567	0.519	0.497	0.476	0.437	0.402	0.370	0.341	0.328	0.315	0.291	0.269	0.223	0.186	0.156	0.132
6	0.942	0.888	0.790	0.705	0.630	0.564	0.507	0.456	0.432	0.410	0.370	0.335	0.303	0.275	0.262	0.250	0.227	0.207	0.165	0.133	0.108	0.088
7	0.933	0.871	0.760	0.665	0.583	0.513	0.452	0.400	0.376	0.354	0.314	0.279	0.249	0.222	0.210	0.198	0.178	0.159	0.122	0.095	0.074	0.059
8	0.923	0.853	0.731	0.627	0.540	0.467	0.404	0.351	0.327	0.305	0.266	0.233	0.204	0.179	0.168	0.157	0.139	0.123	0.091	0.068	0.051	0.039
9	0.914	0.837	0.703	0.592	0.500	0.424	0.361	0.308	0.284	0.263	0.225	0.194	0.167	0.144	0.134	0.125	0.108	0.094	0.067	0.048	0.035	0.026
10	0.905	0.820	0.676	0.558	0.463	0.386	0.322	0.270	0.247	0.227	0.191	0.162	0.137	0.116	0.107	0.099	0.085	0.073	0.050	0.035	0.024	0.017
11	0.896	0.804	0.650	0.527	0.429	0.350	0.287	0.237	0.215	0.195	0.162	0.135	0.112	0.094	0.086	0.079	0.066	0.056	0.037	0.025	0.017	0.012
12	0.887	0.788	0.625	0.497	0.397	0.319	0.257	0.208	0.187	0.168	0.137	0.112	0.092	0.076	0.069	0.062	0.052	0.043	0.027	0.018	0.012	0.008
13	0.879	0.773	0.601	0.469	0.368	0.290	0.229	0.182	0.163	0.145	0.116	0.093	0.075	0.061	0.055	0.050	0.040	0.033	0.020	0.013	0.008	0.005
14	0.870	0.758	0.577	0.442	0.340	0.263	0.205	0.160	0.141	0.125	0.099	0.078	0.062	0.049	0.044	0.039	0.032	0.025	0.015	0.009	0.006	0.003
15	0.861	0.743	0.555	0.417	0.315	0.239	0.183	0.140	0.123	0.108	0.084	0.065	0.051	0.040	0.035	0.031	0.025	0.020	0.011	0.006	0.004	0.002
16	0.853	0.728	0.534	0.394	0.292	0.218	0.163	0.123	0.107	0.093	0.071	0.054	0.042	0.032	0.028	0.025	0.019	0.015	0.008	0.005	0.003	0.002
17	0.844	0.714	0.513	0.371	0.270	0.198	0.146	0.108	0.093	0.080	0.060	0.045	0.034	0.026	0.023	0.020	0.015	0.012	0.006	0.003	0.002	0.001
18	0.836	0.700	0.494	0.350	0.250	0.180	0.130	0.095	0.081	0.069	0.051	0.038	0.028	0.021	0.018	0.016	0.012	0.009	0.005	0.002	0.001	
19	0.828	0.686	0.475	0.331	0.232	0.164	0.116	0.083	0.070	0.060	0.043	0.031	0.023	0.017	0.014	0.012	0.009	0.007	0.003	0.002	0.001	
20	0.820	0.673	0.456	0.312	0.215	0.149	0.104	0.073	0.061	0.051	0.037	0.026	0.019	0.014	0.012	0.010	0.007	0.005	0.002	0.001		
21	0.811	0.660	0.439	0.294	0.199	0.135	0.093	0.064	0.053	0.044	0.031	0.022	0.015	0.011	0.009	0.008	0.006	0.004	0.002	0.001		
22	0.803	0.647	0.422	0.278	0.184	0.123	0.083	0.056	0.046	0.038	0.026	0.018	0.013	0.009	0.007	0.006	0.004	0.003	0.001	0.001		
23	0.795	0.634	0.406	0.262	0.170	0.112	0.074	0.049	0.040	0.033	0.022	0.015	0.010	0.007	0.006	0.005	0.003	0.002	0.001			
24	0.788	0.622	0.390	0.247	0.158	0.102	0.066	0.043	0.035	0.028	0.019	0.013	0.008	0.006	0.005	0.004	0.003	0.002	0.001			
25	0.780	0.610	0.375	0.233	0.146	0.092	0.059	0.038	0.030	0.024	0.016	0.010	0.007	0.005	0.004	0.003	0.002	0.001	0.001			
26	0.772	0.598	0.361	0.220	0.135	0.084	0.053	0.033	0.026	0.021	0.014	0.009	0.006	0.004	0.003	0.002	0.002	0.001				
27	0.764	0.586	0.347	0.207	0.125	0.076	0.047	0.029	0.023	0.018	0.011	0.007	0.005	0.003	0.002	0.002	0.001	0.001				
28	0.757	0.574	0.333	0.196	0.116	0.069	0.042	0.026	0.020	0.016	0.010	0.006	0.004	0.002	0.002	0.001	0.001	0.001				
29	0.749	0.563	0.321	0.185	0.107	0.063	0.037	0.022	0.017	0.014	0.008	0.005	0.003	0.002	0.002	0.001	0.001					
30	0.742	0.552	0.308	0.174	0.099	0.057	0.033	0.020	0.015	0.012	0.007	0.004	0.003	0.002	0.001	0.001	0.001					
40	0.672	0.453	0.208	0.097	0.046	0.022	0.011	0.005	0.004	0.003	0.001	0.001										
50	0.608	0.372	0.141	0.054	0.021	0.009	0.003	0.001	0.001	0.001												

Table 22-2   Present Value of $1.00 Received Annually for t Years

$$PV = \left(\frac{1}{1+i}\right)^1 + \left(\frac{1}{1+i}\right)^2 + \cdots + \left(\frac{1}{1+i}\right)^t$$

Years (t)	1%	2%	4%	6%	8%	10%	12%	14%	15%	16%	18%	20%	22%	24%	25%	26%	28%	30%	35%	40%	45%	50%
1	0.990	0.980	0.962	0.943	0.926	0.909	0.893	0.877	0.870	0.862	0.847	0.833	0.820	0.806	0.800	0.794	0.781	0.769	0.741	0.714	0.690	0.667
2	1.970	1.942	1.886	1.833	1.783	1.736	1.690	1.647	1.626	1.605	1.566	1.528	1.492	1.457	1.440	1.424	1.392	1.361	1.289	1.224	1.165	1.111
3	2.941	2.884	2.775	2.673	2.577	2.487	2.402	2.322	2.283	2.246	2.174	2.106	2.042	1.981	1.952	1.923	1.868	1.816	1.696	1.589	1.493	1.407
4	3.902	3.808	3.630	3.465	3.312	3.170	3.037	2.914	2.855	2.798	2.690	2.589	2.494	2.404	2.362	2.320	2.241	2.166	1.997	1.849	1.720	1.605
5	4.853	4.713	4.452	4.212	3.993	3.791	3.605	3.433	3.352	3.274	3.127	2.991	2.864	2.745	2.689	2.635	2.532	2.436	2.220	2.035	1.876	1.737
6	5.795	5.601	5.242	4.917	4.623	4.355	4.111	3.889	3.784	3.685	3.498	3.326	3.167	3.020	2.951	2.885	2.759	2.643	2.385	2.168	1.983	1.824
7	6.728	6.472	6.002	5.582	5.206	4.868	4.564	4.288	4.160	4.039	3.812	3.605	3.416	3.242	3.161	3.083	2.937	2.802	2.508	2.263	2.057	1.883
8	7.652	7.325	6.733	6.210	5.747	5.335	4.968	4.639	4.487	4.344	4.078	3.837	3.619	3.421	3.329	3.241	3.076	2.925	2.598	2.331	2.108	1.922
9	8.566	8.162	7.435	6.802	6.247	5.759	5.328	4.946	4.772	4.607	4.303	4.031	3.786	3.566	3.463	3.366	3.184	3.019	2.665	2.379	2.144	1.948
10	9.714	8.983	8.111	7.360	6.710	6.145	5.650	5.216	5.019	4.833	4.494	4.192	3.923	3.682	3.571	3.465	3.269	3.092	2.715	2.414	2.168	1.965
11	10.368	9.787	8.760	7.877	7.139	6.495	5.988	5.453	5.234	5.029	4.656	4.327	4.035	3.776	3.656	3.544	3.335	3.147	2.757	2.438	2.185	1.977
12	11.255	10.575	9.385	8.384	7.536	6.814	6.194	5.660	5.421	5.197	4.793	4.439	4.127	3.851	3.725	3.606	3.387	3.190	2.779	2.456	2.196	1.985
13	12.134	11.343	9.986	8.853	7.904	7.103	6.424	5.842	5.583	5.342	4.910	4.533	4.203	3.912	3.780	3.656	3.427	3.223	2.799	2.468	2.204	1.990
14	13.004	12.106	10.563	9.295	8.244	7.367	6.628	6.002	5.724	5.468	5.008	4.611	4.265	3.962	3.824	3.695	3.459	3.249	2.814	2.477	2.210	1.993
15	13.865	12.849	11.118	9.712	8.559	7.606	6.811	6.142	5.847	5.575	5.092	4.675	4.315	4.001	3.859	3.726	3.483	3.268	2.825	2.484	2.214	1.995
16	14.718	13.578	11.652	10.106	8.851	7.824	6.974	6.265	5.954	5.669	5.162	4.730	4.357	4.003	3.887	3.751	3.503	3.283	2.834	2.489	2.216	1.997
17	15.562	14.292	12.166	10.477	9.122	8.022	7.120	6.373	6.047	5.749	5.222	4.775	4.391	4.059	3.910	3.771	3.518	3.295	2.840	2.492	2.218	1.998
18	16.398	14.992	12.659	10.828	9.372	8.201	7.250	6.467	6.128	5.818	5.273	4.812	4.419	4.080	3.928	3.786	3.529	3.304	2.844	2.494	2.219	1.999
19	17.226	15.678	13.134	11.158	9.604	8.365	7.366	6.550	6.198	5.877	5.316	4.844	4.442	4.097	3.942	3.799	3.539	3.311	2.848	2.496	2.220	1.999
20	18.046	16.351	13.590	11.470	9.818	8.514	7.469	6.623	6.259	5.929	5.353	4.870	4.460	4.110	3.954	3.808	3.546	3.316	2.850	2.497	2.221	1.999
21	18.857	17.011	14.029	11.764	10.017	8.649	7.562	6.687	6.312	5.973	5.384	4.891	4.476	4.121	3.963	3.816	3.551	3.320	2.852	2.498	2.221	2.000
22	19.660	17.658	14.451	12.042	10.201	8.772	7.645	6.743	6.359	6.011	5.410	4.909	4.488	4.130	3.970	3.822	3.556	3.323	2.853	2.498	2.222	2.000
23	20.456	18.292	14.857	12.303	10.371	8.883	7.718	6.792	6.399	6.044	5.432	4.925	4.499	4.137	3.976	3.827	3.559	3.325	2.854	2.499	2.222	2.000
24	21.243	18.914	15.247	12.550	10.529	8.985	7.784	6.835	6.434	6.073	5.451	4.937	4.507	4.143	3.981	3.831	3.562	3.327	2.855	2.499	2.222	2.000
25	22.023	19.523	15.622	12.783	10.675	9.077	7.843	6.873	6.464	6.097	5.467	4.948	4.514	4.147	3.985	3.834	3.564	3.329	2.856	2.499	2.222	2.000
26	22.795	20.121	15.983	13.003	10.810	9.161	7.896	6.906	6.491	6.118	5.480	4.956	4.520	4.151	3.988	3.837	3.566	3.330	2.856	2.500	2.222	2.000
27	23.560	20.707	16.330	13.211	10.935	9.237	7.943	6.935	6.514	6.136	5.492	4.964	4.524	4.154	3.990	3.839	3.567	3.331	2.856	2.500	2.222	2.000
28	24.316	21.281	16.663	13.406	11.051	9.307	7.984	6.961	6.534	6.152	5.502	4.970	4.528	4.157	3.992	3.840	3.568	3.331	2.857	2.500	2.222	2.000
29	25.066	21.844	16.984	13.591	11.158	9.370	8.022	6.983	6.551	6.166	5.510	4.975	4.531	4.159	3.994	3.841	3.569	3.332	2.857	2.500	2.222	2.000
30	25.808	22.396	17.292	13.765	11.258	9.427	8.055	7.003	6.566	6.177	5.517	4.979	4.534	4.160	3.995	3.842	3.569	3.332	2.857	2.500	2.222	2.000
40	32.835	27.355	19.793	15.046	11.925	9.779	8.244	7.105	6.642	6.234	5.548	4.997	4.544	4.166	3.999	3.846	3.571	3.333	2.857	2.500	2.222	2.000
50	39.196	31.424	21.482	15.762	12.234	9.915	8.304	7.133	6.661	6.246	5.554	4.999	4.545	4.167	4.000	3.846	3.571	3.333	2.857	2.500	2.222	2.000

(c) <u>My Son, the Doctor, maybe</u>. The senior Schmidts were considering with son
     Hermann whether he should go on to medical school or enter the family
     business. They estimated that if he went on to medical school (four years),
     internship (one year), and a residency for surgical training (four years), the
     opportunity cost would be $10,000 a year--mostly for reduced earnings for the
     nine years. It was estimated that from the tenth to the fortieth year, his
     earnings in medicine would exceed his business earnings by $10,000 a year.
     Mother Schmidt argued for the prestige of the M.D., but Father wanted
     assurance that his investment in Hermann would yield at least 6 percent.
     Would it? What is it estimated to yield?

4.   <u>Marginal Efficiency of Capital Calculations</u>
     Suppose that a firm currently maximizes profits with a capital stock of $10,000.
     The MEC of this capital stock is 10 percent, as is shown in the diagram below.
         Now assume that the market rate of interest falls to 8 percent and the firm
     reassesses the level of the capital stock. It is possible to invest in a machine
     costing $1,000 that, when added to the current capital stock, yields $1,080 in
     additional net revenue for one year. Thereafter it yields nothing and has no
     scrappage value.

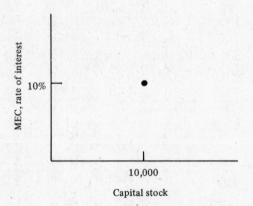

(a) Before the interest rate changed, what must have been the level of the market
     rate of interest?

(b) Calculate the MEC of the $1,000 machine. Show this value with the associated
     level of the capital stock in the diagram.

(c) Should the firm buy this machine?

5. **Constructing a Net PV Curve**

If you are not convinced that interest rates and PV are inversely related, perhaps this exercise will eliminate your doubt. Let us define <u>net PV</u> as the discounted income stream (PV) minus the acquisition cost of the asset. Suppose that an asset that can be acquired for $500 is expected to yield $400 after one year and and $200 after two years.

(a) Calculate the total PV of the expected income stream using an interest rate of 2 percent. Subtract $500 from this amount and call this the net PV at an interest rate of 2 percent.

(b) Calculate the net PV for interest rates of 4 percent, 8 percent, 15 percent, and 18 percent.

(c) Plot the relationship between net PV and the interest rate in the diagram below.

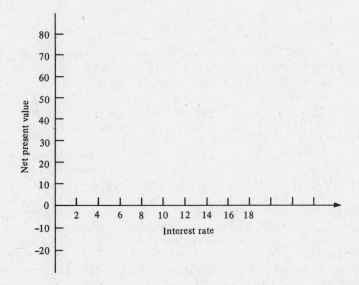

(d) Suppose that for some reason the return in the second year increased from $200 to $260, but the first-year return remained at $400. What do you think will happen to the net PV curve? Demonstrate this by calculating the new net PV values for interest rates of 8 percent and 15 percent.

Poverty, Inequality, and Mobility | 23

KEY CONCEPTS AND DEFINITIONS

1. The concept of <u>poverty</u> involves relative and absolute levels of income. A minimum living standard required by a family is defined as the <u>poverty line</u> below which a family is said to be poor. As of 1979, about 12 percent of Canadian families were classified as living in poverty.

2. The <u>incidence of poverty</u> is higher in rural areas, in the Atlantic provinces, and among those who are old, unemployed, and members of a large family.

3. The extent of poverty is affected by the performance of the economy. The <u>occasionally poor</u> are those who are temporarily below the poverty line because of spells of unemployment caused by a downturn in economic activity. <u>Persistently poor</u> are those who are virtually permanently poor regardless of economic conditions.

4. Antipoverty programs have included retraining programs to improve job opportunities, <u>social insurance</u> (Old-age Pension, Canada Pension Plan, unemployment insurance), and other welfare programs administered by provincial and/or municipal governments.

5. Some argue that antipoverty programs have certain important <u>disincentive effects</u>. These include (a) reducing the willingness of those on welfare to work, (b) generating various attitudes about work and willingness to learn skills on the part of second-generation welfare recipients, and (c) creating a heavy tax burden on citizens who pay for welfare programs.

6. Employment opportunity programs include promoting economic growth, avoiding general unemployment, and retraining programs.

7. Market conditions exercise a powerful influence on factor earning, particularly for nonhuman factors such as land and raw materials. For labour, the influence of nonmonetary considerations is important. Nevertheless, the competitive theory of factor markets and a bit of monopoly theory appear to explain a good part of the variation in the relative earnings of different groups in the labour force.

8. In the case of nonhuman factors of production, there is strong evidence that mobility is high in response to changes in earnings. Labour movement in

response to earnings differentials occurs, but it does not always occur rapidly enough to avoid regional pockets of extreme unemployment and poverty.

9. Several programs have been put into place in order to deal with the problem of regional disparities in income and employment. These have included mobility programs, relocation policies, tax incentives and subsidies, and capital expenditure programs. However, the evidence indicates that regional differences have hardly changed since such policies were introduced.

MULTIPLE-CHOICE QUESTIONS

1. The incidence of poverty tends to be highest for those persons (families) who
   (a) live in urban areas
   (b) have few children
   (c) are not in the labour force
   (d) have a male head of the family

2. An economic downturn is likely to
   (a) increase the number of occasionally poor families
   (b) decrease the number of occasionally poor families since members of the family opt out of the labour force
   (c) decrease unemployment insurance benefits to unemployed workers
   (d) have no effect on poverty since unions protect their members

3. A scheme that reduces welfare payments by a greater proportion for every dollar that the recipient earns is most likely to
   (a) increase the work effort of recipients on average
   (b) increase the tax burden of citizens
   (c) decrease the opportunity cost of working
   (d) decrease the work effort of recipients on average

4. One reason why income differentials do not generate movements of the labour factor as readily as they stimulate movements of nonhuman factors is that
   (a) labour is made less mobile because of nonpecuniary considerations
   (b) people do not really care much about making money
   (c) nonhuman factors are typically small and easily shipped around the country
   (d) nonhuman factors are owned by profit-maximizing people

5. The Canadian government in 1968 established the Department of Regional Economic Expansion, which
   (a) uses compulsion as a means of reallocating labour
   (b) introduces nonmarket policies designed in part to compensate for the immobility of labour
   (c) shifts the demand curve for labour to the left
   (d) has brought unemployment rates in the Atlantic Provinces to the national average

6. The poverty level established by Statistics Canada is the level of a family that spends on the basic necessities of food, clothing, and shelter
   (a) 50 percent of income
   (b) 60 percent or more of income
   (c) 30 percent of income
   (d) less than 50 percent of income

7. The poverty level for a family of three in Canada in 1979 is calculated to be
   (a) $5,000
   (b) $7,200
   (c) $8,500
   (d) $4,500

8. The highest incidence of poverty occurs in
   (a) the Maritime Provinces
   (b) British Columbia
   (c) Quebec
   (d) Prairie Provinces

9. The earnings of university-trained graduates fell relative to other workers during the 1970s because
   (a) the demand for university graduates increased
   (b) the supply of workers increased more than the supply of university graduates
   (c) the supply of university graduates grew significantly but employment opportunities fell for them
   (d) university graduates increasingly moved to other countries

10. The high economic activity in western Canada in the 1970s and 1980s has
    (a) increased net in-migration to western Canada
    (b) decreased the willingness of western Canadians to leave western Canada
    (c) decreased net in-migration to Ontario
    (d) all of the above

EXERCISES

1. The following exercise combines your knowledge of the theories of human capital and net advantage.

   Suppose that John Smith, who currently lives in Nova Scotia, conducts some job and information searches in the labour markets in Nova Scotia and Ontario. John is assumed to be an income maximizer in the sense that nonmonetary considerations do not influence his locational choice of employment.

   John estimates that he will receive $8,000 per year for the next thirty years if he works in Nova Scotia. If he moves to Ontario his income flow is estimated to be $8,500 per year for the next thirty years. However, his total moving costs are estimated to be $1,000 over the first year in Ontario. Moving is a risky business and so John decides to use a 10 percent discount rate when computing the present value of both income streams. Should John move to Ontario? Use the PV tables in Chapter 22 for your analysis.

2. The Incidence of Poverty According to Occupations in Canada
    Table 23-1 in the text illustrates some of the major characteristics of families
    whose 1979 income was below some cutoff point called the poverty line. We now
    consider an additional characteristic: the main occupation of the head of the
    family. In the table below we have shown the incidence of low income according to
    the main occupation of the head of the family in 1967. For this year, the
    proportion of Canadian families who were below the poverty line was 18 percent.
    The figures in the table give rough indications of the chances, or "probabilities,"
    of poverty according to various occupations. For example, we can say that there is
    about a 3 percent probability of being poor if you have a professional or technical
    occupation.

INCIDENCE OF LOW INCOME, CANADA, 1967*

Occupation of Head	Percentage
Managerial	6.7
Professional and technical	3.3
Clerical	5.6
Sales	7.2
Service and recreation	16.7
Transporation and communication	14.9
Farmers and farm workers	52.8
Loggers and fishermen	42.3
Miners	8.9
Craftsmen	9.6
Laborers	21.4

*Source: Statistics on Low Income in Canada, 1967,
Statistics Canada, 1971.

(a) In Chapter 22 you were introduced to the concept of investments in human
     capital. Specifically, academic and vocational education along with
     apprenticeship programs are examples of investments in human capital that
     improve individual skills and crafts. In turn, higher income is obtained for
     the improvement in skills. By inspecting the table above, select those
     occupations that most likely involve the greatest amounts of investments in
     human capital. Are the probabilities of poverty relatively high or low for
     these occupations?

(b) If an individual finds himself continually unemployed and/or hired for
     particular seasons, his income is likely to be low. In your opinion, which of
     the above occupations tend to have the highest levels of unemployment and/or
     seasonality? Give reasons for your choices. What relationship exists between
     your choices and the incidence of poverty?

Microeconomic Policy I: Benefits and Costs of Government Intervention in the Market Economy

24

KEY CONCEPTS AND DEFINITIONS

1. The market system constitutes a system of <u>signals and responses</u>. Production levels of firms respond to consumer preferences through the demand signals of households.

2. A market system, functioning properly, has the following characteristics: <u>coordination</u>, <u>impersonal relationships</u>, <u>efficient resource allocation</u>, and the tendency to <u>correct for disequilibrium situations</u>.

3. In a market system, firms are <u>intermediaries</u> combining resources to produce the goods and services demanded by households.

4. The concept of <u>laissez faire</u> refers to an economic environment in which government does not interfere with the market system.

5. <u>Market failure</u> refers to situations in a market economy that prevent achieving the best attainable outcome.

6. In a market system, unfettered by government, pricing policies are ultimately based on costs as determined by the producer. Such private costs reflect the best alternative of any resource to the producer. However, this cost may not reflect the best alternative use to society as a whole. A cost that measures the value of a resource to society is known as a <u>social cost</u>.

7. The market system equates <u>private benefits</u> and private costs. Should these be different from <u>social benefits</u> and social costs, the market system fails from the viewpoint of society in allocating resources in the best possible way. A divergence between social and private benefits or costs may be generated by what is called an <u>externality</u>.

8. Externalities are also referred to as <u>third party effects</u> because individuals or firms who are not the primary participants in a transaction are affected by the transaction.

9. A <u>common property resource</u> is one to which it is not possible to assign private ownership.

10. A <u>collective consumption good</u> is a good or service which once made available to one person, is available to a large group of people at no additional cost.

11. <u>Transaction costs</u> refer to the costs that are incurred to complete an exchange or market transaction.

154

12. In an attempt to prevent or offset the effects of market failure, governments can alter the market system through (i) provision of public goods, (ii) redistribution of wealth, (iii) regulations, (iv) incentives.

13. Proscriptive rules governing the economy are similar to laws that define the sphere of activity for private economic transactions, while prescriptive rules replace private decision making.

14. Government intervention is an attempt to internalize certain externalities resulting from private economic action.

15. If there exists adverse or negative external effects, then net social benefit equals net private benefit minus the external effects.

16. The act of intervention by government may itself impose costs on society in the form of lost productivity, compliance expenses, and time. In addition, government itself may, like a market that is not functioning as desired, be imperfect.

MULTIPLE-CHOICE QUESTIONS

1. An increase in the demand for wood-burning stoves will likely
   (a) cause the price of fuels other than wood to rise
   (b) increase the production of certain types of steel
   (c) lower the price of stoves
   (d) leave unchanged the price of firewood

2. If supply and demand schedules for product x are elastic, a shift in the demand schedule to the right
   (a) will leave the price and output of x unchanged
   (b) will result in a temporary disequilibrium that the market will eliminate through a rise in price and output
   (c) will result in a disequilibrium price that will require intervention to correct
   (d) will, in the short run, result in a surplus output

3. If there is an unanticipated increase in the demand for new homes, we would expect the market system to respond by
   (a) producing new homes at the current average price
   (b) allocating homes on a personal selective basis
   (c) producing more materials and labour for housing construction
   (d) producing more apartments

4. If a ton of newspaper costs $350 to produce and in the process causes $10 worth of damage to the environment,
   (a) the private cost is $360 per ton
   (b) the social cost is $10 per ton and the private cost is $350 per ton
   (c) the private cost is $350 per ton and the social cost is $340 per ton
   (d) the social and private costs per ton are $360 and $350, respectively

5. An individual who decides to drive his (her) car to work rather than take the subway
   (a) is maximizing private utility
   (b) is creating an externality
   (c) creates a situation in which social cost exceeds private cost
   (d) all of the above

6. When both the public and private sector can produce a commodity, the choice of how it is to be supplied
   (a) may depend upon the transaction costs
   (b) can be a matter of the specific type of commodity
   (c) may be based on whether or not there are externalities
   (d) all of the above

7. If there are positive externalities associated with an economic activity and that
    activity is carried out until net private benefits equal zero,
    (a) that activity should be subsidized
    (b) net social benefits will still be positive
    (c) output should be restricted
    (d) private costs are above social costs

Questions 8 and 9 refer to the diagram below.

8. The demand and supply schedules for a perfectly competitive industry (which causes
    air pollution) are shown below. In such a situation,
    (a) private output is less than the socially desirable level
    (b) the existing market price is below the socially desirable price
    (c) pollution must be reduced to zero to ensure that social and private benefits
         are equalized
    (d) the firm's output must be regulated

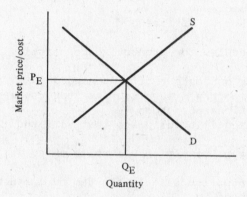

9. If a tax per unit of output is levied on an industry (elasticity of supply and
    demand greater than zero but less than infinity),
    (a) output will fall and price will remain constant
    (b) both producers and consumers will share the burden of the tax
    (c) the industry will be in a permanent disequilibrium
    (d) price will rise by the amount of the tax and output will be stimulated

10. Government intervention may fail in its objective for all but one of the following
     reasons:
     (a) lack of knowledge as to the extent of an externality
     (b) undesirable income redistribution due to intervention
     (c) inflexibility of rules
     (d) political constraints

11. If pollution abatement becomes increasingly expensive with increasing levels of
     abatement,
     (a) the optimal level of pollution is not likely to be the maximum attainable
     (b) the optimal level of pollution reduction will depend on the benefits from
          pollution abatement
     (c) optimal pollution will not be zero pollution
     (d) all of the above

156

EXERCISES

1. Assume that Mr. Maple has access to his wooded retreat by way of a 2-km road that he and another individual, Mr. Oak, must maintain. The demand for the quality of the road on the part of Mr. Oak and Mr. Maple is shown below, where Q^* is some "maximum" quality of the road. The cost of increasing the quality is shown as $S = MC$. (We assume that "zero" quality implies the road is passable.)

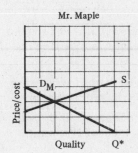
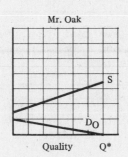
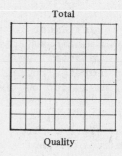

      Mr. Maple   Mr. Oak   Total

(a) What quality level will Mr. Maple maintain?

(b) How would you illustrate the social demand for road quality? Use graph 3. (Hint: Recall the discussion in the text on collective consumption goods.)

(c) Given the costs involved as shown, would the socially desirable quality result in an improvement in the quality of the road?

(d) If the level of road quality given by (c) was produced, and the costs shared, would Mr. Maple pay more or less than in (a)?

2. The following are examples of possible government intervention in the economy. In a word or two, predict the effect on relative profitability of the indicated industries.
    (a) The Province of Ontario passes new laws reducing allowed length and weight of trucks on provincial highways. Effect on:
    trucking _____
    railroads _____

(b) The government of Canada imposes a tax on gasoline that applies only to
individuals who use gasoline for noncommercial purposes. Effect on:
private gasoline consumption _____
trucking _____

(c) The Federal Department of Transport announces a new policy of letting aviation
pay its own way; federal aid to airport construction and air-traffic control
will be financed from higher taxes on airline fares, aviation gasoline, and
airport taxes, instead of from general taxation revenues. Effect on:
airlines _____
railroads _____

(d) Parliament legislates new laws that disallow tax advantages that various U.S.
magazines (Reader's Digest and Time) had in Canada and gives subsidies to
Canadian publications. Effect on:
foreign publishers _____
Canadian publishers _____

3. The following schedule shows (a) how the cost of resources increases as a pulp and
paper firm expands output and (b) the effect of pollution from the firm on
commercial fishing in the area.

Output (tons/wk)	Total Private Cost	Dollar Value of Fishing Loss Due to Pollution
0	0	0
1	500	100
2	550	225
3	620	365
4	710	515
5	820	675
6	1050	845
7	1350	1025

(a) Complete the table below and graph your results on the following page.

Average Private Cost (APC)	Marginal Private Cost (MPC)	Average Social Cost (ASC)	Marginal Social Cost (MSC)
_____	_____	_____	_____
_____	_____	_____	_____
_____	_____	_____	_____
_____	_____	_____	_____
_____	_____	_____	_____
_____	_____	_____	_____

(b) If the firm was producing four tons of output per week, what price would they
require to cover their private cost? What price would they require to cover
the social cost?

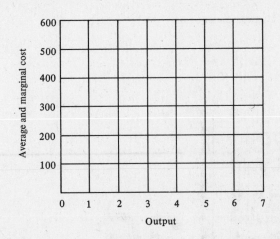

(c) If pricing were based on the average costs and <u>all</u> costs of producing pulp and
paper were considered, then the price of pulp and paper would always
be _____ than the case in which only private costs are considered.

Microeconomic Policy II: Public Finance and Public Expenditure

25

KEY CONCEPTS AND DEFINITIONS

1. A tax concession designed to encourage individuals or firms to take specific action in terms of their expenditure or saving behaviour is a tax expenditure.

2. If as income rises, tax paid is a declining share of income, the tax is regressive; if tax paid is a constant share of income, the tax is proportional; and if tax paid is a rising share of income, the tax is progressive.

3. A person's average tax rate is equal to the ratio of tax paid to income. The percentage of an increase in income that goes to taxes is the marginal tax rate.

4. The progressivity of the system refers to how the rate of tax paid to income changes as income rises.

5. The Laffer curve is a graph that relates income tax revenue to the level of the marginal tax rates.

6. A negative income tax is a system whereby the government makes a payment to an individual or family whose income falls below some prescribed level.

7. The tax base is the amount of taxable income to which tax rates are applied. It is equal to income received minus deductions and exemptions. Comprehensive income taxation would raise the tax base by lowering the exemptions and deductions permitted.

8. Taxes will affect prices, output levels, and incomes to factors of production. They thereby exert allocative effects in the economy through changing the net rewards to factors of production.

9. Tax incidence refers to who ultimately shoulders the burden of the tax, and may differ from how the tax is imposed or collected.

10. A tax on profits as defined by the tax authorities does affect resource allocation, while a tax on pure profits does not.

11. Government spending can be classified into two broad categories: transfer payments and expenditure on goods and services. Only the latter represents a direct or indirect purchase of factors of production from the economy.

12. Within a federation, the central government may adopt policies to redistribute wealth on a geographical basis from wealthy to less wealthy jurisdictions in the country. In Canada, such payments take the form of equalization payments. An

additional <u>conditional grant</u> may be used to encourage particular kinds of expenditure by provincial or local governments.

13. <u>Established Programs Financing (EPF)</u> refers to the introduction of a federal-provincial cost-sharing arrangement with respect to hospital insurance, Medicare, and post-secondary education.

14. Government expenditures benefit individuals in various ways. Similar to taxes, they can be classified, at least conceptually, as being progressive, regressive, or proportional.

MULTIPLE-CHOICE QUESTIONS

1. If as income rises, the amount of tax paid increases,
   (a) the tax is proportional
   (b) the tax is progressive
   (c) the tax is regressive
   (d) one cannot say with certainty what pattern it exhibits

2. If when income rises from $10,000 to $20,000 to $30,000, tax paid increases from $1,000 to $3,000 to $5,000
   (a) the tax is a progressive one
   (b) the tax is a proportional one
   (c) the marginal rate of tax is constant
   (d) the average rate of tax is constant

3. At $10,000 of income, tax paid is $2,000. At $11,000 of income, tax paid is $2,300.
   (a) The marginal tax rate is 20.9 percent.
   (b) The marginal tax rate is 30.0 percent.
   (c) The average tax rate at $11,000 is 20 percent.
   (d) The average tax rate equals the marginal tax rate.

4. A marginal rate of tax of 50 percent at an income level of $40,000 means
   (a) all income is taxed at 50 percent
   (b) total tax paid is $20,000
   (c) income above $40,000 is taxed at a 50 percent rate
   (d) the average tax rate is constant for incomes equal to and above $40,000

5. In Canada, it is generally believed that
   (a) tax rates are at their revenue-maximizing level
   (b) tax rates could be reduced and tax revenue would rise
   (c) an increase in tax rates would produce more tax revenue
   (d) the Laffer curve holds true

6. Comprehensive income taxation
   (a) refers to the taxation of all income
   (b) requires that there be many different taxes
   (c) means a fixed proportional tax rate
   (d) refers to reducing the difference between the tax base and total income

7. A tax concession that would permit the deduction of mortgage interest from income when computing taxable income
   (a) would be neutral in terms of allocative effects
   (b) would allocate resources away from rental housing
   (c) would increase the tax base
   (d) all of the above

8. The problem of tax incidence refers to
   (a) the question of who ultimately pays the tax
   (b) the size of the tax base relative to income
   (c) the type of tax and its allocative effects
   (d) how higher taxes eventually reduce tax revenue

Questions 9 and 10 refer to the diagram below.

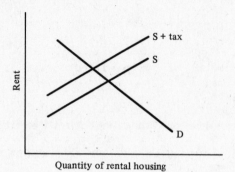

9. A tax on landlords in the market described in the diagram
   (a) would be paid entirely by landlords
   (b) would be paid entirely by renters
   (c) would be shared by landlords and tenants
   (d) would produce a leftward shift in the demand schedule

10. In the situation described by the diagram,
    (a) the amount of rental housing demanded remains the same before and after the tax
    (b) the quality of rental housing would improve
    (c) the quantity of rental housing demanded would fall
    (d) the quantity of rental housing that landlords would be willing to supply does not change

11. Understanding the difference between pure profits and profits defined by the tax authority is most important for
    (a) questions related to the impact of taxes on government revenue
    (b) questions related to the impact of taxes on factor allocation
    (c) understanding how the tax system as a whole functions
    (d) deciding on what tax is the most equitable

12. Transfer payments in Canada have grown rapidly in recent years for all but one of the following reasons:
    (a) changes in regulations regarding eligible recipients
    (b) taxes used to pay for transfer payments have risen rapidly
    (c) more concern in society for low-income families
    (d) unemployment compensation has increased due to higher rates of unemployment

13. Equalization payments
    (a) redistribute income from wealthy individuals to poorer individuals directly
    (b) involve a federal provincial agreement over the sharing of tax fields
    (c) are payments from Ottawa to provinces with below-average tax capacity
    (d) have declined during the past ten years due to increasing wealth in Alberta

162

14. Decentralization of government economic activity can be justified by all but which of the following?
    (a) regional preferences
    (b) income redistribution
    (c) particular local needs for public expenditure
    (d) cultural differences within the country

15. Increasing amounts of tax revenue have been transferred to the provincial and municipal governments for all but which of the following reasons?
    (a) Expenditure needs of urban areas are rapidly growing.
    (b) Municipal revenue sources have been growing slowly.
    (c) Provincial and municipal governments do not collect tax revenue.
    (d) The federal government has greater access to the high-growth tax sources.

EXERCISES

1. The three diagrams below represent three different market situations with respect to the supply and demand for rental accommodation in the short run. Assume that a property tax of equal value is imposed in all three situations.

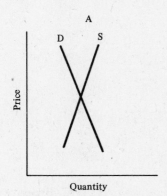
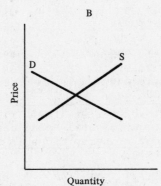
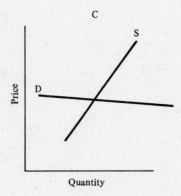

   (a) In which market situation will the landlord bear most of the tax burden? Why is this the case?

   (b) In which market situation is there the smallest change in the quantity of accommodation? Why is this the case?

   (c) Suppose that in Case B rent controls had "fixed" rent or price at the original equilibrium, pre-tax rate. Is the tax burden shouldered by the landlord in Case B altered because of the existence of rent control?

2. (a) The table on the following page provides information on the taxes paid by four individuals in different income categories. For each of the three taxes, A, B, and C, indicate whether the tax is proportional, regressive, or progressive.

163

Tax	Income Category and Tax Paid			
	$5,000	10,000	20,000	30,000
A	500	1,000	2,000	3,000
B	400	700	1,300	1,800
C	200	500	1,300	2,000

Tax A is _____ .

Tax B is _____ .

Tax C is _____ .

(b) Taking all taxes together (A + B + C), is the tax system progressive, regressive, or proportional? _____

3. A study by the Province of Ontario produced data (which are summarized in the following table) illustrating the relationship between household income and property taxes in Guelph, Ontario.

Household Income (class)	Average Property Tax Paid
$ 2,500-4,999	$275
5,000-6,999	279
7,000-9,999	319
10,000-11,999	355
12,000-14,999	417
15,000-19,999	495
20,000-24,999	581
25,000-49,999	650
50,000-99,999	836

Source: Ministry of Treasury, Economics and Intergovernmental Relations; Analysis of Property Taxes in Guelph, October 1972.

(a) Given these data, does the property tax appear to be regressive, proportional, or progressive? Why? (To make your calculations, use the mid-point of the income range.)

(b) To make a tax a proportional one at a tax rate roughly equal to 4 percent, what kind of subsidies and additional taxes would the government need to impose at each household income level?

Part Eight

Resource Allocation in an Open Economy

| International Trade and Protection | **26** |

KEY CONCEPTS AND DEFINITIONS

1. <u>International trade</u> is the exchange of goods and service across international boundaries. Such exchange can result in advantages for countries that trade, advantages that are known as the <u>gains from trade</u>.

2. An important aspect of trade is that one country can specialize in producing things where it has an advantage to do so, and thus purchase from elsewhere things it cannot produce efficiently.

3. For <u>absolute advantage</u> to exist, one country can produce more of a particular good from a given quantity of resources than another country using the same bundle of resources.

4. <u>Comparative advantage</u> arises when the margin of absolute advantage differs for two commodities in two countries.

5. The degree of specialization and resulting gains from trade depend upon the pattern of comparative, not absolute, advantage. More precisely, the gains are related to the differences in opportunity cost between countries.

6. In addition to comparative and absolute advantage, gains from trade can originate from long experience in producing things and economies of large-scale production.

7. The <u>terms of trade</u> are defined as the quantity of domestic goods that must be exported to get a unit of imported goods. An <u>index of the terms of trade</u> is computed as $(P_M/P_X) \cdot 100$, where P_M is the index of import prices and P_X the index of export prices. If the index rises, a country experiences a <u>favourable change</u> in the terms of trade, and an <u>unfavorable change</u> if the index falls.

8. <u>Protectionism</u> describes how a country protects its domestic industries from foreign competition. <u>Free trade</u> occurs where there is no protectionism.

9. An <u>ad valorem tariff</u> is a tax on imported goods, usually a percentage of the producer's price. Further methods of protectionism are <u>import quotas</u> (limits on the number of foreign goods permitted to be sold) and the use of <u>foreign exchange limitations</u> to buy certain goods.

10. In theory, free trade permits a country to maximize its consumption by specialization and by sale of what it does not consume for goods it wishes to consume.

11. Protectionism is not an irrational policy if there are social goals other than maximizing production and consumption. Such goals may involve economic diversification and cultural objectives.

12. The infant industry argument for protection is based on the notion that certain industries need time to establish domestic and international markets, reaping economies of scale and low costs. Short-run protection affords this opportunity.

13. A country's standard of living depends on what it can consume. Exports, for which a country receives foreign exchange, allow for the purchase of imports, often at a cost much lower than if they were produced domestically.

14. The General Agreement on Tariffs and Trade (GATT) refers to the post-1945 agreement involving major trading countries to reduce tariffs and meet periodically to consider continuous reductions.

15. Extraterritoriality refers to the application of foreign laws to branches of foreign-owned companies producing in the domestic country.

16. The Foreign Investment Review Act of 1973 established an agency to approve and monitor take-over bids and the establishment of foreign-owned companies in Canada.

MULTIPLE-CHOICE QUESTIONS

1. Absolute advantage
   (a) occurs when one country can produce a greater quantity of all goods than another country
   (b) refers to the cost of factors of production
   (c) is a synonym for gains from trade
   (d) occurs if one country, using a given bundle of resources, can produce more of a good than another country using the same bundle of resources

2. International specialization
   (a) guarantees a higher standard of living
   (b) guarantees increased consumption
   (c) results in gains if trade takes place
   (d) is determined entirely by natural resource endowments

3. Country A has a comparative advantage over country B
   (a) if, for two goods, A produces more of both commodities than does B
   (b) if the margin of absolute advantage differs for two commodities produced by both countries
   (c) if A's output of one commodity exceeds that of B for the same commodity
   (d) all of the above

Questions 4 through 7 refer to the following table.

	One Unit of Resources can Produce	
	Lumber (bd.m)	Aluminum (kg)
Australia	4	9
Canada	9	3
Brazil	3	2

4. In the situation described above, considering Australia and Canada,
   (a) Australia has an absolute advantage in lumber
   (b) Australia has an absolute advantage in aluminum
   (c) there are no gains from trade to be realized through specialization
   (d) Canada should specialize in aluminum production

166

5. Considering Canada and Brazil,
   (a) Brazil has an absolute advantage in lumber
   (b) Brazil has a comparative advantage in aluminum
   (c) Canada has an absolute advantage in only one commodity
   (c) there are no gains from trade due to specialization

6. In Australia, the opportunity cost of 1 board metre of lumber is
   (a) 2.25 kg of aluminum
   (b) 0.44 kg of aluminum
   (c) 0.36 kg of aluminum
   (d) 3.60 kg of aluminum

7. In Canada, the opportunity cost of 1 kg of aluminum is
   (a) 0.33 bd.m of lumber
   (b) 2.70 bd.m of lumber
   (c) 3.0 bd.m of lumber
   (d) 3.33 bd.m of lumber

8. Gains from international trade arise when
   (a) opportunity costs across countries differ
   (b) countries generate, through experience, lower costs of production for certain domestic commodities
   (c) countries can realize economies of scale with respect to certain commodities
   (d) all of the above

9. The terms of trade refer to
   (a) specific trade agreements between two countries
   (b) the ratio of opportunity costs within a country
   (c) the quantity of domestic goods that must be exported to get a unit of imported goods
   (d) the inverse of the opportunity costs between two products

10. Referring to the table preceding question 4, Canada would export lumber and import aluminum if the terms of trade were
    (a) 3 bd.m of lumber for 3 kg of aluminum
    (b) 3 bd.m of lumber for 1 kg of aluminum
    (c) 6 bd.m of lumber for 2 kg of aluminum
    (d) 1 bd.m of lumber for 1/10 kg of aluminum

11. If, for country A, the opportunity cost of a unit of Z is .25 units of Y and the terms of trade are such that a unit of Y can be bought on the world market for 3 units of Z,
    (a) country A will not export Y
    (b) country A will export Z
    (c) country A will be better off if it exports Z
    (d) all of the above

12. Which of the following is not a protectionist policy?
    (a) an ad valorem tariff on finished lumber products
    (b) a limit on the volume of Italian shoes sold in Canada per year
    (c) a sales tax on hotel rooms rented by foreigners
    (d) a limit on foreign exchange purchases by importers

13. Free trade
    (a) guarantees considerable diversity in any one economy
    (b) maximizes the opportunity for expanding consumption
    (c) is only advantageous to countries experiencing absolute advantage
    (d) is always advantageous to everyone

14. The infant industry argument for protection
    (a) applies to small firms that will never be able to compete internationally
    (b) is a permanent protectionist policy
    (c) is based on the notion that protection will be withdrawn once an efficient scale of operation has been reached
    (d) has little justification in developing countries

15. Which of the following statements is a valid description of free trade?
    (a) Free trade benefits all countries.
    (b) A greater degree of specialization will occur with free trade than without it.
    (c) The introduction of free trade in Canada would be easily accomplished at no cost.
    (d) Free trade maximizes gross national product.

16. Which of the following is not a valid reason for protectionism?
    (a) Protectionism in the short run is useful to stimulate new industry.
    (b) A protectionist policy encourages domestic spending and keeps the money at home.
    (c) Protectionist policies may be needed to diversify an economy away from one or relatively few specialized industries.
    (d) Cultural traditions may require protectionist policies.

17. Nonresident ownership in Canada
    (a) is concentrated in the service sector, such as restaurants
    (b) is very high in the petroleum and coal industry
    (c) is not more than 25 percent in any sector
    (d) has been of little concern to policy-makers

18. Problems associated with extraterritoriality
    (a) are not in evidence in Canada
    (b) involve Canadian ownership in the United States
    (c) are associated with countries where trade is minimal
    (d) involve the application of foreign laws in other countries where there is foreign ownership

19. The Foreign Investment Review Act
    (a) sets limits on the degree of foreign ownership in Canada
    (b) has been in effect since the 1930s
    (c) established a screening device to evaluate potential foreign ownership
    (d) limits foreign investment to only a few sectors of the economy

EXERCISES

1. For each of the situations below, determine which commodity each country should specialize in and trade.
    (a) One unit of resources can produce:

	Wheat (100 bushels)	Beef (hundredweight)
Canada	2	4
Argentina	3	1

The opportunity costs are:

	Wheat/100 bushels	Beef/hundredweight
Canada	_____	_____
Argentina	_____	_____

Canada should specialize in the production of _____.
Argentina should specialize in the production of _____.

(b) One unit of resources can produce:

	Wheat (100 bushels)	Beef (hundredweight)
Canada	2	4
Argentina	1	3

The opportunity costs are:

	Wheat/100 bushels	Beef/hundredweight
Canada	_____	_____
Argentina	_____	_____

Canada should specialize in the production of _____.
Argentina should specialize in the production of _____.

(c) One unit of resources can produce:

	Wheat (100 bushels)	Beef (hundredweight)
Canada	2	4
Argentina	1	2

The opportunity costs are:

	Wheat/100 bushels	Beef/hundredweight
Canada	_____	_____
Argentina	_____	_____

Canada whould specialize in the production of _____.
Argentina should specialize in the production of _____.

2. Below are the production patterns with respect to wheat and wool for Canada and Australia.

	One Unit of Resources Will Produce	
	Wheat (bu)	Wool (kg)
Canada	10	2
Australia	12	6

(a) Do these data suggest the existence of strictly absolute advantage alone or comparative advantage?

(b) What is the opportunity cost of wheat, in terms of wool, for both countries?

(c) Is a gain from trade possible? Why?

(d) If Canada moved 1/2 unit of resources from wool to wheat and Australia moved 1/4 unit of resources from wheat to wool, complete the table below. What has happened to world output of both products?

PATTERN OF WHEAT AND WOOL PRODUCTION
After Resource Transfer

	Wheat	Wool
Canada	_____	_____
Australia	_____	_____
World	_____	_____

169

Let us define the terms of trade for either country as

<u>necessary bushels of wheat exported</u>
1 kg wool received

(e) If the terms of trade for Canada were 4:1, would Canada wish to trade? Why?

(f) If the terms of trade were the same for Australia, would Australia want to trade? Why?

3. (a) The table below provides data on the index of merchandise import prices and the index of merchandise export prices. Using the definition of the terms of trade that involves indexes, complete the fourth column and plot the terms of trade.

Year	Index of Export Prices	Index of Import Prices	Terms of Trade
1970	100.6	98.6	_____
1971	100.0	100.0	_____
1972	103.3	102.3	_____
1973	118.1	110.0	_____
1974	157.1	135.6	_____
1975	173.2	156.6	_____
1976	176.6	157.9	_____
1977	189.4	177.0	_____
1978	205.4	200.7	_____
1979	248.4	229.0	_____

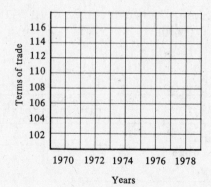

170

(b) For the periods listed, indicate if the change in the terms of trade was favourable (F) or unfavourable (U).

1970-1975   _____
1972-1973   _____
1975-1979   _____
1971-1979   _____
1974-1978   _____

(c) Setting the terms of trade equal to 100 in 1974, what would be the terms of trade in 1975? _____
If in 1974 the export of 50 units of pulp and paper was required to import 10 units of automobiles, how many units of pulp and paper were needed in 1975 to buy the same quantity of imported automobiles?

4. (a) The three diagrams below illustrate the demand for and supply of an imported commodity Z, given free trade. Revise these diagrams according to the protectionist policy outlined below each diagram and indicate what the new price (P*) and quantity exchanged (Q*) will be.

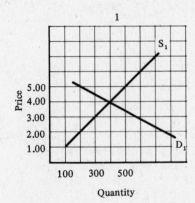

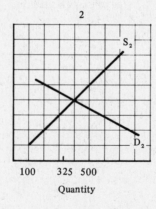

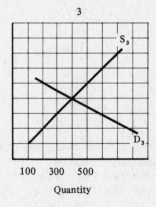

The government restricts importers to purchasing only 1/2 of what they previously purchased, at any price.

The government imposes a quota of 325 units of Z that can be imported.

The government imposes a tariff at $1.00 per unit of the foreign good.

(b) If the demand for Z was highly inelastic, which policy would government likely <u>not</u> choose if it wanted to maximize its restriction on the amount of the import purchased? Why?

(c)   Which policy would the government likely choose if it was concerned that restricted or protectionist policies might be inflationary? Why?

5.   The diagram below illustrates the domestic supply of steel (S_D), the foreign supply of steel (S_F) and the domestic demand (D).
   (a)   Draw the total supply curve for steel and establish the domestic output (Q_D) and overall price (P_O).

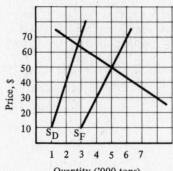

Quantity ('000 tons)

   (b)   The "domestic" government now levies a tariff of $20 per ton of steel on foreign suppliers. Using a broken line, draw the "after-tariff" supply curve for foreigners and the new total supply curve, labelling them S_F' and S_{D+F}'. Label the new price P_1.
   (c)   What happens to the total revenue of domestic steel producers? Does the change in output for domestic producers depend on the elasticity of the domestic steel supply curve? Explain.

6.   Let us assume that 0.2 is the opportunity cost of hydroelectric power with respect to automobiles, for Canada. For the United States, let us assume the opportunity cost of hydroelectric power with respect to automobiles is 2.5.
   (a)   Assuming they are straight lines, draw Canada's and the United States' production (and consumption) possibility curves. Label them PC_{CAN} and PC_{US}.

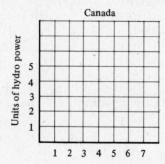

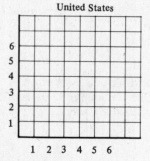

Units of automobile production

172

(b)   Suppose Canada could specialize in hydropower production only, trading
      hydropower for automobiles at the U.S. opportunity cost, and the United States
      could specialize in automobile production, trading automobiles for hydropower
      at the Canadian opportunity cost. Draw the consumption possibilities curves
      that would exist in both countries. Label them PC_{CAN}^* and PC_{US}^*. Which
      country is now better off and why?

(c)   If Canada could specialize in hydropower and trade at an opportunity cost
      (hydropower in terms of automobiles) of 1.0, and the United States could
      specialize in automobiles and trade at an opportunity cost of 0.8, would both
      countries gain? Explain. Draw in the new production-consumption
      possibilities curves, labelling them PC'_{CAN} and PC'_{US}.

Energy Policy:
A Case Study

27

KEY CONCEPTS AND DEFINITIONS

1. The two-price system for energy is a policy that in Canada has ensured that certain domestic energy prices are below those of the world.

2. Self-sufficiency in energy means that any energy exports equal energy imports.

3. The import compensation scheme introduced in 1974 subsidized firms that were importing oil to keep domestic prices below world prices.

4. To finance the import compensation scheme, a tax on the export of oil was levied on Canadian production sold abroad.

5. The blended price of oil (paid by the consumer) is the wellhead price (received by the producer) plus a tax.

6. Oil price parity refers to raising the price of oil in Canada to that of the world price.

7. The opportunity cost of oil to Canada is what we could sell it for to the rest of the world: the world price.

8. A two-price system for oil means that too little oil is produced in Canada and too much is consumed. Resources are therefore being used where their marginal product is lower than would be otherwise.

9. Going to the world price for oil will have distributional consequences, but there are more efficient methods to achieve distributional objectives than subsidizing the price of oil.

10. The two-price system leads to a misallocation of labour resources since the private and social marginal revenue products of labour in oil-producing regions are different.

11. The two-price system does mean lower energy prices for Canadian manufacturers, but the effect on expanding exports is relatively small.

12. The Petroleum Compensation Charge, part of the 1980 National Energy Program, is paid by domestic refineries and is equal to the difference between the blended oil price, which consumers would pay, and the wellhead price.

13. A depletion allowance is a tax-deductible expense equal to a given percentage of exploration and development expense.

174

MULTIPLE-CHOICE QUESTIONS

1. The two-price system for oil in Canada from 1974 to 1981 involved
   (a) a policy of different prices for oil for different consumers
   (b) a significantly higher price for oil east of the Ottawa Valley compared to the rest of Canada
   (c) a policy whereby the price of oil to Canadians was below world price
   (d) a policy whereby the price of oil in Canada was always 85 percent of the world price.

2. The 1974 import compensation scheme
   (a) has never had any impact on government resources because the tax always equaled the subsidy
   (b) subsidized those refineries that used oil that had to be purchased at world prices
   (c) applied only to residential heating fuel oil
   (d) ensures an efficient allocation of oil supply

3. For an oil exporting country, an oil export tax has all but one of the following effects.
   (a) It reduces domestic prices.
   (b) It increases domestic consumption.
   (c) It will raise exports of oil.
   (d) It reduces domestic production.

4. The difference between the wellhead price of oil and the blended price of oil is
   (a) the cost of transportation
   (b) the tax that drives a wedge between the price received by the producer and paid by the consumer
   (c) the world price minus the domestic price of oil
   (d) equal to the import subsidy

5. For a country that is a net exporter of oil, a production tax (royalty) and an export tax of equal value per barrel of oil
   (a) will always generate equal revenue for the government
   (b) have the same impact on domestic oil consumption
   (c) generate different amounts of revenue for the government
   (d) will both always cause production of oil to decline

6. The magnitude of the allocative distortion due to the two-price system
   (a) varies indirectly with the elasticities of supply and demand
   (b) is equal to the difference between the domestic and world price of oil
   (c) is larger, the higher the elasticity of demand and/or supply
   (d) can be reduced by an import subsidy

7. The main arguments against moving to parity with respect to the world price of oil include
   (a) the world price is not the true price of oil and will eventually be lower
   (b) lower oil prices allow us to have greater export revenues and fewer imports
   (c) the undesirable effects that parity would have on income distribution and exports
   (d) Canada can set its own price because it is self-sufficient and has plenty of other energy resources

8. If oil is priced lower than its true opportunity cost and is not produced in equal quantities within a country, then it follows that
    (a) there will be an inefficient allocation of labour within the country
    (b) the private marginal revenue product (MRP) of labour in the oil-producing region will be less than the SRP of labour
    (c) labour mobility will be less than it would be at world price
    (d) all of the above

9. The true cost of oil use today is
    (a) the cost of extracting the oil plus any taxes
    (b) the price set by the OPEC cartel
    (c) the cost of extraction, processing, and the cost of less oil in the future
    (d) the cost of the closest substitute

10. A key argument for the establishment of a crown corporation in the oil industry is that
    (a) it allows society to obtain true information on the cost of extracting and processing crude oil
    (b) the profits of the corporation can be used to subsidize low-income families
    (c) there is a lack of financial capital to explore for oil
    (d) the government firm will be more efficient in the allocation of the oil

EXERCISES

1. In the diagram below, the domestic price of oil is determined by supply and demand conditions (domestically). The world price of oil is shown as P_W.

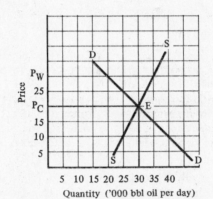

Quantity ('000 bbl oil per day)

    (a) Given that any excess production can always be sold at the world price, what will be the domestic consumption of oil if this country goes to world price?

    (b) What will be the volume of exports of oil?

    (c) What is the net gain in efficiency in terms of going to world price? (Indicate on diagram.)

176

2. In the diagram below, DD and SS represent the demand for and supply of oil in Canada. Any output over and above that which Canadians wish to purchase at the world price of $25/bbl is sold to the world at the world price.

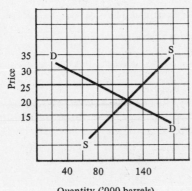

Quantity ('000 barrels)

The government is debating whether or not to impose an export tax (paid by the producer) of $10/bbl or a royalty of $5/bbl.
(a) How much revenue would be generated by the export tax?

(b) With the royalty of $5, what would domestic consumption become? What would be the volume of exports?

(c) How much revenue would the government collect if it imposed the royalty?

3. The Canadian energy policy of the mid-1970s was complex in that it involved an export tax and an import subsidy. Recall from the text that
(i) a subsidy is needed to give consumers a lower than world price for imported oil
(ii) a tax on exports is needed to ensure that Canadian producers do not sell in international markets where world price > domestic price.
In the diagram below, S is the domestic supply curve for oil and D is the domestic demand. Demand that cannot be met from domestic production can be satisfied by imports. Any domestic producer can sell in Canada or on the international market.

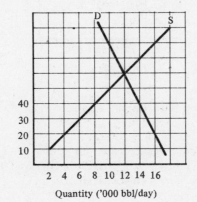

Quantity ('000 bbl/day)

177

(a) If world price is $40/bbl, what will Canadian demand be per day? How much will
be imported?

(b) If Canada introduced an import subsidy of $10/bbl of oil, what would Canadian
demand be per day? _____ Would Canadian oil producers sell oil
in Canada? Explain.

(c) Canadian policy is changed to include an export tax of $10/bbl levied on
Canadian producers. Would Canadian producers sell in Canada now? Explain.

(d) Given the diagram on the preceding page, calculate (i) the cost of the import
subsidy and (ii) the revenue from the export tax.

4. Figure 27-4 in the text describes in detail the gains and losses associated with a
movement to parity with the world price of oil. The following exercise is similar
to that analysis, except that you are required to make the numerical calculation
given the information below. We assume in this example that Canada is a net
exporter of oil.

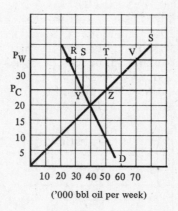

('000 bbl oil per week)

The world price is $35/bbl and the Canadian price is $25/bbl due to an export tax of
$10/bbl.
(a) At P_C, export tax revenues are $ _____ with Canadian producers
selling _____ barrels a week to Canadians. A move to the world price
by eliminating the tax results in domestic demand becoming _____
barrels a week and total exports rising to _____ barrels a week.

178

(b) The move to the world price creates a producer's surplus equal to the area _____, while consumer's surplus falls by the area _____. The difference between the two areas is _____ .

(c) The export tax is paid by foreigners who, at a price P_C, purchase _____ barrels of oil per week. A move to world price means the loss of export taxes equal to the area _____ .

(d) The net gain as a result of the move to world prices is producer's surplus <u>minus</u> consumer's surplus <u>minus</u> lost tax revenue. This is equal to the area _____ .

Part Nine

National Income and Fiscal Policy

<table>
<tr><td>

Aggregate Demand and Aggregate Supply

</td><td>

28

</td></tr>
</table>

KEY CONCEPTS AND DEFINITIONS

1. The general price level, a macroeconomic variable, is measured by any index of the economy's prices. The annual rate of inflation is the percentage change in a price index from one year to the next.
2. National income (or output) refers to the total market value of goods and services produced in the economy. The notion of market value incorporates both the prices as well as the physical output of goods and services.
3. One commonly used measure of national income is the gross national product (GNP). When it is measured in current dollars, it is called nominal GNP or current dollar GNP. When it is measured in constant dollars, it is referred to as real GNP or constant dollar GNP.
4. Potential or full-employment GNP is what the economy would have produced if its productive resources were fully employed at their normal intensity of use. The GNP gap is the difference between potential GNP and actual GNP.
5. Employment denotes the number of adult workers who hold full-time civilian jobs; unemployment denotes the number of persons who are not employed and are actively searching for a job; and the labour force is the total number of the employed in civilian jobs and the unemployed.
6. The unemployment rate is the percentage of the labour force that is unemployed.
7. The aggregate demand (AD) curve shows a relation between the total amount of all real output (Y) that will be demanded by purchasers and the price level (P) of that output. The AD curve typically slopes downward to the right for three reasons: (1) substitution for "foreign goods"; (2) money and interest rate effects; and (3) direct money balance effects on expenditures.
8. The aggregate supply (AS) curve shows a relation between the total amount of real output (Y) that will be produced and the price level (P) of that output. A composite AS curve is a short-run relation between the price level and national income (product). It has three ranges: a Keynesian range, where P is constant but Y can vary; an intermediate range, where P and Y vary directly; and a classical range, where Y is constant but P varies.

9. The <u>Keynesian</u> portion of the AS curve assumes the <u>downward rigidity</u> of wages and prices even though excess supply (unemployment) exists. When demand falls, firms reduce output but do not reduce prices.
10. The <u>ratchet effect</u> refers to the fact that the horizontal, Keynesian portion of the AS curve shifts up whenever the actual price level rises (due to a demand increase). The price level will not fall should demand subsequently decrease due to the assumption of the downward rigidity of wages and prices.

MULTIPLE-CHOICE QUESTIONS

1. If the price index increases from x to y from one year to the next, then the rate of inflation is
   (a) y - x
   (b) (y - x)/x
   (c) (y/x) times 100%
   (d) [(y - x)/x] times 100%

2. National income in nominal terms refers to
   (a) the total purchasing power of the household
   (b) the total market values in current prices of goods and services produced in the economy
   (c) the physical output of all goods and services produced in the economy
   (d) the total market value in current prices of goods and services consumed by the household

3. Decreases in real GNP reflect
   (a) price level decreases
   (b) output decreases
   (c) output increases and price decreases
   (d) none of the above

4. A GNP gap exists when
   (a) actual GNP is less than potential GNP
   (b) actual GNP and potential GNP are equal
   (c) there are no unemployed resources
   (d) current dollar GNP is the same as real GNP

5. The labour force is defined as
   (a) the total adult population in an economy
   (b) the number of civilian, adult workers who are employed
   (c) the number of civilian, adult employed workers minus the number of unemployed workers
   (d) none of the above

6. The domestic labour force will increase by 10 if
   (a) 10 unemployed workers become employed
   (b) 10 unemployed workers leave the country
   (c) 10 twenty-year-old females leave school and obtain employment
   (d) all of the above

7. The unemployment rate is defined as
   (a) the percentage of the labour force who are unemployed
   (b) the total number of unemployed workers
   (c) the percentage of employed workers who are unemployed
   (d) the percentage of the adult population who are unemployed

8. The AD curve is usually depicted as
   (a) a direct relationship between the total amount of real output (Y) that will be demanded by purchasers and the price level (P)
   (b) a direct relationship between nominal GNP that will be demanded by purchasers, and P
   (c) an inverse relationship between current dollar GNP that will be demanded and P
   (d) an inverse relationship between real GNP that will be demanded and P

9. The Canadian AD curve is likely to be downward sloping because Canadians will buy more imported goods and foreigners will purchase fewer Canadian-produced goods if
   (a) the Canadian price level falls and the foreign price level remains constant
   (b) the Canadian price level rises and the foreign price level remains constant
   (c) the Canadian inflation rate is equal to the foreign inflation rate
   (d) the Canadian inflation rate is less than the foreign inflation rate

10. The Keynesian portion of a composite AS curve portrays an economic situation in which
   (a) prices are constant but real output can vary
   (b) there are unemployed resources
   (c) there is a downward rigidity of wages and prices in the economy
   (d) all of the above

11. The classical range of a composite AS curve portrays an economic situation in which
   (a) prices vary but Y is constant
   (b) Y is at its full-employment level
   (c) both (a) and (b)
   (d) answer (a) but not (b)

Questions 12 through 17 refer to the diagram below.

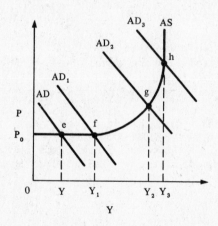

12. Assuming the aggregate demand curve shifts to the right from AD to AD_1,
   (a) there are unemployed resources at f
   (b) prices and output rise
   (c) prices remain constant but output increases
   (d) the horizontal portion P_0f shifts up

13. Assuming the aggregate demand curve shifts to the right from AD to AD_2,
   (a) there are unemployed resources at g
   (b) prices and output increase
   (c) nominal GNP increases but not real GNP
   (d) the horizontal portion P_0f shifts down if the ratchet effect is operative

182

14. Assuming the aggregate demand curve shifts to the right from AD to AD_3,
    (a) full-employment income results
    (b) prices and real output rise
    (c) the horizontal portion P_0f shifts up and passes through point h
    (d) all of the above

15. If the aggregate demand curve shifts to the left from AD_1 to AD,
    (a) prices and output fall
    (b) prices stay constant but output falls
    (c) it is likely that there will be less unemployed resources
    (d) the horizontal portion P_0f shifts down

16. Point g is in the
    (a) Keynesian range of the AS curve
    (b) classical range of the AS curve
    (c) intermediate range of a composite AS curve
    (d) GNP gap

17. Capacity or maximum national income is
    (a) Y_3
    (b) Y_2
    (c) Y_1
    (d) unknown

EXERCISES

1. You are given the following price indices for various years. The base year has an index of 100.

Year	Price Index	Annual Inflation Rate (%)
7	118.1	NA
8	121.9	_____
9	125.1	_____
10	_____	1.1

   (a) Calculate the annual inflation rate (to one decimal) for years 8 and 9 and fill in the third column.

   (b) What was the total inflation rate from the base year through year 9?

   (c) Calculate (to one decimal) the price index for year 10.

2. The table on the following page provides information about the Canadian economy for six years.
   (a) Fill in the missing values in the table.

183

Date	Constant $ GNP (billions)	Constant $ Potential GNP (billions)	Labour Force (thousands)	Unemployed (thousands)	Employed (thousands)	Unemployment Rate (%)
1974	111.7		9,639	514	9,125	_____
1975	113.0	115.7	9,974	690	_____	6.918
1976	119.1	121.4	10,206	___	9,479	7.123
1977	121.9		_____	850	_____	8.097
1978	126.1		10,882	___	_____	8.362
1979	129.8		11,207	838	_____	_____

(b) Calculate the percentage change in real (constant dollar) GNP between 1978 and 1979. Compare this value with the percentage change in employment in this time period.

(c) Does there appear to be a direct or indirect relationship between real GNP and employment over the period?

(d) Between 1977 and 1978 the unemployment rate increased while employment increased. How is this possible?

(e) Calculate the values of the real income per member of the labour force for 1974 and 1979.

(f) Calculate the values of the GNP gap for 1975 and 1976.

3. You are given the following schedules for AD and AS. For mathematical simplicity, the AS curve is not the composite version discussed in the text.

Price	Aggregate Demand (AD) Output (Y)		Price	Aggregate Supply (AS) Output (Y)	
	(1)	(2)		(3)	(4)
90	0	15	90	30	33
72	9	24	72	24	33
54	18	33	54	18	33
30	30	45	30	10	33
0	45	60	0	0	33

(a) Inspecting the values in column (1) for AD and the column of prices, is there an inverse relationship between Y and P? Provide three theoretical reasons for the inverse relationship.

(b) Inspecting the values in column (3) for AS and the column of prices, what type of relationship exists between output supplied (Y) and P? This AS curve is similar to that portrayed in Figure 28-6 of the text.

(c) Inspecting column (4) for the AS and the price column, identify the range of the composite AS curve that this relationship portrays.

(d) Using the values in column (1) for AD and those in column (3) for AS, determine the equilibrium values for Y and P. Equilibrium is where, for a given level of P, quantity supplied equals quantity demanded.

(e) Using the values in column (2) for AD and those in column (3) for AS, determine the equilibrium values of Y and P.

(f) Compare your answers to (d) and (e). You should have concluded that the equilibrium Y and P values for the AD curve column (2) were higher than those for the AD curve column (1). Discuss this result in relation to Figure 28-8 in the text.

4. The aggregate demand curve is given by the expression $P = 40 - 2Y$, and the aggregate supply curve is given by the following:

   (i) $P = 20$ for $0 \leq Y \leq 30^*$, and

   (ii) $P = 5 + .5Y$ for $30 \leq Y \leq 50$, and

   (iii) $Y = 50$ for $P \geq 30$

$^*0 \leq Y \leq 30$ means output has the range greater than or equal to zero but less than or equal to 30.

(a) Plot the AD curve in the diagram on the following page and carefully indicate the intercept values.

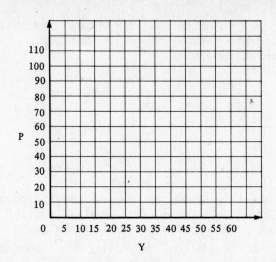

(b) Plot the AS curve in the diagram. Indicate the Keynesian, intermediate, and classical ranges.

(c) Referring to the diagram, what are the equilibrium levels of P and Y? Prove algebraically that the intersection of equation (i) and the AD expression yields these equilibrium values.

(d) Suppose the expression for the AD curve became $P = 80 - 2Y$. Plot this expression in the diagram and discuss the changes that occurred to the equilibrium values of P and Y.

(e) Suppose the AD expression became $P = 105 - 2Y$. Plot this relationship and determine the equilibrium levels of P and Y.

(f) Assuming the AD curve changes from $P = 80 - 2Y$ to $P = 105 - 2Y$, what changes in equilibrium values do you observe?

(g) If the ratchet effect is operative for your answer to part (f), what will be the new algebraic expression for the Keynesian range?

The Concepts of National Product and National Income

29

KEY CONCEPTS AND DEFINITIONS

1. National product is the market value of all the production in the economy over a year. National income is the value of all the claims generated by that production. By accounting convention, these two values must be equal.

2. National income (product) may be calculated either by the output-expenditure approach or by the factor-income approach.

3. The output-expenditure approach calculates the total expenditure needed to purchase the nation's output. The value of output of final goods and services can be found by taking the sum of the value added. Value added is the value of the firm's output minus the value of inputs that it purchases from other firms. These inputs used to produce the final product are referred to as intermediate goods. Therefore, the value-added approach avoids double-counting of output.

4. The major components of expenditure are consumption by households, denoted by C, investment in inventories and/or capital goods by firms, denoted by I, government expenditures on goods and services (but excluding government transfer payments), denoted by G, and net exports (exports minus imports), denoted by

5. The total investment that occurs in the economy is called gross investment. It consists of two parts: replacement investment (that which is necessary to maintain the existing capital stock intact), or what is referred to as either the capital consumption allowance or depreciation, and net investment (additions to the capital stock). By definition, net investment is equal to gross investment minus the capital consumption allowance.

6. From the output-expenditure approach, the total value of expenditure (AE) that measures national income and national product in an open economy (one which engages in foreign trade) is $AE = C + I + G + (X - M)$. This national income measure is called gross national product (GNP).

7. The factor-income approach measures the total value of factor payments that were involved in producing national output. The four main components of factor incomes are: rent (the payment for services of land and other factors that are rented); wages and salaries (payments for the services of labour); interest (pay-

187

ment to those who lend money); and _profits_, which are payments to the owners of capital.

8. Other related measures of national income are: _net national product (NNP)_, which is GNP minus the capital consumption allowance; _personal income_, which is the income earned by or paid to individuals before allowances for personal income taxes; and _disposable income_, which is GNP _minus_ any part of it that is not actually paid over to individuals (business earnings retained by corporations and taxes paid by business) _minus_ the personal income taxes paid by households _plus_ government transfer payments (including government payments of interest) received by households.

9. Changes in GNP are caused by variations in market prices as well as changes in the quantities of output. Changes in the latter kind are defined as real or constant dollar changes.

10. _Per capita GNP_ is GNP divided by the total population in an economy.

11. Various activities such as illegal, unreported, and nonmarketed activities are omitted from measures of GNP.

MULTIPLE-CHOICE QUESTIONS

1. Value added in production is equal to
   (a) purchases from other firms
   (b) profits
   (c) total output
   (d) total value of output minus purchases from other firms

2. Which of the following about savings is _not_ true?
   (a) It is the same as investing.
   (b) It is the result of not spending all of one's income.
   (c) It is often used to finance investment by business firms.
   (d) It is done by businesses as well as households.

3. Mass marriages of men to housekeepers
   (a) would reduce national income as now measured
   (b) would increase national income as now measured
   (c) would leave national income the same
   (d) cannot tell the effect on GNP

4. National income can be measured in all but which of the following ways?
   (a) by the flow of goods and services
   (b) by the payments made to purchase this flow of goods and services
   (c) by adding all money transactions in the economy
   (d) by the value of payments made to factors of production that have been used to produce final goods and services

5. Which of the following is _not_ a part of the total of final goods and services included in the national income?
   (a) government transfer payments to households
   (b) goods sold to government and foreign countries
   (c) increases in purchases of business equipment
   (d) additions to inventories

6. The difference between GNP and net national product is
   (a) depreciation or capital consumption allowance
   (b) total taxes paid to governments
   (c) net exports
   (d) personal savings

7. Personal disposable income is
   (a) the same as personal income
   (b) income that is used only for consumption
   (c) income paid to individuals minus personal taxes plus transfer payments paid to
        households
   (d) exclusive of welfare payments

8. If GNP in current pesetas in 1970 was 500 billion while GNP in constant (1960)
   pesetas was 200 billion in 1970,
   (a) real GNP doubled over the decade 1960-1970
   (b) the price level more than doubled over the decade
   (c) real income declined slightly over the decade
   (d) it is impossible to estimate what happened to prices over the decade; more
        information is needed

9. If nominal GNP rises from $100 billion to $115 billion and the GNP deflator rises
   from 125 to 150,
   (a) real GNP has risen
   (b) real GNP has fallen
   (c) real GNP is unchanged
   (d) it is impossible to tell the change in real GNP

10. Which of the following is not a component of expenditure by households?
    (a) new television sets produced in Kitchener, Ontario
    (b) vacation trips to Cape Breton Island
    (c) purchases of Canada savings bonds
    (d) apples from British Columbia

11. Gross investment is defined as
    (a) net investment plus dividend payments by firms
    (b) net investment minus the capital consumption allowance
    (c) net investment minus replacement investment
    (d) net investment plus depreciation

12. Which of the following is not a component of investment expenditure?
    (a) unintended inventory increases
    (b) planned inventory increases
    (c) new residential construction
    (d) purchases of Dome Petroleum stocks

13. An open economy is one that
    (a) engages in foreign trade and AE equals C + I + G
    (b) does not engage in foreign trade and AE equals C + I + G
    (c) engages in foreign trade and AE equals C + I + G + (X - M)
    (d) does not engage in foreign trade and AE = C + I

14. Which of the following is not included in measuring GNP from the factor-income
    approach?
    (a) personal income taxes
    (b) wages and other labour income
    (c) investment and miscellaneous investment income
    (d) indirect taxes

15. Which of the following is omitted from measured GNP?
    (a) winnings from illegal gambling
    (b) tradesmen who do not report earnings from moonlighting
    (c) volunteer work for the Canadian Cancer Society
    (d) all of the above

16. The GNP deflator is defined as
    (a) GNP in constant dollars divided by GNP in current dollars
    (b) GNP in current dollars divided by GNP in constant dollars
    (c) GNP in current dollars divided by GNP in constant dollars times 100
    (d) the consumer price deflator times current GNP in dollars

EXERCISES

1. Suppose that the following items represent the expenditures and factor incomes for
    an economy in 1973. By selecting the appropriate items, calculate the value for
    GNP using both the factor-income approach and the output-expenditure approach.
    (Figures are in billions of dollars.)

Government purchases of goods and services	$277.1
Wages and employee compensation	785.3
Net exports of goods and services	4.6
Income of proprietors	84.3
Indirect business taxes	117.8
Gross private investment	201.5
Capital consumption allowances	109.6
Corporate profits	126.4
Personal consumption expenditures	805.0
Rental and interest income	75.5
Adjustment on factor-income accounts	-10.7

2. You are given the following national income accounting items for an economy in a
    particular year.

Gross national product	$2,369
Capital consumption allowances	243
Retained earnings	126
Government transfers to individuals	304
Business taxes	379
Personal income taxes	300
Personal expenditure	1,510

    (a) Calculate NNP.

    (b) Using the value for net national income (NNP), calculate personal income and
         personal disposable income.

    (c) What was the magnitude of personal saving?

190

3. (a) Complete the following table using the figures given to fill in the missing values.

Year	Canadian GNP in Current Dollars (billions)	Canadian GNP in Constant Dollars (billions)	GNP Deflator
1971	94.45		100
1972	105.23	100.25	
1974	147.53		132.1
1975		113.13	146.2
1976	191.49	119.39	160.4

(b) What was the base year? Constant dollars refer to what year?

(c) What was the percentage increase in current dollar GNP between 1971 and 1976? What was the percentage increase in constant dollar (real) GNP in the same period?

4. From 1950 to 1970, personal disposable income in Canada rose from $12.69 billion to $53.60 billion. Population increased from 13.71 million to 21.41 million in the same period. The consumer price index increased from approximately 100.0 to 142.2. What was the total percentage increase in the per capita standard of living as measured by per capita real personal disposable income from 1950 to 1970?

5. (a) Identify the items in the statements below according to the following code. Some statements have more than one answer.

C	Consumption	S_p	Savings of persons or households
I	Investment	M	Imports
G	Government spending on goods and services	X	Exports
		F	Factor-income payments
T	Taxes	N	None of the above
S_b	Saving of business		

_____ (1) A student gets a haircut from a self-employed barber.

_____ (2) The barber buys some clippers from the Short-Cut Clipper Company (Toronto).

_____ (3) Out of each day's revenue, the barber sets aside $5 in his piggybank.

_____ (4) When he has enough set aside, the barber buys a share of Royal Bank of Canada stock.

_____ (5) The Royal Bank expands its computer facilities in its head office.

_____ (6) The Royal Bank pays municipal taxes to the City of Montreal.

_____ (7) The Royal Bank sets aside some of its income as depreciation reserves.

_____ (8) The Short-Cut Clipper Company has profits of $50,000 after paying provincial and municipal taxes.

_____ (a) It pays $17,500 in corporate profits taxes to the federal government.

191

_____ (b) It pays dividends of $20,000.

_____ (c) It retains the rest and adds it to its surplus.

_____ (9) Canadians go to London, England, and stay at the Savoy Hotel.

_____ (10) Russia buys beef cattle from Alberta beef-cattle farmers.

_____ (11) Acme Construction Company builds 1,000 new houses to put on the market.

_____ (12) The Province of Saskatchewan builds a new highway.

(b) Which of the above would be included in the output-expenditure approach to measuring national income?

What Determines National Income? | 30

KEY CONCEPTS AND DEFINITIONS

1. National income accounts measure <u>actual expenditures</u>, whereas the theory of national income determination deals with <u>desired expenditures</u>. Desired expenditure refers to what decision-makers want to spend given the resources at their command. Desired and actual expenditure need not be equal. For example, if firms unintentionally produce more than they sell, the unsold goods represent undesired or unintended inventory accumulation.

2. Households decide how much of their income they wish to <u>consume</u>, and they <u>save</u> the rest.

3. The <u>consumption function</u> describes the relationship between consumption expenditure and all the factors that determine it. One of the most important determinants of consumption is <u>household disposable income</u> (Y_d).

4. Two technical terms are used to describe the relationship between consumption and disposable income. The <u>average propensity to consume (APC)</u> is total consumption divided by total disposable income. The <u>marginal propensity to consume (MPC)</u> relates the <u>change</u> in consumption to the change in disposable income that brought it about.

5. <u>The 45° line</u> is a useful construction line in a consumption function diagram. It is a line that connects all points where desired consumption expenditure (measured on the vertical axis) equals disposable income (measured on the horizontal axis). It helps locate the <u>break-even level</u> of income at which consumption expenditure equals disposable income.

6. The <u>savings function</u> is a relationship between desired savings and the factors that determine it, including disposable income. The <u>average propensity to save (APS)</u> is total desired saving divided by total disposable income. The <u>marginal propensity to save (MPS)</u> is the change in total desired saving related to the change in disposable income that brought it about.

7. The analysis in this chapter assumes that government and investment expenditure, as well as exports, are constant and do not depend on the level of income. However, consumption expenditure and imports are both assumed to be directly related to income.

8. The aggregate expenditure (AE) function relates the level of desired expenditure to the level of national income. The marginal propensity to spend is the ratio of the change in spending to the change in income that brought it about. The remainder is the marginal propensity not to spend (or the marginal propensity to withdraw).

9. Equilibrium national income exists when desired expenditure equals total national output; i.e., Y = C + I + G + (X − M). The 45° line is a locus of equilibrium points; that is, any point on this line represents a situation in which desired aggregate expenditure (on the vertical axis) equals national output (on the horizontal axis).

10. The AE diagram analyzes the determination of equilibrium income on the assumption that firms are able and willing to produce whatever is demanded at the going price level. In contrast, the AD diagram shows for each price level the equilibrium income that would equate desired expenditure with actual income if firms were willing to produce that level of income at that price level.

MULTIPLE-CHOICE QUESTIONS

1. The aggregate expenditure function is a relationship between
   (a) actual expenditure and real national income
   (b) desired expenditure and nominal national income
   (c) actual expenditure and nominal national income
   (d) desired expenditure and real national income

2. The theory of income determination deals with
   (a) the desired levels of the components of aggregate expenditure
   (b) the actual levels of the components of aggregate expenditure
   (c) only the desired level of consumption and investment expenditure
   (d) only the actual level of consumption and investment expenditure

3. Which of the following is not a component of aggregate expenditure?
   (a) investment in plant and equipment
   (b) government expenditure on goods
   (c) personal taxes
   (d) imports

4. The average propensity to consume out of disposable income is defined as
   (a) the ratio of total consumption to total national income
   (b) the ratio of total consumption to total disposable income
   (c) the ratio of the change in consumption to total disposable income
   (d) $\Delta C / \Delta Y$

5. If households consume 80¢ out of every additional dollar of disposable income they receive, we can say that
   (a) the marginal propensity to consume is 8
   (b) the marginal propensity to consume is 0.2
   (c) the marginal and average propensities are necessarily both equal to 0.8
   (d) the marginal propensity to consume is 0.8

6. Below the break-even level of disposable income, households
   (a) dissave
   (b) consume less than their disposable income
   (c) save
   (d) spend an amount on goods and services equal to the value of their disposable income

7. For the short-run consumption functions depicted in the text, it is likely that as disposable income rises, the APC value
   (a) falls
   (b) rises
   (c) is constant
   (d) is zero

8. Disposable income will be less than national income
   (a) if there are positive personal income taxes
   (b) if personal income taxes are greater than transfer payments to households
   (c) if both (a) and (b)
   (d) if personal taxes are equal to transfer payments

9. If the marginal propensity to save out of disposable income is 0.25, then the MPC is
   (a) 0.25
   (b) 0.75
   (c) 1.0
   (d) 0.33

10. If $Y_d = .8Y$ and consumption was always 80 percent of disposable income, then the marginal propensity to consume out of total income would be
    (a) 0.8
    (b) 0.2
    (c) 1.0
    (d) 0.64

11. Aggregate expenditure is equal to
    (a) C + I + G + (X − M) + transfer payments
    (b) C + I + G + (X + M)
    (c) C + I + G + (X − M)
    (d) C + I + G + (M − X)

12. Equilibrium national income occurs when
    (a) Y = C + I + G + (X − M)
    (b) the average propensity to spend is one
    (c) desired aggregate expenditure equals national income
    (d) all of the above

13. If desired aggregate expenditure exceeds national income, there will be a tendency for
    (a) output and income to contract
    (b) output and income to expand
    (c) output and income to remain constant
    (d) an equilibrium to exist in the economy

14. The AE diagram analyzes the determination of equilibrium income on the assumption that firms are able and willing to produce whatever is demanded
    (a) at all levels of prices
    (b) at the going price level
    (c) at all levels of wages
    (d) at a given output level

Questions 15 through 23 refer to the diagram on the following page.

195

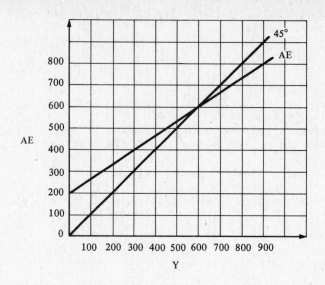

15. When national income (Y) is 0, desired aggregate expenditure is
    (a) 0
    (b) equal to actual output
    (c) 200
    (d) 300

16. When national income is 600, desired aggregate expenditure is
    (a) 600
    (b) less than income
    (c) 300
    (d) greater than income

17. If actual national income was 400, desired aggregate expenditure
    (a) exceeds income, and hence output and income are likely to contract
    (b) is less than income, and hence income is likely to contract
    (c) exceeds income, but equilibrium exists
    (d) exceeds income, and hence output and income are likely to expand

18. When actual (measured) national income is equal to 700, desired aggregate
    expenditure
    (a) is less than income, and hence inventories are likely to fall unintentionally
    (b) is less than income, and hence inventories are likely to accumulate
         unintentionally
    (c) is less than income, but no change in inventory occurs
    (d) is equal to 700

19. According to the diagram, the marginal propensity to spend is
    (a) two-thirds and constant
    (b) less than one but variable according to the level of income
    (c) one-third and constant
    (d) always equal to the average propensity to spend

20. The marginal propensity to withdraw in this case is
    (a) two-thirds
    (b) one-third
    (c) equal to one
    (d) a variable fraction

196

21. The equilibrium level of national income is
    (a) 500
    (b) necessarily equal to full employment
    (c) in the range 400 to 500
    (d) 600

22. At a national income level of 300, desired aggregate expenditure equals
    (a) 400 and the average propensity to spend is 0.75
    (b) 400 and the average propensity to spend is two-thirds
    (c) 400 and the average propensity to spend is less than the marginal propensity
         to spend
    (d) 400 and the average propensity to spend is four-thirds

23. At a national income level of 600, the value of the average propensity to spend is
    (a) equal to the value of the marginal propensity to spend
    (b) unity
    (c) less than the value of the marginal propensity to spend
    (d) less than unity

EXERCISES

1. The first two columns of the following schedule depict the relationship between
    desired consumption expenditure (C) and disposable income (Y_d).

Y_d	C	APC	ΔY_d	ΔC	MPC	S
0	80	N.A.	100	50	0.50	−80
100	130	1.30	60	30	0.50	−30
160	___	1.00		20	0.50	
200	180	___	___		0.50	20
400	___	0.70	350	___		120
750	455	___		___	___	___

(a) Fill in the missing values for the change in disposable income (ΔY_d).

(b) Fill in the missing values for C using the formula $C = 80 + .5Y_d$.

(c) Using the definition for the average propensity to consume (APC), fill in the
     missing values for APC. What did you notice happened to the value of APC as
     the level of Y_d increased?

(d) Fill in the missing values for ΔC.

(e) Using the definition for MPC, calculate it for the income change from 400 to
     750.

197

(f) Using the definition for saving $S = Y_d - C$, fill in the missing values in the table. Using the formula $\Delta S/\Delta Y_d$, prove that the marginal propensity to save is constant and equal to 0.5.

(g) What is the break-even level of disposable income? What is the level of saving at this level of Y_d?

(h) Plot both the consumption and savings function in the diagram below. In addition, draw the 45° line in the diagram and prove that this line intersects the consumption function at a level of Y_d for which $S = 0$.

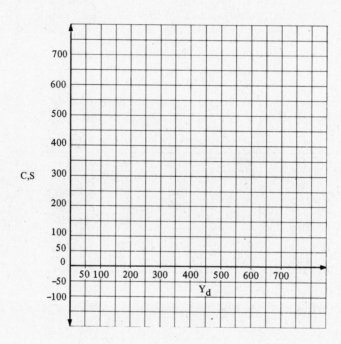

2. You are given the following information:

Y	Y_d	C	APC	$S = Y_d - C$
100	70	100	1.43	-30
200	140	156	____	-16
314.3	220	220	____	0

(a) What relationship exists between Y and Y_d? Why is Y_d less than Y?

(b) Prove that the marginal propensity to consume out of disposable income is constant and equal to 0.80.

(c)   Calculate the marginal propensity to consume out of income (Y).

(d)   Calculate the values for APC out of disposable income (the fourth column).

(e)   What is the marginal propensity to save out of disposable income?

(f)   What is the break-even level of disposable income? Total national income?

3.   Question 2 is based on specific mathematical relationships. The relationship between Y and Y_d is $Y_d = .7Y$, and the consumption function is given by $C = 44 + .8Y_d$. The coefficient .8 is the slope of the consumption function, or what is called the MPC out of disposable income. You may wish to recheck your answers to question 2 using these equations.

(a)   Suppose Y = 400. Calculate the values for Y_d and C. Do the same for Y = 500 and Y = 600.

(b)   Now assume that the relationship between Y and Y_d becomes $Y_d = .6Y$, but the consumption function remains the same. What factor might have caused the change? Recalculate the values of C and Y_d for levels of income of 400, 500, and 600. Compare these values with the values in part (a).

(c)   Suppose the consumption function becomes $C = 44 + .9Y_d$ while the relationship between Y and Y_d given in part (a) still holds ($Y_d = .7Y$). What is the value of the MPC out of disposable income? Out of total income? Calculate the values for C when Y has values of 400, 500, and 600.

4.   As an economy expands in terms of real income, the balance of trade (or for our purposes, net exports) falls. If (X - M) is negative, a _deficit_ in the balance of trade is said to exist. To understand this we present the following hypothetical schedule.

Y	X	M	(X - M)
0	40	0	___
100	40	10	___
200	40	20	___
400	40	40	___
800	40	80	___

(a) Exports are assumed to be autonomous (independent of the level of Y). However, what specific relationship exists between M (imports) and Y? Identify some factors that explain the direct relationship between imports and real national income.

(b) Calculate the values for (X - M). Does the balance of trade fall (become smaller) as Y increases?

5. (a) The aggregate-expenditure schedule below shows the relationship between the various components of desired aggregate expenditure and real national income. Fill in the blanks and plot the values of total aggregate expenditure (AE) associated with levels of Y on the graph.

Y	C	I	G	(X - M)	AE	ΔY	ΔAE
0	90	10	30	20	___		
100	150	10	30	10	___	___	___
200	210	10	30	0	___	___	___
300	270	10	30	-10	___	___	___
400	330	10	30	-20	___	___	___

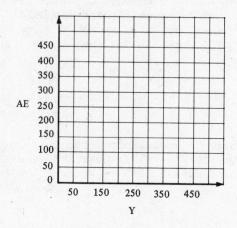

200

(b) National income is in equilibrium at a level of _____. Explain.

(c) Suppose actual (measured) national income was 400. What is the value of desired aggregate expenditure at that level? What does the residual amount (Y – AE) represent? Is national output likely to expand or contract in this situation? Explain.

(d) Calculate the values for ΔY and ΔAE and fill in the table. Prove that the marginal propensity to spend is constant and equal to .50. The slope of the AE function you plotted should be one-half.

(e) The marginal propensity to withdraw is _____.

(f) Draw the 45° line on the graph and demonstrate that it intersects the AE function at the equilibrium level of Y you solved for in part (b).

6. An Algebraic Determination of Equilibrium National Income
You are given the following information about behaviour in an economy:

Equation 1: the consumption function

$$C = 100 + .7Y_d$$

Equation 2: the relationship between Y and Y_d

$$Y_d = .8Y$$

Equation 3: the investment function

$$I = 56$$

Equation 4: the net export function

$$(X - M) = 10 - .1Y$$

Equation 5: the government expenditure function

$$G = 50$$

(a) Referring to the consumption function, what does the coefficient .7 mean?

(b) What components of aggregate expenditure depend upon national income?

201

(c) Aggregate expenditure is the algebraic sum of the various components. Derive this expression.

(d) Equilibrium national income is where Y = AE. This is the expression for the 45° line. Equate your expression for AE in part (c) with Y. Solve for Y.

(e) Derive the marginal propensity to spend. (Hint: substitute values for Y equal to 100 and 200 into the algebraic expression for AE and then calculate $\triangle Y$ and $\triangle AE$.

7. The Relationship Between Aggregate Demand and Aggregate Expenditure

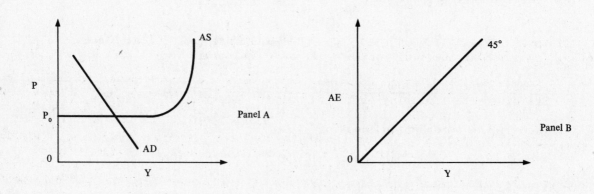

(a) According to panel A, what is the equilibrium level of Y? Denote it as Y_0. What is the equilibrium value of price?

(b) Draw a rough sketch of an AE curve in panel B that has a slope of .5, a positive value of AE for Y = 0, and intersects the 45° line at the appropriate equilibrium level of national income.

Changes in National Income | 31

KEY CONCEPTS AND DEFINITIONS

1. A movement along an expenditure curve is caused by a change in national income. A _shift_ in the expenditure curve is caused by an increased desire to spend at _each level of national income_, including the present one. The latter causes national income to move from one equilibrium level to another.

2. Marginal propensities relate to movements along curves and tell us how much a particular component of desired expenditure responds to a change in income.

3. A rise in the amount of desired consumption, investment, government, or export expenditure associated with each level of income will cause the AE curve to shift upward in a parallel fashion and thereby will increase equilibrium national income, other things being equal. A fall in these components associated with each level of income will shift the AE curve downward and hence will lower equilibrium national income.

4. A rise (fall) in tax rates, savings, or imports will cause the AE curve to shift downward (upward) and will therefore lower (raise) the level of national income, other things being equal.

5. _The paradox of thrift_ states that, other things being equal, the more frugal and thrifty are spending units, the lower will be the level of national income and total employment. The prediction of the paradox of thrift depends on two assumptions. First, it assumes that the economy is on the Keynesian portion of an AS curve. Second, it assumes that the volume of investment is at least partly independent of the volume of saving.

6. A central prediction of national income theory is that an increase (decrease) in autonomous expenditure will cause an increase (decrease) in national income that is greater than the initial increase (decrease) in expenditure. The _multiplier_ is the ratio of the change in national income to the initial change in expenditure that brings it about.

7. The larger the marginal propensity to spend (the steeper the aggregate expenditure function), the _larger_ is the value of the multiplier.

8. The size of the multiplier (K) is given by the mathematical formula $1/(1 - n)$, where n is the marginal propensity to spend. The value $(1 - n)$ is the _marginal propensity to withdraw_ and is denoted by w. Hence the multiplier is also given by the expression $1/w$.

9. The <u>kinked aggregate supply curve</u> contains only a Keynesian portion and a classical portion. It makes a sharp distinction between situations of unemployment, where the price level is fixed and real output is variable (the Keynesian range), and situations of full employment, where real national income is fixed at its full-employment level while the price level is variable (the classical range).

10. The extent to which actual national income is below its full-employment level is called the <u>GNP gap</u>. It measures the lost output that could have been produced if full employment had been achieved.

11. <u>The deflationary gap</u> measures the extent to which the aggregate expenditure schedule would have to shift upward to produce the full-employment level of national income.

12. <u>The inflationary gap</u> measures the extent to which the aggregate expenditure schedule would have to shift downward to produce the full-employment level of national income without inflation.

MULTIPLE-CHOICE QUESTIONS

1. A change in the equilibrium level of national income is caused by
   (a) a shift in the aggregate expenditure curve
   (b) a movement along the aggregate expenditure curve
   (c) an increase in output but expenditure remains constant
   (d) shift in the 45° line

2. The greater the value of the marginal propensity to spend out of national income,
   (a) the greater the value of the marginal propensity to withdraw
   (b) the smaller the value of the multiplier
   (c) the flatter the aggregate expenditure curve
   (d) the steeper the aggregate expenditure curve

3. Increases in national income are predicted to be caused by increases in all but which of the following, other things being equal:
   (a) taxes
   (b) exports
   (c) government expenditure
   (d) investment

4. Increases in national income are predicted to be caused by decreases in all but which of the following, other things being equal:
   (a) the marginal propensity to save
   (b) tax rates
   (c) imports
   (d) exports

5. A decrease in the marginal propensity to spend out of national income will cause the AE curve to
   (a) shift upward in a parallel fashion
   (b) shift downward in a parallel fashion
   (c) have a lower slope
   (d) have a steeper slope

6. The effect on national income of a fall in investment could be offset by
   (a) a rise in saving at each level of income
   (b) a rise in the tax rate
   (c) a rise in G
   (d) a rise in imports at each level of income

7. The paradox of thrift states that, other things being equal, the more frugal and thrifty are spending units,
   (a) the higher will be the level of national income and total employment
   (b) the greater is the marginal propensity to spend
   (c) the lower will be the level of national income and total employment
   (d) the smaller is the marginal propensity to withdraw

8. The multiplier measures
   (a) the rise in investment resulting from an increase in Y
   (b) the ratio of total income to total aggregate expenditure
   (c) the reciprocal of the value of the marginal propensity to spend
   (d) the extent to which income will change as a result of a change in expenditure that brings it about

9. Which of the following formulae is the correct expression for the multiplier?
   (a) $1/(1 - n) = K$
   (b) $1/(1 - w) = K$
   (c) $\Delta A/\Delta Y = K$
   (d) $K = (\Delta A + \Delta N)/\Delta N$

10. If no expenditure in the economy depended upon the level of income, the value of the multiplier would be
    (a) zero
    (b) unity
    (c) infinity
    (d) - 1

11. If the marginal propensity to withdraw is .2, the multiplier is
    (a) equal to the marginal propensity to spend
    (b) 2.0
    (c) 5.0
    (d) 1.25

12. The kinked AS curve
    (a) has only a Keynesian portion
    (b) has only a classical portion
    (c) has only a Keynesian and classical portion
    (d) allows for situations of the coexistence of inflation and unemployment

13. An inflationary gap is defined as the extent to which the
    (a) aggregate expenditure schedule would have to shift downward to produce full-employment income but a lower inflation rate
    (b) aggregate expenditure schedule would have to shift downward to produce full-employment income without inflation
    (c) GNP gap exceeds inflation
    (d) inflation rate has changed

14. A deflationary gap is
    (a) the extent to which the AE schedule would have to shift upward to achieve full-employment income
    (b) the difference between the full-employment level and a lower equilibrium level of national income divided by the value of the multiplier
    (c) both a and b
    (d) neither a nor b

Questions 15 through 25 refer to the diagram below. Assume that a <u>kinked AS curve</u> exists.

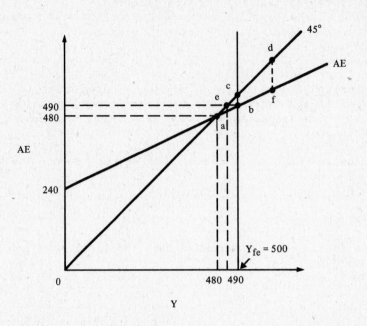

15. With the aggregate expenditure labelled AE, the current equilibrium level of national income is
     (a) 500
     (b) 480
     (c) 490
     (d) at point b

16. AE has a slope of
     (a) 0.5
     (b) 2.0
     (c) 12/25
     (d) 0.6

17. The value of the multiplier is
     (a) 2.0
     (b) 0.5
     (c) 2.5
     (d) 1.9

18. the value of the GNP gap is
     (a) 500
     (b) 20
     (c) 2.0
     (d) the distance ac

19. In the current situation, unemployment and a(n)
     (a) deflationary gap measured by the distance bc exist
     (b) deflationary gap of 20 exist
     (c) inflationary gap of 20 exist
     (d) deflationary gap measured by the distance ac exist

20. To solve this gap problem, the aggregate expenditure curve must
    (a) shift upward by 20
    (b) shift upward by 2
    (c) shift upward by 10
    (d) remain unchanged, but output must increase by 20 thereby causing a movement
        along AE from point a to point b

21. Suppose that government expenditures increased by 5 at all levels of Y. The
    aggregate expenditure curve would
    (a) shift upward by 10 and have a slope of .6
    (b) shift upward by 5 and have a slope of .5
    (c) intersect the 45° line at point c
    (d) shift upward by 5 in a parallel fashion and intersect the 45° line at point c

22. The increase in government expenditure of 5 causes national income to
    (a) increase in total by 5
    (b) increase by the autonomous increase 5 plus another 5 of increased induced
        expenditure
    (c) decrease in total by 10
    (d) increase in total by the amount 2.5

23. To solve the current gap problem, the government should
    (a) increase its expenditure by 10
    (b) increase its expenditure by 20
    (c) increase its expenditure by 5
    (d) reduce the tax rate such that the marginal propensity to spend out of national
        income becomes 1.0

24. To solve the current gap problem, the government might change tax rates in such a
    way that
    (a) the marginal propensity to spend falls
    (b) the marginal propensity to spend increases and the AE shifts up in a parallel
        fashion
    (c) the marginal propensity to spend increases and the AE curve has a lower slope
    (d) the marginal propensity to spend increases and the AE pivots upward
        intersecting the 45° line at point c

25. If the AE curve intersected the 45° line at point d, the economy would experience
    (a) unemployment of resources
    (b) an inflationary gap of df
    (c) an inflationary gap of dc
    (d) a deflationary gap of df

EXERCISES

1. You are given the following information about an economy. The data labelled case A
   represent the initial situation in the economy.

		CASE A				CASE B		CASE C		CASE D	
Y	C	I	G	(X − M)	AE	I	AE	(X − M)	AE	C	AE
0	10	50	10	10	80	60	90	−10	60	10	80
200	190	50	10	−10	240	60		−30		150	
300	280	50	10	−20	320	60	__	−40	__	220	__
400	370	50	10	−30	400	60	__	−50	__	290	__
450	415	50	10	−35	440	60	__	−55	__	325	__

(a) For case A, determine the equilibrium level of national income and the marginal propensity to spend.

(b) Plot the aggregate expenditure curve in the diagram below and indicate the equilibrum level of national income.

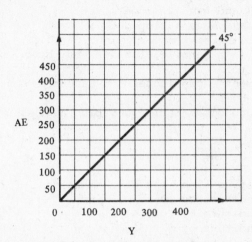

(c) Now assume that a change occurs in the economy such that case B holds. Case B is identical to case A except that investment at every level of Y increases from 50 to 60. Fill in the missing values for AE and plot the new aggregate expenditure curve in the diagram above. What has happened to the aggregate expenditure curve? (Compare case A with case B.)

(d) Using the AE curve for case B, what is the value of desired AE at a level of national income of 400? What do you predict will happen to the equilibrium level of national income in this situation? Explain.

(e) What is the equilibrium level of national income for case B? What has been the total change in national income (ΔY) between case A and B? Calculate the ratio $\Delta Y / \Delta I$ from A to B. This is the value of the multiplier.

(f) Calculate the value of the marginal propensity to spend (denoted as n in the text) for case B. Calculate the marginal propensity to withdraw (w) for case B. Using the two formulae $K = 1/(1 - n)$ and $K = 1/w$, confirm your answer for the value of the multiplier in part (e).

(g) The total change in income is composed of two parts: the change in the autonomous component of AE (ΔA), which in this case is ΔI, and the <u>induced</u> change in aggregate expenditure (ΔN). What is the value for ΔN? What was the change in consumption? The change in (X − M)?

2. Assume that case A is the initial situation and that exports <u>at every level of income</u> fall such that a new (X − M) has fallen by 20 at every level of Y.
   (a) Fill in the missing values of AE for case C. What is the new equilibrium level of income? What is the marginal propensity to spend?

   (b) Comparing case A with case C, what is the total change in Y? Calculate the value of the multiplier. Calculate the change in ΔA (in this case Δ(X − M) and ΔN).

   (c) What happened to the AE curve? (Compare case A with case C.)

3. Assume that case A is the initial situation but that factors in the economy change such that case D applies. Case D is identical to case A except that the consumption schedule is now quite different.
   (a) Calculate the marginal propensities to consume out of national income for both cases and indicate the nature of the behavioural change between the two cases.

   (b) Fill in the missing values of AE for case D. Plot the new aggregate expenditure curve in the diagram on page 208 and compare it with that for case A.

   (c) Calculate the marginal propensity to spend for case D and compare it with that for case A. Calculate the multiplier value and compare it with the multiplier for case A.

   (d) What is the equilibrium value of national income for case D? Does case D depict an example of the paradox of thrift? Explain.

4. Suppose that the economy behaves as follows: Whenever national income rises (falls) by $1, disposable income rises (falls) by 90¢, induced consumption expenditure on domestically produced goods and services rises (falls) by 80¢, and induced import expenditures and savings each rise (fall) by 5¢.

(a) What is this economy's marginal propensity to spend out of national income?

(b) Now suppose that autonomous expenditure decreases because the federal government decides to spend $4 million less on national defense. National income initially _falls_ by $4 million. But that is not the end of the process. In the table below, fill in the values for the decreases in disposable income and expenditure for three rounds.

	Decreases in Y_d (thousands of dollars per year)	Decreases in Expenditure (thousands of dollars per year)
Assumed decrease in government expenditure per year		4000.0
2nd round (decrease in Y_d and expenditure)	3600.0	3200.0
3rd round " "	2880.0	_____
4th round " "	_____	_____
5th round " "	_____	_____
Sum of first five rounds		_____

(c) Using the formula $\Delta Y = K \cdot \Delta A$, where ΔA is -4 million and K is the value of the multiplier, calculate the final change in national income (ΔY).

5. You are given the following equations:
Equation 1: the consumption function

$$C = 30 + .9Y_d$$

Equation 2: the relationship between Y_d and Y

$$Y_d = .8Y$$

Equation 3: the investment function

$$I = 40$$

Equation 4: the government expenditure function

$$G = 20$$

Equation 5: the net export function

$$(X - M) = 20 - .12 Y$$

Equation 6:   the AE expenditure function

$$AE = C + I + G + (X - M)$$

Equation 7:   the equilibrium condition

$$AE = Y$$

(a)   Substitute equation 2 into equation 1 and solve for C in terms of Y. Call this equation 8.

(b)   Substitute equations 8, 3, 4, and 5 into the right-hand side of equation 6. What is the value of the slope of the AE function ($\Delta AE/\Delta Y$)? This is the marginal propensity to spend.

(c)   Using equation 7, solve for the equilibrium level of Y.

(d)   Now suppose that the federal government raised the personal income tax rate such that equation 2 changed to $Y_d = .689Y$. Call this equation 9.

   (i)   Substitute equation 9 into equation 1 and solve for C in terms of Y. Call this equation 10.

   (ii)   Substitute equations 10, 3, 4, and 5 into the right-hand side of equation 6. What is the slope of this AE function? Compare it with the value you obtained for part (b).

   (iii)   Using equation 7 and the new expression for the aggregate expenditure function, solve for the equilibrium level of Y. Compare this with your answer to part (c).

(e)   Calculate and compare the value of the multipliers before and after the tax rate increase.

211

6. Suppose the country of Econ has an aggregate supply curve that is referred to in the text as a kinked aggregate supply curve. Full-employment or potential national income is given as 609 and is assumed constant. The current equilibrium national income level is 603, the price level is 2, and Econ's marginal propensity to spend out of national income is constant and equal to 2/3.

   (a) Draw the AS and the AE curves in the appropriate diagram below. The equilibrium level of Y must be identical in the two diagrams.

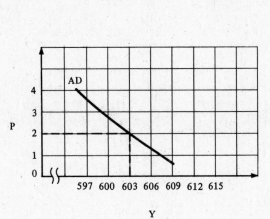
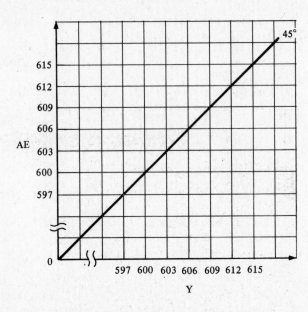

   (b) Using the information you have been given regarding the AS curve, label the full-employment level of national income as Y_{fe} in both diagrams.

   (c) What is the quantitative magnitude of the GNP gap? Show it in the diagrams.

   (d) Does a deflationary or inflationary gap exist? Label this gap in the AE diagram.

   (e) The quantitative magnitude of this gap is given by the formula gap = GNP gap divided by the value of the multiplier. Calculate the value.

   (f) Would an increase in autonomous expenditure of 1 solve the gap problem without generating inflation? Would an increase of 2 solve the gap problem? Explain.

(g) What would happen to Econ if government expenditure increased by 3 (assuming the initial equilibrium national income level was 603)? Explain. Draw the new AE curve in the preceding diagram. What happens to the AD curve?

7. Fill in the following table.

	Nature of Change	Shift in Curve		Change in Slope of AE Curve
		AE	AD	
(a)	Increase in G at every level of Y	upward	upward	no change
(b)	Decrease in M at every level of Y	_____	_____	_____
(c)	Increase in MPC out of national income	_____	_____	_____
(d)	Decrease in I at every level of Y	_____	_____	_____
(e)	Increase in the personal tax rate	_____	_____	_____

213

Cycles and Fluctuations in National Income

32

KEY CONCEPTS AND DEFINITIONS

1. Short-term fluctuations in GNP are often caused by variations in aggregate demand and aggregate supply. These fluctuations are often referred to as business cycles.

2. Shifts in the consumption function may generate business cycles. Shifts are caused by changes in the income distribution, availability and terms of credit, expectations about the future, changes in personal income taxes, and changes in consumer attitudes such that the relationship between consumption and disposable income changes.

3. Ceteris paribus, if households expect inflation, they may purchase new goods they would otherwise buy sometime in the relatively near future.

4. Shifts in exports can generate business cycles. Since about one-half of all goods are exported, fluctuations in the national income of other countries can be transmitted to the Canadian economy through fluctuations in their demand for Canadian exports. This process is known as the international transmission of fluctuations through exports.

5. A major source of business cycles is changes in investment expenditure. Components of investment are business fixed investment (machinery, equipment, and nonresidential construction), changes in inventories, and residential construction.

6. Changes in business inventories are very volatile and therefore contribute importantly to shifts in the investment schedule. They respond directly to changes in sales and the level of production and inversely to the interest rate.

7. Investment in residential construction depends on various demographic factors as well as economic factors. Specifically, expenditures for residential construction relate directly with changes in average income and inversely with interest rates. The interest rate importantly determines residential construction because interest payments are a large fraction of mortgage payments, which affect the household's ability to buy a house.

8. Business fixed investment is the largest component of domestic investment. It depends upon the rate of innovation, expectations about future profits, changes in the level of national income, and the rate of interest.

214

9. A decrease in the rate of interest increases the desired stock of capital. However, investment may not expand immediately because of supply constraints in the capital-goods industry. Thus decreases in the interest rate can have a major effect on the length of the backlog for capital equipment rather than on the level of investment in a particular year.

10. The accelerator theory relates net investment to change in the level of national income on the assumption of a fixed capital-output ratio. The chief prediction of the accelerator theory is that rising income is required to maintain a positive level of investment.

11. Economists have developed a vocabulary to describe the different stages of a business cycle: trough (the bottom), expansion, peak (upper turning point), and recession (downward-turn and sustained contraction).

12. The combination of the multiplier and the accelerator can cause upward or downward movements in the economy to be cumulative.

13. Several types of cycles are possible. Inventory cycles are fluctuations in inventory holdings caused by changes in national income. A building cycle caused by an accelerator process can occur in the residential construction sector.

MULTIPLE-CHOICE QUESTIONS

1. The largest component of aggregate expenditure in Canada is
    (a) consumption
    (b) government expenditure
    (c) net exports
    (d) investment expenditure

2. Assume that households expect prices of household appliances to rise rapidly but are confident about the adequacy of their future income. It is likely that current purchases of appliances will
    (a) be postponed until the future
    (b) be high and as a consequence future purchases will tend to be lower
    (c) not be affected and households will allow their present appliances to age
    (d) be equal to current real income

3. Which of the following would have the effect of shifting the consumption function upward?
    (a) Borrowing rates increase.
    (b) Governments increase tax rates.
    (c) Prices of consumer goods are expected to fall in the future.
    (d) Income is redistributed from households with low marginal propensities to consume to households with high ones.

4. Increasing the marginal propensity to consume out of GNP by lowering the tax rate will cause the consumption function to
    (a) shift upward in a parallel fashion
    (b) shift upward but have a steeper slope
    (c) shift upward but have a lower slope
    (d) be unchanged since the MPC out of disposable income is equal to less than unity

5. Which of the following will tend not to increase Canadian exports?
    (a) a depreciation in the price of the Canadian dollar
    (b) a decrease in the price of Canadian prices relative to foreign ones
    (c) an increase in the preference for Canadian products by foreigners
    (d) a recession in the United States

6. If you were determining the total investment expenditure, which of the following would you not include?
   (a) purchase of stocks and bonds
   (b) changes in inventories
   (c) new residential construction
   (d) new plant and equipment

7. Inventories tend to vary
   (a) directly with the level of sales, inversely with the rate of interest
   (b) inversely with sales and the interest rate
   (c) directly with sales and the interest rate
   (d) inversely with sales and directly with the interest rate

8. Which of the following is likely to increase residential construction?
   (a) a decrease in the marriage rate
   (b) an increase in the mortgage rate
   (c) an increase in family income
   (d) a declining population

9. The desired stock of capital depends
   (a) directly on profitability expectations
   (b) directly on the cost of borrowing
   (c) inversely on the level of sales
   (d) all of the above

10. If the rate of interest falls, causing the desired stock of capital to rise by 30 million, then in the short run
    (a) actual investment will necessarily be 30 million
    (b) actual investment will accelerate
    (c) actual investment may be less than 30 million because of capacity constraints in the capital goods industries
    (d) investment is not affected

11. According to the accelerator theory, investment is a function of
    (a) the level of income
    (b) changes in income and a constant capital-output ratio
    (c) savings
    (d) changes in income and a variable capital-output ratio

12. Suppose that Canadian unemployment insurance benefit payments to unemployed workers fall when national income expands. It can be argued that these transfer payments are
    (a) countercyclical since they fall relative to GNP when GNP is rising
    (b) procyclical since they rise relative to GNP when GNP is rising
    (c) countercyclical since they rise relative to GNP when GNP is rising
    (d) procyclical since they fall relative to GNP when GNP is rising

13. A trough is characterized by
    (a) high unemployment of labour
    (b) large amounts of unused industrial capacity
    (c) low business profits and pessimistic expectations about future profits
    (d) all of the above

14. The upper turning point will not include which of the following:
    (a) a high degree of utilization of existing capacity
    (b) a high unemployment rate
    (c) shortages of certain key raw materials
    (d) all of the above

15. The multiplier and accelerator effects operating together
    (a) tend to cancel out
    (b) help to explain why recoveries, once started, continue upward
    (c) make the amplitude of cycles less than they otherwise would be
    (d) tend to keep growth going perpetually

EXERCISES

1. Illustrating the Accelerator Principle.
   The table below shows the hypothetical situation for a firm that requires 1 machine
   for every 1,000 units of product it turns out annually. As it increases its output
   and sales in response to changing demand, show how its investment will be
   affected. Replacement for depreciation is 1 machine per year throughout.

Year	Annual Output (units)	Units of Capital Needed	New Machines Required	Replacement Machines	Total Machines to Be Purchased (Desired Investment)
1	10,000	10	0	1	1
2	10,000	___	___	1	___
3	11,000	___	___	1	___
4	12,000	___	___	1	___
5	15,000	___	___	1	___
6	17,000	___	___	1	___
7	18,000	___	___	1	___
8	18,000	___	___	1	___

(a) Between year 2 and year 5, output increased by what percent? _____
(b) In the same period, total investment spending by this firm increased by what
    percent? _____
(c) Plot the cyclical fluctuation in desired investment in the diagram below.

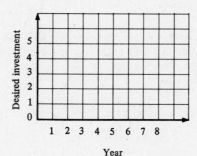

2. A seller of shirts has had weekly sales of 100 and tries to keep inventory on his
   shelves equal to twice his weekly sales, adjusting his weekly orders from the jobber
   according to the current week's sales. Complete the table on the following page,
   showing how his actual inventory and orders from his supplier would change as his
   weekly sales change.

217

Week	Weekly Sales	Actual Inventory, End of Week	Inventory/ Sales Ratio	Desired Inventory	Desired Inventory Plus Expected Sales	Weekly Orders for Next Week
1	100	200	2	200	300	100
2	100	200	2	200	300	100
3	110	190	1.7	220	330	140
4	110	220	2	220	330	110
5	120	210				
6	120	240				
7	110	250				
8	110	220				
9	100	230				

(a) The range of weekly sales was from _____ to _____.

(b) The range of weekly orders was from _____ to _____.

(c) How do these findings help to explain the cause of economic fluctuations?

3. Assume there are two consumers in any economy, Tom and Kerry. Their consumption schedules as well as the average aggregate schedule are illustrated below.

Kerry		Tom		Average Aggregate	
C	Y_d	C	Y_d	C	Y_d
80	0	80	0	80	0
980	1,000	580	1,000	780	1,000
1,880	2,000	1,080	2,000	1,480	2,000
2,780	3,000	1,580	3,000	2,180	3,000

(a) Calculate the marginal propensities to consume for Kerry and Tom as well as for the average aggregate schedule.

(b) Suppose that the goverment taxes Tom at a rate of 10 percent for each level of Y_d and gives all of this tax revenue to Kerry. Assuming that the MPC values do not change for either Tom or Kerry, calculate the new values of C and Y_d and fill in the table below.

AFTER INCOME DISTRIBUTION

Kerry		Tom		Average Aggregate	
C	Y_d	C	Y_d	C	Y_d
80	0	80	0	80	0
1,070	1,100	530	900	800	1,000

(c) Calculate the MPC for the average aggregate after the income redistribution program and compare it with the original value.

(d) What has happened to the aggregate consumption function?

4. Since approximately 30 percent of GNP is comprised of exports, Canada's economic activity depends critically on foreigners' willingness to buy Canadian goods and services. As the text explains, foreign business cycles can be transmitted to Canada via fluctuations in exports, other things being equal. One determinant of foreigners' ability to buy Canadian goods is their national income, which itself can display cyclical activity.

You are given the following hypothetical relationship between foreign income and Canadian exports. In addition you are told that the marginal propensity to spend in Canada is .8.

Year	Foreign GNP	Canadian Exports	Δ in Canadian GNP
1	100	10	--
2	150	15	+25
3	200	20	____
4	180	18	____
5	100	10	____
6	100	10	____

(a) Deduce the relationship between foreign GNP and Canadian exports. List some factors that explain why foreign income might determine Canadian exports.

(b) Assume that if exports change between two years, the multiplier process works itself through by the end of the second year. On this basis, fill in the missing values for the change in the Canadian GNP.

(c) Has a business cycle been transmitted to Canada? Does it have the basic characteristics of the foreign business cycle?

5. Changes in Desired Capital Stocks
You are given two schedules that relate desired capital stock to the interest rate.

Schedule A		Schedule B	
Capital Stock	Interest Rate (%)	Capital Stock	Interest Rate (%)
100	20	150	20
200	18	250	28
300	14	350	14
400	8	450	8
500	1	550	1

(a)   Inspecting both schedules, does an inverse or direct relationship exist
      between the desired capital stock and the rate of
      interest? _____

(b)   Assuming schedule A applies, if the current rate of interest falls from 20
      percent to 18 percent, what is the change in the desired capital stock?
      Desired investment? Would firms necessarily be able to achieve this level of
      investment in the current time period?

(c)   Suppose that the schedule given by A suddenly changed to that given by
      schedule B. With a current interest rate of 14 percent, what is the new
      magnitude of the desired capital stock? Does the change in the schedule imply
      new desired investment activity? Indicate two factors that may have caused
      the schedule to change.

6.   The Multiplier-Accelerator Interaction Model
     The multiplier when combined with the accelerator may generate fluctuations in
     national income. For this model we have assumed: (1) the marginal propensity to
     consume is .5; (2) consumption in time period t depends on the level of income one
     period past (t - 1); (3) the capital-output ratio, or what is often referred to as
     the accelerator coefficient, is 1; and (4) investment in time period t depends on
     an autonomous amount, 100, plus the difference in income between t - 1 and t - 2.
     These assumptions are expressed by the following equations:

$$C_t = .5Y_{t-1}$$

and

$$I_t = 100 + 1(Y_{t-1} - Y_{t-2})$$

Therefore, since Y = C + I,

$$Y_t = .5Y_{t-1} + 100 + 1(Y_{t-1} - Y_{t-2})$$

     The economy is assumed to be at an equilibrium level of income of 200 in the
current time period 0 and has been at that level for two previous periods, -2 and
-1. In period 1 autonomous investment increases from 100 to 200 and stays at that
level permanently.
     The effect of this increase shows up in national income in period 1 as simply
an increase of 100. Why? Since consumption depends on last period's income
(period 0), and income is 200, the consumption level remains at a level of 100.
Furthermore, there is no accelerator effect in period 1 since the difference
between income in period 0 and period -1 (one period and two periods removed from
period 1, respectively) is zero.
     However, interesting things start to occur to national income thereafter. We
have started the process by completing the entries until period 6.
(a)   Fill in the missing values for periods 6 through 9 in the chart on the
      following page.
(b)   Identify by period(s) the trough of the cycle, the peak, the expansion phase,
      and the recession phase.

220

| | Consumption | Investment (I_t) | | National Income |
Period	$C_t = .5Y_{t-1}$	Autonomous	Accelerator $1(Y_{t-1} - Y_{t-2})$	$Y_t = C_t + I_t$
-2	100	100	0	200
-1	100	100	0	200
0	100	100	0	200
1	100	200	0	300
2	150	200	100	450
3	225	200	150	575
4	287.5	200	125	612.5
5	306.3	200	37.5	543.8
6	_____	200	_____	_____
7	_____	200	_____	_____
8	_____	200	_____	_____
9	_____	200	_____	_____

(c) Did the accelerator process counteract or reinforce the multiplier process during the expansion phase? The recession phase?

(d) Assume that the autonomous element of investment is sensitive to the rate of interest. What changes in the level of the rate of interest might the government of this economy pursue in periods 2 to 4 and periods 5 to 8 to "smooth out" this business cycle?

221

National Income, International Trade, and the Balance of Payments

33

KEY CONCEPTS AND DEFINITIONS

1. The balance of trade is the difference between the dollar value of exports and imports in a given year. An excess of exports over imports is referred to as a surplus in the balance of trade, while an excess of imports over exports is called a deficit. A situation in which exports are equal to imports is a situation of balanced trade.

2. Importables refer to goods actually imported as well as close substitutes produced in Canada that compete with imports. Exportables refer to goods actually exported as well as the production and consumption of these goods by Canadians.

3. Since imports are determined (induced) by Canadian GNP, the value of the multiplier is smaller than it would otherwise be if imports were autonomous (independent of GNP). Thus induced imports act as a built-in stabilizer.

4. The net-export (X - M) function relates the balance of trade surplus (as deficit is a negative surplus) to the level of national income. Net exports (assuming exports are exogenous) are inversely related to the level of Y.

5. The value of exports depends upon the level of foreign income and on the terms of trade (the price of Canadian goods relative to foreign goods). Differences in foreign and domestic inflation rates and changes in the exchange rate are the prime ways in which the terms of trade change.

6. Movements along the net export function are caused by changes in real GNP. Shifts in the function are caused by changes in foreign income, changes in domestic and foreign prices, and changes in the exchange rate.

7. Domestic absorption (A) is the total expenditure on all goods and services (domestic and foreign) for use within the economy, or $A = C + I + G$. At equilibrium, $Y = A + (X - M)$, or $(X - M) = Y - A$. Net exports can be positive only if Y is greater than A.

8. A shift in the net-export function, ceteris paribus, causes a shift in the AD function.

9. Internal balance (full-employment national income) and external balance (trade balance) may be conflicting goals.

10. The balance-of-payments accounts record the actual transactions between Canada and all other countries. Any transaction that is expected to lead to a payment

to other nations is classified as a debit because, ceteris paribus, it subtracts from Canada's foreign exchange reserves. Key examples of debits are imports and capital outflows. Any transaction that is expected to lead to a payment by foreigners to Canadians is classified as a credit item because, ceteris paribus, it adds to Canada's foreign exchange reserves. Key examples are exports and capital inflows to Canada.

11. Because the amount of dollars actually bought must equal the amount of dollars actually sold, the balance of payment, in an accounting sense, always balances.

12. There are three divisions in the balance-of-payments accounts: (a) the current account, which records all payments made because of current purchases of goods and services; (b) the capital account, which records all transactions related to international movements of financial capital; and (c) official reserves account, which records changes in gold and foreign exchange reserves held by the central authorities. In Canada, these reserves are managed by the Bank of Canada.

13. The current account is subdivided into trade balances on visibles (goods that can be seen and touched when they cross international borders) and invisibles (services that cannot be seen or touched). The balance of trade refers to only net exports of visibles.

14. The capital account is subdivided into short-term and long-term capital movements. The long-term component is subdivided into direct investment and portfolio investment. Direct investment refers to changes in nonresident ownership of domestic firms and changes in resident ownership of foreign firms. Portfolio investment is investment in bonds or a minority holding of shares that does not involve legal control.

15. International capital movements are influenced by differences in rates of returns among countries. Ceteris paribus, international capital will flow to the country where the return is highest.

16. If payments (debits) are greater than receipts (credits) on the combined current and capital accounts, there will be a reduction in the holdings of official reserves (gold and foreign currencies). In this case a balance-of-payments deficit is said to exist.

17. Permanent deficits on the balance-of-payments accounts (the sum of current plus capital) cannot be maintained, because the official reserves that are needed to finance such deficits are sure to be exhausted. A permanent surplus also cannot be sustained indefinitely unless the surplus country is prepared to give its trading partners (who have deficits) the money or allow them to increase their debts without limit. These conditions are not feasible in the long run.

18. Government policies to correct a deficit or a surplus include import and export restrictions, changes in interest rates, policies that alter the level of national income, and exchange rate changes.

19. Ceteris paribus, a surplus country should allow its currency to appreciate relative to other currency. A deficit country should allow its currency to depreciate. In either case, if exchange rates are completely free to vary, balance-of-payments deficits will be eliminated through exchange rate adjustments.

MULTIPLE-CHOICE QUESTIONS

1. The higher the propensity to buy additional imports out of increases in national income, the
   (a) lower will be the marginal propensity to withdraw
   (b) greater the value of the multiplier
   (c) more effective are domestic policies that attempt to change the level of domestic income
   (d) lower the value of the multiplier and the higher the marginal propensity to withdraw

2. The net-export function is typically
   (a) downward sloping because as Y increases the balance-of-trade surplus declines
   (b) downward sloping because as Y increases exports fall
   (c) downward sloping because as relative prices rise imports rise and exports fall thereby reducing the balance-of-payments surplus
   (d) horizontal with respect to the horizontal axis even though imports are induced by changes in Y

3. Which of the following will not cause the net-export function to shift upward?
   (a) a fall in terms of trade
   (b) a devaluation (or depreciation) of the domestic currency
   (c) an increase in national income
   (d) a higher foreign inflation rate relative to the domestic inflation rate

4. If at equilibrium Y equals 400 and (X - M) equals 30, then domestic absorption is equal to
   (a) 30
   (b) 400
   (c) 430
   (d) 370

5. The AE curve is usually flatter than the absorption curve because
   (a) the marginal propensity to spend is less than the marginal propensity to withdraw
   (b) net exports are inversely related to Y
   (c) the slope of the AE curve excludes the marginal propensity to import
   (d) the absorption curve is net of imports

6. Net exports can only be positive if
   (a) A exceeds Y
   (b) A = Y
   (c) Y exceeds A
   (d) full employment has been attained

7. If exports increase by 20 and relative prices and the exchange rate are unaffected by this increase, then net exports will eventually
   (a) increase only by 20
   (b) increase by more than 20 since Y increases by a multiple
   (c) increase by less than 20 because additional imports will be induced by the increased value of Y caused by the multiplier
   (d) increase by more than 20 because domestic absorption falls

8. If the economy was always in the Keynesian portion of the AS curve, a devaluation of its currency would likely cause
   (a) an increase in national income and net exports
   (b) an increase in domestic inflation and a decline in net exports
   (c) a rise in Y but no change in (X - M)
   (d) an upward shift in the (X - M) function and a downward shift to the left of the AD function

9. If full employment occurs at a level of income below that consistent with a balance of trade, an increase in government expenditure designed to achieve full employment will lead to:
   (a) a balance-of-trade surplus
   (b) a balance-of-trade deficit
   (c) a capital outflow
   (d) an increase in exports

10. If there is a current-account deficit, the sale of Canadian-government bonds to U.S. citizens will
    (a) guarantee a balance on the balance of payments
    (b) increase the likelihood of a balance-of-payments deficit,
    (c) be recorded as a payment on the capital account
    (d) offset totally or in part the deficit on the current account

11. Which of the following will not be recorded as a credit in the Canadian current account?
    (a) Labatt's purchase of a brewery firm in California
    (b) Russian purchases of Saskatchewan potash
    (c) Japanese tourist expenditures in Vancouver
    (d) British merchants pay Canada Steamship Co. to transport Hamilton-produced steel through the St. Lawrence seaway

12. Which of the following statements about the balance of payments is true?
    (a) Current-account debits must equal current-account credits.
    (b) Current-account deficits must always equal capital-account surpluses.
    (c) Total debits must equal total credits.
    (d) Desired payments must equal actual payments.

13. A balance-of-payments deficit is
    (a) impossible since the balance of payments always balances
    (b) an overall deficit (debit) position in the combined current and capital accounts
    (c) always caused by a deficit on the current account
    (d) when a current-account deficit is equal to the capital account surplus

Questions 14 through 22 refer to the balance-of-payments items listed below:

(a)	Long-term capital receipts	$ 1,305
(b)	Merchandise exports	17,785
(c)	Freight and shipping receipts	1,170
(d)	Freight and shipping payments	1,147
(e)	Short-term capital receipts	1,182
(f)	Changes in official reserves	+777
(g)	Merchandise imports	15,556
(h)	Long-term capital payments	814
(i)	Short-term capital payments	1,158
(j)	Interest and dividend receipts	545
(k)	Interest and dividend payments	1,613
(l)	Other current-accounts payments	721
(m)	Net travel payments	201

14. The value of merchandise net exports (balance of trade visibles) is
    (a) 33,341
    (b) -2,229
    (c) 2,229
    (d) 1,307

15. Which of the following is not a credit item in the current account?
    (a) item (m)
    (b) item (b)
    (c) item (j)
    (d) item (c)

16. The value of the current-account balance is a
    (a)   deficit of 262
    (b)   surplus of 262
    (c)   debit of 262
    (d)   surplus of 380

17. A surplus in the current account must be matched by
    (a)   a deficit in the capital account
    (b)   an increase in international reserves
    (c)   either (a) or (b)
    (d)   always (b) but never (a)

18. Which of the following is not a capital account item?
    (a)   item (f)
    (b)   item (i)
    (c)   item (e)
    (d)   item (h)

19. The value of the capital-account balance is a
    (a)   deficit of 515
    (b)   surplus of 515
    (c)   deficit of 262
    (d)   surplus of 262

20. Excluding item (l), the current-account balance of invisibles is a
    (a)   credit of 1,246
    (b)   debit of 1,045
    (c)   credit of 1,045
    (d)   deficit of 1,246

21. In the current situation, the sum of the current and capital accounts indicates that the balance of payment is in a
    (a)   surplus position of 777
    (b)   deficit position of 777
    (c)   balanced position of 0
    (d)   deficit position of 530

22. The value of the balance-of-payments position in the last question is reflected by the fact that official reserves
    (a)   increased by 777
    (b)   decreased by 777
    (c)   decreased by 530
    (d)   did not change because the balance of payments always balances by accounting convention

23. If a country has a balance-of-payments surplus and allows its currency to fluctuate freely on foreign-exchange markets, its currency will
    (a)   depreciate relative to other currencies
    (b)   remain constant since the surplus will eventually become a deficit
    (c)   reach a higher equilibrium value in foreign-exchange markets
    (d)   appreciate initially but then fall back to its original level once a balance has been restored.

226

1. You are given the following information about the economy of Oz:
   (a) the AS curve is horizontal at P = 2 for Y values equal to and less than 180;
   (b) the exchange rate is fixed at a given level;
   (c) $Y_{FE} = 180$;
   (d) the schedule of Y and expenditures shown below.

Y	C	I + G	X	M	(X − M)	AE	Absorption (A)
0	40	23	22	5	17	80	63
100	100	23	22	15	7	130	123
120	112	23	22	17	5	140	135
160	136	23	22	21	1	160	
170	142	23	22	22		165	___
180	148	23	22	23	___	170	$\overline{171}$

(a) Coming to Grips With the Current Situation
    Calculate the following information for Oz:

   (i) Equilibrium national income is _____.
  (ii) Domestic absorption at the equilibrium level of Y is _____.
 (iii) The marginal propensity to spend is _____.
  (iv) The multiplier value is _____.
   (v) The marginal propensity to consume is _____.
  (vi) The balance of trade at the equilibrium level of Y is _____.
 (vii) For every 10 increase in Y, net exports (increase/decrease)
        by _____.
(viii) Domestic absorption is _____ at Y = 170.
  (ix) (X − M) is _____ at Y = 180.
   (x) The slope of the absorption function is _____.
  (xi) The GNP gap is _____. The deflationary gap is _____.

(b) Plot the net-export function in the diagram below.

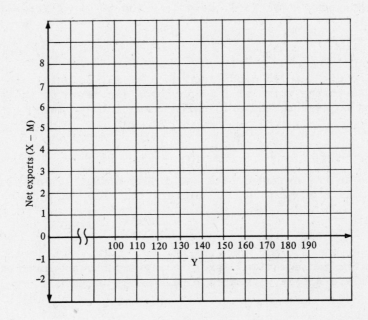

(c) Suppose that exports increased from 22 to 25 at every level of national income. Calculate
   (i) the new equilibrium level of Y. _____
   (ii) domestic absorption at the new equilibrium Y _____.
   (iii) net exports at the new equilibrium Y _____.

(d) Plot the new net-export function in the diagram above. Demonstrate that at the new equilibrium Y level net exports increased less than the export increase of three. Explain.

(e) Identify two factors (recalling the assumptions that have been made) that might have caused exports to increase.

(f) What increase in (I + G) from the initial level of 23 (X = 22) is necessary to achieve Y_{FE}? What is the value of (X − M) at Y_{FE}? You should have noticed that the achievement of internal balance (full employment) created an external imbalance (a trade-balance deficit).

2. Suppose that the (real) export function for Canadian goods is given by $X = .1Y_{for} - 20R$ and the (real) import function for Canada is given by $M = .2Y + 30R$, where Y_{for} is the level of foreign income in Canadian dollars and R is the ratio of the price of Canadian goods in dollars to the price of foreign goods in Canadian dollars (the terms of trade).
   (a) If the price of one unit of foreign exchange is $2 (Canadian), and the average price of Canadian goods is $2 while the average price of foreign goods (in terms of their currency) is 1, calculate the terms of trade (R).

   (b) If the price of Canadian goods increased to $3, calculate the new value of R. What changes in the price of foreign goods (in terms of their currency) would be required to restore the original R value in part (a)?

   (c) What change in the exchange rate would just offset an increase in the price of Canadian goods from $2 to $3 to maintain the value of R in part (a)?

   (d) Inspecting the two equations, explain why exports are inversely related to R and imports are directly related to R.

(e) Using the values Y_{for} = 1,000, Y = 100, and R = 1 [according to the information in part (a)], calculate the values of X, M, and $(X - M)$.

(f) Recalculate the values of X, M and $(X - M)$ for Y = 200, Y_{for} = 1,000, and R = 1. You may assume that the increase in Canadian GNP had no effect on R or Y_{for}.

(g) Recalculate the values of X, M, and $(X - M)$ for Y = 100, Y_{for} = 1,000, and R = 1.5.

(h) Identify three separate factors that might have caused R to increase from 1 to 1.5.

(i) For Y_{for} = 1,000 and Y = 100, calculate the (arc) elasticity of net exports for an increase in R from 1 to 1.5.

(j) Fill in the table below by indicating the effect of each event on the net-export function.

| | Net-Export Function | |
Event	Movement Along	Shift (Up, Down)
(i) An increase Y_{for}		
(ii) A decrease in Y		
(iii) Canadian dollar depreciates in terms of foreign currencies		
(iv) Foreign prices of goods (in their currency) decrease		
(v) Inflation rate in Canada is greater than foreign inflation rate		

3. The Effect of a Devaluation on an Economy at Full Employment
Suppose that an economy's export and import functions are given by $X = 70 - 20R$ and $M = .2Y + 30R$, respectively, where R is the terms of trade. The economy is initially at full employment of 100 with a price level of 2, as portrayed on the following page. The level of foreign prices is 1 (in terms of foreign currency) and the price of foreign currency in terms of the domestic currency is 2.

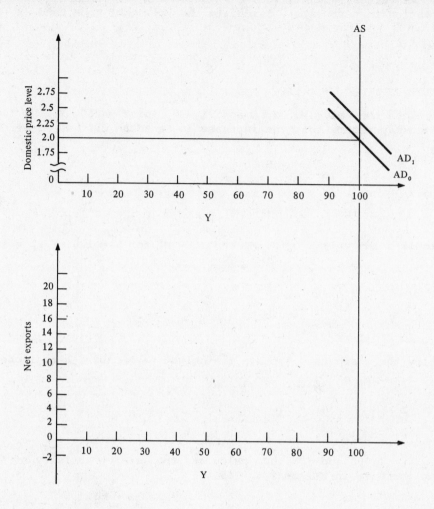

(a) Given the information above, plot the net-export function and demonstrate that net exports are initially zero.

(b) Suppose that a devaluation occurs such that the price of foreign currency in terms of the domestic currency rises from 2 to 2.5. Remember that a rise in the price of foreign currency is equivalent to a fall in the price of the domestic currency. Recalculate the value of R (assuming the domestic price level does change yet) and use this value to recalculate the new values of (X − M) at Y = 100 and Y = 90. Plot the new net-export function at these values of Y.

(c) Since the net-export function has shifted upward, the AD curve will shift upward. In this case we assume that the AD curve becomes AD_1. The domestic price level becomes 2.25, but the economy is still at full employment. A rise in the domestic price will cause exports to fall and imports to rise through the influence of R. Recalculate the value of R, and then recalculate the values of (X - M) at Y = 100 and Y = 90. Plot the new net-export function at these values of Y.

(d) What is the final effect on domestic absorption and net exports after devaluation?

4. You are given the following demand and supply curve for a country's currency.

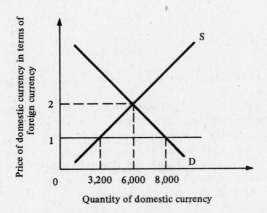

(a) If the exchange rate is 1, what balance-of-payments situation exists?

(b) In this situation the price of domestic currency is likely to (appreciate/depreciate) to a price of _____, at which the balance of payments is (in a deficit position/in a surplus position/in a balanced position).

(c) Capital inflows and exports are determinants of the (demand for/supply of) domestic currency on foreign exchange markets. A fall in foreign income is likely to shift the (demand/supply) curve for domestic currency in a(n) (upward/downward) fashion. If the equilibrium price of 2 still holds, the shift in the curve will cause an initial (deficit/surplus) in the balance of payments. If the price is free to move, the price of the domestic currency will (depreciate/appreciate) on world markets.

Fiscal Policy | 34

1. Fiscal policy is the deliberate use of public expenditures or taxes to alter the level of aggregate demand.
2. The budget balance is the difference between tax revenue and public expenditure. If tax revenue exceeds expenditure, there is a budget surplus; if revenue falls short of expenditure, there is a budget deficit and the government is said to be deficit financing. If a change in expenditure is matched by a change in tax revenue, there is a balanced budget change in spending.
3. To remove an inflationary gap, the appropriate fiscal policy would be to change expenditures and/or taxes so as to move the budget toward a surplus. The reverse procedures would be followed in an attempt to remove a deflationary gap.
4. Expenditure and tax changes of equal magnitude have different impacts on national income. The net effect of a balanced budget change in spending is measured by the balanced budget multiplier.
5. If small changes in fiscal policy are made in response to small deviations in national income from its desired level, the government is said to be "fine tuning" the economy.
6. Built-in stabilizers may be present on both the expenditure and tax side of the budget. They operate in such a manner as to dampen an expansion in income and cushion a decline without the need for the government to make a policy change. Discretionary fiscal policy refers to the decision by the government to change a tax rate or level of expenditure through legislative action.
7. Because tax revenues respond to changes in national income, the combination of fixed government expenditure and rising national income eventually creates a surplus, referred to as fiscal drag.
8. The budget surplus function relates the difference between tax revenues and expenditures to national income. Endogenous changes in the budget balance resulting from changes in national income produce movements along the function. Discretionary changes in tax rate of levels of expenditure will change the function.

232

9. The <u>full-employment surplus</u> is the potential budget balance that would result if (a) the economy were at full employment and (b) all policies related to expenditure and taxation were unchanged.

10. The efficacy with which discretionary fiscal tax policy works may depend upon the specific relationship between consumption and disposable income. Consumption behaviour based on a <u>permanent income</u> concept may be less responsive to short-term tax changes than one based on changes in current absolute income.

11. The coexistance of inflation and unemployment, known as stagflation, has limited the use of discretionary fiscal policy.

12. A policy that balances the budget annually would, in some years, require discretionary policies that would be pro-cyclical, thereby accentuating swings in national income.

13. In addition to raising taxes, an expenditure increase can be financed by borrowing money from persons and corporations, at home and abroad, or through the creation of new money.

14. The national debt represents the cumulative result of all past borrowings by government that have not yet been repaid.

MULTIPLE-CHOICE QUESTIONS

1. Fiscal stabilization policy refers to
   (a) government's attempt to regulate prices
   (b) budget results that change pro-cyclically
   (c) the use of tax and expenditure policies to reach desired levels of GNP
   (d) government's attempt to stabilize tax rates and expenditure

2. The budget balance of a government
   (a) is the difference between revenues and expenditures
   (b) refers to a situation in which revenues equal expenditures
   (c) can only be maintained if there is a surplus
   (d) all of the above

3. If the government spends more than it receives in taxes and other revenues,
   (a) it is obviously spending too much
   (b) national income will surely rise
   (c) there will be a surplus in the budget
   (d) there will be a deficit in the budget

4. If an expenditure increase by government is matched by an equal increase in tax revenue,
   (a) there has been a balanced budget change in spending
   (b) a deficit will eventually arise
   (c) national income will fall
   (d) the ratio of government spending to GNP will rise

5. A budget deficit will increase GNP only if
   (a) the government borrows money that otherwise would have been spent on investment
   (b) the government borrows money that otherwise would not have been spent at all
   (c) the government borrows from households money that otherwise would have been lent to firms
   (d) the government spends more money abroad than at home

6. When government expenditure exceeds tax revenue, the government can
   (a) sell treasury bills to financial institutions
   (b) sell bonds to individuals
   (c) borrow from the Bank of Canada
   (d) all of the above

233

7. It is possible that government spending, even if financed wholly out of taxes, will increase incomes if
   (a) taxpayers would have saved some of the money they had to pay in taxes
   (b) only high-income levels are taxed
   (c) prices rise as a result
   (d) investment declines by an equivalent amount

8. The balanced budget multiplier
   (a) applies only when government expenditures are equal to taxes
   (b) is larger than the multiplier for government expenditures
   (c) applies when additional tax receipts are equal to additional government expenditures
   (d) is the same as the multiplier for government expenditures

9. If government expenditure and tax revenue are both reduced by $50M and national income falls by $75M,
   (a) the inflationary gap is reduced
   (b) the balanced budget multiplier is 1.5
   (c) the balanced budget multiplier is 2/3
   (d) the budget balance is reduced

10. Fiscal "fine-tuning" calls for
    (a) no change in taxes or expenditure unless actual GNP is far from its desired level
    (b) using tax rates only to stabilize the economy
    (c) minor changes in fiscal variables whenever actual GNP deviates slightly from its desired level
    (d) a passive role on the part of the government in terms of influencing aggregate expenditures

11. Built-in fiscal stabilizers
    (a) reduce the marginal propensity to spend out of national income
    (b) keep aggregate demand constant
    (c) operate only on the tax side of the budget
    (d) reduce fluctuations in national income by one-half

12. Which of the following is not a built-in stabilizer?
    (a) a change in tax rates
    (b) unemployment insurance payments
    (c) the income tax
    (d) agricultural subsidies

13. The marginal propensity to consume out of disposable income is .75. If the tax rate of 10 percent of national income is increased to 20 percent,
    (a) the value of the multiplier falls from 3.1 to 2.5
    (b) the value of the multiplier remains constant
    (c) the value of the multiplier increases from 4 to 5
    (d) the value of the mulitplier falls to one-half its original value

14. Fiscal drag
    (a) slows economic expansion
    (b) increases the government surplus automatically as income rises
    (c) results from taxes being a function of income
    (d) all of the above

15. Discretionary expenditure changes are favoured over discretionary tax changes as fiscal measures
    (a) because they are politically more acceptable
    (b) because they have shorter decision lags
    (c) because of their impact on aggregate demand
    (d) when the location of the impact is important

16. Tax rate changes are preferred to expenditure changes as fiscal measures
    (a) because the execution lag is short
    (b) because people can see a tax change
    (c) when taxes are high
    (d) only when there is a recession

17. The impact of temporary income tax rate changes may be small
    (a) when incomes are high
    (b) when consumption is geared to lifetime income rather than current income
    (c) when the rate change is large
    (d) if the economy is close to full employment

18. An observed increase in personal income tax revenue indicates
    (a) tax rates have increased
    (b) incomes have increased
    (c) tax rates have increased and income has remained constant
    (d) any of the above is a possible explanation

19. The budget surplus function
    (a) relates taxes to income
    (b) shows the size of the surplus when tax revenue exceeds expenditure
    (c) is graphically a stright line for most economies
    (d) relates the net result of (tax revenue minus government expenditure) to national income

20. If total government expenditure (goods and services plus transfers) (G) = 20 − .05Y and T = .10Y where Y is national income, then the budget surplus function (B) is equal to
    (a) B = 20 − .10Y
    (b) B = −20 + .15Y
    (c) B = 20 − .05Y
    (d) B = 20 + .05Y

21. A decline in the full-employment surplus means that
    (a) a countercyclical fiscal policy is being followed
    (b) the budget will be in surplus at all levels of GNP
    (c) government spending must have declined
    (d) there may be fiscal drag in the tax structure

22. Stagflation
    (a) implies that fiscal policy will not work
    (b) refers to the coexistence of inflation and high unemployment
    (c) means inflation cannot be cured by fiscal policy
    (d) means economic growth is the economy's major problem

23. If the objective of government policy was to balance the budget every year,
    (a) taxes could not be changed
    (b) either tax rates would have to be raised or expenditures cut in a period recession
    (c) the budget surplus function would be a straight line
    (d) fluctuations in national income would be reduced

24. Interest on the federal debt
    (a) has risen in relation to GNP since 1945
    (b) represents a transfer from taxpayers to bondholders
    (c) is borne only by the losers
    (d) is almost always less than the economic benefits

25. From the Keynesian viewpoint, an important signal to a country that the public debt was too large would be
    (a) when the rates of debt to GNP increased
    (b) when individuals and institutions demand a significant risk premium to hold government debt
    (c) when interest payments as a percent of GNP increased
    (d) when deficits occurred at full-employment GNP

EXERCISES

1. You are given that the actual equilibrium GNP (Y) is $200 billion and full-employment GNP (Y_F) is $250 billion. The aggregate expenditure function has a slope of .5.
   (a) On the graph below plot the actual aggregate expenditure function. (Label it AE_O).
   (b) What is the magnitude of the GNP gap?

   (c) By how much must government expenditure rise to achieve Y_F? Indicate what the new AE schedule would look like and label it AE_1.

   (d) If taxes were reduced to achieve Y_F, illustrate the AE function that would be required to achieve full employment and label it AE_2.

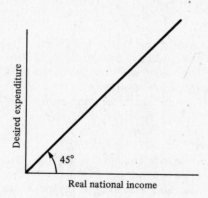

2. Suppose that the government wishes to close a GNP gap of $500 million by raising government spending and the tax rate such that the increase in tax revenue equals the increase in government expenditure. The marginal propensity to consume out of

236

disposable income is .50. If the balanced budget multiplier is 1.0, what increase in government expenditure and tax revenue is necessary to achieve the goal?

3. The following table provides information on a hypothetical economy. (The symbols Y, Y_d . . . I are those used in the text.)

Y	Y_d	T	C	G	I
100	80	20	40	40	80
200	160	40	80	40	80
300	240	60	120	40	80
400	320	80	160	40	80

(a) What is the specific functional relationship between Y and Y_d?

(b) What is the tax rate in this economy?

(c) What is the government's budget balance at equilibrium GNP?

(d) Suppose the tax rate was cut to 10 percent. What would the new equilibrium level of Y become? (Recall that you must determine the new relationship between Y and Y_d).

(e) How much tax revenue would be collected at the new equilibrium level of GNP? What would be the budget balance?

4. (a) The graph on the following page illustrates the current aggregate expenditure schedule. The tax rate is 10 percent. Illustrate what happens to the AE schedule when the government raises the tax rate to 40 percent and then, after the new equilibrium Y is reached, raises spending by $20 million. (Label the after-tax-change schedule AE_T and the after-the-expenditure-change AE_G. Try to graph the new AE schedules as accurately as possible using the graph paper).

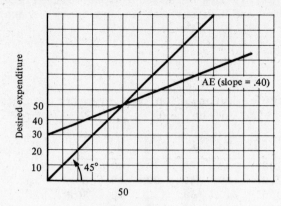

Real national income

(b)   What approximately is the new GNP?

5.   <u>Automatic Stabilizers</u>
It is possible to set government expenditures equal to some fixed amount or to allow a portion of the expenditure to be related to changes in national income. Let these two options, or expenditure functions, be described as

$$(1)\quad G = 10$$

$$(2)\quad G = 20 - .1 \; (AE - G)$$

where AE is aggregate expenditure and G is government expenditure.

(a)   Complete the last column in each table.

(1) G = 10				(2) G = 20 - .1 (AE - G)		
(AE - G)	G	AE		(AE - G)	G	AE
100	10	___		100	10	
120	10	___		120	8	___
120	10	___		120	8	___
110	10	___		110	9	___

(b)   Which of these government expenditure functions provides built-in stability? Explain your answer, relating it to the definition of automatic stabilizers in the text.

6.   Assume that the government's tax function is T = .05Y and that government expenditure is fixed at G = $100 million. The budgetary surplus function (B) is defined as B = T - G.

238

(a) For the following levels of Y, calculate and plot B. Label it B₁.

Y ($M)	B ($M)
1000	_____
1500	_____
2000	_____
2500	_____
3000	_____

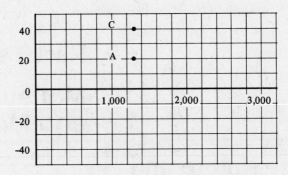

(b) If the tax rate is increased to 7 percent, plot the new budgetary surplus function (or as much of it as you can) and label it B₂.

(c) If we observed from one year to the next a movement from A to C on the graph could we conclude that the government has adopted a more restrictive fiscal policy? Explain.

239

Part Ten

Money, Banking, and Monetary Policy

<table>
<tr><td>

The Nature and Importance of Money

</td><td>

35

</td></tr>
</table>

KEY CONCEPTS AND DEFINITIONS

1. <u>Money</u> is defined as any generally accepted medium of exchange. It has three main functions: to act as a <u>medium of exchange</u>, as a <u>store of value</u>, and as a <u>unit of account</u>.

2. An important function of money is to facilitate <u>exchange</u> and avoid <u>barter</u> transactions. With money as a medium of exchange, everyone is free to specialize in the direction of one's natural abilities, and hence the production of all commodities increases.

3. As a <u>store of value</u>, money is a convenient way of storing purchasing power when the price level is relatively stable.

4. As a <u>unit of account</u>, money is used to measure the value of goods and services.

5. Money has evolved from coins of precious metals to paper money fully <u>convertible</u> to precious metal, to <u>fiat money</u>, and to <u>deposit money</u>.

6. The early experience of currency debasement led to a famous economic law known as <u>Gresham's Law</u>. The hypothesis is that bad money drives out good.

7. When a country's money is convertible into gold, the country is said to be on the <u>gold standard</u>.

8. A money is <u>legal tender</u> if you are offered it in payment for debt and you refuse to accept it, then the debt is no longer legally collectible.

9. <u>Deposit money</u>, a liability of a bank, will often allow an individual to write cheques in order to make payments.

10. <u>Near money</u> is an asset that serves as a store of value and is readily converted into a medium of exchange but is not itself a medium of exchange.

11. Things that serve as a temporary medium of exchange but are not a store of value are sometimes called <u>money substitutes</u>.

12. Early economic theory regarded the economy as being divided into a <u>real part</u> and a <u>money part</u>. The allocation of resources, depending on the structure of <u>relative prices</u>, is determined in the real part of the economy. The monetary part determined the <u>absolute level of prices</u> at which the real transactions (production, resource allocation, distribution) took place. This was determined by the <u>quantity of money</u>.

13. The effects of unanticipated inflation are (1) resource reallocation by changing relative prices and wages, (2) redistribution of wealth from lenders to borrowers, and (3) reduction in the living standards of those on fixed incomes.

14. The quantity theory of money provided early economists with a link between the money supply and the price level.

15. The reason originally stressed in the quantity theory for wanting to hold money is the so-called transactions motive. The need to finance transactions forces firms and households to hold money balances called transactions balances. The level of transactions balances is directly related to the level of national income.

16. The quantity theory of money is represented by the expressions $M = kPY$ or $MV = PY$, where V is the velocity of circulation. Furthermore, $V = 1/k$.

17. Given the assumptions that the AS curve is vertical (national income is at its full-employment level) and that k is constant, the quantity theory of money predicts that changes in the money supply lead to proportional changes in the price level with no changes in real output.

MULTIPLE-CHOICE QUESTIONS

1. For money to serve as an efficient medium of exchange, it must have all but which one of the following characteristics?
   (a) general acceptability
   (b) convertibility into precious metals
   (c) high value for its weight
   (d) divisibility

2. The value of money depends primarily on
   (a) the gold backing of the currency
   (b) the gold backing of the currency and bank deposits
   (c) its purchasing power
   (d) who uses it

3. To be a satisfactory store of value, money must have
   (a) a relatively stable value
   (b) A direct relationship to GNP
   (c) a highly volatile value over time
   (d) no interest payment for holding it

4 Debasing the coinage leads to a
   (a) fall in prices in the economy
   (b) rise in prices in the economy
   (c) constant level of prices
   (d) loss to the person issuing the coins

5. Whenever a person gets hold of an undebased coin, he will
   (a) pass it on and hold onto debased coins when he receives them
   (b) hold onto it and also hold onto debased coins when he receives them
   (c) pass it on
   (d) hold onto it and pass on debased coins when he receives them

6. A requirement for the gold standard was that
   (a) the price level be stable
   (b) there be no paper money
   (c) the paper money be convertible into gold
   (d) gold coinage be 100 percent of the money supply

7. A fractionally backed paper money system is when paper money has
   (a) a 100-percent backing in precious metals
   (b) less than a 100-percent backing in precious metals
   (c) a direct relationship to GNP
   (d) a fixed relationship to the quantity of coinage

8. Today, paper money in Canada is issued by
   (a) the banks
   (b) the central bank of Canada (the Bank of Canada)
   (c) the Queen
   (d) the Department of Finance

9. All Canadian currency (coins plus paper notes) is
   (a) fractionally backed by gold
   (b) fractionally backed by gold and silver
   (c) interest bearing
   (d) fiat money

10. Which of the following is an example of near money?
    (a) a deposit at a trust company
    (b) a personal chequing account at a bank
    (c) foreign currency
    (d) Gulf Oil stocks

11. A money substitute is something that serves as a
    (a) store of value
    (b) unit of account
    (c) temporary medium of exchange but not as a store of value
    (d) temporary medium of exchange and also as a store of value

12. The relative price of chicken to lamb will fall if
    (a) chicken and lamb prices double
    (b) lamb prices rise
    (c) chicken and lamb prices halve
    (d) chicken prices rise

13. The doctrine of the neutrality of money states that the quantity of money influences
    (a) the level of money prices but has no effect on the real part of the economy
    (b) the real part of the economy but has no effect on the money part of the economy
    (c) both the real and money parts of the economy in an identical fashion
    (d) neither the real nor the money part of the economy

14. Unanticipated inflation adversely affects a
    (a) debtor
    (b) borrower
    (c) tenant who has a long-term lease
    (d) creditor

15. Which of the following is not an assumption of the simple quantity theory of money?
    (a) The economy is at full employment except for very temporary periods.
    (b) People try to hold a fairly constant fraction of their income in money.
    (c) Changes in the supply of money relative to the demand for money result in changes in expenditure.
    (d) The supply of money depends directly on the price level.

16. The amount of money held for transactions balances
    (a) will vary in the same direction as nominal income
    (b) will vary in the same direction as the opportunity cost of holding money
    (c) will be larger the shorter the interval between paydays
    (d) all of the above

17. When firms and households have more money than they wish to hold, they
    (a) reduce their expenditures in order to reduce their unwanted money balances
    (b) raise their expenditures
    (c) reduce their expenditures in order to increase their money balances
    (d) permanently increase the proportion of their income they hold in money

18. For a given money supply, the aggregate demand for goods is
    (a) directly related to the price level
    (b) inversely related to the price level
    (c) directly related to the interest rate
    (d) equivalent to full-employment national income

19. Assuming that the AS curve is vertical, a halving of the money supply will cause
    (a) prices to halve
    (b) prices to double
    (c) real output to halve
    (d) real output to double

20. If, in the short run, k falls but the money supply rises, then it is possible that
    (a) real income may rise
    (b) prices and real income fall
    (c) real output and prices remain unchanged
    (d) full-employment changes

21. If the value of k rises, other things being equal,
    (a) V will rise
    (b) price will rise
    (c) the money supply will rise
    (d) V will fall

EXERCISES

1. Indicate which of the three functions of money is demonstrated in each of the
   following transactions. Use the appropriate letter: (a) medium of exchange; (b)
   store of wealth; (c) unit of account; (d) none.

   _____ (1) Farmer Brown puts cash in his mattress.
   _____ (2) Storekeeper Brown adds up his total sales for the day.
   _____ (3) Sue Brown withdraws cash and buys a government bond.
   _____ (4) Traveling salesman Brown uses his credit card to buy gas for his car.
   _____ (5) Mrs. Brown buys a good oriental rug with the thought that it will keep
              its value for a long time.

2. If k = .20, price level is unity, real income is $100 billion, and potential real
   GNP is $100 billion, what will be the desired or equilibrium amount of the money
   supply? What is the income velocity of money? _____

Suppose that the actual money supply is $25 billion. Outline the expected reactions in the economy and the likely final effects in the economy.

3. Suppose that a household is paid $1,000 at the beginning of each month. The household spends all of its income on the purchase of goods and services each month. Furthermore, assume that these purchases are at a constant rate throughout the month.
    (a) What is the value of cash holdings at the beginning of the month? At the end of the first week? At the end of the third week? At the end of the month?

    (b) What is the magnitude of the average cash holdings over the month?

    (c) Suppose that the household's income increases to $1,200 and purchases of goods and services during a month are equal to this amount. What is the average cash holding?

    (d) Suppose that the household is paid $1,000 over the month but in installments of $500 at the beginning of the month and $500 at the beginning of the third week. What is the magnitude of the average cash holdings per month?

4. Indicate whether the probable effect of unanticipated inflation for the following will be favourable, unfavourable, or neutral.
    (a) A tenant who signs a three-year lease on an apartment for $300 per month _____
    (b) The landlord in the above agreement _____
    (c) A university student who receives a provincial scholarship for $2,500 per year over the next four years _____
    (d) A graduate student who receives a three-year award that is adjusted for the annual rate of inflation per year _____
    (e) Quebec government tax revenue from a provincial sales tax on consumer goods _____
    (f) A Toronto Blue Jay baseball player who receives $300,000 for the next five years _____
    (g) A retired person whose primary source of income is from a portfolio of Canada Savings bonds _____
    (h) A real estate salesman's income from commissions _____

5. Olympic Coins

The Olympic Committee announced early in 1973 that they intended to finance the 1976 Olympic Games in Montreal partly by the sale of about $240 million in special Olympic coins. A similar scheme had been successfully used by the Munich Olympic Committee in 1972.

The federal government agreed to instruct the Mint in Ottawa to produce the coins in various face values. The coins were sold to the Olympic Committee at cost, which was well below the total face value of the coins. The Olympic Committee then sold the coins to the public at their face value. Furthermore, the coins were declared legal tender by the federal government.

(a) If the Olympic Committee sold all of the coins, would the money supply increase? Explain.

(b) According to the details you have been given, does it appear that the value of the coins depended on the value of their metallic content? What did their value depend upon?

(c) Suppose that these coins became valuable collectors' items so that their market price (the price determined on the coin collectors' market) doubled. Would the money supply double?

(d) Suppose that the price of the metals used to produce these coins increased tenfold so that the metallic price of the coins became greater than their face value. How do you think the holders of these coins would react?

6. Canada's Income Velocity of Money

Below are some relevant data for recent years. M_1 is the measure of the money supply: currency and demand deposits. The velocity here is income velocity (GNP/M_1).

Year	M_1($B)	GNP($B)	V
1968	8.9	72.7	8.17
1969	9.2	79.7	
1970	9.7	85.7	
1971	11.4	94.5	
1972	12.9	105.2	
1973	14.4	123.6	
1974	15.3	147.2	
1975	18.8	165.4	
1976	19.2	191.5	
1977	21.5	210.1	

Source: Statistics Canada, Canadian Statistical Review, various issues.

(a) Calculate the velocity values and fill in the table on the previous page.

(b) For a velocity of 8.0, what is the fraction of income held in money balances?

(c) What role might higher interest rates on savings deposits, wider use of credit cards, and price inflation in the late 1960s and 1970s have played in the higher V_{M_1}?

International Monetary Systems | **36**

KEY CONCEPTS AND DEFINITIONS

1. Under the <u>gold standard</u>, the central authorities of each country kept their paper currency <u>convertible</u> into gold at a fixed rate, and the "gold content" of each currency established fixed rates of exchange between all the currrencies. Because all currencies were freely convertible into gold, they were also freely convertible into each other.

2. A country having balance-of-payment deficits would lose gold, thereby shrinking its money supply and causing domestic prices to fall. This in turn would stimulate the country's exports and reduce imports. A country experiencing surpluses in the balance of payments would receive gold and increase its money supply, causing prices to rise. In both cases, the relationship between gold and prices is called the <u>gold flow, price level mechanism</u>.

3. In the 1920s, the gold standard failed because price level adjustments could not take place fast enough and because governments were unwilling to allow their price levels to change solely because of the balance of payments.

4. The gold standard was abandoned and many experiments were tried throughout the 1920s. One policy, the beggar-my-neighbor policy, involved attempting to reduce exports in order to reduce imports. This had the effect of shifting unemployment onto another country.

5. From 1944 to the early 1970s, the international monetary system was the <u>Bretton Woods</u> system. It put the world on an <u>adjustable peg</u> (pegged against short-term fluctuations but adjusted from time to time), <u>gold exchange standard</u> (reserves of gold, pound sterling, and U.S. dollars). To fix their exchange rates relative to the U.S. dollar, foreign monetary authorities held reserves of gold, pounds, and U.S. dollars.

6. Exchange rates were only to be changed in the face of a <u>fundamental disequilibrium</u> (a persistent, long-run problem) in the balance of payments.

7. The <u>International Monetary Fund (IMF)</u> was the major institution of the Bretton Woods system.

8. Three major problems with any adjustable peg system are (1) to provide sufficient international reserves both for short-run and long-run needs, (2) to handle periodic speculative crises, and (3) to adjust to long-term trends in receipts and payments.

247

9. The Bretton Woods system broke down under a series of speculative crises that stemmed from the failure of the system to provide sufficient international reserves and to accommodate devaluations of the U.S. dollar, which was the currency to which all other countries pegged their exchange rates.
10. The two major events in the transition from the Bretton Woods system to the present one were the abandonment of gold convertibility of dollars held by central banks in 1971 and the drift toward managed flexibility of exchange rates.
11. A managed float or a dirty float is an aspect of the present system in which an exchange rate floats because it is not pegged at any publicly announced par value. However, the central bank does intervene in the foreign exchange market to reduce short-term fluctuations and sometimes to resist long-term trends.
12. The present system, a dollar standard with managed flexibility of exchange rates, is under heavy strains because of the current-account deficits of the oil-importing countries, the lack of an alternative to the dollar as a reserve currency, and the enormous excess purchasing power (petrodollars) in the hands of oil-producing countries.

MULTIPLE-CHOICE QUESTIONS

1. Under the gold standard
    (a) exchange rates fluctuated frequently
    (b) equilibrium was produced by changes in fixed exchange rates
    (c) crises of confidence were met quickly despite the small amount of gold relative to claims on it
    (d) equilibrium was supposed to be reached by changes in domestic price levels

2. During the monetary crisis and the depression of the 1930s
    (a) most countries stayed on the gold standard despite the difficulties
    (b) competitive currency devaluations were frequent
    (c) U.S. tariff policy became less protectionist
    (d) international trade was stimulated because of the low prices of goods

3. Under the Bretton Woods agreement
    (a) most countries returned to the gold standard
    (b) countries were given almost complete freedom to let their currencies float
    (c) all exchange rates were tied to the U.S. dollar
    (d) gold was completely abandoned as an international means of payment

4. Among postwar international developments were all the following except
    (a) the dollar shortage confronting war-torn countries that needed U.S. goods
    (b) the dollar surplus Europe and Japan accumulated as they recovered
    (c) prompt upward adjustments of undervalued currencies
    (d) considerable international cooperation to maintain stable exchange rates

5. The International Monetary Fund
    (a) is a fund for long-term development projects
    (b) was designed to assist in making exchange rates more readily flexible
    (c) was designed to help maintain fixed exchange rates in the face of short-term fluctuations
    (d) was abandoned after the dollar shortage of the early postwar years

6. Destabilizing speculation occurs when
    (a) lower exchange rates increase the quantity of a currency demanded
    (b) higher exchange rates increase the quantity of a currency supplied
    (c) there is no expectation that fixed exchange rates will be changed
    (d) a change in exchange rates leads to expectation of further changes in the same direction

248

7. Floating exchange rates
    (a) are the same as fixed rates
    (b) describe the fluctuations around fixed rates permitted by IMF rules
    (c) are necessarily destabilizing
    (d) are determined in international exchange markets by competitive demand and
         supply conditions

8. Special drawing rights are
    (a) supplementary reserves with the IMF that member countries can use to finance
         balance-of-payments deficits
    (b) demand deposits that central banks hold in the World Bank
    (c) special credit given to importers in IMF countries
    (d) long-term reserves available to member countries in return for gold

9. The "dirty" float of currencies means that
    (a) currencies are officially pegged but a large black market exists
    (b) the official price at which gold is being sold is allowed to fluctuate
    (c) currencies are officially floating but are being influenced unofficially by
         central bank policies
    (d) none of the above

10. A workable international monetary system must be able to deal with all but which
    one of the following?
    (a) short-term fluctuations in trade and capital movements
    (b) long-term changes in trade and payments patterns
    (c) the necessity of gold as a source of confidence in the value of currencies
    (d) speculative crises

Questions 11 through 15 refer to the diagram below.

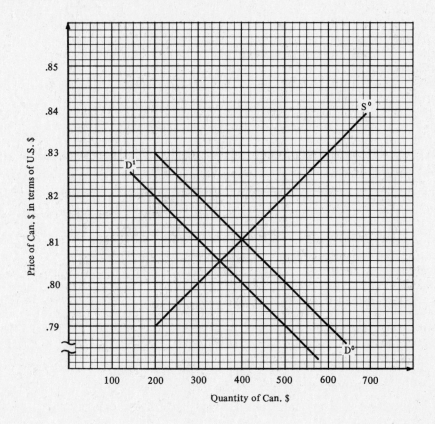

249

11. Referring to the curves labeled with the superscript ^{0} and assuming a floating exchange rate system existed, the price of the Canadian dollar per U.S. dollar would be
    (a) 400
    (b) .81
    (c) 1.81
    (d) .81 cents

12. If the demand curve shifted downward to D^1, this might be explained by the fact that
    (a) Canadian export sales fell
    (b) Canadian export sales rose
    (c) imports to Canada rose
    (d) imports to Canada fell

13. Because of the decrease in demand, the price of the Canadian dollar is likely to
    (a) fall to U.S. $.80
    (b) fall to U.S. $.805
    (c) stay at U.S. $.81
    (d) rise to U.S. $.805

14. The central bank (the Bank of Canada) pursuing a dirty-float policy might try to maintain a price of $.81 for a short period of time by
    (a) selling 100 Canadian dollars
    (b) selling 50 Canadian dollars
    (c) buying 100 Canadian dollars
    (d) buying 50 Canadian dollars

15. The decrease in demand might also cause speculators to forecast
    (a) a further decline in the Canadian dollar, and hence they would buy Canadian dollars now
    (b) a further decline in the Canadian dollar, and hence they would sell U.S. dollars now
    (c) a further decline in the Canadian dollar, and hence they would sell Canadian dollars now
    (d) a further decline in the price of the U.S. dollar

EXERCISES

1. Indicate with an "X" which characteristics apply to each of the monetary arrangements listed below.

	Gold standard	Bretton Woods system	Current monetary arrangements
International Monetary Fund			
Effective fixed gold content for U.S. dollar			
Fluctuating exchange rate			
Special drawing rights			
Dollar convertible to gold domestically			
Adjustable peg			
"Dirty" float			
Free market for gold			
Fixed exchange rates			

250

2. During the late 1977 and early 1978 period, the U.S. price of the Canadian dollar fell dramatically, reaching a low of 80.8 cents. This low had not been experienced since September 1931. Several factors contributed to this decline, including increased unemployment, the national unity crisis, poor domestic inflation experience, low forecasts of domestic investment in 1978, adverse speculation, and a poor trade sale performance.

   (a) As a Canadian who is engaged in importing goods from abroad, what guarantees might you try to obtain concerning the goods that you are planning to buy during 1978 and early 1979? Why might you wish such guarantees?

   (b) As a speculator in the foreign-exchange market, what activity might you become engaged in if you anticipated a worsening in Canadian economic activity and export sales and a growing dependence on foreign oil? If your behavior was a general tendency, what would happen to the price of the Canadian dollar?

3. Oil Price Increases and Recycling Petrodollars
   The foreign-exchange reserve positions of a number of countries are shown below. (Figures are in billions of U.S. dollars.)

	1973	1974	1975
Canada	$ 5.8	$ 5.8	$ 5.3
United States	14.4	16.1	15.9
United Kingdom	6.5	6.9	5.3
Japan	12.2	13.5	12.8
Oil-exporting countries (mostly OPEC countries)	14.5	46.4	55.4

   (a) Explain why the rise in the price of oil imposed by the OPEC countries during this period contributed to the significant difference in the reserve positions of the first four countries in the table and the OPEC countries.

   (b) Describe the adjustment process that would have occurred over this period if the world had operated under the gold standard, with the free convertibility of currencies into gold and fixed rates with each other.

(c) In the text, the authors point out that these reserves or petrodollars will eventually be recycled by the way of trade and investment between the OPEC and other countries. Some OPEC countries are interested in investing substantial amounts in Canada. If this were to occur, how might it affect:

(i) Canada's employment situation?

(ii) Canada's foreign-reserve position?

(d) Some of the petrodollar investments in Canada may be in the form of short-term capital, including deposits in Canadian banks. If this were to occur and the OPEC countries suddenly withdrew their OPEC dollar investments from Canada, what would happen to the price of Canadian dollars under the current international monetary system? What type of foreign-exchange speculation might occur as a result of the withdrawal of OPEC dollars?

The Banking System and the Supply of Money | 37

KEY CONCEPTS AND DEFINITIONS

1. The total stock of money in the economy at any moment of time is called the money supply.
2. There are many definitions of the money supply. The most commonly used measure in Canada is M_1, which is defined to include currency (coins and Bank of Canada notes) and demand deposits at banks.
3. The measure M_1 concentrates on the medium-of-exchange function of money. Funds held in demand deposits can be transferred by cheque or withdrawn on demand (i.e., without prior notice being given). Broader definitions of money add in savings accounts and term deposits, which serve the temporary store-of-value function.
4. The banking system in Canada consists of 11 chartered banks. The central bank in Canada, which regulates the activities of the banks, is the Bank of Canada.
5. The chartered banks are profit-seeking institutions that allow their customers to transfer demand deposits from one bank to another by means of cheques. The banks are differentiated from other financial institutions (trust companies, credit unions, etc.) because they are the only institutions that accept demand deposits.
6. The principal assets of the banks are securities, loans, and cash reserves. Cash reserves include notes and deposits with the Bank of Canada. Because of the Bank of Canada's policy, banks must hold a certain fraction of their deposits in reserves. This fraction is called the cash reserve ratio.
7. Those reserves that the banks are required to hold under the Bank Act are called required reserves. Any reserves that a bank holds over and above the required reserves are called excess cash reserves.
8. The major liabilities of the banks are the public's deposits.
9. Because most customers of the banks are content to pay their transactions by cheques rather than by currency, the banks need only keep a small cash reserve against their deposit liabilities. Because of this fact plus the fact that the cash reserve ratio is a fraction, when banks receive new deposits the banking system will end up creating new deposits by some multiple of the initial increase in deposits.

10. The amount of new deposits created depends on the cash reserve ratio, the <u>currency drain</u> (the amount of currency the public wishes to hold rather than holding demand deposits), and whether the banks are motivated to hold excess reserves.

11. Assuming no cash drain or excess reserve holdings, the money-creation multiplier is $1/r$, where r is the cash reserve ratio.

12. If banks lose deposits and are not holding excess reserves, there will be a multiple contraction of the money supply.

13. A central bank has four main functions: to serve as banker for banks, as a bank for the government, as a controller of the nation's supply of money, and as a supporter of financial markets. The major tool that the central bank uses to affect the money supply is <u>open-market operations</u>.

14. Open-market operations involve purchases and sales by the central bank of government securities in financial markets. If the central bank <u>purchases</u> securities on the open market, this <u>increases</u> the reserves of the banks and permits them to <u>expand</u> deposits by a <u>multiple</u>, thereby increasing the money supply by a multiple.

15. If the central bank <u>sells</u> securities on the open market, it <u>decreases</u> the reserves of the banks and forces them to <u>contract</u> loans. This causes a <u>multiple contraction of the money supply</u>.

MULTIPLE-CHOICE QUESTIONS

1. The measure of M_1 includes
    (a) paper notes and all deposits at banks
    (b) demand deposits at all financial institutions
    (c) currency and demand deposits at banks
    (d) paper notes and all deposits in the financial institutions

2. The key distinguishing feature between a bank and other institutions that offer banking services is that only a bank
    (a) accepts deposits
    (b) has its charter granted from provincial legislation
    (c) accepts demand deposits
    (d) extends loans to consumers

3. Which of the following is <u>not</u> an asset of a bank?
    (a) deposits of households
    (b) reserves
    (c) loans
    (d) Government of Canada securities

4. Cash reserves include
    (a) short-term government securities and paper notes
    (b) paper notes and deposits in the Bank of Canada
    (c) paper notes and demand deposits in the banks
    (d) all liquid assets (those that can be readily converted into cash)

5. The cash reserve ratio is
    (a) the fraction of a bank's deposits that it holds in the form of currency
    (b) the fraction of a bank's deposits that it holds in the form of reserves
    (c) the fraction of a bank's assets that it holds in the form of reserves
    (d) the fraction of a bank's reserves that it holds in the form of deposits with the Bank of Canada

6. The process of creation of deposit money by banks
   (a) is possible because of the fractional-reserve requirement
   (b) is consciously undertaken by each bank
   (c) always occurs if there are excess reserves
   (d) permits only small, gradual changes in the supply of money

7. If a bank's deposits are $40 million and the cash reserve ratio is 10 percent, required reserves are
   (a) $40 million
   (b) 10 percent of assets
   (c) $4 million
   (d) always equal to excess reserves of $4 million

8. A reduction in bank reserves by payments to foreigners, for example,
   (a) will always cause a multiple contraction in deposits
   (b) will cause a multiple contraction in deposits only if there are no excess reserves
   (c) will not affect domestic deposits
   (d) will not affect the availability of domestic credit

9. Which one of the following is not a function of the central bank?
   (a) to provide banking services for the federal government
   (b) to act as lender of last resort to banks
   (c) to control the supply of money and credit
   (d) to lend to business firms

10. A bank that has insufficient reserves may
    (a) borrow from the Bank of Canada
    (b) call in loans
    (c) sell securities
    (d) do all of the above

11. The existence of a cash drain will
    (a) reduce the ability of the banking system to expand or contract the money supply by a multiple
    (b) have no effect on the ability of the banking system to contract the money supply by a multiple
    (c) have no effect on the ability of the banking system to expand the money supply by a multiple
    (d) increase the ability of the banking system to expand or contract the money supply by a multiple

12. Purchase and resale agreements involve
    (a) sales and purchases of securities between chartered banks
    (b) sales and purchases of securities between the Bank of Canada and the chartered banks
    (c) sales of securities by investment dealers to the Bank of Canada with agreement to repurchase them at a later date
    (d) sales of securities by investment dealers to the Government of Canada with agreement to repurchase them at a later date

13. If bank reserves increase by $10 million and r = .10, the maximum change in the money supply is
    (a) an increase of $100 million
    (b) a decrease of $100 million
    (c) an increase of $11.1 million
    (c) a decrease of $11.1 million

14. The money-expansion multiplier is given by the expression
    (a) $1/(1-r)$
    (b) r
    (c) $(1/w) \times r$
    (d) $1/r$

15. Open-market operations are
    (a) purchases and sales by the central bank of government securities in financial markets
    (b) sales of government securities by investment dealers to the Bank of Canada
    (c) total purchases and sales of government securities in the bond market
    (d) purchases and sales by banks of government securities in financial markets

16. If the Bank of Canada purchases bonds from the banks,
    (a) bank reserves fall
    (b) bank reserves rise
    (c) the money supply will fall by a maximum of $1/r$ times the value of the purchase of bonds
    (d) the money supply will rise only by the value of the purchase

17. Which of the following is not a policy of the central bank?
    (a) raising the tax rate on interest payments
    (b) moral suasion
    (c) open-market operations
    (d) establishing the secondary reserve requirement

18. The bank rate is defined as
    (a) the interest rate charged to prime lenders at the banks
    (b) the cash reserve ratio times the rate on three-month Treasury Bills
    (c) the interest rate charged by banks for overdrafts
    (d) the interest rate at which the central bank makes advances to the banks

Questions 19 through 24 refer to the balance sheets below.

All Banks (millions of dollars)				Bank of Canada (millions of dollars)		
Reserves	$100	Deposits	$500	Securities	$100	Deposits of Banks: $100
Loans	300					
Securities	100					

Note: (i)   There is no cash drain
       (ii) The cash reserve ratio is constant

19. If the banking system is currently holding no excess reserves, it follows that the cash reserve ratio is
    (a) 20 percent
    (b) 10 percent
    (c) indeterminant
    (d) 0

20. If the Bank of Canada sold $10 million of securities to the banks,
    (a) reserves and securities in the banks would each rise by $10 million
    (b) reserves would fall by $10 million and securities held by banks would rise by $10 million
    (c) security holdings by the Bank of Canada would increase by $10 million and deposits of the banks in the Bank of Canada would be unaffected
    (d) deposits in the banking system would immediately fall by $10 million

21. The immediate effect of this transaction is to create a deficient reserve position in the banking system of
    (a) $10 million
    (b) $8 million
    (c) $50 million
    (d) 0

22. Banks will react to this situation by
    (a) holding onto any excess reserves they receive
    (b) extending loans in a magnitude equal to excess reserves
    (c) buying back the bonds they sold
    (d) calling in loans to increase their reserve position

23. The maximum final effect of this transaction on the money supply is a
    (a) $10 million increase
    (b) $12.5 million increase
    (c) $50 million decrease
    (d) $50 million increase

24. If the problem had allowed for a 5-percent cash drain, the final effect on the money supply of this transaction would have been
    (a) less than a $10 million increase
    (b) more than a $50 million decrease
    (c) more than a $50 million increase
    (d) less than a $50 million decrease

EXERCISES

Exercises 1 through 4 involve banking problems in the absence of Bank of Canada policies; Exercises 5 through 7 involve open-market operations and the Bank of Canada.

1. From the data below*, calculate the magnitudes of M_1, M_{1B}, and M_2. (All figures are in millions of dollars as of November, 1980.)

Currency outside the banks	$ 9,850
Demand deposits	16,606
Chequeable savings deposits	8,333
Personal savings deposits	66,905
Nonpersonal notice deposits	2,034

   *Source: Bank of Canada Review, November 1980.

   M_1 = _____
   M_{1B} = _____
   M_2 = _____

2. Arrange the following items on the proper side of a bank's balance sheet.

(a)	Demand deposits	$5,000,000
(b)	Savings deposits	1,000,000
(c)	Currency in vaults	60,000
(d)	Deposits in the Bank of Canada	1,000,000
(e)	Loans to public	4,000,000
(f)	Security holdings, Canadian government, provincial, municipal, and other	1,500,000
(g)	Banking building and fixtures	360,000
(h)	Capital and surplus	920,000

257

Assets	Liabilities

3. We use "T-account," abbreviated balance sheets for a bank to show changes in bank reserves, loans, and deposits. Make the entries on the T-accounts below, using + and − signs to show increase or decrease, for each of the following independent events. (Remember that all changes must balance.)

	Event	Assets	Liabilities
(a)	You deposit your pay cheque of $100 at your bank	Reserves: Loans and securities:	Deposits:
(b)	A bank sells $10,000 of government bonds in the market to replenish its reserves.	Reserves: Loans and securities:	Deposits:
(c)	A bank makes a loan of $5,000 to a local businessman and credits it to his chequing account.	Reserves: Loans and securities:	Deposits:
(d)	A bank sells $50,000 of securities to the Bank of Canada and receives deposits in the Bank of Canada.	Reserves: Loans and securities:	Deposits:
(e)	A businessman uses $5,000 of his demand deposit to pay off a loan from the same bank.	Reserves: Loans and securities:	Deposits:
(f)	A bank orders $5,000 in currency from the Bank of Canada.	Reserves: Loans and securities:	Deposits:

4. Suppose that bank A, a Canadian bank, begins with the T-account shown below. The cash reserve ratio is assumed to be 10 percent. Joe Doe, a holder of a deposit in bank A, withdraws $1,000 and deposits this amount in a commercial bank in a foreign country. Thus $1,000 has been taken out of the Canadian banking system.

Bank A (initial situation)			Bank A (after the withdrawal)	
Reserves:	$10,000	Deposits: $100,000	Reserves: $	Deposits: $
Loans:	90,000		Loans:	

(a) What were bank A's required reserves? Did it have excess reserves initially?

(b) Show the immediate effect of the withdrawal from bank A.

(c) What is the magnitude of bank A's reserve deficiency?

(d) Bank A reacts by calling in a loan equal to the amount of its reserve
     deficiency that it had made to Mary Smith. Mary repays the loan by writing a
     cheque on her account in bank B, another Canadian bank. Bank B's initial
     T-account is shown below. Fill in the T-accounts below for the effects of
     bank A's receiving the payment from Mary and of bank B's losing Mary's deposit.

	Bank B (initial situation)			Bank B (after losing Mary's deposit)	
Reserves:	$ 5,000	Deposits: $ 50,000	Reserves:	$	Deposits: $
Loans:	45,000		Loans:		

	Bank A (after receiving loan repayment)	
Reserves:	$	Deposits: $
Loans:		

(e) After this transaction, does bank A have deficient reserves? Bank B?

(f) In fact, bank B has a deficiency of reserves. It reacts by calling in a loan
     equal to the amount of the deficiency made to Peter Piper. Peter cashes in a
     savings deposit that he held in Bank C; that is, Bank C loses a deposit and
     Peter repays bank B. Bank C's initial situation is shown below. Fill in the
     T-accounts for the effects of bank B's receiving the loan repayment and bank
     C's losing Peter's savings deposit.

	Bank C (initial situation)			Bank C (after losing Peter's deposit)	
Reserves:	$ 7,000	Deposits: $ 70,000	Reserves:	$	Deposits: $
Loans:	63,000		Loans:		

	Bank B (after receiving loan repayment)	
Reserves:	$	Deposits: $
Loans:		

(g) After this transaction, does bank B have deficient reserves? Bank C?

(h) After this transaction, the reduction in the money supply has been Joe's
     original withdrawal plus $_____ in other deposits. Loans have been
     reduced by $_____.

(i) The process will continue until the total reduction in the money supply will
     be $ _____. The total reduction in loans will be $ _____.

5. Indicate on which side of the Bank of Canada's balance sheet the following items
    should go.

(a) Chartered bank reserves
(b) Currency in circulation
(c) Canadian government deposits
(d) Government securities
(e) Foreign currency assets
(f) Advances to chartered banks

	Bank of Canada	
	Assets	Liabilities

6. The Bank of Canada decides to purchase $100 million of Canadian government securities from the nonbank public for open-market operations. Show the effect of this first step on the banking system. (Be sure to use + and - to indicate changes, not totals.) Assume that the public holds all their money in bank deposits.

(a)

Bank of Canada		All Banks	
Securities:	Bank reserves:	Reserves:	Demand deposits:

(b) If the reserve ratio is 20 percent, it is now possible for deposits to increase by a total of _____ (including the original increase).

(c) What is likely to happen to the level of interest rates?

7. Suppose the Bank of Canada sells $150 million of Canadian government securities to the chartered banks. Show the immediate effect of this transaction in the balance sheets below. The cash reserve ratio is assumed to be .10.

Bank of Canada		Banking System	
Securities:	Bank reserves:	Reserves: Loans: Securities:	Deposits:

(a) Is the money supply immediately changed? Why or why not?

(b) After this transaction, what is the level of deficient reserves in the banking system? What is the total amount of loans that will be called in initially?

(c) What will be the final change in the money supply?

38

The Macroeconomic Role of Money and the Theory of Monetary Policy

KEY CONCEPTS AND DEFINITIONS

1. Many assets are components of a household's stock of wealth. These may be categorized into: assets that serve as a medium of exchange (money); financial assets that yield interest returns and have a fixed money value at some future maturity date, and whose price before maturity may fluctuate on the open market (bonds); and claims on real capital.

2. The liquidity of an asset is the degree of ease and certainty with which an asset can be turned into a given amount of an economy's medium of exchange. Money is perfectly liquid but earns no interest. Bonds are less liquid but earn an interest return.

3. A bond is a promise by the issuer to pay a stated sum of money as interest each year and to repay the face value of the bond at some future redemption date. The time until the redemption date is called the term to maturity or the term of the bond.

4. The rate of interest and bond prices vary inversely with each other. The closer to the present date is the redemption date of a bond, the less the bond's value will change with a change in the rate of interest.

5. The demand for money includes the transactions motive, the precautionary motive, and the speculative motive.

6. The transactions demand for money is directly related to the level of national income at current market prices and inversely related to the rate of interest. Since wealth held as money is not earning interest, an increase in interest rates increases the opportunity cost of holding money, and hence money balances will be reduced.

7. Precautionary balances in money are held because of the uncertainty about the degree to which payments and receipts will synchronize. The magnitude of precautionary balances is also directly related to the value of national income at current market prices.

8. The motive that leads firms to hold more money in order to avoid the risks inherent in a fluctuating price of bonds is called the speculative motive. Many firms and households are assumed to be risk averse; they prefer to avoid the possibility that they may have to sell bonds in the future at a price that cannot be predicted in advance.

9. The speculative motive leads a decision maker to add to his money holdings until the reduction in risk obtained by the last dollar added is just balanced by the cost in terms of the interest foregone on that dollar. A fall in the interest rate will cause decision makers to hold more money.

10. The function relating money demand to the rate of interest is called the liquidity preference (LP) function.

11. A monetary disequilibrium is a situation in which the demand for money does not equal the supply of money. A monetary equilibrium is a situation in which the two magnitudes are equal. A monetary disequilibrium will cause interest rates to change.

12. The mechanism by which excess demand for or supply of money affects the aggregate expenditure function is called the transmission mechanism.

13. There are two components of the transmission mechanism: the link between monetary disequilibrium and the interest rate, and the link between the interest rate and the aggregate expenditure function.

14. An excess demand (supply) for (of) money will cause interest rates to rise (fall). As interest rates rise (fall), the quantity of money demanded will fall (rise) in order to restore monetary equilibrium.

15. Changes in interest rates cause changes in investment expenditure. The inverse relationship between the two is called the marginal efficiency of investment (MEI) function. A change in interest rates causing a change in investment expenditure will shift the AE and AD functions.

16. Monetary policy (the central bank's policy to influence the money supply and interest rates) seeks to create a monetary disturbance that will work through the transmission mechanism to shift the aggregate expenditure and aggregate demand functions and so change equilibrium national income. An increase in the money supply is expansionary, a decrease is contractionary.

17. A given change in the money supply will have larger effects on national income the steeper is the LP functon and the flatter is the MEI function.

18. The inverse relation between P and equilibrium Y shown by the AD curve occurs because (money supply assumed constant) a rise in P raises the demand for money, and this shifts the AE curve downward and lowers equilibrium national income.

19. The monetary adjustment mechanism is a process that will eliminate an inflationary gap provided that the money supply is held constant.

20. The ultimate objectives of monetary policy are called policy variables. Both real national income and the inflation rate are policy variables. The variables that the Bank of Canada controls directly to achieve certain objectives are called policy instruments.

21. Intermediate targets are variables that are neither directly controlled nor for which there is any ultimate desired value for them to attain, but which, nevertheless, play a key role in the execution of monetary policy.

APPENDIX

1. The IS curve is a relationship between interest rates and real national income. It shows combinations of Y and r for which AE = Y in the economy. It is usually downward sloping.

2. An increase (decrease) in government expenditure causes the IS curve to shift upward (downward) to the right (left).

3. The LM curve is a relationship between interest rates and real national income and shows combinations of Y and r for which money supply equals the total demand for money. It is upward sloping.

4. An increase (decrease) in the supply of money causes the LM curve to shift downward (upward) to the right (left).

5. The intersection of the LM and IS curves indicates the only combination of Y and r for which AE = Y and the demand for money is equal to the supply.

1. If the price of a bond that has a large (long) term falls on the open market, the rate of interest on the bond will
    (a) fall
    (b) increase
    (c) not be affected
    (d) equal the new price of the bond

2. Which of the following assets has no risk as defined in the text?
    (a) equities
    (b) bonds
    (c) land
    (d) money

3. A promise to pay $200 one year hence is worth $178.57 when the interest rate is
    (a) 89 percent
    (b) 12 percent
    (c) 11 percent
    (d) .89 percent

4. If the interest rate increases,
    (a) the transactions demand for money rises
    (b) the precautionary demand for money rises
    (c) national income will rise
    (d) the quantity of money demanded will fall

5. If there is an excess supply of money, households and firms will
    (a) sell bonds and add to their holdings of money, thereby causing the interest rate to fall
    (b) purchase bonds and reduce their holdings of money, thereby causing the interest rate to rise
    (c) purchase bonds and reduce their holdings of money, thereby causing the price of bonds to rise
    (d) purchase bonds and reduce their holdings of money, thereby causing the price of bonds to fall

6. A fall in the interest rate will cause
    (a) a shift in the MEI function to the left
    (b) a shift in the MEI function to the right
    (c) a movement down the MEI functon
    (d) a movement up the MEI function

7. The MEI function is a relation between interest rates and
    (a) the capital stock
    (b) investment expenditure
    (c) real national income at which AE = Y
    (d) the quantity of money demanded

8. A given money supply increase will decrease interest rates to a greater degree the
    (a) flatter is the LP function
    (b) greater is the upward shift in the LP curve
    (c) steeper is the LP function
    (d) b and c

9. A decrease in the money supply will cause the
    (a) AE function to shift upward
    (b) LP function to shift leftward
    (c) AD and AE functions to shift downward
    (d) AE function to shift downward, but the AD curve will be unaffected

10. Assuming the economy is currently at less than full employment, a monetary
    expansion is likely to cause
    (a) real national income to fall
    (b) bond prices to fall
    (c) inflation but no change in real output
    (d) real national income to rise

11. If an inflationary gap exists, the central bank may wish to
    (a) purchase bonds in the open market
    (b) sell bonds in the open market
    (c) lower the cash reserve ratio
    (d) lower the bank rate

12. If prices rise and the money supply is constant, the demand for money will
    (a) rise and so will interest rates
    (b) fall and so will interest rates
    (c) rise but interest rates will fall
    (d) rise and national income will also increase

13. The monetary adjustment mechanism in an inflationary gap is such that price rises
    may eliminate the gap by
    (a) increasing the money supply
    (b) decreasing investment because of interest rate increases
    (c) decreasing investment by increasing real output
    (d) changing the marginal propensity to spend

14. Open-market sales of securities by the central bank will tend to
    (a) lower the price of bonds
    (b) lower interest rates
    (c) increase the price of bonds
    (d) increase bank reserves

15. Which of the following has not been a policy variable of the Bank of Canada?
    (a) inflation rate
    (b) the level of real national income
    (c) the exchange rate
    (d) the price of imported oil

16. Base control is said to exist when the central bank
    (a) sets the price at which it sells or buys bonds on the open market
    (b) uses a base year to determine its monetary rule
    (c) debases currency and destroys the public's confidence in it
    (d) sets the quantity of open-market sales or purchases

17. Expansionary monetary policy will encounter problems in influencing national income
    when
    (a) the LP function is flat
    (b) the MEI function is very steep
    (c) both a and b
    (d) neither a nor b

18. A monetary rule, a preference by some monetarists, is when the central bank
    (a) expands the money supply in a year depending on the growth rate of Y in that year
    (b) maintains a constant supply of money over a period of time
    (c) expands the money supply in each year at a constant rate equal to the growth rate of the demand for money in that year
    (d) expands the money supply every year at a constant rate equal to the growth rate of real income

19. If government expenditure decreases, the
    (a) IS curve shifts upward to the right
    (b) LM curve shifts upward to the right
    (c) LM curve shifts downward to the left
    (d) IS curve shifts downward to the left

20. If the money supply increases, the
    (a) LM curve shifts upward to the left
    (b) LM curve shifts downward to the right
    (c) IS curve shifts downward to the left
    (d) IS curve shifts upward to the right

21. For a given LM curve, if the IS curve shifts upward to the right
    (a) interest rates and real income will fall
    (b) interest rates will rise, real income will fall
    (c) interest rates and real income will rise
    (d) the money supply will rise causing interest rates to fall but real income to rise

EXERCISES

1. Calculate the interest rate for each of the following assets:
    (a) a perpetuity that pays $450 a year and has a face value of $3,000
    (b) a perpetuity that pays $450 a year and has a face value of $4,500
    (c) a bond that promises to pay $100 one year from now and is purchased for $87.72 today
    (d) a bond that promises to pay $100 one year from now and is purchased for $89.29 today
    (e) a bond that promises to pay $100 two years from now and is purchased for $79.72 today

2. Calculate the present value for each of the following assets:
    (a) a bond that promises to pay $100 three years from now and has a yearly interest rate of 2 percent
    (b) a bond that promises to pay $100 two years from now and has a yearly interest rate of 3 percent
    (c) a perpetuity that pays $100 a year and has an interest rate of 17 percent

3. Two liquidity preference curves are drawn below.

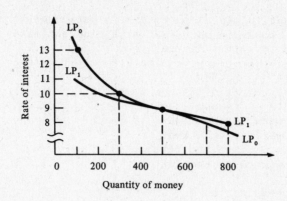

(a) Using your knowledge of the transactions and speculative motives for money,
     explain why the quantity of money demanded falls when interest rates rise.

(b) If the money supply is 500 and constant at all levels of interest rates, what
     interest rate is associated with monetary equilibrium? Plot the supply of
     money function in the above diagram and indicate the monetary-equilibrium
     interest rate.

(c) Suppose that the monetary authority decreased the money supply from 500 to
     300. At an interest rate of 9 percent, what kind of situation exists in the
     money market? Would households and firms tend to buy or sell bonds?
     Explain. Predict what is likely to happen to bond prices and interest rates.

(d) As interest rates rise, what happens to the quantity of money demanded?
     Predict the new equilibrium level of interest rates using LP_0. Using LP_1.

(e) What increase in the money supply would be necessary to achieve an equilibrium
     interest rate of 8 percent if LP_0 applies? If LP_1 applies? Comment on
     how the shape of the LP function affects the effectiveness of monetary policy.

4. Suppose the Bank of Canada purchases 1 million dollars of securities from the public. You may assume that the cash reserve ratio is 10 percent and that all the assumptions involved in the money process hold (no cash drain and banks have no excess reserves at the outset).

(a) What will be the final change in the money supply?

(b) What will be the final change in the quantity of money demanded? What factors explain the change?

(c) What will tend to happen to the level of interest rates? Explain carefully.

5. Suppose that the economy is currently experiencing unemployment. The central bank considers full-employment income to be the policy variable. The economy's liquidity preference curve is that labeled as LP_0 in question 3, and the current money supply is 500. Other information about the economy is described below.

(i) The cash reserve ratio is 10 percent.
(ii) The marginal propensity to spend is .50.
(iii) The full-employment level of national income is 1,600.
(iv) The MEI function is given by the following schedule.

Investment Expenditure	Interest Rate (%)
160	13
180	11
200	9
210	8

(v) Aggregate expenditures are depicted by the following schedule.

Y	C	I	G	(X – M)	AE
1,520	912	200	300	138	1,550
1,540	924	200	300	136	1,560
1,560	936	200	300	134	1,570
1,580	948	200	300	132	1,580
1,600	960	200	300	130	1,590

(vi) The LP curve is not influenced by changes in the level of national income.
(vii) The AS curve is horizontal at a price level of 2.0 for all levels of national income less than full employment. It is vertical at the full-employment level of Y, which in this case is equal to 1,600.

The central bank sets its research department to work in order to establish accurate information about the current situation and to suggest what it should do in order to eliminate unemployment.

(a)   Referring to the LP diagram in Exercise 3, what is the current equilibrium level of the interest rate?

(b)   Given the interest rate, what is the level of investment expenditure according to the MEI schedule?

(c)   What is the current equilibrium value of national income? What is the value of the GNP gap? The deflationary gap?

(d)   What is the value of the multiplier? What change in autonomous expenditure is required for the economy to achieve full employment without inflation?

With all of the information, the research department is in a position to recommend policy changes for the central bank. Its principal instrument is open-market operations that will affect intermediate target variables, the money supply, and the interest rate.

(e)   Should the money supply be increased or decreased? Should the interest rate be increased or decreased?

(f)   Changes in the money supply and the interest rate will change the level of investment. How much must investment be increased from its current level in order to achieve full-employment national income?

(g)   To achieve this higher level of investment, what is the required level of the interest rate? (Refer to the MEI schedule.)

(h)   Given the required level of the interest rate, what must the money supply be in order to achieve equilibrium in the money market at that interest rate? Refer to the LP function in question 3. What change in the current money supply is necessary?

(i)   To achieve the larger money supply, should the central bank purchase or sell bonds in the open market? What quantity? Explain.

Suppose that the open-market operation is successful in increasing the money supply and investment by the appropriate magnitudes. It follows that national income should increase by a multiple and attain a level of 1,600.

(j) Calculate the new level of consumption expenditure and calculate the aggregate level of expenditure at Y = 1,600. Is this an equilibrium situation?

(k) Illustrate the change in the AE and AD functions in the diagrams below.

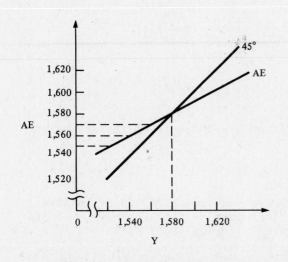
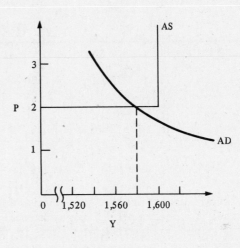

6. The Shape of the Aggregate Demand Curve

(i) The Effects of Changes in the Price Level on Investment

LP SCHEDULE			MEI SCHEDULE	
Rate of	Quantity Demanded		Rate of	
Interest (%)	P = 1	P = 2	Interest (%)	Investment
4	80	100	10	180
6	70	90	11	179
8	60	80	12	177
10	50	70	13	174
12	40	60	14	170
14	30	50		

Assume that the supply of money is fixed at a value of 50.

(a) Assuming the price level is 1.0, what is the interest rate? Investment expenditure?

(b) Assume that for some reason the price level becomes 2.0. For a given level of real income, what will happen to the demand for money? What will happen in the bond market? Explain.

(c)   Using the LP schedule for P = 2, determine the new equilibrium interest rate.

(d)   Given this change in the interest rate, what is the new level of investment expenditure?

(ii)   The Effects of Changes in Investment on Y

Y	C	I (interest = 10%)	AE (r = 10%)	AE (r = 14%)
340	170	180	350	
350	175	180	355	
360	180	180	360	
370	185	180	365	

(e)   What is the equilibrium level of Y associated with an interest rate of 10 percent and a price level of 1.0?

(f)   Given the interest rate increase because of a doubling of the price level, what is the level of investment? Fill in the values for the new level of aggregate expenditure. What is the new equilibrium level of Y?

(iii)   Synthesis: The Relationship Between P and Y
(g)   Plot the inverse relationship between P and Y for this problem. (Use your answers to parts (e) and (f).)

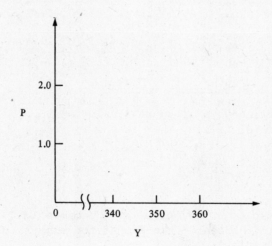

270

Part Eleven

Macroeconomic Policy

The Nature of Unemployment and Inflation

39

KEY CONCEPTS AND DEFINITIONS

1. <u>Voluntary unemployment</u> occurs when there is a job available but the unemployed person is not willing to accept it at the going wage rate for persons now employed.

2. <u>Involuntary unemployment</u> occurs when a person is willing to accept a job at the going wage rate but no such job can be found.

3. There are four major types of unemployment: <u>frictional</u>, <u>structural</u>, <u>deficient-demand</u>, and <u>search</u>.

4. <u>Frictional unemployment</u> is associated with the normal turnover of labour. Persons are frictionally unemployed in the course of finding new jobs.

5. <u>Structural unemployment</u> is said to exist when there is a mismatch between the unemployed and the available jobs. In a sense, structural unemployment is really long-term frictional unemployment.

6. <u>Deficient-demand unemployment</u> occurs because there is insufficient aggregate demand to purchase full-employment output. A useful measure of this is the difference between the number of persons seeking jobs and the number of vacancies.

7. <u>Search unemployment</u> occurs when a person who could find work remains unemployed in order to search for a better offer than he or she has so far received. The basic cause of search unemployment is imperfect information about job opportunities.

8. In the text the authors define <u>inflation</u> as a rise in the price level. The increase may be sustained or nonsustained. Seven causes of inflation are: <u>demand-pull</u>, <u>wage cost-push</u>, <u>price-push</u>, <u>import cost-push</u>, <u>structural rigidity</u>, <u>expectational</u>, and <u>inertial</u>.

9. The <u>demand-pull</u> inflation theory says that changes in prices are caused by changes in aggregate demand. An increase in aggregate demand in a situation of full employment will create excess demand and prices will rise.

10. <u>Supply-side theories</u> of inflation look to shifts in the aggregate supply curve as the initiating cause of inflation. The <u>wage cost-push</u> theory says that rises in wage costs not themselves associated with excess demand are the initiating cause of inflation. The <u>price-push</u> theory is similar to the wage cost-push

theory except that it identifies firm's pricing policies as the initiating cause of inflation. An import cost-push is a rise in a country's price level due to a rise in the prices of important imported goods and services.

11. Structural rigidity, another supply-side theory of inflation, assumes that resources do not move quickly from one use to another. When patterns of demand and costs change, real adjustments occur very slowly and shortages occur in expanding sectors, causing prices to rise.

12. Demand-supply theories of inflation say that the initiating cause of price rises is shifts in aggregate demand, but eventually aggregate supply shifts as well. The two main theories of this type are expectational inflation and inertial inflation.

13. The expectational theory of inflation says that if decision makers expect a certain future inflation they will use this value as a base from which to negotiate price and wage increases in the current time period. In a sense, expectational inflation is forward-looking.

14. Inertial inflation depends on backward-looking comparisons. Wage and price setters look at recent wage settlements and price decisions for closely related labour groups and products when setting their own wages and prices.

15. When inflation is allowed to persist because the government permits the money supply to expand at the same rate as the inflation, economists speak of the inflation as being validated by increases in the money supply. When inflation is not accompanied by increases in the money supply, the inflation is unvalidated.

16. The Phillips curve relates national income to the rate of change in the price level. The AS curve relates national income to the price level.

17. Whenever the economy comes to rest on the intermediate portion of the aggregate supply curve, the curve itself starts to shift upward. As a consequence, increases in output caused by a movement into the intermediate section of the AS curve are transitory as long as the inflation is unvalidated.

18. If demand-pull inflation is validated by monetary expansion, the Phillips curve suggests a long-term trade-off between national income and the rate of inflation. However, the Phelps-Friedman theory states that it is impossible for the economy to sustain a level of Y that is above Y_F in the long run since expectations are formed about price rises. According to this theory, the attempt to hold national income above Y_F leads to an ever-accelerating rate of inflation. How fast it accelerates depends on how fast current inflationary expectations adjust to past actual rates.

19. Stagflation is the coexistence of high rates of inflation and high rates of unemployment.

MULTIPLE-CHOICE QUESTIONS

1. Voluntary unemployment
   (a) occurs when there is a job available at the going wage but the unemployed person is unwilling to accept it
   (b) is of more concern to policy makers than involuntary unemployment
   (c) increases substantially during a deep recession
   (d) occurs when a person is willing to accept a job at the going rate but no such job can be found

2. Unemployment that occurs as a result of the normal turnover of the labour force as people move from job to job is called
   (a) involuntary unemployment
   (b) structural unemployment
   (c) search unemployment
   (d) frictional unemployment

3. Structural unemployment means that
   (a) there is an inadequate number of jobs in the economy
   (b) there are not enough employees
   (c) the building trades workers are suffering from high unemployment rates
   (d) certain resources have been unable to adjust to changing economic conditions

4. Search unemployment
   (a) tends to increase as the costs of search increase
   (b) will tend to be higher with more generous unemployment insurance benefits
   (c) is socially undesirable even if a better job is obtained as a result of additional search
   (d) tends to be reduced as the prevalence of multiworker households increases

5. The unemployment rate is defined as
   (a) the percentage of unemployed to employed workers
   (b) the percentage of the adult population who are unemployed
   (c) the percentage of the labour force who are unemployed
   (d) the percentage of the unemployed who are collecting unemployment insurance

6. Deficient-demand unemployment exists when the number of unemployed is
   (a) greater than the number of available vacancies
   (b) equal to the number of available jobs
   (c) less than the number of available vacancies
   (d) greater than zero

7. Demand-pull inflation occurs when
   (a) aggregate demand is greater than the value of full-employment GNP
   (b) aggregate demand and employment are rising at equivalent rates
   (c) a rise in the demand for goods is coupled with a decrease in demand for factors of production
   (d) aggregate demand exceeds current GNP but is less than potential GNP

8. Which of the following is not a supply-side theory of inflation?
   (a) structural rigidity
   (b) inertial
   (c) import cost-push
   (d) price-push

9. Structural inflation arises when
   (a) the rate of monetary expansion is greater than the demand
   (b) wages in key industrial sectors cause prices to rise
   (c) monopolistic firms raise their prices in order to increase their profits
   (d) shortages appear in potentially expanding sectors and prices rise because the slow movement of resources prevents these sectors from expanding

10. When decision makers raise current wages and prices in anticipation of general price rises during the contract period, it is possible that inflation of the following variety will result.
    (a) inertial
    (b) wage cost-push
    (c) expectational
    (d) price-push

11. The initial consequence of bringing a cost-push inflation to a halt by refusing to increase the money supply will be
    (a) a rise in output
    (b) to accelerate inflation
    (c) to validate the inflation in the short run
    (d) a fall in output

12. If government spending were suddenly reduced, the greatest impact would probably be toward
    (a) reducing price-push inflation
    (b) decreasing the money supply
    (c) reducing demand-pull inflation
    (d) reducing structural inflation

13. The intermediate section of the aggregate supply curve allows in the short run an increase in aggregate demand to generate
    (a) output increases only
    (b) price increases only
    (c) output and price increases
    (d) an increase in full-employment or potential output

14. The Phillips curve shows
    (a) the relation between rate of change of national income and the price level
    (b) the relation between national income and the price level
    (c) the relation between national income and the rate of change in the price level
    (d) the relation betweeen the growth rate in national income and prices

15. The short-run Phillips curve is based on the fact that
    (a) inflation will correct itself through changes in real market forces
    (b) expectations about future inflation are zero
    (c) the natural rate of unemployment is changing
    (d) none of the above

16. The demand-pull component of inflation
    (a) equals actual inflation minus expected inflation
    (b) equals actual inflation plus expected inflation
    (c) occurs only at the natural rate of unemployment
    (d) equals the expected inflation of the last period

17. The adaptive expectations theory assumes that people's expectations of the future inflation rate are based on
    (a) recent inflation rates in the past
    (b) current monetary and fiscal policies
    (c) only the current inflation rate
    (d) a random sample of prediction errors from future expectations

18. Which of the following is not an implication of the Phelps-Friedman theory?
    (a) Monetary policies cannot control inflations in the long run.
    (b) The long-run Phillips curve is vertical at full-employment income.
    (c) The natural rate of unemployment is the only acceptable target for long-run stabilization policy.
    (d) Attempts to reduce unemployment below its natural rate will eventually cause the rate of inflation to accelerate.

EXERCISES

1. Classify the following situations as frictional unemployment, structural unemployment, search unemployment, or deficient-demand unemployment, and briefly explain your choice:
    (a) An auto assemblyman is laid off because auto sales decrease with a slowdown in economic activity.

(b) A chartered accountant is unable to find a job in her current location at an acceptable pay rate.

(c) A social worker is laid off because the government has cancelled the Local Initiatives Program (LIP).

(d) A mechanic in London, Ontario, is laid off when a bus manufacturing firm relocates in Montreal.

(e) A business analyst quits one job and has so far been unsuccessful in finding a new job.

2. What type of government policy would be appropriate for each of the following?
   (a) Demand-pull inflation

   (b) Structural inflation

   (c) Deficient-demand unemployment

   (d) Expectational inflation

3. Suppose that there are two labour markets in an economy, each of which is characterized by a rigid money wage that deviates from the equilibrium wage and a completely inelastic supply curve of labour. The total demand for labour in the economy is the sum of the two demand-for-labour curves in the two markets. The demand for labour is equal to unfilled vacancies plus employment. The supply of labour is equal to employment plus unemployment.

   The initial situation for the demand for labour in each market is given by the superscript 0.

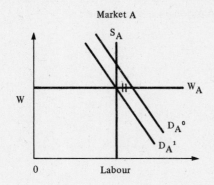

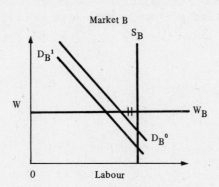

(a) What initial situation exists in market A? In market B?

(b) The authors of the text indicate that a measure of deficient-demand unemployment is unemployment minus job vacancies. Accordingly, what is the level of deficient-demand unemployment at the initial conditions?

(c) What market adjustments might occur to solve the unemployment and unfilled vacancies problem? (Two answers.)

(d) Under what conditions might labour be totally immobile, as is indicated in the example above?

(e) Suppose aggregate demand for labour decreased and this overall decrease was shared equally in the two markets. The situation is depicted by the curves with superscripts [1]. What would happen to the national unemployment rate? Unfilled vacancies? Deficient-demand unemployment?

(f) Suppose that the labour demand curves shifted from D_A^1 to D_A^0 and D_B^1 to D_B^0. What would happen in Market A if the wage was allowed to change? What would happen in Market B? What do you predict will happen to the economy's inflation rate? What type of inflation does this represent?

4. Suppose an economy has an aggregate demand function P = 8 - .02Y, and an aggregate supply function P = 2 (for Y ≤ 300) and Y = 300 (for P ≥ 2). Full-employment income is 300.
    (a) Plot the AD and AS curves in the diagram below and determine the equilibrium levels of Y and P.

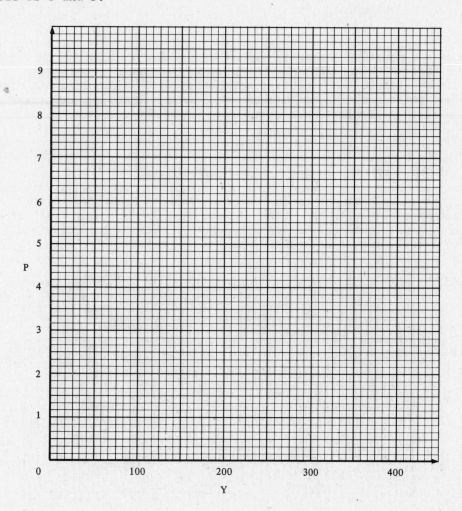

    (b) Suppose that investment expenditure increases such that the aggregate demand function becomes P = 9 - .02Y. Draw this function in the diagram and determine the new equilibrium values for P and Y. What is the inflation rate? What kind of inflation is this?

    (c) What will happen to the AS curve as a result of the demand curve shift? Show this in the diagram.

(d) Because inflation has been generated, suppose that expectations of future inflation change such that the AS curve becomes P = 4 (for Y ≤ 300) and Y = 300 (for P ≥ 4). What will happen to the level of real output?

(e) Suppose the monetary authority wishes to prevent a situation in which real output is less than full employment, as is the case for part (d). It must therefore <u>validate</u> the expectational inflation by increasing the money supply. Determine the new AD curve that will sustain expectational inflation but maintain national income at Y_{FE}.

5. <u>The Phillips Curve and the Phelps-Friedman Hypothesis</u>
   Can an economy permanently have a level of national income that is greater than Y_F and a constant rate of change in the price level? According to the Phelps-Friedman hypothesis, the answer is no. Let us carefully work through this proposition. A particular economy has the following Phillips curve at which expectational inflation is zero ($P_e = 0$).

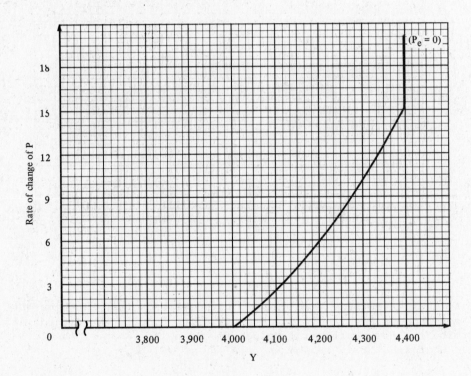

(a) According to the diagram, what is the level of full-employment income? The level of maximum national income? How is it possible for an economy to attain a higher level of national income beyond its full-employment level?

(b) Suppose the monetary authority expands the money supply such that Y increases from 4,000 to 4,200. Does this policy create excess demand or excess supply in the economy? According to the diagram, what will be the rate of change in the price level? What kind of inflation does this represent?

(c) As long as no inflationary expectations are formed by firms and workers and the monetary authority continues to validate this inflation rate, the Phillips curve analysis suggests that the economy can operate at a level of Y greater than Y_F but, of course, with some inflation. However, the Phelps-Friedman hypothesis argues that this situation is only transitory, since workers and firms will form new inflationary expectations when they observe the current inflation rate. What level of inflation will they expect?

(d) Firms will charge higher prices as a consequence. The actual rate of change in the price level is equal to expectational inflation plus demand-pull inflation. What will be the actual inflation rate?

(e) When expectations change at a given level of Y, the Phillips curve shifts upward. Draw the new Phillips curve (with the new expectational inflation) in the diagram on the previous page.

(f) But the process is not yet completed. As long as the monetary authority attempts to keep the economy at Y = 4,200, new expectations will be formed. What will they be? What will happen to the actual inflation rate as a result? What will happen to the Phillips curve?

(g) The process described above suggests that <u>accelerating</u> inflation will occur if the government attempts to maintain a level of national income above Y_F in the long run. What will be the long-run Phillips curve according to the Phelps-Friedman hypothesis? Draw it in the diagram. If inflation does occur, what type of inflation does it represent?

6. Below are data on actual inflation, price expectations, and excess demand inflation.

Time Period	Excess Demand Inflation	Expected Inflation = Previous Period Actual Inflation	Actual Inflation = Excess-Demand Inflation + Expected Inflation
0	0	0	0
1	0	0	0
2	5	0	5
3	5		
4	5	_____	_____
5	5	_____	_____
6	5	_____	_____

(a) It is assumed that expected inflation in any period is equal to actual inflation in the previous period and that actual inflation in a given period equals the excess demand inflation plus the expected inflation in that same period. Complete the table above.

(b) If the persistent excess demand suggested in the table is consistent with a 4-percent rate of unemployment, what would the long-run Phillips curve look like for period 2 through period 6?

(c) If the excess demand were removed after period 6 by, let us say, restrictive fiscal policy, what would happen to expected inflation and the actual rate of inflation?

Macroeconomic Policy and the Balance of Payments

40

KEY CONCEPTS AND DEFINITIONS

1. Persistent balance-of-trade deficits arise for a particular country because (a) the demand elasticity for its exports is less than the demand elasticity for the goods it imports, (b) the country's comparative advantage deteriorates over time, and (c) its inflation rate is greater than the inflation rate in other countries.

2. Use of monetary or fiscal policy to eliminate an inflationary or deflationary gap will also influence the balance of trade. A trade account deficit combined with a deflationary gap poses a conflict because the expansion of Y to eliminate the gap leads to an increase in imports and hence a worsening of the trade deficit. A trade account surplus combined with an inflationary gap also poses a conflict because the contraction of Y to eliminate the gap leads to a reduction in imports and hence an increase in the trade balance surplus.

3. Policies that maintain the level of aggregate desired expenditure but influence its composition between domestic absorption and net exports are called expenditure-switching policies. Policies that change aggregate desired expenditure are called expenditure-changing policies. Both policies operate by influencing domestic absorption, but an expenditure-switching policy also involves an offsetting shift in the net-export function.

4. In a situation of unemployment and a balance-of-trade deficit, expansionary policies (increases in G, lower taxes, or increases in the money supply) of the expenditure-changing variety will lead to a deterioration in the trade balance. These policies should be combined with expenditure-switching policies (tariffs, devaluation) in order to switch domestic absorption into net exports. Thus internal and external balance can be achieved simultaneously.

5. Fiscal policy can indirectly affect the capital-account balance. Increases in G or tax cuts raise national income. With a fixed money supply, interest rates will rise and hence capital inflows will rise and capital outflows will fall. These two improve the capital-account surplus.

6. Since capital flows respond to changes in interest rates, monetary policy will also influence the capital account. A reduction in the money supply will increase domestic interest rates and lead to an increase in capital inflows and a reduction in capital outflows.

7. Under a fixed exchange rate there is very little scope for the use of monetary policy for domestic stabilization purposes. An increase in the money supply (to reduce unemployment) causes capital outflows (depending on the interest elasticity) and this tends to reduce the domestic money supply. To counteract this reduction, the central bank must conduct sterilization policies, which in this case means purchasing bonds.

8. Under a fixed exchange rate, interest-sensitive international capital flows stabilize the domestic interest rate and enhance the effectiveness of fiscal policy.

9. Under a flexible exchange rate, fiscal policy will be offset by a crowding-out effect unless monetary policy accommodates the fiscal policy change. For example, increases in government expenditures, with a fixed money supply, cause interest rates to rise. Depending on the interest elasticity of investment, domestic investment will fall, thus negating the expansionary effect of the fiscal policy.

10. Under a flexible exchange rate, monetary policy is a powerful tool. If capital flows are highly interest elastic and monetary policy is expansionary, the interest rate decline stimulates domestic spending and also increases imports and capital outflows, which in turn cause a depreciation of the exchange rate. This depreciation stimulates exports and decreases imports.

MULTIPLE-CHOICE QUESTIONS

1. Which of the following is likely to cause a country to have a persistent balance-of-trade deficit?
    (a) a lower inflation rate than its trading partners
    (b) an improvement in the country's productive capacity
    (c) a lower elasticity for its exports than the elasticity of the goods it imports
    (d) all of the above

2. A country that has a trade-balance deficit and inflationary gap may solve both problems if
    (a) government expenditures increase
    (b) tax increases are implemented
    (c) tax cuts are put into place
    (d) government expenditures are financed by an increase in the money supply

3. An example of an expenditure-switching policy is
    (a) a reduction in the money supply
    (b) a cut in the personal tax rate
    (c) an increase in defense expenditures
    (d) a tariff on imported goods

4. A conflict arises when an expenditure-changing policy involves a situation in which national income must be
    (a) increased and the trade balance must be reduced
    (b) decreased and the trade balance must be increased
    (c) increased by complementary monetary and fiscal policies
    (d) decreased along with the trade balance

5. If an economy has an inflationary gap and a balance-of-trade surplus, both internal and external balance may be attained if
   (a) a contractionary expenditure-changing policy is combined with an expenditure-switching policy that involves devaluation of the domestic currency
   (b) a contractionary expenditure-changing policy is combined with an expenditure-switching policy that involves a reduction in tariffs
   (c) a contractionary monetary policy is combined with a contractionary fiscal policy
   (d) a contractionary expenditure-changing policy is combined with an expenditure-switching policy that involves export subsidies

6. The capital account is affected by an expansion in government expenditures because
   (a) foreign-produced defense equipment is purchased by the federal government
   (b) national income will increase and domestic households will travel abroad more frequently
   (c) a current-account surplus that is generated by the fiscal policy change must necessarily affect the capital account since the balance of payments must balance
   (d) an increase in the rate of interest, assuming a fixed money supply, will trigger additional capital inflows.

7. To solve a capital-account deficit, the central bank should
   (a) buy bonds in the open market
   (b) increase bank reserves
   (c) sell bonds in the open market
   (d) reduce interest rates when foreign central banks raise their interest rates

8. To sterilize the monetary effects of balance-of-payments deficit under a fixed exchange regime, the central bank should
   (a) sell bonds in the open market
   (b) increase the price of bonds by open-market operations
   (c) decrease the price of bonds by open-market operations
   (d) decrease reserves of the banks

9. The effectiveness of monetary policy to solve domestic unemployment when the country is committed to maintain the foreign price of its currency is
   (a) severely reduced because capital outflows will counteract the expansionary monetary policies
   (b) significantly increased because capital inflows will increase thereby adding to the monetary expansion
   (c) as effective as monetary expansion under flexible exchange rates
   (d) powerful because a central bank can indefinitely sterilize any balance-of-payment deficit that may result from an expansion in the money supply

10. The effectiveness of expansionary fiscal policy is enhanced under a fixed exchange rate if
   (a) international capital flows are interest-sensitive
   (b) international capital flows are perfectly interest-inelastic
   (c) the money supply is not allowed to change
   (d) the money supply is simultaneously reduced

11. Suppose a country is operating under a flexible exchange rate and has a deflationary gap problem. An expansionary monetary policy, assuming that capital flows are interest-sensitive, will cause
    (a) imports to rise initially, capital to flow into the country, and the exchange rate to be unaffected
    (b) a capital-account deficit and the exchange rate to appreciate
    (c) an initial current-account deficit, a capital-account deficit, the exchange rate to depreciate, and hence the balance of payments to ultimately be restored
    (d) an initial current-account deficit, a capital outflow, the exchange rate to depreciate, but unfortunately the balance of payments ultimately to be in a deficit overall position

12. Assuming capital flows are totally insensitive to interest rates, the domestic money supply is constant, a flexible exchange rate exists and there is a deflationary gap, a government policy of tax cuts will cause
    (a) income to increase only slightly because the crowding-out effect prevents the exchange rate from depreciating
    (b) income to increase only slightly because the crowding-out effect causes an exchange rate appreciation
    (c) increases in income, and since the crowding-out effect is absent, the exchange rate will depreciate
    (d) income to increase greatly because the crowding-out effect reinforces the exchange rate depreciation

13. In order to counteract the countervailing influence of the crowding-out effect, an expansionary fiscal policy should be accompanied by a(n)
    (a) contractionary monetary policy
    (b) purchase of bonds by the central bank on the open market
    (c) increase in the secondary-reserve requirement
    (d) monetary-base rule that increases the interest rate

EXERCISES

1. Assume that Canada, which is considered to be on a fixed exchange rate system, experiences a balance-of-payments surplus because of increased sales of natural gas to the United States. Americans are assumed to pay Canadians in U.S. dollars, and the Canadian exporting firms wish to convert U.S. dollars into Canadian dollars. Suppose the sale of natural gas is the equivalent of $40 million Canadian dollars.

Public:

Assets		Liabilities
Foreign currency	_____	
Deposits	_____	

Chartered Banks:

Assets		Liabilities	
Reserves with Bank of Canada	_____	Deposits	_____

Bank of Canada:

Assets		Liabilities	
Foreign currency	_____	Chartered bank deposits	_____

(a) Americans pay Canadian exporting firms in U.S. dollars assumed to be the equivalent of $40 million (Canadian). Canadian firms wish to convert this amount into deposits at Canadian banks. Show the effect of this transaction in the balance sheet of the public.

(b) Banks, having purchased the U.S. dollars from firms, wish to sell the $40 million to the Bank of Canada. How does the Bank of Canada pay for these U.S. dollars? Show this transaction in the Bank of Canada's balance sheet.

(c) Finally, after the Bank of Canada has purchased the U.S. dollars from the banks, show the effect on the chartered banks' balance sheet.

(d) What do you predict will finally happen to the level of deposits in the banking system if the cash reserve ratio is .1 and there is no cash drain?

(e) You should have concluded that the money supply (deposits) increases by a multiple. If the Bank of Canada wishes to sterilize this increase, what should it do--buy or sell bonds to the banks?

2. The economy of Man trades with other nations but no international capital flows into or out of Man. The current price levels of goods produced in Man and in other countries are 2.0 and 1.0 (in foreign currency), respectively. The exchange rate that is fixed is 2 units of Man's currency per unit of foreign currency. Hence the current terms of trade, (R), is 1.0. The behavioural relationships in Man are:

$$
\begin{array}{ll}
\text{(i)} & C = 80 + .6Y \\
\text{(ii)} & I + G = 40 \\
\text{(iii)} & X = 80 - 20R \\
\text{(iv)} & M = .1Y + 30R \\
\text{(v)} & Y_{FE} = 310
\end{array}
$$

(a) Formulate the equation for AE. For domestic absorption (A). (Refer to Chapter 33.) What is the marginal propensity to spend?

(b) Using the equilibrium condition Y = AE, calculate the equilibrium value of Y. At this level of Y, calculate the values of A and net exports.

(c) A deflationary gap of _____ exists in Man although the balance of trade is balanced (X - M = 0). What <u>specific expenditure-increasing</u> policy with respect to G would you recommend in order to eliminate unemployment? You may assume that Man's price level doesn't change.

285

(d) Your expenditure-increasing policy has generated a trade-balance deficit of _____ when national income is at its full-employment level. At Y_{FE}, domestic absorption is _____ .

(e) To achieve both internal balance ($Y = Y_{FE}$) and external balance ($X - M = 0$), an <u>expenditure-switching</u> policy must complement an expenditure-increasing policy. Specifically, since $X - M$ is negative at Y_F, the net-export function must be shifted (<u>upward/downward</u>) so that $X - M = 0$ at Y_{FE}. To achieve external balance it is clear that the value of R must be (<u>increased/decreased</u>). This may be accomplished by (<u>devaluing/revaluing</u>) Man's currency in the foreign exchange market.

(f) Suppose that the government of Man devalues its currency so that the exchange rate rises from 2.0 to 2.04 and at the same time increases government expenditures by 4 ($I + G = 44$). Will this combined policy achieve internal and external balance? What is the value of domestic absorption at the new equilibrium level of income?

3. <u>Monetary Policy Under Flexible Rates</u>
This exercise is designed to reinforce your understanding of the analyses associated with Figure 40-2 in the text. Initial conditions have a subscript "0."

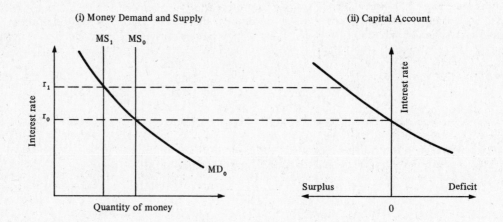

(i) Money Demand and Supply   (ii) Capital Account

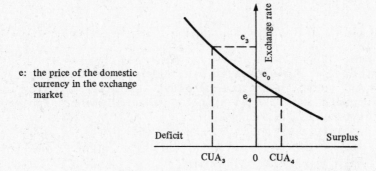

(iii) Current Account

e: the price of the domestic currency in the exchange market

(a) Explain why the capital-account curve is downward sloping.

(b) At an interest rate of r_0, what is the capital-account balance? If the international reserve position at the central bank is not changing, what is implied about the current-account balance?

(c) In fact, the diagram in panel (iii) indicates that at an exchange rate of e_0 the current-account balance is _____ . Why is the current-account curve downward sloping with respect to the exchange rate?

(d) If you had difficulty answering part (c), perhaps your comprehension may be enhanced if you analyze the diagram that underlies the panel (iii) diagram.

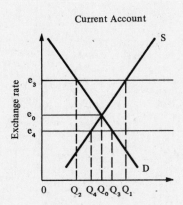

Current Account

Quantity of domestic currency

Answer the following questions:

(i) At e_0, the current account is in a (deficit/surplus/balanced) position.

(ii) At e_3, the quantity demanded of domestic currency is _____ and the quantity supplied is _____ . This represents a situation of a current-account (balance/surplus/deficit) of the magnitude _____ . This amount is exactly equal to the quantity CUA_3 in panel (iii).

(iii) At e_4, the quantity demanded of domestic currency is _____ and the quantity supplied is _____ . This represents a current-account (balance/surplus/deficit) of the magnitude _____ . This amount is exactly equal to the quantity CUA_4 in panel (iii).

287

(e) Suppose the money supply decreases to MS_1 because the central bank (<u>sold/purchased</u>) bonds in the open market. As a result, the equilibrium interest rate (<u>rises/falls</u>) to _____ . This change in the interest rate will lead to more capital (<u>inflows/outflows</u>), and hence the capital account will go into a (<u>balance/surplus/deficit</u>) position. Illustrate the amount in panel (ii).

(f) Because of the capital-account position, the exchange rate will (<u>remain constant/appreciate/depreciate</u>) to a level of e_3, and as a result the quantity demanded for exports will (<u>remain constant/decrease/increase</u>) and the quantity demanded for imports will (<u>remain constant/decrease/increase</u>). The resulting current-account (<u>balance/surplus/deficit</u>) exactly equals the capital-account (<u>balance/surplus/deficit</u>), thereby generating equilibrium in the balance of payments.

<u>Note</u>: Readers should have noted that these diagrams as well as those in Figure 40-2 in the text have been drawn on the assumption that changes in the level of national income do not cause shifts in the curves.

Macroeconomic Experience | 41

KEY CONCEPTS AND DEFINITIONS

1. The period of the 1930s and 1940s seemed to support Keynesian theories: (1) The main problem facing the depression years of the 1930s was a deficiency in aggregate demand; (2) Excess demand at full-employment income in the 1940s was the cause of inflation; (3) Price controls (during the war) designed to suppress demand-pull inflation were a temporary expedient at best. Factors (1) and (2) led to the conclusion that <u>fiscal policy</u> was an effective tool to solve GNP gaps and suppress inflation.

2. Countercyclical fiscal policy, combined with a flexible exchange rate system, was implemented in the 1950s. However, toward the end of the decade there was a tendency for the price level to rise despite a significant GNP gap. This seemed to imply a spontaneous <u>upward shift</u> in the horizontal portion of the <u>AS curve</u>, not associated with any excess demand.

3. Various explanations included structural rigidity and wage cost-push hypotheses. The experience of the late 1950s forced economists to regard the kinked AS curve as an inadequate description of the supply side of the economy. An intermediate section over which the price level and national income could vary simultaneously was suggested. However, the realization that the AS curve would continue to <u>shift upward</u> when equilibrium was on its rising portion and that the AD curve would have to be <u>shifted right</u> by monetary policy to prevent national income from falling led to the formulation of the <u>Phillips curve</u>.

4. The Phillips curve shows an apparent trade-off between national income and inflation; to increase national income is at the cost of more inflation.

5. In the early 1960s, the money supply was expanded and fiscal policy was expansionary. National income expanded because of the expansionary policies, and because a depreciated Canadian dollar increased exports. By 1966, unemployment was low but the inflation rate increased. Hence, the experience of the 1960s seemed to confirm the notion of a stable trade-off between inflation and unemployment and to establish confidence in stabilization macroeconomic policies.

6. In the late 1960s anti-inflationary policies were pursued mainly by a contractionary monetary policy. This led to a significant balance-of-payments surplus, which meant that the Bank of Canada had difficulty in maintaining a

fixed exchange rate. The attempt to inflate at a slower rate of inflation was incompatible with fixed exchange rates; in the face of a high balance-of-payments surplus either the economy had to be expanded faster or the exchange rate had to be freed. The latter was chosen in 1970.

7. However, the Bank of Canada embarked on a policy of a dirty float. Although the Bank was not committed to an explicit value of the Canadian dollar, it pursued policies that prevented the exchange rate from appreciating as much as market forces would have dictated. It did this by setting a low interest-rate target, and hence monetary expansion was high. Canada, therefore, imported U.S. inflation. Although economic activity increased sharply between 1970 and 1973, the unemployment rate barely fell at all and policy-makers wondered what had happened to the Phillips curve.

8. The Phillips curve began to shift upward; a higher inflation rate was associated with a given level of national income. One explanation for this phenomenon was provided by Professors Phelps and Friedman who argued that attempts to maintain national income above its full-employment level (or below the natural rate of unemployment) cause an accelerating inflation. The Phelps-Friedman theory also provided an explanation for bouts of stagflation: strong inflationary expectations can sustain the inflation rate, and rising expectations can increase it temporarily in the face of declining demand and output and hence rising unemployment.

9. In 1973 and 1974 the Canadian economy (as well as most others) experienced severe supply-side shocks; the AS curve shifted upward partly due to OPEC oil-price increases and embargoes and partly due to rising prices of agricultural goods.

10. Because OPEC countries allocated their substantially increased revenues to the purchase of short-term financial securities, gold, and land rather than of currently produced goods, the U.S. aggregate demand curve shifted leftward. Thus the combination of an upward shifting AS curve and a leftward shift in the AD curve led to high inflation and falling U.S. national income (rising unemployment). However, some of the contractionary national income forces were counteracted in Canada by expansionary monetary and fiscal policies. Nevertheless, a low rate of unemployment was accompanied by a high rate of inflation.

11. In the period 1975-1978, persistently high inflation was accompanied by rising unemployment. Canadian policy-makers expected an accelerating wage-push inflation, and hence wage-price controls were initiated in 1975. An Anti-Inflation Board (AIB) was set up with power to control wages and prices for three years. At the same time, the Bank of Canada began to focus on the rate of growth of the money supply, and announced its intention to lower the rate of monetary expansion very slowly. This policy is termed monetary gradualism.

12. The AIB had perhaps its strongest impact on slowing the rate of increases in wages in the public sector. However, the AIB did not control prices directly. It influenced them indirectly by monitoring profits. The controls seemed to have redistributed income from wages to profits.

13. The experience of the last fifty years shows that policy-makers are able to manipulate the AD curve. However, how the effects of a change of AD are distributed between changes in output, real income, and employment on the one hand and inflation on the other is still an unresolved issue.

MULTIPLE-CHOICE QUESTIONS

1. The high unemployment experience of the 1930s indicated that the appropriate public policy stance was
   (a) an expansionary aggregate demand policy
   (b) an outward shift in the AS curve in order to increase output capacity
   (c) a contractionary monetary policy
   (d) permanent wage and price control policies to arrest inflation

2. During the period 1950 to mid-1962, Canada pursued
   (a) a fixed exchange rate policy
   (b) a "dirty float" exchange rate policy
   (c) an exchange rate policy that was characterized by the Bretton Woods agreement
   (d) a flexible exchange rate policy

3. The Phillips curve theory suggested that a reduction in the inflation rate necessitated
   (a) a rise in real output
   (b) a rise in unemployment
   (c) a fall in unemployment
   (d) no sacrifice in real output because the economy was on the vertical portion of the AS curve

4. If the money supply is increased under flexible exchange rates,
   (a) capital inflows occur and the exchange rate appreciates
   (b) the balance-of-trade deficit declines and the exchange rate depreciates
   (c) capital outflows occur and the exchange rate depreciates
   (d) the balance-of-trade deficit is matched by a capital-account surplus

5. Because of a persistent capital-account surplus, in 1970 the Government of Canada
   (a) reiterated its resolve to keep the Canadian dollar at 92.5 cents U.S.
   (b) continued to sell Canadian dollars in the foreign exchange market
   (c) reverted to a floating exchange rate
   (d) revalued the Canadian dollar

6. In order to prevent the Canadian dollar from appreciating in world markets, the Bank of Canada could
   (a) buy Canadian dollars in the exchange market
   (b) sell bonds to foreigners
   (c) purchase bonds from the public
   (d) pursue a higher interest rate than most other countries

7. The period of the 1970s in Canada suggested that the Phillips curve had
   (a) remained the same as in previous periods
   (b) shifted upward to the left
   (c) shifted to the right
   (d) changed such that a higher inflation rate was associated with lower levels of unemployment

8. The Phelps-Friedman hypothesis suggested that
   (a) government attempts to maintain a level of Y above Y_F caused decelerating inflation
   (b) stagflation could never occur in the short run
   (c) a long-run trade-off existed between inflation and real income, but this relationship breaks down in the short run
   (d) stagflation in the short run is possible because of inflationary expectations

9. Assuming that the AD curve is stable, an upward shift in the AS curve causes
   (a) only an increase in inflation
   (b) an increase in unemployment and inflation
   (c) an increase in real output and inflation
   (d) an elimination of a stagflationary period

10. The experience of the Canadian and American economies during the stagflation of 1974-1975 suggests that Canadian output fell less than U.S. output because
    (a) Canadian monetary expansion was much greater than that of the United States
    (b) the Canadian economy did not suffer the same supply-side shocks
    (c) the inflation rate in Canada did not increase as much as the U.S. inflation rate
    (d) wage-price controls were imposed in 1974

11. Monetary gradualism refers to a policy stance in which a central bank
    (a) reduces monetary expansion very slowly
    (b) allows the money supply to decrease for a period of time and then reverses this process gradually
    (c) allows near monies to gradually replace traditional forms of money
    (d) validates inflation gradually

12. Which of the following was not a feature of the AIB?
    (a) Price freezes were applied to essential food items.
    (b) Price changes were indirectly influenced by monitoring profits.
    (c) Wage increases in the public sector were suppressed.
    (d) The majority of wage contracts in the private sector had to be approved by the AIB.

EXERCISES

1. Depression Macroeconomics
   Suppose that an economy has the aggregate supply curve depicted below. Its AD curve is given by the schedule at the right.

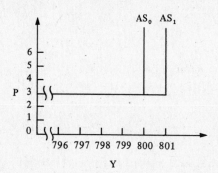

AGGREGATE DEMAND	
Price Level	Real Output (Y)
1	800
2	799
3	798
4	797
5	796

   (a) What are the equilibrium levels of P and Y using the AS curve labeled AS_0? Plot the AD curve in the diagram above.

   (b) What is the value of the GNP gap? If the AS curve becomes AS_1, what is the value of the GNP gap?

   (c) Assume the AS curve labeled AS_0 applies. To solve this gap problem without generating inflation, government expenditure should be (increased/decreased) such that the AD curve shifts (right/left) in order to intersect the AS curve at a level of national income of _____. Show this policy change in the diagram above.

292

(d) However, suppose the government actually increases expenditure such that the new AD curve is given by the expression P = 804 - Y. What are the equilibrium values of P and Y? What will happen to the AS curve? Show this in the diagram.

2. The Canadian Phillips Curve, 1949-1970
As you have seen, the Phillips curve is a relationship between inflation and the level of real national income. However, the Phillips curve can be drawn in several other forms. It can be drawn as a relationship between inflation and the percentage of the labour force employed or the unemployment rate. You are given the data below for the period of 1949-1970.

Year	Percent Change in the CPI	Percent of the Labour Force Employed	Unemployment Rate (%)
1949	3.1	97.2	2.6
1950	2.8	96.4	3.2
1951	10.6	97.6	2.0
1952	2.5	97.1	2.4
1953	-0.9	97.0	2.5
1954	0.6	95.4	4.3
1955	0.2	95.6	4.1
1956	1.4	96.6	3.1
1957	3.2	95.4	4.3
1958	2.7	93.0	6.6
1959	1.1	94.0	5.6
1960	1.2	93.0	7.0
1961	0.9	92.9	7.1
1962	1.2	94.1	5.9
1963	1.7	94.5	5.5
1964	1.8	95.3	4.7
1965	2.5	96.1	3.9
1966	3.7	96.4	3.6
1967	3.6	95.9	4.1
1968	4.1	95.1	4.8
1969	4.5	95.3	4.7
1970	3.3	94.1	5.0

(a) According to the data, in what ways was the period 1957-1970 different from the period prior to it?

(b) As employment expanded from 1962 to 1966, what happened to the inflation rate? What kind of inflation does this represent?

(c) Plot the scatter diagram for the relationship between inflation and the employment rate for the period 1960-1970 in the accompanying graph. Plot the Phillips curve between inflation and the unemployment rate. You should have noticed that there is a direct relationship between the employment rate and the inflation rate and an inverse relationship between inflation and the unemployment rate.

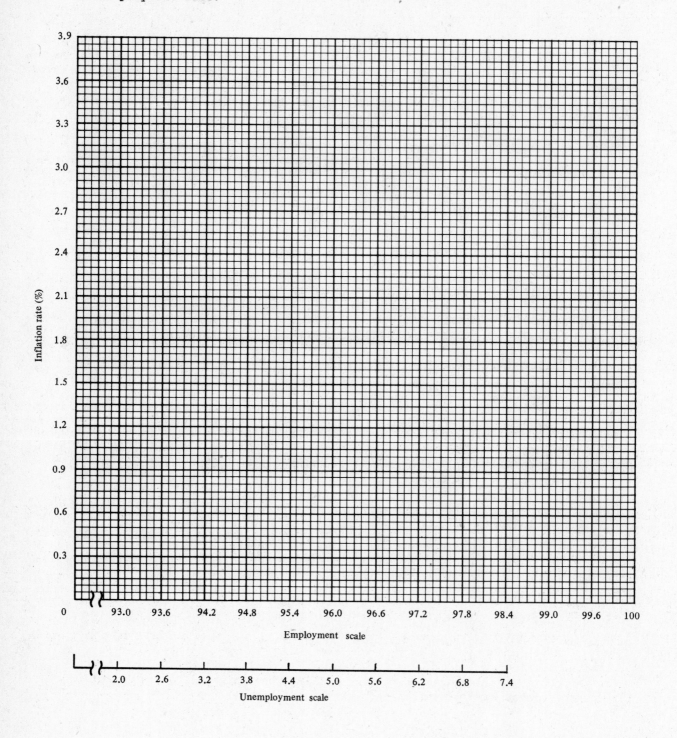

294

3. Suppose the initial conditions in an economy are as depicted below. Explain how each of the following events is likely to influence the price level and real national income. Indicate what curve is affected.

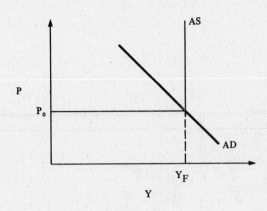

(a) An increase in the price of imported goods.

(b) A major cut in personal taxes.

(c) Wage cost-push inflation that is validated by monetary policy.

(d) A decrease in exports.

(e) An increase in the productive capacity of the economy that increases the value of Y_F.

(f) A permanent increase in the money supply and the imposition of temporary price controls at P_0.

42

Current Issues in Macroeconomic Policy

KEY CONCEPTS AND DEFINITIONS

1. There are two extreme views of macroeconomic policies. The _monetarist_ view (or _monetarism_) is that the economy tends to be relatively self-regulating and hence will naturally tend toward full employment and a relatively stable price level. Government stabilization policies should take a stable stance. Monetarism points to variations in the money supply as the major cause of recessions and inflations. The _Keynesian_ (or neo-Keynesian) view maintains that the free-enterprise economy has weak self-regulatory powers. Active government is therefore vital.

2. All major theories agree that monetary restraint is a _necessary condition_ for slowing inflation. Monetarists believe that the control of the money supply is a sufficient as well as a necessary condition for controlling inflation. An inflationary process triggered by expectations can ultimately be eliminated if the money supply is held constant. The economy will undergo a temporary recession and eventually expectational inflation will cease. Then the money supply can be expanded cautiously to move the economy to full employment without inflation.

3. Neo-Keynesians argue that the process in 2 takes a long time and is much more painful than monetarists suggest. They argue that the increase in unemployment is very large in order to reduce inflation by a small amount. Neo-Keynesians' cures involve the same monetary restraint that monetarists advocate but include an additional technique: _incomes policies_.

4. Incomes policies are any form of direct or indirect intervention by the government into wage-price formation with a view to influencing the rate of inflation. They include wage and price controls and tax incentive programs.

5. _Tax-based incomes policies (TIPs)_, a neo-Keynesian policy, provide tax incentives for management and labour to conform to government-established wage and price guidelines. Increases in wages and prices in excess of the guideline rates are taxed heavily, thereby making firms and unions reluctant to engage in inflation-producing behaviour.

6. Post-Keynesians contend that an upward shift in the AS curve is caused by wage-cost, price-push, and various structural rigidities. These forces will not subside by contractionary monetary policies. Thus, post-Keynesians advocate permanent wage and price controls or TIPS.

7. Monetarists and neo-Keynesians disagree as to the main causes of cyclical fluctuations. Monetarists believe that the major source of business cycles is monetary fluctuations. Major recessions are associated with absolute declines in the money supply and minor recessions with the slowing of the rate of increase in the money supply below its long-term trend. Neo-Keynesian theory emphasizes variations in investment as a cause of business cycles and stresses nonmonetary causes of such variations. In addition, neo-Keynesians believe that an economy may settle into an underemployment equilibrium, where it may stay for a long time unless it is forced out by an active stabilization policy.

8. For neo-Keynesians, fluctuations in national income cause fluctuations in the money supply. This causality is completely opposite to that of monetarists. The neo-Keynesian position stems from the fact that most central banks have pursued an interest-rate target. Thus central banks increase the money supply in upswings and decrease it in downturns.

9. Monetarists believe that national income can be influenced strongly by monetary policy and only weakly by fiscal policy. Keynesians believe that fiscal policy may be more potent than monetary policy. The difference in views hinges on the interest-elasticity of the demand for money and the interest-elasticity of investment expenditure.

10. Keynesians believe that the demand for money is sensitive to interest rates while monetarists believe it is insensitive to interest rates. The reverse holds for investment expenditure; monetarists believe that investment expenditure is highly sensitive to interest rates.

11. Because of the different views regarding interest sensitivity of the demand for money and investment expenditure, monetarists and Keynesians disagree about the effectiveness of monetary policy. Monetarists argue that changes in the money supply cause large changes in the interest rate, which in turn cause large changes in investment expenditure.

12. There is significant disagreement about the effectiveness of fiscal policy. According to the monetarists, changes in government expenditure will induce large increases in the interest rate that in turn cause large offsetting changes in investment expenditure. This reduction in investment is called the crowding-out effect. Neo-Keynesians argue that the crowding-out effect is small when the economy is suffering from a substantial GNP gap.

13. The monetarist macro model is based on a microeconomic model of competitive, full-clearing markets. The only equilibrium of all markets is one of full employment. Departure from this norm occurs because people make mistakes in predicting the price level. According to the theory of rational expectations, people do not make persistent, systematic errors in predicting the overall inflation rate; however, they may make unsystematic errors. Thus there is no need for systematic stabilization policy.

14. The neo-Keynesian model assumes that wages and prices are relatively rigid over the cycle and are not market clearing. Fluctuations in demand cause fluctuations in employment and production (rather than prices) because prices are fixed and firms and labour groups will sell what they can at the going price. Thus, because long systematic disturbances may exist, there is room for offsetting stabilization policies.

15. In the monetarist model, all unemployment is voluntary. Workers decide to be unemployed as a result of the errors they make in predicting the general price level. In the Keynesian model, since wages are assumed rigid, unemployment is involuntary in the sense that unemployed workers would like a job at the going wage rate but cannot find one.

16. The amount of unemployment occurring at Y_F is called the natural rate of unemployment.

297

APPENDIX TO CHAPTER 42

A.1. Since monetarists believe that the interest-elasticity of investment is high, the IS curve becomes relatively flat. The IS curve is relatively steep according to neo-Keynesians.

A.2. According to the monetarists, the LM curve is steep; neo-Keynesians believe that it is relatively flat.

A.3. The different views regarding the shapes of the IS and LM curves generate different views concerning the efficacy of stabilization policy. Given the neo-Keynesian views, the effects of fiscal policy are mainly felt in relatively large changes in national income and relatively small changes in the interest rate. The monetarists believe that fiscal policy has a large effect on interest rates, with little change in national income.

A.4. Given the monetarists' views regarding the shapes of the two curves, the effects of monetary policy are mainly felt in large changes in national income and in the interest rate. Neo-Keynesians believe that monetary policy has a small effect on the interest rate and on national income.

A.5. The neo-Keynesian view (that shifts in the LM curve, which change the price level, have little influence on Y), implies that the AD curve is relatively steep. In addition, fiscal policy leads to large changes in Y while monetary policy leads to only very small changes.

A.6. Monetarists' views imply that the AD curve is relatively flat. Fiscal policy leads to only small shifts in the AD curve while monetary policy leads to large shifts.

MULTIPLE-CHOICE QUESTIONS

1. In the view of the monetarist group of economists,
   (a) changes in the money supply should be used often as a countercyclical tool
   (b) interest rates have very little effect on spending
   (c) the economy will not recover by itself from recessions
   (d) inflation is caused by excessive increases in the supply of money

2. The economists called neo-Keynesians in this chapter
   (a) do not agree with Keynes that investment spending is important in causing a rise in national income
   (b) believe that fiscal policy is a more effective stabilization tool than monetary policy
   (c) are opposed entirely to the use of monetary policy
   (d) believe that investment spending is very interest-elastic

3. The monetary policy advocated by the monetarists
   (a) is one of growth in the money supply at about the rate of growth of real GNP
   (b) would use controls on the changes in interest rates to affect GNP
   (c) would be determined primarily by Parliament
   (d) includes the active use of fiscal policy as well

4. According to the monetarists, the cure for inflation that is caused by an upward shift in the AS curve is
   (a) to impose permanent wage controls
   (b) to tax companies that make excessive profits
   (c) to validate this inflation by increasing the money supply
   (d) to keep the money supply constant until the cause of the initial supply-side inflation has terminated

5. Neo-Keynesians have little faith in expansionary monetary policy because
   (a) they feel that the government is ill-equipped to predict future economic conditions
   (b) they believe that the interest-elastic demand and supply of money will offset the effect of open-market policy on the rate of interest, and hence on national income
   (c) banks will usually maintain only required reserves and thus are responsive to Bank of Canada policy changes
   (d) they believe that since the demand for money is highly interest-elastic and aggregate expenditure is interest-inelastic, the Bank of Canada can induce only small changes in the interest rate, which, in turn, will have a small effect on aggregate expenditure

6. According to Keynesians, active government stabilization policies are warranted because
   (a) an unemployment equilibrium is possible
   (b) cyclical fluctuations are often systematic
   (c) wages and prices are rigid and are not likely to clear markets quickly or at all
   (d) any of the above

7. Because a very large increase in unemployment appears to be required to achieve a small reduction in expectational or inertial inflation, neo-Keynesians argue that
   (a) the economy will have to "bite the bullet" and endure a long recession until inflation has subsided
   (b) permanent wage and price controls must be imposed to stop inflation
   (c) money restraint should be combined with temporary incomes policies
   (d) the price of the domestic currency in world markets should be revalued upward

8. Which of the following is <u>not</u> an argument of supply-side economics?
   (a) The money supply is endogenous and determined by national income.
   (b) Tax cuts may stimulate persons to work more.
   (c) Eliminating certain welfare programs may encourage labour mobility.
   (d) Government regulations that apply to private firms should be reduced.

9. Monetarists believe that a small reduction in the interest rate will
   (a) greatly increase the quantity of money demanded
   (b) increase investment expenditure by a significant amount
   (c) be caused by a substantial increase in the money supply
   (d) not affect national income because of the crowding-out effect

10. The crowding-out effect may apply when increases in government expenditure cause
    (a) significant inflows of migrants into crowded urban centers
    (b) national income increases that eliminate net-export surpluses
    (c) interest rates to fall, thus causing households to buy stocks rather than government bonds
    (d) interest rates to rise, thereby choking off investment expenditure

11. According to the micro foundations of neo-Keynesian theory, wage rigidities arise because
    (a) workers who are prone to unemployment will insist on fixed wages regardless of the phase of the business cycle
    (b) workers who are relatively immune to unemployment wish contracts that reduce the variability of wages over the cycle
    (c) people are temporarily fooled by unexpected wage decreases and hence become voluntarily unemployed
    (d) all of the above

12. An attempt to arrest rising structural unemployment by increasing aggregate demand will
    (a) lead to an inflation accompanying the rising level of unemployment
    (b) reduce national unemployment and therefore, by definition, reduce structural unemployment
    (c) increase Y_F and thus reduce structural unemployment
    (d) cause prices to fall because the economy becomes more efficient

APPENDIX

A.1. A Keynesian view is that the LM curve is
    (a) relatively steep because prices are constant
    (b) relatively flat because income is constant
    (c) relatively flat because the demand for money is highly sensitive to interest rates
    (d) relatively steep because the demand for money is insensitive to interest rates

A.2. A monetarist view is that the IS curve is
    (a) relatively flat because investment expenditure is highly sensitive to interest rates
    (b) relatively steep because investment expenditure is insensitive to interest rates
    (c) relatively flat because prices are constant
    (d) relatively steep because income is constant

A.3. The AD curve will shift further to the right when taxes are cut than when the money supply is increased according to
    (a) both monetarists and Keynesians
    (b) monetarists
    (c) Keynesians
    (d) the rational-expectations hypothesis

EXERCISES

1. Insert an M for monetarist or a K for neo-Keynesian after the statements below.
    (a) The demand for money, especially for the speculative motive, can be quite sensitive to interest rates. _____
    (b) The demand for money is quite insensitive to interest rates but depends mostly on income and the demand for transactions balances. _____
    (c) The cause of inflation and changes in national income is found primarily in changes in the supply of money. _____
    (d) The only equilibrium of all markets is one of full employment. Departures from this are random movements. _____
    (e) Changes in the money supply may be a response to, rather than the cause of, changes in GNP and the price level. _____
    (f) Expansionary fiscal policy only works to the extent that it is financed by monetary expansion. _____
    (g) Because the crowding-out effect is large, fiscal policy is relatively ineffective in changing the level of real GNP. _____
    (h) Contraction of the money supply raises interest rates, but the small rise in interest rates does not do very much to discourage expenditures. _____
    (i) Wages and prices tend to be rigid over cyclical fluctuations in national income. _____
    (j) Fiscal policy has more general effects on the economy, whereas monetary policy affects primarily interest rates and therefore has too much effect on housing and small businesses. _____

2. The Crowding-out Effect
    Suppose that the federal government decides to increase its expenditures by $500
    million permanently. Prices and the exchange rates are assumed constant. The
    marginal propensity to spend is .5, potential GNP is $151 billion, and current
    equilibrium GNP is $150 billion.
    (a) What type of gap exists and what is its magnitude?

    (b) The government assumes that the interest rate will not change due to its
         policy change. If this assumption is correct, will the increase in G solve
         the gap problem?

    (c) In fact, suppose that the demand for money equation is given by the expression
         $D_M = .8Y - 2i$, where Y stands for GNP and i represents the level of the
         interest rate in percentage terms. If the current money supply is $100
         billion and Y = 150, solve for the level of i.

    (d) If the government's policy raised real GNP to $151 billion, what would be the
         effect on the level of the interest rate?

    (e) Suppose you know that every increase in the interest rate of .1 decreased
         investment expenditures by $125 million. Given your answer to part (d),
         what is the total effect on investment expenditures?

    (f) Instead of the relationship given in (e), suppose that for every increase
         in the interest rate of .1, expenditure fell by $25 million. Given your
         answer to part (d), what is the total effect on investment expenditure now?

    (g) What is the extent of the crowding-out effect in part (e)? Part (f)? Which
         result is most likely to reflect the monetarist view?

3. The Association Between the Money Supply and National Income: The Neo-Keynesian View

Most economists agree that the money supply and national income move together through time, but the direction of causality is a matter of considerable debate. Suppose that the demand for money equation is $D_M = .8Y - 2i$, where i is the interest rate. The current (real) money supply is 60 and national income is 100.

(a) What is the current rate of interest? Assume that the central bank is committed to this level regardless of the level of national income.

(b) Suppose that net exports increase such that national income rises from 100 to 101. If interest rates are allowed to change, what is the new equilibrium level of interest rates?

(c) However, given the central bank's policy, what change in the money supply is necessary? As you have seen, the money supply change is caused by an interest-rate target policy and an increase in national income.

4. Monetary Policy: Monetarists Versus Keynesians

You are given two investment schedules and two demand-for-money schedules.

Interest Rate (%)	Demand for Money		Investment	
	Quantity of Money		Investment Expenditure	
	Case A	Case B	Case A	Case B
4	460	412	106	220
5	450	410	105	200
8	420	404	102	140
9	410	402	101	120
10	400	400	100	100
12	380	396	98	60

(a) If the money supply is 400, what are the equilibrium values for the demand for money and investment in both cases? What is the interest rate?

(b) Calculate the (arc) interest elasticity of demand for money between interest rates of 10 percent and 12 percent for Case A and Case B. Which case is likely to represent the monetarist view?

(c) Calculate the (arc) interest elasticity of investment expenditure between interest rates of 10 percent and 12 percent for Case A and Case B. Which case is likely to represent the Keynesian view?

(d) Suppose the money supply increased from 400 to 410. What is the new equilibrium interest rate for Case A? Case B?

(e) Assuming you were a proponent of the monetarist school and referring to Cases A and B, what change in investment expenditure would you predict? If you were a Keynesian?

Part Twelve

Economic Growth and Comparative Systems

Growth in Developed Economies

43

KEY CONCEPTS AND DEFINITIONS

1. Investment has been a major cause of long-term economic growth by increasing the capital stock and hence increasing a nation's capacity to produce and its standard of living. Economic growth is often measured by using rates of change in potential real GNP per person or per man-hour.

2. The cumulative effects of a growth rate become large over periods of a generation or more. For example, after 50 years a growth rate of 3 percent transforms potential real GNP from 100 to 448.

3. The benefits to growth are (1) to raise the general living standards of the population, (2) to make income redistribution easier, and (3) to increase a nation's national defence and prestige.

4. Growth, while often beneficial, is never costless. There can be substantial social and personal costs of growth. Industrialization, unless carefully managed, causes deterioration of the environment. Furthermore, rapid growth requires rapid adjustments, and these can cause upset and misery to the individuals affected.

5. The opportunity cost of growth is the diversion of resources from current consumption to capital formation. Many sectors of society may not wish to incur this sacrifice if they believe that they will not receive the benefits of growth.

6. The theory of economic growth involves understanding the concepts of the utilization of existing investment opportunities and the creation of new investment opportunities.

7. The nineteenth-century view of the growth process involved the utilization of existing investment opportunities. In formal terms, this is portrayed as a process of accumulating capital, increasing the capital-output ratio, and driving the marginal efficiency of capital down to the limit in which it is zero. The prospects for continual growth were therefore not optimistic.

8. Today most economists recognize that many investment opportunities can be created and attention is therefore given to sources of outward shifts in the MEC schedule.

9. Some of the factors that can cause the <u>MEC</u> schedule to shift outward are (1) innovation: (2) improvements in the quality of human capital (education, health); (3) the size of the population and the labour force; (4) social, religious, and legal institutions that are conducive to change and growth; and (5) international trade.

10. Some opponents of growth predict some future "doomsday" because of the complete exhaustion of natural resources given the growth of the world's population. These <u>doomsday</u> models assume (1) there is no technical progress; (2) no new resources are discovered or rendered usable by new techniques; (3) there is no substitution of more plentiful resources for those that become scarce.

11. Increases in productive capacity that are intrinsic to the form of capital goods in use are called <u>embodied technical change</u>. Innovations in the organization of production are called <u>disembodied technical change</u>.

MULTIPLE-CHOICE QUESTIONS

1. Economic growth can best be defined as
   (a) a rise in the GNP as unemployment is reduced
   (b) an increase in real income
   (c) a rise in potential real GNP per capita
   (d) an increase in investment and the capital stock

2. Economic growth has
   (a) characterized most of mankind's history
   (b) recently been most rapid in countries with the most rapidly increasing populations
   (b) been largely independent of social and legal patterns
   (d) been particularly characteristic of Western countries in the last two centuries

3. Output per man-hour increases as a result of
   (a) a rise in the labour force
   (b) a rise in total output
   (c) better machinery and training supplied to workers
   (d) an increase in the level of wages

4. The most important benefit of economic growth has been its role in
   (a) redistributing income among people
   (b) raising living standards
   (c) helping countries defend themselves
   (d) providing for the use of scarce resources

5. An increase in the rate of economic growth
   (a) will usually require a reduction in consumption
   (b) will usually be encouraged by an increase in consumption
   (c) seems to be the result of increased investment alone
   (d) will be aided by high interest rates

6. Without technical change or new knowledge,
   (a) diminishing returns to additional investment will cause the capital-output ratio to rise
   (b) the marginal-efficiency-of-capital schedule will become horizontal
   (c) the shortage of investment will cause interest rates to rise
   (d) the marginal-efficiency-of-capital schedule will shift to the left

7. Classical theories of growth
   (a) predicted a declining return on capital
   (b) predicted an increasing return on capital
   (c) predicted a constant return on capital
   (d) had no prediction for the rate of return on capital

8. The major difference between the earlier classical theory of economic growth and the contemporary view is that
   (a) contemporary economists place much more importance on the quantity of labour than do classical economists
   (b) classical economists ignored the role of capital accumulation
   (c) contemporary economists emphasize the creation of investment opportunities rather than simply the exploitation of existing opportunities
   (d) classical economists emphasized the role of international trade in economic growth

9. An embodied change is one that
   (a) improves the quality of labour
   (b) inheres in the form or nature of capital in use
   (c) is concerned with techniques of managerial control
   (d) is exogenous to the economic system

10. If, for a given state of technology and resource supplies, an increase in population causes a reduction in per capita income,
    (a) investment must have been decreasing
    (b) the optimal population has apparently been exceeded
    (c) labour productivity must have fallen
    (d) inflation is inevitable and will discourage further growth

11. Predictions of future trends based on present rates indicate eventual
    (a) rapidly rising worldwide per capita income
    (b) serious resource shortages from growing population and industrialization
    (c) reversal of damage to the environment with successful and increasing efforts
    (d) leveling off of world population at about 8 billion people

12. The text concludes that the predictions of the doomsday models
    (a) have proved totally incorrect and should be ignored
    (b) were correct until the early 1900s but are now incorrect because of technological change
    (c) place too much weight on gradual reduction in the rate of population growth to be valid in the present world
    (d) may be avoidable in the future with technological advances, but the problem of timing is crucial

13. A growth in the population of 2 percent per year means that population will double in approximately
    (a) 2 years
    (b) 36 years
    (c) 72 years
    (d) 50 years

14. Current net investment will cause the AD curve to
    (a) shift to the right, and in the long run the AS curve will also shift to the right
    (b) shift to the right, but in the long run Y_F will not be influenced
    (c) shift to the left, and Y_F will be increased in the long run
    (d) shift to the right, and the AS curve will shift to the left thereby increasing Y_F

15. If investment occurs less rapidly than the increase in investment opportunities,
    (a) the rate of return will fall because of diminishing marginal productivity of
         capital
    (b) the rate of return will increase
    (c) one of the doomsday predictions will be confirmed
    (d) the economy will undergo a stagflation

EXERCISES

1. Assume that the productivity of labour increases by 2.5 percent a year, the labour
    force increases by 1.75 percent a year, hours worked per member of the work force
    decline by .25 percent a year, and population increases by 1 percent a year.
    Predict:
    (a) The annual increase in real GNP

    (b) The annual increase in output per capita

    (c) The number of years to double real GNP

    (d) The number of years to double output per capita

2. Explain how each of the following factors would affect per capita real GNP, ceteris
    paribus.
    (a) An increase in population

    (b) An increase in current consumption

    (c) A technological innovation

    (d) An increase in current expenditures for education

    (e) An increase in capital stock

    (f) A decrease in the working span of the labour force

Growth and the Less-developed Countries | 44

1. Economic growth is highly uneven in the world. The development gap, the discrepancy between the standards of living in countries at the two ends of the world income distribution, is very large.

2. Income per head may serve as a rough index of the level of economic development. The barriers to economic development are (1) a high rate of population increase; (2) resource limitations including financial, social, and human capital; and (3) inefficiency in the use of existing resources.

3. There are two kinds of inefficiency. Using society's resources to make the wrong products is an example of allocative inefficiency. In terms of the production-possibility boundary, allocative inefficiency represents operation at the wrong place on the boundary. X-inefficiency arises whenever resources are used in such a way that even if they are making the right product, they are doing so less productively than is possible. Recent research suggests X-inefficiency may be of major importance in accounting for low incomes and a slow rate of growth.

4. X-inefficiency can be the product of inadequate education, poor health, cultural attitudes, or ignorance. Consequently, adopting techniques used in more-developed countries may prove disappointingly unproductive in less-developed countries.

5. Economic development policy involves identifying the particular barriers to the level and kind of desired development and then devising policies to overcome them. One of the key considerations in the development strategy is how much government control over the economy is necessary and desirable.

6. The active intervention of the government in the economy rests upon the real or alleged failure of market forces to produce satisfactory results. The major appeal of such intervention is that it can accelerate the pace of economic development and change its direction.

7. Educational policy and population control, although important to long-run economic growth, yield benefits only in the future. As a result, they frequently are bypassed in search of more immediate results.

8. A country has three sources of funds for investment: (1) domestic savings; (2) loans or investment from abroad; and (3) contributions from foreigners.
9. A <u>vicious circle of poverty</u> exists in most developing countries, thereby preventing domestic savings from being a viable source of funds. A country is poor because it lacks capital and it cannot forego consumption to accumulate capital because it is poor.
10. Selecting a pattern of development poses difficult choices. A <u>balanced growth policy</u> involves expanding all sectors of the economy. Another choice is <u>unbalanced growth</u>, which pushes specialization in only certain areas.
11. The <u>theory of comparative advantage</u> provides the traditional case for unbalanced growth. However, there are important reasons for not pushing specialization too far, including the risks of fluctuations or declines in the demand for a country's principal products and the dependence on foreign trade.
12. Much of the current debate about development involves the importance given to (1) agricultural development versus industrialization, (2) reduction of dependence on foreign trade by development of <u>important substitution</u> industries, and (3) development of an industrial capacity that will create new export industries.
13. <u>A New International Economic Order (NIEO)</u>, a resolution of the United Nations, was aimed at <u>wealth transfer</u> policies instead of <u>wealth creation policies</u>. NIEO policies are concerned with more equal distribution of existing wealth rather than economic development.

MULTIPLE-CHOICE QUESTIONS

1. We might define a less-developed country as
   (a) one with a per capita national income of less than $500
   (b) one with substantial quantities of undeveloped resources
   (c) one with a low amount of capital per head
   (d) any of the above

2. In choosing between building a steel industry and investing more in education, a less-developed country
   (a) will be better off with the industry so that it can get cheaper steel
   (b) will probably get greater returns in the long run from more education
   (c) will get immediate short-run returns from education
   (d) finds all of the above true

3. When deciding whether growth should be financed by imported capital or domestic savings, a less-developed country's leaders
   (a) should realize that finance by savings will yield a greater return later on
   (b) should realize that finance by imported borrowed capital will require less financial sacrifice now but more later
   (c) might want to consider noneconomic consequences of each method
   (d) find all of the above true

4. Medical advances in a less-developed country
   (a) increase per capita income
   (b) increase the rate of population growth
   (c) are very expensive to bring about
   (d) have been self-defeating because the death rate from famine has risen equivalently

5. Among the arguments for unbalanced growth are that
    (a) it will insulate the economy from the vagaries of foreign trade
    (b) it will enable the citizens of that country to exercise a wide variety of talents in their work
    (c) it will lead to more rapid growth
    (d) diversification is always more expensive in the long run

6. Developing countries often have balance-of-payments problems because
    (a) as income rises, imports often rise even more rapidly
    (b) most of their exports are primary commodities with low elasticities of demand
    (c) most of their machinery must be imported
    (d) all of the above

7. It is usually important that developing countries improve their agricultural output because
    (a) agricultural surpluses will be needed to feed a growing industrial population
    (b) population is apt to be growing rapidly
    (c) agricultural products may be exported to help pay for needed imports
    (d) all of the above

8. A possible obstacle to scientific agriculture in the less-developed countries is likely to be
    (a) too-small peasant plots or large feudal-type estates
    (b) inadequate capital
    (c) a preference for traditional ways
    (d) all of the above

EXERCISES

1. Why may the gap between the rich and poor countries grow larger, even if both have the same rate of growth? Consider the following example.

	Country A	Country B	Difference
Year X, GNP per capita	$2,000	$100	_____
Annual rate of per capita growth	3%	3%	_____
Year X + 1, real GNP per capita	_____	_____	_____
Year X + 23, real GNP per capita	_____	_____	_____

Use the "rule of 72," recognizing that for continuous compounding, as in population growth, the doubling time is more nearly the number 69 divided by the annual rate.

2. Use the "rule of 72" for the following (assume annual compounding):
    (a) If real GNP is rising at a steady rate of 4 percent, it will be doubled in how many years? _____ If the population is rising steadily at 3 percent per year, it will double itself in how many years? _____ In how many years, then, will real GNP per capita be doubled in this example?

    _____
    (b) It is predicted that at current rates of increase the population of the less-developed countries (the "third world") will double itself by the year 1996. What must be the approximate annual rate of increase in population in these countries? _____(The prediction was made in 1971.)

3. Production Possibilities, Efficiency, and Development
    Suppose that there are two countries, A and B, both of which are less-developed in
    terms of advanced country standards. Both countries have x units of working labour
    and y units of land, but very little capital. Country A has a population of 8 and
    country B has a population of 10. Assume that either country produces and consumes
    only wheat and peanuts. The production possibilities are given in the schedules
    below.

Country A		Country B	
Wheat (bu.)	Peanuts (lb.)	Wheat (bu.)	Peanuts (lb.)
100	0	200	0
90	10	180	18
80	19	160	35
70	27	140	51
60	34	120	66
50	40	100	80
40	45	80	93
30	49	60	105
20	52	40	116
10	54	20	126
0	55	0	135

(a) Plot the schedules on the diagram provided. To obtain successive increases in
     wheat production, what is happening to the rate of loss in peanut production
     in country A? Country B? What can be said about the change in opportunity
     costs?

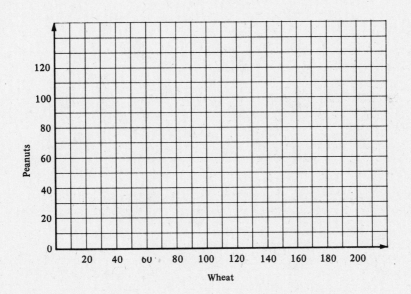

311

(b)   Suppose that production and consumption in country A are 16 pounds of peanuts and 80 bushels of wheat and in country B are 160 bushels of wheat and 35 pounds of peanuts. Does production inefficiency exist in either country? What type?

(c)   If wheat is worth U.S. $ 2 per bushel and peanuts are worth U.S. $ .50 per pound, what is the value of GNP in each country in terms of U.S. dollars? What is the per capita level of GNP in each country?

(d)   Give some reasons why country B is more technically efficient than country A.

(e)   What type of foreign aid could Canada give to country A to increase its per capita income? How would this affect the production-possibility schedule?

Answers

ANSWERS TO CHAPTER 1

MULTIPLE-CHOICE QUESTIONS:

1. (c)   2. (b)   3. (d)   4. (c)   5. (a)   6. (c)   7. (a)   8. (c)   9. (b)
10. (d)   11. (a)   12. (b)   13. (b)

EXERCISES:

1. (1) What goods and services are being produced and in what quantities?
    (2) By what methods are these goods produced?
    (3) How is the supply of goods allocated among the members of the society?
    (4) Are the country's resources being fully utilized, or are some of them lying
         idle and thus going to waste?
    (5) Is the purchasing power of people's money and savings constant, or is it being
         eroded by inflation?
    (6) Is the economy's capacity to produce goods growing or remaining the same over
         time?

    (a) 1   (b) 2   (c) 4   (d) 3   (e) 6   (f) 5   (g) 1   (h) 2

2. (b) yes   (c) no   (c) 2,000 bushels of corn   (e) underutilized

3. (a) The production-possibility frontier shifts to the right with point F being
         unchanged and point M moving to the right.
    (b) A movement along the frontier from right to left.
    (c) A point inside the frontier.

315

MULTIPLE-CHOICE QUESTIONS:

1. (d)   2. (b)   3. (b)   4. (b)   5. (c)   6. (d)   7. (a)   8. (b)   9. (b)
10. (c)   11. (c)   12. (a)
A.1. (b)   A. 2. (b)   A. 3. (c)

EXERCISES:

1. (a) The change in housing starts is related inversely to the change in the average
       mortgage rate.
   (b) Yes. Using the data supplied, one could determine the specific functional
       relationship and then examine the hypothesis in light of the functional
       relationship.

2. (a) endogenous; flow   (b) stock; flow   (c) exogenous; exogenous;
       endogenous   (d) (i) flow   (ii) stock   (iii) flow   (iv) flow

A.1. (a) $X = Y^2$ (b) $X = 20 - 1/2(Z)$; X and Z are inversely related.   (c) Z and
     H are not related.

A.2. Values for X corresponding to Y = 0, 1, 2, 3, 4, 5, are X = 10, 7, -2, -17, -38,
     -65.

ANSWERS TO CHAPTER 3

MULTIPLE-CHOICE QUESTIONS:

1. (b)   2. (a)   3. (c)   4. (a)   5. (c)   6. (b)   7. (c)   8. (b)   9. (d)
10. (c)

EXERCISES:

1. (a) Base year: (3,000 x .3) + (2,500 x .25) + (5,000 x .15) + (100 x .1)
               + (60 x .1) + (300 x .1) = 2,321
       Next year: (3,300 x .3) + (2,500 x .25) + (5,000 x .15) + (110 x .1)
               + (60 x .1) + (330 x .1) = 2,415
   (b) Index = (2,415/2,321) x 100 = 104.0
   (c) No; the prices increased by approximately 4 percent. This is because shelter,
       clothing, and other goods are only 50 percent of total expenditures.
   (d) The price increase from the base year for this group of households (using
       their fixed weights) is 5.5 percent. Hence, the overall price increase
       reflected by the overall price index underestimates the cost-of-living
       increase of this group.
   (e) Most likely shelter and transportation. Weights of shelter and transportation
       might increase and hence other components (food, clothing, entertainment, and
       other) might fall.

2. (a) 1980: Industry A = 6,000/4,000 = 1.5
              Industry B = 21,000/20,000 = 1.05
       1981: Industry A = 8,000/4,000 = 2.0
              Industry B = 25,000/20,000 = 1.25

(b) Value of industry B's output in 1980 = 1.05(6) = \$6.3 million
     Value of total output 1980 = 1.5 (10) + 1.05 (6) = \$21.3 million
                            1981 = 2.0 (10) + 1.25 (6) = \$27.5 million

(c) Index for 1980 = 21.3/16 x 100 = 133.13 approximately. Output increased by 33.13 percent from the base year.

(d) Output increased 71.9 percent from the base year. Output increased 29.1 percent between 1981 and 1980 (171.9/133.13).

3. (a) Per capita consumption was 25,479/17.87 = \$1,425.80. Real per capita C was 1,425.8/.9936 = 1,435. Prices were lower in 1960 compared with 1961.

    (c) They are directly related; as Y_d increases, so does C.

    (d) $\Delta C = 1,435 - 1,142$; $\Delta Y_d = 1,496 - 1,216$; $\Delta C / \Delta Y_d = 1.05$
         For 1960–1970, $\Delta C / \Delta Y_d = (1,858 - 1,435)/(1,994 - 1,496) = .85$

    (e) Slightly below. The distance is $Y_d - C$, which you will discover is saving.

    (f) The slope of the consumption function. The sign is positive because C and Y_d are directly related.

    (g) Ninety-nine percent of the variance in C is explained by the variance of Y_d.

    (h) The hypothesis has not been proven, but given the high value of the coefficient of determination, we can act as if the hypothesis were true.

4. (a) They are inversely related; as P increases, Q_d falls.

    (b) Q_d = 6,000, 4,000 0, and 8,000

    (c) The intercept on the P axis is 2,000, and the intercept on the Q_d axis is 8,000.

    (d) ΔQ_d = (4,000 - 6,000) = -2,000; ΔP = 500; $\Delta Q_d / \Delta P = -4$
         This is the slope of the function. Alternatively, $\Delta P / \Delta Q_d = -1/4$

    (e) $\Delta Q_d / \Delta P$ = (0 - 4,000)/1,000 = -4 and (0 - 6,000)/1,500 = -4. It is a constant -4 value. Therefore, the slope is constant. This is because the expression is linear.

    (f) The intercept on the P axis is 2,500, and the intercept on the Q_d axis is 9,000. The demand curve shifted upward in a parallel fashion.

5. (a) Q = 6,300 when N = 30; Q = 12,500 when N = 50

    (b) 210, 250, 240

    (c)

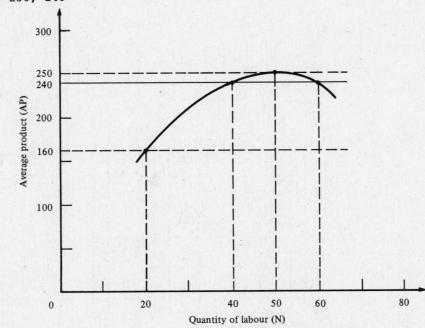

    (d) positive, negative, 50

317

6. (a) When P = 50, quantity supplied is 600 and quantity demanded is 900.
When P = 100, quantity supplied and quantity demanded are 800.
When P = 150, quantity supplied is 1,000 and quantity demanded is 700.
   (b) P = 100, q = 800
   (c) 400 + .5P = 1,000 - 2P. Therefore, P = 240, q = 520.

ANSWERS TO CHAPTER 4

MULTIPLE-CHOICE QUESTIONS:

1. (c)   2. (b)   3. (d)   4. (d)   5. (b)   6. (b)   7. (d)   8. (d)   9. (c)
10. (c)

EXERCISES:

1.

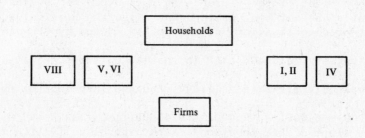

2. (a) III   (b) IV   (c) II   (d) I   (e) V

3. (a) NM, P   (b) NM, R   (c) M, R   (d) M, P   (e) M, P   (f) NM, P

4. increase, decrease, increase, decrease, increase, stay the same, increase, decrease.

ANSWERS TO CHAPTER 5

MULTIPLE-CHOICE QUESTIONS:

1. (b)   2. (a)   3. (b)   4. (b)   5. (c)   6. (a)   7. (a)   8. (c)   9. (c)
10. (a)   11. (c)   12. (a)   13. (c)

EXERCISES:

1. (a)

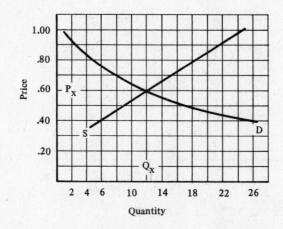

(b) It is zero.

Price	Excess Demand (+) Excess Supply (−)
$1.00	−24
.90	−18
.80	−14
.70	− 7
.60	0
.50	+ 9
.40	+20

(c) If excess demand exists, price is likely to rise; in the event of excess supply, price is likely to fall.

2.

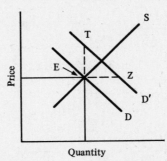

	D	S	P	Q
(a)	0	−	+	−
(b)	+	0	+	+
(c)	+	0	+	+
(d)	+	+	U	+
(e)	−	0	−	−
(f)	0	−	+	−
(g)	+	0	+	+

3. (a) The demand curve would shift right and the equilibrium price and output would be higher.

   (b)

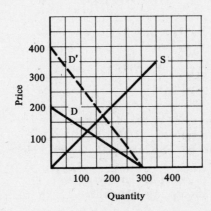

Quantity

The price would rise to the point indicated by T because if the output is fixed at 20,000 cases, only at T would excess demand be eliminated.

   (c) Supply shifts leftward, price rises, and output falls.

4. (a)

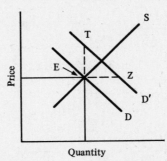

Quantity

(b) At equilibrium, $Q_S = Q_D$; therefore $300 - 1.5P = 1.0P$, and $P = 120$ and $Q = 120$.

(c) Equating the new demand and original supply, $P = 171.43 = Q$.

ANSWERS TO CHAPTER 6

MULTIPLE-CHOICE QUESTIONS:

1. (d)   2. (a)   3. (a)   4. (c)   5. (b)   6. (d)   7. (d)   8. (d)   9. (a)
10. (c)   11. (d)   12. (d)   13. (c)   14. (b)   15. (b)

EXERCISES:

1. (a)

	Price Elasticity of Demand for		Income Elasticity of Demand for		Cross Elasticity of Demand for
	X	Y	X	Y	X
	--	--	--	--	--
	0.929	--	--	--	--
	--	0.332	--	--	0.294
	--	--	1.240	0.296	--
	--	--	--	--	--

(b) The condition of <u>ceteris paribus</u> does not apply. Not only has income changed, but the price of Y has also changed.

2. Starting from the origin for S_1, the elasticities are $\frac{2}{2} = \frac{2/3}{2/3} = \frac{.4}{.4} = 1.0$; and for S_2, the elasticities are $\frac{2}{2} = \frac{2/3}{2/3} = \frac{.4}{.4} = 1.0$.

3. (a) Elasticity measures are $\dfrac{\frac{100}{50}}{\frac{20}{30}} = 13.0$; $\dfrac{\frac{200}{200}}{\frac{20}{50}} = 2.5$; $\dfrac{\frac{200}{400}}{\frac{10}{65}} = .75$

(b) $\dfrac{\frac{100}{350}}{\frac{10}{35}} = 1.0$; total revenue declines

4. (a) = 1 (b) = 4 (c) = 5 (d) = 2 (e) = 3 (f) = 6

5. (a) For D_1: $Q_d = 12 - 1.2P$
   For D_2: $Q_d = 36 - 3.6P$

(b) For D_1: elasticities are 4, 1.25, 0.23
   For D_2: elasticities are 9, 1.78, 0.56, 0.12
   (These values may not be the same as yours, depending on precise values chosen at arrows.)
   The steeper the curve $\Delta P/\Delta Q$, the narrower the range of elasticity values although the basic pattern is the same.

MULTIPLE-CHOICE QUESTIONS:

1. (d) 2. (d) 3. (c) 4. (a) 5. (c) 6. (b) 7. (c) 8. (a) 9. (a)
10. (b) 11. (c) 12. (c) 13. (b) 14. (a) 15. (b) 16. (b) 17. (c)
18. (b) 19. (a) 20. (b)
A.1. (d) A.2. (b) A.3. (a)

EXERCISES:

1. (a) and (b)

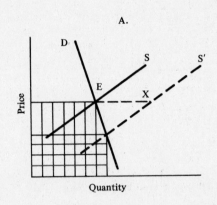

(c) Market A. The demand is inelastic compared to market B.
(d) No. The shift in supply is identical, and at a price equal to original equilibrium price, the quantity of unsold goods (EX in both markets) is the same.

2.

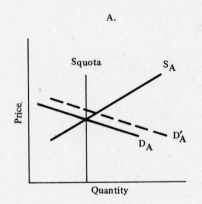
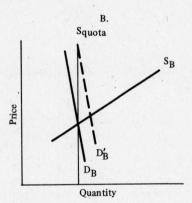

Fix quota at S_{quota}. Shift demand to D_A' and D_B'. Price rises much more in market where there is an inelastic demand.

3. (a) Stock would increase due to the attractiveness of higher prices for rental units. Short-run profits attract new producers.
   (b) The short-run supply would, if it could, have to shift out to where D_3 intersects p^*.

(c) (i) Quantity demanded will occur at intersection of D_3 and p^*, while producers will be willing to supply an amount where p^* intersects S_{LR}.

(ii) Price falls and quantity demanded/sold will increase. Equilibrium will be at intersection of D_3 and S_{LR}.

4.

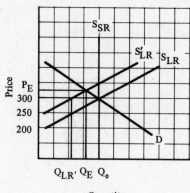

5. (a) $5.25 million   (b) $9 million   (c) falls by 1 million units   (d) 2 million
    (e) $4 million

6. The quota would result in a new price of $1.75 and 40,000 units sold for a revenue of $70,000. A fixed price of $1.50 would result in 45,000 units sold for a revenue of $67,500. The quota would maximize income.

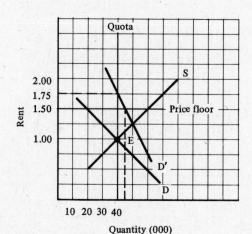

322

A.1.

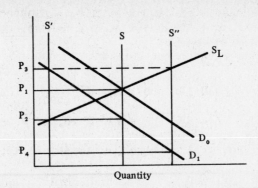

Price falls from P_1 to P_2. At P_2, supply offered is S', generating a rise in price to P_3. Price P_3 elicits a supply of S'' and price falls to P_4.

ANSWERS TO CHAPTER 8

MULTIPLE-CHOICE QUESTIONS:

1. (c)   2. (a)   3. (a)   4. (b)   5. (b)   6. (c)   7. (a)   8. (c)   9. (b)
10. (b)   11. (d)   12. (c)   13. (a)   14. (c)   15. (c)

EXERCISES

1. First of all, draw in a line to represent the terms of trade, 2:1, as shown by tt below.

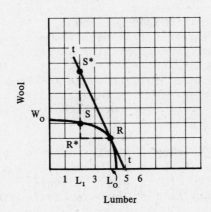

(a) In autarky, the country would have to move to a point on the production frontier above L_1 (shown here as S). More wool would be produced.
(b) Instead, the country could continue to produce at R and export L_0L_1 of lumber in exchange for R^*S^* of wool, which would make them better off than in autarky. Exports = RR^* and imports = R^*S^*.

323

2. (a) Canadian importers need   10,000 x A. $50 = 500,000
                              + 100,000 x A. $ 4 = 400,000

A. $900,000 and will have to pay Can. $1,170,000 for this Australian currency.

Australian importers need 100,000 x 500 x $\frac{1}{1,000}$ = Can. $ 50,000

                                    + 130 x 10,000 = Can. $1,300,000

or Can. $1,350,000 and will have to pay A. $1,038,460.

On balance, Canadian banks will receive $1,350,000
                                            -$1,170,000
                                     Can. $ 180,000

Australian banks lose $1,038,460
                        -$ 900,000
                    A. $ 138,460

Thus Canada will have a trade surplus.

   (b) If the exchange rate changes to A. $1.00 = Can. $1.50 then the Canadian
       importer will require 900,000 x 1.50 = $1,350,000 to obtain Australian
       currency. Since Australians will be purchasing Can. $1,350,000, the balance
       of trade will become zero.
   (c) The price of the Australian dollar has appreciated in terms of the Canadian
       dollar. However, the Canadian dollar has depreciated in terms of the
       Australian dollar. Exports to Australia would rise and imports decline.

3. (a) Depreciated
   (b) from £ 120 per ton to £ 109.09 per ton
   (c) The demand for dollars will rise because more newsprint will be demanded and
       since the Canadian price remains at $300 per ton, more dollars are needed to
       purchase more newsprint.
   (d) The price of the Canadian dollar has fallen from £ 0.40 to £ 0.363 or
       approximately 9 percent. Within an elasticity of -1.2 percent, the volume of
       newsprint purchased would therefore rise to 110.8 tons per month.

4. (a) Demand schedule shifts right; supply schedule shifts right; cannot say what
       new price will be relative to P_1.
   (b) Demand schedule shifts right; supply schedule shifts left; price rises.
   (c) Supply schedule shifts right; demand schedule shifts left; price falls.

5. (a) Sell pounds, thereby shifting supply schedule to the right to intersect demand
       schedule at $2.65. About £ 300 million.
   (b) Demand pounds, thereby shifting demand schedule to the right to intersect
       supply schedule at $2.85. About £ 300 million.

6. (a) The demand schedule will shift to the right (D') to produce a "free" market
        equilibrium at $.89. To prevent this the Bank of Canada will sell Canadian
        dollars, the amount equal to the distance EB.

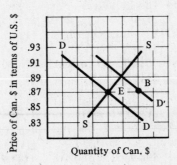

   (b) In order to travel in the United States, Canadians will have to sell Canadian
        dollars and the supply schedule will shift right to S' and a "free" market
        equilibrium of .85. The Bank of Canada will then buy Canadian dollars in the
        amount EB.

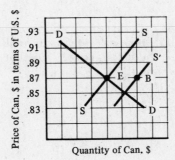

   (c) In this case Canadians will supply fewer Canadian dollars to the exchange
        market and supply shifts to S'. Demand for Canadian dollars will increase
        to D'. The relative sizes of the moves will differ but they will intersect
        at a "free" market equilibrium of .91. The Bank of Canada will therefore sell
        Canadian dollars equal in amount to EB.

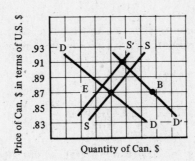

7. (a) Yes; the reciprocal of the dollar price of pounds is 1/2.40, which is equal to .417.
   (b) Yes; the reciprocal of the dollar price of lire is 1/600, which is equal to .00167.
   (c) The pound price of lire is .000833. The lire price of pounds is 1,200. Thus the reciprocal of the latter is 1/1,200, which is equal to .000833.
   (d) No; the cross-rate is .417/600, which is equal to .000695, whereas the pound price of lire is .000833.
   (e) Yes; it could purchase 600,000 lire with $1,000, then purchase £500 with the lire, and then purchase $1,200. The profit is therefore $200.

8. (a) In equilibrium, $Q_s = Q_d$, therefore $1.5 - 1.0P = -0.25 + 1.0P$, and $P = .885$. The equilibrium amount of currency exchanged would be $Q_d = Q_s = 1.5 - 1.0(.875) = 615,000$.
   (b) (i) Increased demand; demand schedule shifts to the right
       (ii) Canadian dollar would appreciate in value to $1.00. (Equate old supply and new demand equation.)
   (c) Highly responsive since the supply schedule would almost be a line perpendicular to the quantity axis.

9. (a) The cost of U.S. $800 per month is determined by multiplying the $800 by the exchange rate. E.g., 800 x .9722 = Can. $777.76 for October. The total cost of doing this is $4,908.
   (b) Liquidation of the $4,667 in savings in October 1976 would have given Smith $4,800.45 to take south. However, by doing so, Smith lost $233.35 in interest (5 percent). Thus the total cost of option (ii) would have been $4,900.35; little difference.

ANSWERS TO CHAPTER 9

MULTIPLE-CHOICE QUESTIONS:

1. (c)   2. (b)   3. (a)   4. (c)   5. (a)   6. (b)   7. (d)   8. (a)   9. (d)
10. (a)   11. (d)   12. (c)   13. (c)   14. (b)   15. (b)   16. (c)   17. (b)
18. (d)   19. (a)   20. (c)

EXERCISES:

1. (a) The graph should show the following points (marginal utility is given in parentheses next to number of milkshakes consumed): 1(50), 2(40), 3(30), 4(10), 5(0), 6(-10).
   (b) After the fifth milkshake.

2. (a) 3 hours on tennis, 2 hours on fishing.
   (b) 2 hours on tennis (T), 3 hours on fishing (F). Utility maximization requires that $MU_T/P_T = MU_F/P_F$. When tennis and fishing are priced the same, (e.g. $1.00 each), the condition is met when 18/1 = 18/1. With the price of tennis increased to $1.19 (19 percent), the condition is met when 19/1.19 = 16/1 (approximately).

3. Case 1: decrease Y and increase X.
   Case 2: increase X and decrease Y.
   Case 3: decrease X and increase Y.
   Case 4: increase Y and decrease X.
   (Note that as you increase the consumption of one good, its MU falls, and as you decrease the consumption of a good, the MU rises.)

4. Commodity A: low elasticity; a small reduction in quantity demanded will raise the MU significantly.
   Commodity B: high elasticity since it will take a large reduction in quantity demanded to generate a rise in the MU.
   Commodity C: close to zero elasticity because a very small reduction in quantity raises the MU significantly.

5. (a) 5 bottles per week
   (b) $2.20
   (c) demand reduced to 3 bottles per week and consumer surplus reduced to $.90.

6. (a) The straight line would start at 40 units on the vertical axis and go to 50 units on the horizontal axis.
   (b) No.
   (c) 25 units of movie-going
   (d) There would be a parallel shift in the budget line to the right and the new line would intersect the vertical axis at 60 units.

7. (a) The budget line starts at 40 units on the vertical axis and goes to 75 units on the horizontal axis.
   (b) 37.5.
   (c) The line starts at 40 units on the vertical axis and goes to 50 units on the horizontal axis. It is the same because although the money value of the budget has risen 50 percent so have all prices.

8. (a)

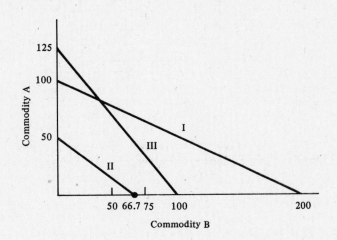

   (b) I : .5
       II : .75
       III : 1.25
   (c) A = 100 − .5B
   (d) 1/3 unit of A

9. (a)

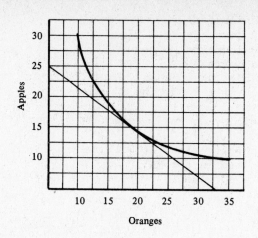

(b) Yes; 15 oranges and 19 apples would give the same utility as 19 oranges and 15 apples. One more apple (15 oranges and 20 apples) would put the consumer on a higher indifference curve.

(c) In the range .75 to .85.

10. (a) and (b)

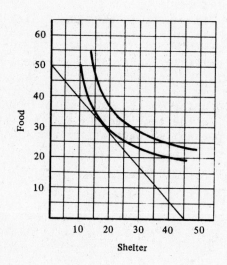

(c) 30 food and 18 shelter. Given the budget constraint, this is the maximum utility attainable. The budget is exhausted at this point of tangency.

11. (a) 18.2 percent

(b) Food: 2.6 percent; clothing: 11.6 percent; transportation: 22.7 percent; alcohol/tobacco: 22.9 percent

(c) Relative price of food and clothing was increased from 1:1 to 2.2:1; for alcohol/tobacco to transportation, relative price fell from 1:1 to 0.6:1.0.

ANSWERS TO CHAPTER 10

MULTIPLE-CHOICE QUESTIONS:

1. (a)   2. (c)   3. (a)   4. (b)   5. (d)   6. (c)   7. (b)   8. (d)   9. (b)

EXERCISES:

1. (a) (i)   income elasticity is .75
      (ii) price elasticity demand is -.45
      (iii) Cannot state price elasticity of demand because both price and income
            have changed. It would appear that the positive income elasticity has
            just offset the negative price elasticity.

2. (a) No. They do not take into account the changes in income or possibly "taste"
           that may well have occurred in each period.
   (b) Given <u>constant</u> real income and no change in tastes in the 1974-1980 period,
       the figure would represent the demand schedule for gasoline.

3. (a) A rightward shift in the demand schedule with a vertical supply schedule.
   (b) They would probably try to stockpile lumber by buying it now in anticipation
       of higher prices. This would shift the demand schedule again to the right,
       further raising prices.

4. (a) The simple graph of these three relationships does not reveal clearly how
       responsive these categories of spending are to changes in real income. The
       calculations in (b) below are more revealing.
   (b) Food and nonalcoholic beverages = 0.40
       Alcohol = 1.16
       Automobiles = 1.43
   (c) Yes, certainly with respect to food and automobiles. (See discussion in the
       text, pages 186 to 187.)

5. (a) Pork: -.68; -.89; -.55
       Eggs: -.02; -.10; -.12
   (b) Eggs are more important in the "basic" food pattern.
   (c) They do in the sense that pork does have a number of close substitutes while
       eggs do not, especially when it comes to the use of eggs in baking and making
       other foods.

ANSWERS TO CHAPTER 11

MULTIPLE-CHOICE QUESTIONS:

1. (b)   2. (c)   3. (b)   4. (c)   5. (c)   6. (c)   7. (a)   8. (c)   9. (b)
10. (a)   11. (c)   12. (c)

EXERCISES:

1. (a) No. Neither method A nor B uses more of both factors than the other.
   (b) Method A, since it is the least-cost method given the price of the two factors.
   (c) Yes. Both methods are the same in terms of this total cost.

2. Revenue from sales   = $ 5.0 million
      less salaries, etc.   = $ 3.0 million
      less depreciation   = $ 0.5 million
   Net profit before tax   = $ 1.5 million   Answer (a)
      less cost of capital   = $ 0.5 million
   Economic profit   = $ 1.0 million   Answer (b)
      less taxes   = $ 0.75 million   (.5 times $1.5 million)
   Economic profit after
      tax   = $ 0.25 million   Answer (c)

3. (a) Approximately 500 square feet.

   (b) The answer would change because it would not be economical to use power tools until the size of the garden reached 1,000 square feet. For both (a) and (b) the answer is derived by computing the cost of production at each garden size, which is the hours of labour times the wage rate plus the depreciation on the tools.

4. (a) It is a legitimate expense since the value of the capital is being used up. If the firm did not own the truck, it would have to rent one.

   (b) $250. No payment for services rendered by the owner has been included. Whatever his opportunity cost, it would be necessary to include it to obtain a true profit figure.

   (c) If profit was regarded as a payment to the owner, it would represent approximately $1.50 per hour ($250 ÷ 160). This hardly seems excessive.

   (d) The decision to return to university occurred after the price of newsprint fell to $30 per ton. This meant a reduction in monthly accounting profits from $250 to $10. In terms of the business then, the opportunity cost was $10 per month.

ANSWERS TO CHAPTER 12

MULTIPLE-CHOICE QUESTIONS:

1. (b)   2. (b)   3. (b)   4. (c)   5. (d)   6. (b)   7. (c)   8. (c)   9. (a)
10. (a)   11. (b)   12. (c)   13. (d)   14. (a)

EXERCISES:

1. (a)

Average Product	Marginal Product
20	20
30	40
40	60
50	80
54	70
54	54
52	40
48	20
44	12
40.4	8

(c)

Output	Fixed Cost	Total Variable Cost	Total Cost	Average Fixed Cost	Average Variable Cost	Average Total Cost	Marginal Cost
20	168	80	248	8.40	4.00	12.40	
60	168	160	328	2.80	2.67	5.46	2.00
120	168	240	408	1.40	2.00	3.40	1.33
200	168	320	488	.84	1.60	2.44	1.00
270	168	400	568	.62	1.48	2.10	1.14
324	168	480	648	.52	1.48	2.00	1.48
364	168	560	728	.46	1.54	2.00	2.00
384	168	640	808	.44	1.67	2.11	4.00
396	168	720	888	.42	1.82	2.24	6.67
404	168	800	968	.42	1.98	2.40	10.00

2. (a)

Output	Total Cost	Average Total Cost
1	$ 3.50	$3.50
2	5.00	2.50
3	6.00	2.00
4	7.25	1.81
5	9.00	1.80
6	11.50	1.92

(c) Minimum average total cost is at 5 units of output.

3. (a) AFC = $102.22;   AVC = $72.22
    (b) $204.44
    (c) Zero
    (d) No. Even if the airline could fill the remaining 40 seats at the regulated price of $204.44, the total cost of the flight would not be covered.

4. (a)

Q	FC	VC	TC	MC	AFC	AVC	ATC
0	50	0	50				
1	50	4	54	4	50	4	54
2	50	10	60	6	25	5	30
3	50	18	68	8	16.07	6	22.07
4	50	28	78	10	12.50	7	19.50
5	50	40	90	12	10	8	18
6	50	54	104	14	8.33	9	17.33
7	50	70	120	16	7.14	10	17.14
8	50	88	138	18	6.25	11	17.25
9	50	108	158	20	5.56	12	17.56
10	50	130	180	22	5	13	18
.	.	.	.		.	.	.
.	.	.	.		.	.	.
.	.	.	.		.	.	.
20	50	460	510		2.50	23	25.50

(b) 7
    (c) 18
    (d) No.
    (e) Although average fixed costs are declining because of the 50 being spread over more and more units of output, average variable costs are rising and at some point (output level of 8) they offset the falling average fixed costs.

5. (a) 8   (b) 6 to 7   (c) 8

ANSWERS TO CHAPTER 13

MULTIPLE-CHOICE QUESTIONS:

1. (b)   2. (a)   3. (a)   4. (a)   5. (c)   6. (c)   7. (b)   8. (d) 9. (d)
10. (d)   11. (c) 12. (d)   13. (d)   14. (c)   15. (c)   16. (a)   17. (b)
18. (b)

EXERCISES:

1. (a)

Method	ΔCapital	ΔLabour	Rate of Substitution
A			
B	+ 5	−22	− .23
C	+10	−18	− .55
D	+15	−16	− .94
E	+18	− 9	−2.00
F	+22	− 6	−3.67

2. (b) one unit of capital and three units of labour
   (c) No. The isocost line would be a straight line passing through not only the original combination of capital and labour (1 and 3 units, respectively) but also through two other combinations of capital and labour that produce 100 units of output. Thus, in this "unusual" configuration of inputs, the new relative price is compatible with three combinations of factors.

3. (a) one unit of capital and two units of labour
   (b) two units of capital and two units of labour

4. (a) At the 6 output levels (including 10,000), the LRAC are: $.50; $.46; $.39; $.35; $.46; $.52.
   (b) 60,000
   (c) It varies slightly, which, given no change in factor prices, might be expected according to the theory in the text.

ANSWERS TO CHAPTER 14

MULTIPLE-CHOICE QUESTIONS:

1. (b) 2. (d) 3. (d) 4. (c) 5. (c) 6. (d) 7. (d) 8. (c) 9. (d)
10. (b) 11. (a) 12. (a) 13. (a) 14. (d) 15. (b) 16. (b)
A.1. (a) A.2. (d) A.3. (b)

EXERCISES:

1.		$12	$ 8	$ 5
	(a)	100	80	60
	(b)	1,200	640	300
	(c)	825(approx)	640	510
	(d)	375	0	−210
	(e)	3.75	0	−3.50

2. (a)

Output	TC	AVC	ATC	MC
0	20	--	--	
				15
1	35	15	35	
				9
2	44	12	22	
				6
3	50	10	$16\frac{2}{3}$	
				18
4	68	12	17	
				27
5	95	15	19	
				45
6	140	20	$23\frac{1}{3}$	

The firm should go out of business since a price of $8 does not even cover AVC.

(b) No. It is approximately at minimum ATC and therefore maximizing profits.

(c) Short-run windfall profits. New entrants would be attracted to the market, increasing supply and placing downward pressure on price.

3. (a) and (b): The ATC at an output level of 5,000 is $.90, so profits are being made, given a market price of $1. However, the firm's MC exceeds price and thus a reduction to an output level where P = MC would be profit maximizing.

4. (a) Above-normal profits.

(b) No, not in a perfectly competitive industry, because the abnormal profits will attract firms into the industry and the expanded market size will drive the price back to a level where all firms make only normal profits.

5. (a) Yes. Briefly, there are no excess profits for the firms; they are price takers; any individual firm has a very small share of the total market.

(b) Price and output will rise and firms will be enjoying above-normal profits: e.g., revenue over and above that sufficient to cover average total costs.

(c) The market-supply schedule would shift to the right because of the entry of new firms until it intersects the D' schedule at such a point so as to produce a price (equilibrium) the same as the initial price in the market.

6.

Firm A		Firm B		Firm C	
Output	MC	Output	MC	Output	MC
30		25		36	
	4		.5		4
40		30		40	
	5		2.5		5
50		35		44	
	7		8		7
60		40		48	
	10		12		10
70		45		52	
	14		18		14
80		50		56	

The industry supply curve is derived by selecting a given price and adding together what each firm would offer at that price according to its MC. It will, roughly, look as follows if one takes P = MC at $2, 4, 6, 8, 10, 12.

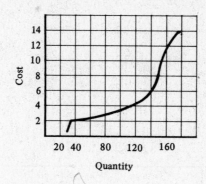

ANSWERS TO CHAPTER 15

MULTIPLE-CHOICE QUESTIONS:

1. (b)   2. (c)   3. (c)   4. (a)   5. (d)   6. (c)   7. (c)   8. (c)   9. (a)
10. (c)   11. (d)   12. (a)   13. (c)   14. (d)   15. (b)

EXERCISES:

1. (a) 60   (b) $11   (c) $660   (d) $480   (e) $180   (f) 25 and 90   (g) $7.50

2. (a) Marginal and average cost and marginal and total revenue.
   (b)

TR	MR	MC	ATC	Output
0			0	0
	18	4		
18			24	1
	14	3		
32			13.50	2
	10	5		
42			10.67	3
	6	7		
48			9.75	4
	2	9		
50			9.60	5
	-2	11		
48			9.83	6

   (c) Between 3 to 4 units.
   (d) Between $12 and $14.
   (e) Between 3 and 4 units of output, total revenue is $42 to $48. Total cost is $32 to $39, and home profits would be $9 to $10.

3. (a) and (b)

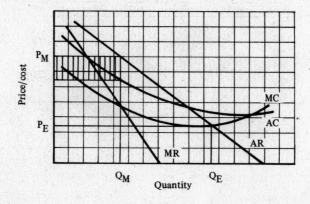

(c) No, it would not, because the ATC exceeds the price and business could not be sustained for long.

4. (a) and (b)

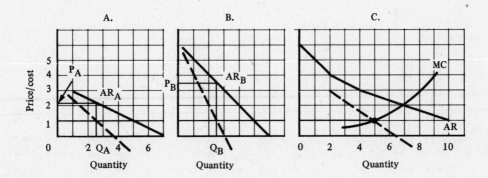

The horizontal summation of AR_A and AR_B will produce AR, as shown in C. The MR for the market is the broken line in C. Next it is necessary to calculate the MR schedules for the individual demand schedules, and these are shown as broken lines in A and B. Relating MC = MR in C to the MR's in A and B produces Q_A and Q_B with the different prices P_A and P_B.

5. (a)

Output	ATC	MC
0		
		2
5	10	
		3
10	6.5	
		5
15	6.0	
		8
20	6.5	
		12
25	7.6	
		17
30	9.2	

(b) See diagram below.

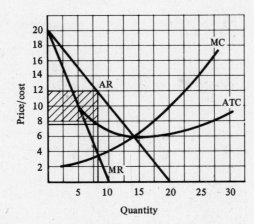

(c) Yes. Output would be reduced and price increased because the tax would raise the MC schedule by $4 and intersect the MR at a new point, indicating that price should rise and output be cut.

335

MULTIPLE-CHOICE QUESTIONS:

1. (d)   2. (b)   3. (a)   4. (b)   5. (b)   6. (c)   7. (c)   8. (d)   9. (c)
10. (a)   11. (b)   12. (a)   13. (c)   14. (d)   15. (b)   16. (d)
A.1. (b)   A.2. (b)

EXERCISES:

1. (a) $6
   (b) $100
   (c) No. New firms will reduce profits.
   (d) The ATC: advertising would raise total ATC but not MC, and if all firms did
        this, there would be little effect on the demand curves of each firm.
   (e) The demand curve for this firm would shift left and profits would be reduced.

2. (a) 3   (b) 4   (c) 5   (d) 3   (e) 1   (f) 2

3. (a)

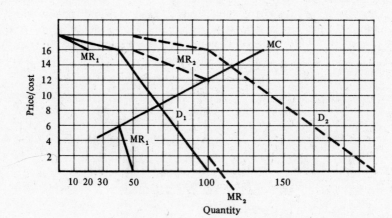

   (b) $16; $16   (c) fall; be unchanged   (d) be unchanged; be higher
   (e) oligopoly

ANSWERS TO CHAPTER 17

MULTIPLE-CHOICE QUESTIONS:

1. (d)   2. (b)   3. (c)   4. (c)   5. (d)   6. (b)   7. (b)

EXERCISES:

1. (a) P = $5 and Q_d = 4
   (b) P = $6; Short-run Q_d = 3.5. In the long run, Q_d will be 2 because the
   long-run demand curve is more elastic than the short-run curve, causing quantity to
   adjust to the higher price.

2. (a) -$35.63; -18 percent (b) -1.25; -$225 (c) -5.6 percent; +$98.75

3. (a)   Excess demand = XZ

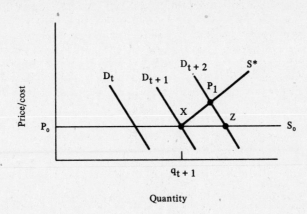

(b)   market price = P_1
(c)   The elasticity of the long-run demand curve is greater than that suggested by D_{t+2}.

ANSWERS TO CHAPTER 18

MULTIPLE-CHOICE QUESTIONS:

1. (c)   2. (b)   3. (c)   4. (b)   5. (a)   6. (d)   7. (b)   8. (b)   9. (c)
10. (b)   11. (a)

EXERCISES:

1. (a)   natural monopoly or public utility
   (b)   where MC = AR
   (c)   where AR = ATC; Price is higher than (b) and output less.

2. (a) $10; 200 units   (b) $13; 125   (c) $3

3. In the diagram illustrating monopoly, draw in MR and equate to MC to set price and output. Shift MC curve up by one. In the diagram illustrating competition, equate S = D to get price and output. Shift supply curve up by one. Visual inspection should show smaller responses in the case of monopoly.

ANSWERS TO CHAPTER 19

MULTIPLE-CHOICE QUESTIONS:

1. (b)   2. (c)   3. (b)   4. (d)   5. (d)   6. (d)   7. (b)   8. (a)   9. (c)

EXERCISES:

1. In sales maximization, price would be "set" between B (profit maximization) and D (full cost pricing with zero markup). Both represent prices lower than and output greater than in the case of a strict profit maximizer.

337

2. (1) Per unit tax = $.50 shifts up MC and ATC by $.50. Profit maximizer reduces
        output and raises price by less than amount of the tax. Sales maximizer was
        earning profits of $1.50 x 4,000 = $6,000 before tax. A tax of $.50 per unit
        would cut this profit to $4,000, the minimum, and hence no change in price.
        Full cost pricing requires the tax be shifted to price completely.

   (2) The profit maximizer does not adjust price. Neither does the full cost firm,
        so it has no excess profit to be taxed. The sales maximizer sees profit cut to
        $3,000 so he will raise price to generate, if possible, $8,000 in pre-tax
        profits.

ANSWERS TO CHAPTER 20

MULTIPLE-CHOICE QUESTIONS:

1. (b)   2. (b)   3. (d)   4. (a)   5. (b)   6. (c)   7. (c)   8. (c)   9. (c)
10. (c)   11. (c)   12. (d)   13. (a)   14. (c)   15. (b)   16. (b)   17. (a)
18. (d)   19. (c)   20. (b)   21. (a)   22. (b)

EXERCISES:

1. (a) APP: 21.4; 19.6   MPP: 10; 8; 6; 2; -2
   (b) Case A: ARP 42.8; 39.2   MRP: 20; 16; 12; 4; -4
        Case B: MRP: 11.6; 8.4; 2.7; -2.5
   (c) The demand curve for labour is the MRP curve, which lies below the ARP curve
        and for which MRP values are positive. In this case, the MRP curve between the
        quantities of labour of 3 to 12 is the demand curve for labour.
   (d) MRP declines in both cases because of diminishing marginal productivity.
        However, the MRP declines in Case B also because MR falls as output increases.
   (e) Case A: about 8 workers because MRP = the wage = $20.
        Case B: about 6 workers because MRP is approximately equal to $20.
   (f) Case A: about 6 workers because MRP is equal to $28.
        Case B: about 4 workers because MRP is approximately equal to $28.
        The arc elasticity is (6 - 8)/7 ÷ (28 - 20)/24 = -.857.
   (g) About 8 workers because MRP = 30 for 8 workers while the wage rate is $28.

2. (a) The demand curve for labour has an intercept of 95 on the quantity axis and a
        slope of -4. Case A supply curve of labour has an intercept of 20 on the wage
        axis and a slope of 2. Case B supply curve of labour is vertical at 60 units
        of labour.
   (b) Cases A and B have equilibrium values of W = 140 and L = 60.
   (c) The total economic rents in Case A are given by the area above the supply
        curve, equal to and below the horizontal line at W = 140, and the equilibrium
        point W = 140 and L = 60; this is a triangle. All earnings are economic rents
        since the supply curve of labour is perfectly inelastic. The transfer earnings
        of the 60th worker in Case A are equal to the market wage of 140.
   (d) W = 160 and L = 70. The total economic rents of the workers who were already
        in this labour market are 1,200 (60 times 160 - 140).
   (e) W = 160 and L = 75. Since the wage rate is the same before and after the
        policy change, no additional economic rents have been created by this policy.

3. (a) At a wage of w_0 the total supply is $h_1 + h_2$. At a wage of w_1,
        individuals A and B increase their hours and individual C is now prepared to
        supply some hours. In the range $w_1 w_2$, the total labour supply curve is
        upward sloping.

(b) Hours have increased because the participation rate has increased and individuals A and B have also increased hours supplied to the market.

(c) Only individual B is prepared to work at a wage of w_1. Hence the participation rate is one-third.

ANSWERS TO CHAPTER 21

MULTIPLE-CHOICE QUESTIONS:

1. (c)   2. (c)   3. (d)   4. (a)   5. (b)   6. (b)   7. (a)   8. (c)   9. (b)
10. (d)   11. (c)   12. (a)   13. (d)   14. (b)   15. (b)   16. (b)   17. (c)
18. (a)   19. (b)

EXERCISES:

1. Total Cost: $80.00; 94.50; 110.00; 126.50; 144.00; 162.50; 182.00
   Marginal Cost: $14.50; 15.50; 16.50; 17.50; 18.50; 19.50

2. (a) $0w_3$; $0q_4$
   (b) $0q$; $0q_5 - 0q$; horizontal at w_6 to q_5 and thereafter corresponding to the labour supply curve.
   (c) $0w$; $0w_2$; $0w_5$; $0q_2$; $0w_1$; $0w_4$; $0w_4$. The wage is lower (compare $0w_1$ with $0w_3$), and employment is lower (compare $0q_2$ with $0q_4$).
   (d) $0q_4$
   (e) The supply curve shifts leftward halfway to the origin. All wage predictions are raised, and employment levels are lowered.

3. (a) The wage levels are $168 and $140 in X and Z, respectively. The differential is therefore $28. The employment levels are 64 and 50 in X and Z, respectively.
   (b) If workers from Z are able to obtain X-specific skills by moving to X, the differential is likely to be eliminated over time. In this case the differential is said to be a dynamic differential. However, if there is no mobility of workers from Z to X, the differential is likely to be an equilibrium differential.
   (c) The wage will be $180 and $132 in X and Z, respectively. The differential is therefore $48. Notice that 4 green-eyed workers were laid off in X and were hired in Z.
   (d) The minimum wage generates total unemployment of 8 in market Z. This is because the minimum wage is greater than the new competitive wage after the inflow of green-eyed workers. Labour supply at a wage of $140 is 58, but the demand is 50. The minimum wage has no effect on market X, since the market wage is greater than the minimum.

ANSWERS TO CHAPTER 22

MULTIPLE-CHOICE QUESTIONS:

1. (b)   2. (a)   3. (a)   4. (c)   5. (b)   6. (d)   7. (b)   8. (c)   9. (c)
10. (c)   11. (d)   12. (a)   13. (b)   14. (b)   15. (c)   16. (b)   17. (c)
18. (d)   19. (d)

EXERCISES:

1. (a) $7.47   (b) 1 percent   (c) 50   (d) $10

2. (a) $42.12   (b) 1 percent   (c) 50   (d) $10

3. (a) Just barely; the annual income flow is $13,587 (100,000 divided by 7.36).
   (b) Yes, but it just meets the 14-percent requirement. The annual savings would
       have a PV of $14,000 x 5.216, which equals $73,024. The $10,000 salvage value
       has a PV of $2,700. The total is $75,724.
   (c) At 6 percent the PV of the cost of the medical education is (6.802 x $10,000),
       or $68,020. The worth of the extra medical earnings is (15.046 - 6.802) x
       ($10,000) or approximately $82,440. The return is therefore over 6 percent.
       At 8 percent the cost is $62,470 and the estimated worth is $56,780. The
       return is therefore slightly less than 8 percent, enough for Mr. Schmidt to
       give his blessing to Hermann's medical career.

4. (a) 10 percent, since the firm had reached its profit-maximizing capital stock at
       which MEC equals the market rate of interest.
   (b) 8 percent; solve the equation $1,000 = 1,080/(1 + MEC)$. The MEC of 8 percent is
       associated with a capital stock of 11,000.
   (c) Yes, because the MEC is at least equal to the new market rate of interest.

5. (a) Total PV is $400 x .98 plus $200 x .961, or $584.2. Net PV is $84.20.
   (b) at i = 4 percent, net PV = $69.80
       at i = 8 percent, net PV = $41.80
       at i = 15 percent, net PV = -$0.80
       at i = 18 percent, net PV = -$17.60
   (d) The net PV curve shifts to the right. Net PV values are $93.22 and $44.56 for
       interest rates of 8 percent and 15 percent, respectively.

ANSWERS TO CHAPTER 23

MULTIPLE-CHOICE QUESTIONS:

1. (c)   2. (a)   3. (d)   4. (a)   5. (b)   6. (b)   7. (c)   8. (a)   9. (c)
10. (d)

EXERCISES:

1. The PV of expected income in Nova Scotia is $8,000 x 9.427 = $75,416. The PV of
   expected income in Ontario is ($8,500 - $1,000) x .909 plus ($8,500 x 8.518) =
   $79,221. Yes, John should move.

2. (a) Largest investments in formal education are likely to have been made by
       individuals whose occupations are managerial, professional, and clerical in
       nature. Craftsmen are likely to have undergone the greatest degree of
       on-the-job training. All of these occupations are characterized by low
       probabilities of poverty.
   (b) Farmers and farm workers, loggers and fishermen, and recreation workers are
       likely to be subject to large seasonal demands. Services and general labourers
       are likely to be low-skilled workers. These workers tend to be laid off first
       if cutbacks in production are necessary. For all of these occupations, the
       incidence of poverty tends to be high relative to others.

MULTIPLE-CHOICE QUESTIONS:

1. (b)   2. (b)   3. (c)   4. (d)   5. (d)   6. (d)   7. (b)   8. (b)   9. (b)
10. (b)   11. (d)

EXERCISES:

1. (a) Where the demand and S = MC schedules intersect for Mr. Maple.
    (b) Add the demand schedules vertically; that is, find out the total willingness
         to pay for each level of quality from 0 to Q*.

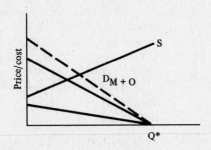

    (c) Yes. The S = MC would intersect the D_{M+O} to indicate an increase in
         quality.
    (d) Less. The new cost would be only slightly above what Mr. Maple paid before,
         but half the cost would be borne by Mr. Oak.

2. (a) trucking down; railroads up
    (b) private gasoline consumption down; trucking unaffected
    (c) airlines down; railroads up
    (d) foreign publishers down; Canadian publishers up

3. (a)

APC	MPC	ASC	MSC
	500		600
500		600	
	50		175
275		387.50	
	70		210
206.67		328.33	
	90		240
177.50		306.25	
	110		270
164		299	
	230		400
175		315.83	
	300		480
192.86		339.29	

    (b) $177.50 and $306.25, respectively
    (c) greater

ANSWERS TO CHAPTER 25

MULTIPLE-CHOICE QUESTIONS:

1. (d)   2. (a)   3. (b)   4. (c)   5. (c)   6. (d)   7. (b)   8. (a)   9. (c)
10. (c)   11. (b)   12. (b)   13. (c)   14. (b)   15. (c)

EXERCISES:

1. (a) Situation C. Demand is very elastic, and quantity of accommodation would decline significantly with little rise in price.
   (b) Situation A. Demand is inelastic and does not respond significantly to the higher price.
   (c) In the short run the landlord would shoulder all the tax.

2. (a) Tax A is proportional.
      Tax B is regressive.
      Tax C is progressive.
   (b) For each income group the tax rates are: 22 percent for $5,000, 22 percent for $10,000, 23 percent for $20,000, and 22.7 percent for $30,000. The tax system is close to being proportional.

3. (a) The ratio of tax paid to income for the nine income classes shown are, from lowest to highest income groups, 7.3, 4.7, 3.8, 3.2, 3.1, 2.8, 2.6, 1.7 and 1.1 percent, suggesting a regressive tax.
   (b) Taking again the mid-points of these income ranges, such a scheme suggests a subsidy for the first two income groups of ($3,750)(.073 − .040) = $123.75 and ($6,000)(.047 − .040) = $42. All other groups would pay an additional tax as follows:

Income Group	Additional Tax	
$ 7,000- 9,999	(8,500)(.040 − .038) = $	17.00
10,000-11,999	(11,000)(.040 − .032) =	88.00
12,000-14,999	(13,500)(.040 − .031) =	121.50
15,000-19,999	(17,500)(.040 − .028) =	210.00
20,000-24,999	(22,500)(.040 − .026) =	315.00
25,000-49,999	(37,500)(.040 − .017) =	862.50
50,000-99,999	(75,000)(.040 − .011) =	2,175.00

ANSWERS TO CHAPTER 26

MULTIPLE-CHOICE QUESTIONS:

1. (d)   2. (c)   3. (b)   4. (b)   5. (b)   6. (a)   7. (c)   8. (d)   9. (c)
10. (a)   11. (d)   12. (c)   13. (b)   14. (c)   15. (b)   16. (b)   17. (b)
18. (d)   19. (c)

EXERCISES:

1. (a) Canada 2.0; 0.5
      Argentina 0.33; 3.0
      Canada should specialize in the production of beef; Argentina should specialize in the production of wheat.
   (b) Canada 2.0; 0.5
      Argentina 3.0; 0.33
      Canada should specialize in the production of wheat; Argentina should specialize in the production of beef.
   (c) Canada 2.0; 0.5
      Argentina 2.0; 0.5
      Canada should specialize in the production of neither; Argentina should specialize in the production of neither.

2. (a) Comparative advantage exists.
   (b) .2 (Canada) and .5 (Australia)
   (c) Yes; the opportunity costs differ between the two countries.
   (d)

	Wheat	Wool
Canada	15	1
Australia	9	7.5
World	24	8.5

   (e) Yes. Domestically, Canada would have to sacrifice 5 bushels of wheat to obtain 1 kg of wool. On the world market, 5 bushels of wheat would generate in return 1.25 kg of wool.
   (f) No. Australia can domestically obtain one kg of wool for 2 bushels of wheat. On the world market, Australia would have to give up 4 bushels of wheat to get 1 kg of wool.

3. (a) Terms of trade: 98.0; 100; 99.0; 93.1; 86.3; 90.4; 89.4; 93.5; 97.7; 92.2
   (b) 1970-1975: F   1972-1973: F   1975-1979: U   1971-1979: F   1974-1978: U
   (c) 104.8; 52.35 (This is obtained by multiplying 50 by 1.048.)

4. (a)

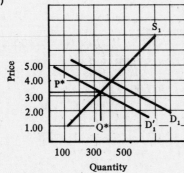 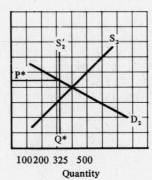 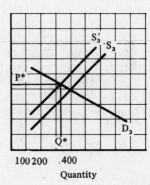

   (b) It would not choose the tariff policy. The price might rise by almost the amount of the tariff, but there would be little reduction in imports.
   (c) Policy 1, a restriction on demand, not only reduces the amount of imports but also lowers the price.

5. (a)

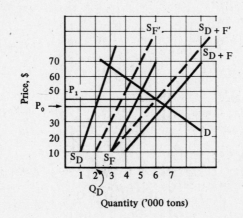

   (b) See diagram above.

343

(c) Revenue rises because domestic steel producers supply more at the higher price. Yes, it does depend on the elasticity. In this case the supply schedule is rather inelastic. A more elastic schedule would result in a greater output of domestic steel.

6. (a) The curves PC_{CAN} and PC_{US} do not have to be exactly like these as long as the slopes are as shown.

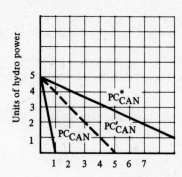 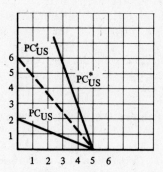

Units of automobile production

(b) See above. Both countries are better off because, for a given level of hydro power, they can now have more automobiles than would be possible without trade. One can always find a point on PC_{CAN}^*, for example, that is preferred to a point on PC_{CAN}.

(c) Yes, again both countries gain because they can, with trade, be better off than without trade.

ANSWERS TO CHAPTER 27

MULTIPLE-CHOICE QUESTIONS:

1. (c)   2. (b)   3. (c)   4. (b)   5. (c)   6. (c)   7. (c)   8. (d)   9. (c)
10. (a)

EXERCISES:

1. (a) 20,000 bbls/day
   (b) 15,000 bbls/day
   (c) The area ERZ.

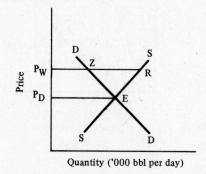

Quantity ('000 bbl per day)

2. (a) 60,000 x 10 = $600,000
    (b) 40,000 bbls. The volume of exports would rise to 120,000 bbls.
    (c) The royalty would produce 160,000 x $5 = $800,000.

3. (a) 14,000 bbl/day; 6,000 bbl/day
    (b) 15,000 bbl/day; No. If they could get $40/bbl on the world market, that is
         where they would sell.
    (c) Yes. The after-tax price for selling oil to foreigners would be $40 - $10 =
         $30/bbl, the same price as the domestic price. They might as well sell in
         Canada rather than abroad.
    (d) (i)   import subsidy = (amount of oil imported at $30/bbl) x ($10) = 9,000
              bbl x 10 = $90,000.
         (ii) export tax = zero, because the existence of the tax will see Canadian
              producers sell all their output (6,000 bbls) in Canada at $30/bbl and
              thus avoid the export tax by not exporting.

4. (a) (50,000 - 35,000)($10) = $150,000; 35,000; 25,000; (70,000 - 25,000) = 45,000
    (b) $P_C ZVP_W$; $P_C YRP_W$; YZVR
    (c) 15,000; YZTS
    (d) RSY + TVZ

ANSWERS TO CHAPTER 28

MULTIPLE-CHOICE QUESTIONS:

1. (d)   2. (b)   3. (b)   4. (a)   5. (d)   6. (c)   7. (a)   8. (d)   9. (b)
10. (d)   11. (c)   12. (c)   13. (b)   14. (d)   15. (b)   16. (c)   17. (a)

EXERCISES:

1. (a) 3.2 percent and 2.6 percent
    (b) 25.1 percent
    (c) 126.5

2. (a) Labour Force: 10,498 = (850 - .08097)
         Unemployed: 727; 910   (910 = 10,882 x .08362)
         Employed: 9,284; 9,648; 9,972; 10,369
         Unemployment rate: 5.333 percent, 7.478 percent
    (b) Percent change in real GNP = 2.93; percent change in employment = 3.98
    (c) direct relationship; real output and employment increase together
    (d) The labour force increased more in percentage terms than did employment. That
         is, more of those who entered the labour force became unemployed than employed.
    (e) 1974 = 11,588; 1979 = 11,582
    (f) 1975: GNP gap is 115.7 - 113 = 2.7
         1976: GNP gap is 121.4 - 119.1 = 2.3

3. (a) An inverse relationship; the three reasons are cited in number 7 of the Key
         Concepts section.
    (b) A direct relationship.
    (c) Since output in real terms is constant for all price levels, this AS curve is
         similar to the classical portion of the composite curve.
    (d) Y = 18 when P = 54
    (e) Y = 24 when P = 72

345

(f) Prices and real output have increased. The aggregate demand curve has shifted to the right. Referring to Figure 28-8 in the text, this result is similar to those for shifts in the AD curve (AD_2 to AD_3) which represent increases in price and output.

4. (a) The AD curve has the following intercept values: when Y = 0, P = 40; when P = 0, Y = 20. The slope is -2.
    (b) The Keynesian range is a horizontal line at P = 20 for Y values from zero to 30. The intermediate range is an upward sloping line (slope of .5) from Y = 30 to Y = 50. The classical range is a vertical line at Y = 50.
    (c) Y = 10 and P = 20; The equilibrium values are in the Keynesian range. Notice, 20 = 40 - 2Y means Y = 20.
    (d) The AD curve has the following intercept values: when Y = 0, P = 80; when P = 0, Y = 40. The slope is -2. This AD curve lies to the right of that in part (b). The equilibrium values are Y = 30 and P = 20. Hence real output has increased but prices have remained constant.
    (e) The AD curve has the following intercept values: when Y = 0, P = 105; when P = 0, Y = 52.5. The slope is -2. The new equilibrium values are Y = 40 and P = 25.
    (f) This AD curve lies to the right of that in part (d). Hence the AD curve has shifted to the right once again. Both output and prices have increased. The new equilibrium point lies in the intermediate range.
    (g) The Keynesian range will shift up vertically. It will be a horizontal line at P = 25 and will have the range $0 \leq Y \leq 40$.

ANSWERS TO CHAPTER 29

MULTIPLE-CHOICE QUESTIONS:

1. (d)   2. (a)   3. (a)   4. (c)   5. (a)   6. (a)   7. (c)   8. (b)   9. (b)
10. (c)   11. (d)   12. (d)   13. (c)   14. (a)   15. (d)   16. (c)

EXERCISES:

1. output-expenditure: (277.1 + 4.6 + 201.5 + 805.0) = 1288.2
    factor-income: (785.3 + 84.3 + 117.8 + 109.6 + 126.4 + 75.5 - 10.7) = 1288.2

2. (a) NNP = 2369 - 243 = 2126
    (b) 2126 - 126 - 379 = 1621 (personal income)
        1621 - 300 + 304 = 1625 (personal disposable income)
    (c) 1625 - 1510 = 115

3. (a) 1971: 94.45   1972: 105.0   1974: 111.68   1975: 165.4
    (b) 1971, since the GNP deflator was 100; 1971
    (c) 102.7 percent increase in current dollar GNP; 26.4 percent increase in constant dollar GNP.

4. Real disposable per capita income was 925.60 and 1760.55 in 1950 and 1970, respectively. The percentage increase was 90.2 percent.

5. (a) (1) C for student, F for barber   (2) I for barber   (3) S_b or S_p
        (4) N   (5) I   (6) T   (7) S_b and F   (8)(a) T   (b) F   (c) S_b
        (9) M and C   (10) X   (11) I   (12) G
    (b) 1, 2, 5, 9, 10, 11, 12

MULTIPLE-CHOICE QUESTIONS:

1. (d)   2. (a)   3. (c)   4. (b)   5. (d)   6. (a)   7. (a)   8. (c)   9. (b)
10. (d)   11. (c)   12. (d)   13. (b)   14. (b)   15. (c)   16. (a)   17. (d)
18. (b)   19. (a)   20. (b)   21. (d)   22. (d)   23. (b)

EXERCISES:

1. (a) 40, 200
    (b) 160, 280
    (c) .90, .61; the value of APC progressively fell.
    (d) 100, 175
    (e) .50 = 175 ÷ 350
    (f) 0, 295. The marginal propensity to save is .50 and is constant. For an
         increase in Y_d from 0 to 100, saving increases from −80 to −30. The ratio
         of the changes is .50.
    (g) 160, at which S = 0.
    (h)

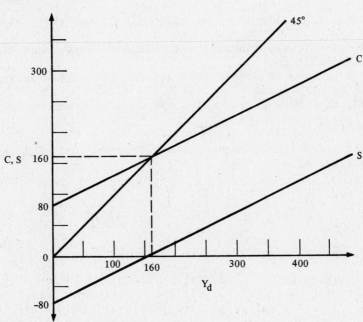

2. (a) There is a direct relationship given by the expression Y_d = .7Y. Personal
         taxes are likely to be present.
    (b) $\Delta C / \Delta Y_d$ = 56/70 and 64/80
    (c) $\Delta C / \Delta Y$ = 56/100 = 64/114.3 = .56
    (d) APC = 156/140 = 1.11; APC = 220/220 = 1.00
    (e) .2 = 1 − .8
    (f) When C = Y_d, which is 220; when C = Y, which is 100

3. (a) When Y = 400, Y_d = 280 and C = 268; when Y = 500, Y_d = 350 and C = 324;
         when Y = 600, Y_d = 420 and C = 380

(b) The tax rate has likely increased. When Y = 400, Y_d = 240 and C = 236. When Y = 500, Y_d = 300 and C = 284. When Y = 600, Y_d = 360 and C = 332. For a given level of Y, both Y_d and C have fallen.

(c) MPC out of Y_d is .9, while the MPC out of total income is .63 (= .9 times .7). When Y = 400, 500, and 600, C values are 296, 359, and 422, respectively.

4. (a) Imports are directly related to national income by the expression M = .1Y. As national income rises, households buy more imported goods; business firms, in order to produce more goods, require more imported inputs; and it is possible for governments and firms to import various imported machines, goods, and services as part of their investment and expenditure programs.

(b) 40, 30, 20, 0, -40. Yes, because imports rise as income rises.

5. (a) AE values are 150, 200, 250, 300, 350.

(b) Equilibrium is 300 because AE(C + I + G + X - M) = Y.

(c) AE = 350 (330 + 10 + 30 - 20). Y - AE = 50 is the amount of unintended inventory accumulation. Since there are costs associated with holding high levels of unplanned inventory, firms are likely to reduce production and lay off factors of production. As a consequence, income falls.

(d) $\triangle Y$ = 100, 100, 100, 100; $\triangle AE$ = 50, 50, 50, 50; MPC = 50/100 = .5.

(e) The marginal propensity to withdraw is equal to (1 - .5) = .5.

6. (a) The coefficient .7 is the marginal propensity to consume out of disposable income.

(b) Net exports (most likely imports) and consumption (through disposable income) depend on national income.

(c) AE = 100 + .7 (.8Y) + 56 + 50 + 10 - .1Y, or AE = 216 + .46Y

(d) 216 + .46Y = Y, or Y = 400

(e) When Y = 100, AE = 262; when Y = 200, AE = 308. Hence, $\triangle AE/\triangle Y$ = 46/100 = .46.

7. (a) The equilibrium level of Y occurs at the intersection of AD and AS. The equilibrium value of price is P_0.

ANSWERS TO CHAPTER 31

MULTIPLE-CHOICE QUESTIONS:

1. (a)   2. (d)   3. (a)   4. (d)   5. (c)   6. (c)   7. (c)   8. (d)
9. (a)   10. (b)   11. (c)   12. (c)   13. (b)   14. (c)   15. (b)   16. (a)
17. (a)   18. (b)   19. (a)   20. (c)   21. (b)   22. (b)   23. (a)   24. (d)
25. (b)

EXERCISES:

1. (a) AE = Y at 400. The marginal propensity to spend is .80 and is constant ($\triangle AE$ = 160, $\triangle Y$ = 200, $\triangle AE/\triangle Y$ = .80).

(b) The AE curve has an intercept value of 80 on the vertical axis, a slope of .80, and intersects the 45° line at an income level of 400.

(c) AE : 90, 250, 330, 410, 450. The AE curve shifts vertically upward by 10 in a parallel fashion.

(d) AE = 410 when Y = 400. Since AE is greater than national income, output and employment will rise.

(e) AE = Y at 450. The change in income is 50 and $\Delta Y/\Delta I$ = 5. The value of the multiplier is 5.

(f) The marginal propensity to spend is .80. The marginal propensity to withdraw is .20.

(g) Since the total change in income is 50 and ΔI = 10, the value of ΔN is 40. The value 40 is composed of ΔC = 45 and $\Delta(X - M)$ = -5.

2. (a) AE : 60, 220, 300, 380, 420. Equilibrium is Y = 300. The marginal propensity to spend remains at .80.

(b) Y fell by 100. The multiplier is $\Delta Y/\Delta(X - M)$ = -100/-20 = 5. The change in income was distributed -10 for (X - M) and -90 for C. The change in autonomous (X - M) was -20, but since Y fell, (X - M) only fell by -10. The rest of ΔN is consumption.

(c) The AE curve shifts down by 20 in a parallel fashion.

3. (a) Case A: MPC = .90; Case D: MPC = .70. Consumers have become more frugal; they are saving a higher proportion of national income.

(b) AE : 80, 200, 260, 320, 350. The new AE has an intercept of 80 on the vertical axis, a slope of .60, and intersects the 45° line at Y = 200. The AE curve for case D is flatter than that for case A.

(c) The marginal propensity to spend for case D is .60, which is lower than .80 for case A. The multiplier for case D is therefore 1/(1 - .60) = 2.5.

(d) AE = Y when Y = 200. Yes; consumers became more frugal and as a result national income fell.

4. (a) The marginal propensity to spend out of national income is .80.

(b)

	ΔY_d	ΔAE
3rd round	2,880.0	2,560.0
4th round	2,304.0	2,048.0
5th round	1,843.2	1,638.4
Sum		13,446.4

(c) ΔY = 5.(-4) = -20 million

5. (a) C = 30 + .9(.8Y)
        = 30 + .72Y : Equation 8

(b) AE = 30 + .72Y + 40 + 20 + 20 - .12Y
        = 110 + .60Y
    The slope of the AE function is .60

(c) 110 + .6Y = Y or Y = 275

(d) (i)   C = 30 + .9(.689Y)
            = 30 + .62Y (approximately): Equation 10

    (ii)   AE = 30 + .62Y + 40 + 20 + 20 - .12Y
              = 110 + .50Y
          The slope is .50.

    (iii) Y = 110 + .50Y or Y = 220. National income has fallen from 275 to 220.

(e) The multipliers before and after the tax rate increase are 2.5 and 2.0, respectively.

6. (a)

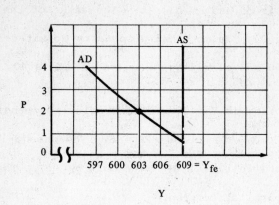

(b) Y_{fe} = 609 in both diagrams.
(c) The GNP gap is 609 - 603 = 6.
(d) A deflationary gap of a magnitude of 2 exists.
(e) Deflationary gap = 6/3 = 2.
(f) An increase in autonomous expenditure of 1 would increase Y by 3. This would not solve the gap problem. However, an increase of 2 would solve the gap problem.
(g) The AE curve would shift upward by 3. Equilibrium Y would be at 603 + 9 = 612. Although full employment is achieved, inflation is now present. An inflationary gap of 1 exists. The AD shifts upward such that a higher price level occurs.

7. (b) upward, upward, no change
   (c) upward, upward, slope gets steeper
   (d) downward, downward, no change
   (e) downward, downward, slope gets flatter

ANSWERS TO CHAPTER 32

MULTIPLE-CHOICE QUESTIONS:

1. (a)   2. (b)   3. (d)   4. (b)   5. (d)   6. (a)   7. (a)   8. (c)   9. (a)
10. (c)   11. (b)   12. (a)   13. (d)   14. (b)   15. (b)

EXERCISES:

1.

Year	Capital Needed	New Machines	Total Machines
2	10	0	1
3	11	1	2
4	12	1	2
5	15	3	4
6	17	2	3
7	18	1	2
8	18	0	1

(a) 50 percent
(b) 300 percent

2.

Week	Inventory/ Sales Ratio	Desired Inventory	Desired Inventory Plus Expected Sales	Weekly Orders for Next Week
5	1.8	240	360	150
6	2	240	360	120
7	2.3	220	330	80
8	2	220	330	110
9	2.3	200	300	70

(a) 100 to 120
(b) 70 to 150
(c) Orders for inventory fluctuate more widely than sales. This variation in investment spending is a major factor behind economic fluctuations.

3. (a) Kerry: .90   Tom: .50   average aggregate: .70

    (b)

Kerry		Tom		Average	Aggregate
C	Y_d	C	Y_d	C	Y_d
80	0	80	0	80	0
1,070	1,100	530	900	800	1,000
2,060	2,200	980	1,800	1,520	2,000
3,050	3,300	1,430	2,700	2,240	3,000

(c) The MPC increases from .70 to .72.
(d) The consumption function has shifted upward and has a steeper slope.

4. (a) Canadian exports are directly related to foreign GNP. It appears that exports are 10 percent of foreign income. Foreign households will tend to buy more Canadian products when their incomes rise; foreign firms require more Canadian-produced inputs in order to expand their production.

(b)   Year 3: Δ in Can. GNP = 5/(1 − .80) = +25
       Year 4: Δ in Can. GNP = −2/(1 − .80) = −10
       Year 5: Δ in Can. GNP = −8/(1 − .80) = −40
       Year 6: Δ in Can. GNP = 0

(c)   Clearly, a business cycle has been transmitted from abroad. The cycles of
       both economies are similar; they peak and trough in similar fashions.

5. (a) Inverse
    (b) Capital stock increases from 100 to 200. Desired investment is 100. No; it
         depends on the availability of capital goods from capital-producing firms.
    (c) Desired capital is 350. Yes, desired investment increases by 50. Profit
         expectations may have improved because of new innovations and/or there are
         more optimistic forecasts about future sales.

6. (a)

Period	C_t	Autonomous	Accelerator	Y_t
6	271.90	200	− 68.70	403.20
7	201.60	200	−140.60	261.00
8	130.50	200	−142.20	188.30
9	94.15	200	− 72.70	221.45

(b)   Trough: period 8;   peak: period 4;   expansion phase: periods 2 and 3;
      recession phase: periods 5, 6, and 7.
(c)   Without the accelerator, the multiplier process would have increased Y by
      200(100/1 − .50). The accelerator process reinforced the multiplier during
      the expansion phase but caused a recessionary phase later on.
(d)   During periods 2 to 4, the government should increase the interest rate to
      dampen investment. During periods 5 to 8, it should reduce the interest rate
      to increase investment.

ANSWERS TO CHAPTER 33

MULTIPLE-CHOICE QUESTIONS:

1. (d)   2. (a)   3. (c)   4. (d)   5. (b)   6. (c)   7. (c)   8. (a)   9. (a)
10. (d)   11. (a)   12. (c)   13. (b)   14. (c)   15. (a)   16. (b)   17. (c)
18. (a)   19. (b)   20. (d)   21. (a)   22. (a)   23. (c)

EXERCISES:

1. (a) (i)   160 because Y = AE
         (ii)   159 = C + I + G
         (iii) .5 and constant
         (iv)   2 = 1/(1 − .5)
         (v)   .6
         (vi)   surplus of 1
         (vii) decrease by 1
         (viii) 165 = C + I + G
         (ix)   deficit of 1 (−1 surplus)
         (x)   .6
         (xi)   20(180 − 160); 10 = 20/2

(c) (i)   Y = 166; ΔY = 6 = (3 x 2)
     (ii)   C = 139.6 at Y = 166 and (I + G) = 23. Hence A = 162.6
     (iii) (X − M) = 166 − 162.6 = 3.4

(d) Although exports rose by 3, additional imports of .6 were induced by the
     multiplied increase in Y. Since ΔY = 6, imports rose by .6. Net exports
     increased by only 2.4.

(e) Foreign income rose or foreign prices rose.

(f) An increase in (I + G) of 10 is required to increase Y from 160 to 180.
     (X − M) at Y = 180 is −1.

2. (a) R = 1 = 2/(2 x 1)

    (b) R = 1.5 = 3/(2 x 1); an increase of foreign prices from 1 to 1.5.

    (c) Exchange rate must increase from 2 to 3. This represents a depreciation of
         the Canadian dollar and an appreciation of the foreign currency.

    (d) As R increases, foreigners buy fewer Canadian exports and Canadians buy more
         imported goods.

    (e) X = .1(1,000) − 20(1) = 80
         M = .2(100) + 30(1) = 50
         (X − M) = 80 − 50 = 30

    (f) X = .1(1,000) − 20(1) = 80
         M = .2(200) + 30(1) = 70
         (X − M) = 80 − 70 = 10

    (g) X = .1(1,000) − 20(1.5) = 70
         M = .2(100) + 30(1.5) = 65
         (X − M) = 70 − 65 = 5

    (h) domestic price increase, foreign price reduction, Canadian dollar appreciation
         (or foreign currency depreciation)

    (i) elasticity is (5 − 30)/17.5 ÷ (1.5 − 1)/1.25 = −1.43/.4 = −3.58

    (j) (i)   shift up
         (ii)   movement along
         (iii) shift up
         (iv)   shift down
         (v)   shift down

3. (a) at Y = 100: X = 70 − 20(1) = 50
                      M = .2(100) + 30(1) = 50
                      (X − M) = 0

    (b) R = 2/(2.5 x 1) = 0.8
         at Y = 100: X = 70 − 20(.8) = 54
                      M = .2(100) + 30(.8) = 44
                      (X − M) = 10
         at Y = 90:   X = 54
                      M = .2(90) + 24 = 42
                      (X − M) = 12

    (c) R = 2.25/2.5 x 1 = .9
         at Y = 100: X = 70 − 20(.9) = 52
                      M = 20 + 30(.9) = 47
                      (X − M) = 5
         at Y = 90:   X = 52
                      M = .2(90) + 27 = 45
                      (X − M) = 7

    (d) Since (X − M) = 7 and Y remains at 100, domestic absorption falls by 7.

4. (a) a surplus of 4,800

    (b) appreciate, 2, in a balanced position

    (c) demand for, demand, downward, deficit, depreciate

MULITPLE-CHOICE QUESTIONS:

1. (c)   2. (a)   3. (d)   4. (a)   5. (b)   6. (d)   7. (a)   8. (c)   9. (b)
10. (c)   11. (a)   12. (a)   13. (a)   14. (d)   15. (d)   16. (a)   17. (b)
18. (d)   19. (d)   20. (b)   21. (d)   22. (b)   23. (b)   24. (b)   25. (b)

EXERCISES:

1. (a)

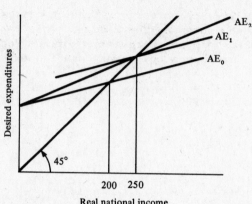

(b) $50 billion
(c) $25 billion. See AE_1 on graph above.
(d) See AE_2 on graph above.

2. An increase in government expenditures of $1,000 million along with a tax increase of the same size raises aggregate spending by $[1,000 - .5(1,000)] = 500$; with a multiplier of one, income will rise by $500 million.

3. (a) $Y_d = .80Y$
    (b) Tax rate is 20 percent of Y.
    (c) Equilibrium GNP is where desired expenditure = real income and occurs at Y = 200. The budget balance here is zero.
    (d) The marginal propensity to spend out of disposable income is .5. With a tax rate of 10 percent, $Y_d = .90Y$. Thus $C = .5Y_d$ and substituting for Y_d, C = .45Y. Since Y = C + I + G, we can substitute and solve for the new Y, which is 218.
    (e) Taxes would be 21.8 and the budget balance -18.2.

4.

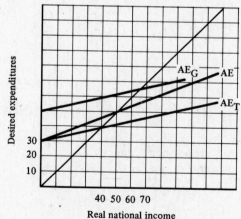

354

(a) The slope of the AE schedule is .40 and the tax rate is 10 percent. Thus $C = .40Y$ and $Y_d = .9Y$, giving $C = .44Y_d$. With a tax of 40 percent, $Y_d = .6Y$ and thus $C = .26Y$, causing the AE schedule to become AE_T. Raising G by $20M shifts the new schedule to AE_G.

(b) Between $60 and $70 million.

5. (a)

(1) AE	(2) AE
110	110
130	128
130	128
120	119

(b) Function 2 provides built-in stability since government expenditure responds inversely to change in private spending. Looking at the completed column above, function 2 <u>reduces</u> the fluctuations in <u>total</u> aggregate demand.

6. (a)

B($M)
− 50
− 25
0
+ 25
+ 50

(b)

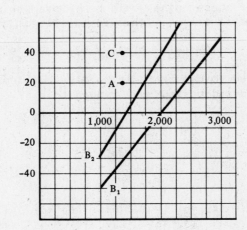

(c) A move A to C could only occur if either expenditure was cut, tax increased, or some combination to raise the surplus at Y = 1,300. The move would be restrictive policy.

<u>ANSWERS TO CHAPTER 35</u>

MULTIPLE-CHOICE QUESTIONS:

1. (b)   2. (c)   3. (a)   4. (b)   5. (d)   6. (c)   7. (b)   8. (b)   9. (d)
10. (a)   11. (c)   12. (b)   13. (a)   14. (d)   15. (d)   16. (a)   17. (b)
18. (b)   19. (a)   20. (a)   21. (d)

EXERCISES:

1.   (1) b   (2) c   (3) a   (4) d   (5) a

2. M_d = .2(100) = 20. The money supply is therefore 20. The income velocity is 1 ÷ .2 = 50. If the money supply is actually 25, an excess supply of money exists. Money holders will reduce their cash holdings and try to purchase more goods and services. However, since the economy is at full employment, prices will have to rise. In fact the price level will rise from 1.0 to 1.25.

3. (a) $1,000, $750, $250, 0
   (b) $1,000/2 = $500
   (c) $1,200/2 = $600
   (d) $500/2 = $250

4. (a) favorable (b) unfavorable (c) unfavorable (d) neutral
   (e) favorable (f) unfavorable (g) unfavorable (h) favorable or
   neutral, depending on the relationship between the inflation rate on real estate and goods and services in general

5. (a) Yes, by $240 million, because the coins were declared legal tender.
   (b) No; their value is determined by the monetary unit ascribed to them, which exceeds the value of the metal content.
   (c) No; their nominal value was fixed by the government.
   (d) If the metal content value exceeds the nominal value and/or the collectors' price, holders of these coins would be tempted to melt down the coins and sell them for their metal value. (This is an illegal act!)

6. (a) 8.17; 8.66; 8.84; 8.29; 8.16; 8.58; 9.62; 8.80; 9.97; 9.77
   (b) 12.5 percent = 1/8
   (c) People have tended to reduce their holdings of demand deposits. Their balances in savings deposits have tended to rise.

ANSWERS TO CHAPTER 36

MULTIPLE-CHOICE QUESTIONS:

1. (d) 2. (b) 3. (c) 4. (c) 5. (c) 6. (d) 7. (d) 8. (a) 9. (c)
10. (c) 11. (b) 12. (a) 13. (b) 14. (c) 15. (c)

EXERCISES:

1.

	Gold Standard	Bretton Woods System	Current Monetary Arrangements
International Monetary Fund		X	X
Effective fixed gold content for U.S. dollar	X		
Fluctuating exchange rate			X
Special drawing rights		X	X
Dollar convertible to gold domestically	X	X	X
Adjustable peg		X	
"Dirty" float			X
Free market for gold			X
Fixed exchange rates	X	X	

2. (a) If you anticipated a further decline in the price of the Canadian dollar, you might try to negotiate a fixed price of imports in terms of Canadian dollars. Hence, if the price of the Canadian dollar declines even further, you have protected yourself. The importer bears the risk of the exchange rate change. Of course, if you anticipate that the price of the Canadian dollar is going to rise, there is no need to protect yourself. You gain!

(b) You would be selling your Canadian dollars and buying foreign currencies that are either going to appreciate or maintain their value. If you are typical of all speculators, the price of the Canadian dollar would fall in the absence of Bank of Canada policy to maintain the current price.

3. (a) Since the demand for oil tends to be fairly inelastic, importers had to pay more for the same amount of oil. _Ceteris paribus_, this caused greater balance-of-payments deficits and hence the reserve positions of the oil-importing countries fell over the period 1974-1975. Of course, the reserve position of the oil-exporting countries rose substantially.

(b) Under the gold standard, the deficits of the oil-importing countries should generate a decrease in their money supplies and hence a reduction in the prices of their products. Exports to the oil-producing countries should rise and exports of oil should fall. The money supply in the oil-producing countries should be increased, generating inflation in those countries.

(c) If the petrodollars were recycled into investment projects in Canada, (i) employment in Canada should rise by the multiplier process, and (ii) Canada's reserves should increase.

(d) The price of the Canadian dollar would surely fall, _ceteris paribus_. The Bank of Canada, under a dirty-float system, might attempt to maintain the price of the Canadian dollar by buying Canadian dollars in the world exchange market. This means, however, that the reserve holdings of foreign currencies would fall. Speculators might pick up this piece of information and speculate that the Canadian authorities will not be able to protect the price of the Canadian dollar continually. Hence, they will sell Canadian dollars and buy other currencies. The Bank of Canada will have a much more difficult time protecting the price of the Canadian dollar.

ANSWERS TO CHAPTER 37

MULTIPLE-CHOICE QUESTIONS:

1. (c)　　2. (c)　　3. (a)　　4. (b)　　5. (b)　　6. (a)　　7. (c)　　8. (b)　　9. (d)
10. (d)　　11. (a)　　12. (c)　　13. (a)　　14. (d)　　15. (a)　　16. (b)　　17. (a)
18. (d)　　19. (a)　　20. (b)　　21. (a)　　22. (d)　　23. (c)　　24. (d)

EXERCISES:

1. M_1 = 26,456　(9,850 + 16,606)
M_{1B} = 34,789　(26,456 + 8,333)
M_2 = 103,728　(34,789 + 66,905 + 2,034)

2.

Assets		Liabilities	
Currency in vaults	$ 60,000	Demand deposits	$5,000,000
Deposits in B of C	1,000,000	Notice deposits	1,000,000
Loans to public	4,000,000		
Security holdings	1,500,000		
Banking building and fixtures	360,000	Capital and surplus	920,000
	$6,920,000		$6,920,000

3. (a) Reserves +100; deposits +100
    (b) Reserves +10,000; securities -10,000
    (c) Loans +5,000; deposits +5,000
    (d) Reserves +50,000; securities -50,000
    (e) Loans -5,000; deposits -5,000
    (f) Total reserves unchanged; currency +5,000 and reserve deposits with the Bank of Canada, -5,000

4. (a) Required reserves = $10,000. No.
    (b) Deposits -1,000 to 99,000 and reserves -1,000 to 9,000
    (c) Required reserves = 9,900; actual reserves = 9,000; hence reserve deficiency = 900.
    (d) Bank A: reserves +900; loans -900. Bank B: reserves -900; deposits -900.
    (e) No, but Bank B has a deficiency of 810.
    (f) Bank B: reserves +810; loans -810. Bank C: reserves -810; deposits -810.
    (g) No, but bank C has a deficiency of 729.
    (h) (-900 + -810 + -729) = 2,439. Loans down by 1,710.
    (i) 10,000; 9,000

5. Assets: (d), (e), (f); liabilities: (a), (b), (c).

6. (a)

Bank of Canada			All Banks		
Securities: +100	Bank reserves +100		Reserves: +100	Deposits +100	

    (b) $500 million.
    (c) Interest rates are likely to fall because banks wish to make new loans and hence reduce the loan rate. All interest rates will fall because other institutions will want to be competitive with the banks.

7. Bank of Canada: Securities, - $150 million; Bank Reserves, - $150 million
    Banking System: Securities, + $150 million; Reserves, - $150 million
    (a) No; deposits have not been affected.
    (b) Deficient reserves are equal to 150 million. Loans will be reduced by this amount.
    (c) Final decrease in the money supply is 10 times 150, or 1,500 million.

ANSWERS TO CHAPTER 38

MULTIPLE-CHOICE QUESTIONS:

1. (b)   2. (d)   3. (b)   4. (d)   5. (c)   6. (c)   7. (b)   8. (c)   9. (c)
10. (d)   11. (b)   12. (a)   13. (b)   14. (a)   15. (d)   16. (d)   17. (c)
18. (d)   19. (d)   20. (b)   21. (c)

EXERCISES:

1. (a) 15 percent   (b) 10 percent   (c) 14 percent   (d) 12 percent   (e) 12 percent; $100/(1.12)^2 = 79.72$

2. (a) $94.23 = 100/(1.02)^3$
    (b) $94.26 = 100/(1.03)^2$
    (c) $100/.17 = 588.24

3. (a) As the opportunity cost of money rises, people will tend to economize on their transactions demand for money. In addition, they are prepared to take more risk (and therefore buy more bonds) since the return on bonds has risen.

(b) Demand (either LP_1 or LP_0) equals supply at r = 9 percent.

(c) At r = 9 percent, an excess demand for money exists. Households and firms would sell bonds to satisfy their increased demand for money. Hence bond prices would fall and interest rates would rise.

(d) As interest rates rise, the quantity demanded falls until demand equals the lower value of the money supply. Interest rates would equal 10 percent and 9.5 percent for LP_0 and LP_1, respectively.

(e) If LP_0 applies, the money supply must be 700. If LP_1 applies, the money supply must be 800. Monetary policy aimed at lowering interest rates would be more effective if LP_0 applied since it takes only an increase in the money supply of 200 (700 - 500) rather than 300 (800 - 500).

4. (a) An increase of $10 million (1 x 1/.10 = 10).

(b) Since money supply increased by 10, the quantity demanded must increase by 10. This will be accomplished by a decrease in the interest rate and an increase in real national income.

(c) The interest rate will fall for several reasons. First, the Bank of Canada will increase the price of bonds to induce the public to sell their bonds. Secondly, since the banks have more reserves and extend more loans, the interest rate on loans will fall.

5. (a) 9 percent, at which demand is equal to supply.

(b) 200

(c) When Y = 1,580, AE = Y. The GNP gap is 1,600 - 1,580 = 20. The deflationary gap is 10.

(d) K = 1/(1 - .5) = 2. Autonomous expenditure must increase by 10 to achieve an increase in Y of 20.

(e) Since AE must increase, the interest rate must fall and hence the money supply must rise.

(f) 10

(g) The interest rate must fall from 9 percent to 8 percent.

(h) According to the diagram in exercise 3, the money supply must increase from 500 to 700: an increase of 200.

(i) Given the money expansion multiplier (1/.1 = 10) and the fact that the money supply must increase by 200, it follows that the Bank of Canada must purchase 20 of bonds from the open market.

(j) When Y = 1,600, C = 960 and AE = Y. This is equilibrium.

(k)

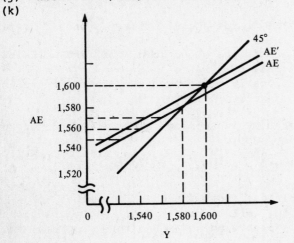
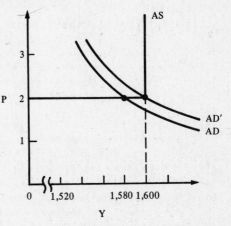

6. (a) Demand equals supply (50) at an interest rate of 10 percent. Investment is therefore 180.
   (b) If price increases, the LP shifts upward (the demand for money increases at every interest rate). Hence, decision-makers will sell their bonds and this drives the price of bonds down. As a consequence, the interest rate increases.
   (c) The new equilibrium interest rate is 14 percent.
   (d) The new level of investment is 170.
   (e) Y = AE at 360 (r = 10 percent and P = 1.0).
   (f) Investment is now 170. AE : 340, 345, 350, 355. AE = Y at 340. Income has fallen by 20.
   (g)

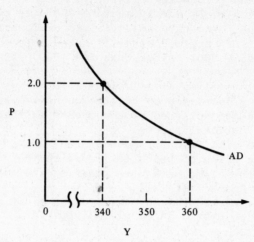

ANSWERS TO CHAPTER 39

MULTIPLE-CHOICE QUESTIONS:

1. (a)   2. (d)   3. (d)   4. (b)   5. (c)   6. (a)   7. (a)   8. (b)   9. (d)
10. (c)   11. (d)   12. (c)   13. (c)   14. (c)   15. (b)   16. (a)   17. (a)
18. (a)

EXERCISES:

1. (a) Deficient-demand because of the slowdown in economic activity.
   (b) Search, perhaps because of change in location or unwillingness to accept lower pay.
   (c) Frictional if short-term; structural if the social worker is unable to find work after a prolonged search.
   (d) Frictional if short-term; structural if the mechanic cannot find work in London or refused to move to Montreal.
   (e) Frictional because prospects are probably quite good that the business analyst will find a suitable job in a short period of time.

2. (a) Reduce the level of aggregate demand by increasing taxes, lowering government expenditure, and reducing the money supply.
   (b) Programs designed to change the structure of the economy, such as retraining and relocation policies.
   (c) The opposite of part (a).
   (d) Policies designed to convince decision-makers in the economy that the government is serious about reducing inflation; for example, contractionary monetary policy, higher taxes, lower government expenditure programs, and perhaps wage and price controls.

360

3. (a) Market A has excess demand; market B has excess supply.
    (b) Since the excess demand in A is equal to the excess supply in B, aggregate excess demand is zero and hence no deficient-demand unemployment exists. Another way of looking at this is to say that unfilled vacancies in A equal unemployed in B.
    (c) First, wages should rise in A and fall in B. This will cure the excess demand in A and excess supply in B. Second, labour in B should move to A. This will shift the supply curve of labour to the right in A and shift the supply curve in B to the left. Vacancies are filled in A and unemployment is eliminated in B.
    (d) People refuse to leave their current jobs because of nonmonetary considerations: do not know about job availabilities in other markets; are not qualified in terms of skills required by other markets.
    (e) The national unemployment rate would increase because unemployment is increased in market B. According to the diagram for market A, unfilled vacancies are eliminated. Since deficient-demand unemployment is defined by the difference between unfilled vacancies and unemployment, and given the fact that vacancies are zero and unemployment has risen, deficient-demand unemployment exists for the first time.
    (f) The wage in market A would rise, but the wage in market B stays the same. If wages rise it is likely that prices will also rise, and hence the inflation rate will increase. This inflation has the characteristics of structural inflation. If the excess supply of labour could have been transferred to market A, wages would not have risen in market A.

4. (a) The AD curve intersects the Y axis at 400 and the P axis at 8. The intersection of the AD and AS curves occurs at P = 2 and Y = 300.
    (b) The new equilibrium is P = 3 and Y = 300. The price level has risen. The inflation rate is 50 percent [(3 − 2) ÷ 2)]. The inflation is of the demand-pull variety.
    (c) The horizontal portion of the AS curve will shift up to P = 3.
    (d) Since the AS curve shifts up (the horizontal portion is now P = 4), there will be a movement up the AD curve P = 9 − .02Y. As a result, Y falls from 300 to 250.
    (e) The AD curve must become P = 10 − .02Y.

5. (a) Y_{FE} = 4,000 (there is no excess demand at that level of Y) and max Y = 4,400. It may be possible for firms to increase their capacity by using their capital more intensively and by obtaining overtime hours from their workers.
    (b) Excess demand has been created and as a result inflation has become 6 percent, which is of the demand-pull variety.
    (c) Since they observe the current inflation rate of 6 percent, they will come to expect future inflation of 6 percent.
    (d) If expectations become 6 percent, the actual inflation rate will become 12 percent, which consists of 6 percent of excess demand and 6 percent of expectational inflation.
    (e) The Phillips curve will shift upward such that at Y = 4,200 the rate of inflation is 12 percent.
    (f) When workers observe an actual inflation rate of 12 percent they will revise their expectations upward to 12 percent. They will negotiate wage increases that take into account 12 percent for expected inflation and 6 percent for excess-demand pressure, for a total of 18 percent. The Phillips curve will shift upward again such that at Y = 4,200 the rate of inflation is 18 percent.
    (g) The long-run Phillips curve is a vertical line at Y = 4,000. Any inflation that occurs will be of the expectational variety.

6. (a)

Time Period	Expected Inflation (%)	Actual Inflation (%)
3	5	10
4	10	15
5	15	20
6	20	25

   (b) Vertical at a 4-percent rate of unemployment.
   (c) Expectational inflation would be reduced. Actual inflation would eventually fall, perhaps to zero after a period of time.

ANSWERS TO CHAPTER 40

MULTIPLE-CHOICE QUESTIONS:

1. (c)   2. (b)   3. (d)   4. (d)   5. (b)   6. (d)   7. (c)   8. (b)   9. (a)
10. (a)   11. (c)   12. (c)   13. (b)

EXERCISES:

1. (a) Once the public has sold the foreign currency to the banks, their holdings of foreign currency fall by $40 million and their holdings of deposits rise by $40 million. Hence, the public has converted one asset into another.
    (b) The Bank of Canada simply increases the reserves of the banks by $40 million. Recall that reserves are deposits with the Bank of Canada. The Bank of Canada's holdings of foreign exchange increase by $40 million and the deposits of the banks in the Bank of Canada increase by $40 million.
    (c) The reserves of the banks increase by $40 million and the deposits of the public in the banks also increase by $40 million.
    (d) The banks now have excess reserves. Required reserves (additional) are $4 million and hence excess reserves are $36 million. The money supply will increase by $400 million ($40 million x 1/.1).
    (e) To prevent the money supply from increasing, the Bank of Canada should sell bonds to the banks or the public.

2. (a) AE = .5Y + 80 + 40 + (60 - 30). A = 120 + .6Y. The marginal propensity to spend is .5.
    (b) Y = 150/.5 = 300. Absorption (A) equals 300 and therefore net exports are zero.
    (c) Deflationary gap is 10/2 = 5. Increases in I and G are necessary. The needed change is equal to the value of the deflationary gap, which is equal to 5.
    (d) X still equals 60, but imports are now .1(310) + 30, or 61. Hence net exports are -1, a trade deficit. Domestic absorption is 311 = [125 + .6(310)].
    (e) upward; decreased; devaluing
    (f) Yes; exports will increase from 60 to 60.4. This is because the new terms of trade are 2/(2.04 x 1), which equals .98. Imports also increase from 60 to 60.4. This is because national income is 310 and the terms of trade are .98. Domestic absorption is also 310.

3. (a) The capital-account curve is downward sloping because as the domestic interest rate falls, capital outflows occur and less capital comes into this country. Hence the capital account surplus falls as the domestic interest rate falls.
    (b) The capital account is balanced. The current account is also balanced.

(c) balanced. As the exchange rate falls, exports rise and imports fall and hence the current-account surplus increases.
(d) (i) balanced
(ii) $0Q_2$; $0Q_1$; deficit; $0Q_2 - 0Q_1$
(iii) $0Q_3$; $0Q_4$; surplus; $0Q_3 - 0Q_4$
(e) sold; rises; r_1; inflows; surplus
(f) appreciate; decrease; increase; deficit; surplus

ANSWERS TO CHAPTER 41

MULTIPLE-CHOICE QUESTIONS:

1. (a)   2. (d)   3. (b)   4. (c)   5. (c)   6. (c)   7. (b)   8. (d)   9. (b)
10. (a)   11. (a)   12. (a)

EXERCISES:

1. (a) $Y = 798$, $P = 3$. The AD curve is downward sloping and linear.
   (b) GNP gap equals $800 - 798 = 2$. If the AS curve is AS_1, the GNP gap is 3.
   (c) increased, right, 800
   (d) $Y = 800$, $P = 4$. The horizontal portion of the AS curve shifts upward to $P = 4$ for levels of income less than and equal to 800.

2. (a) As the text explains, the period 1949-1956 represented full employment without inflation (except for 1951). Minor changes in aggregate demand caused fluctuations in employment and inflation. However, in the period 1957-1970, there was a tendency for the price level to rise despite a significant GNP gap (high unemployment). This seemed to imply a spontaneous upward shift in the horizontal portion of the AS curve <u>not</u> associated with any excess demand. Hence, in order to reduce inflation, it was necessary to reduce real output and generate higher unemployment.
   (b) Inflation increased from 1.2 to 3.7 percent. This inflation is of the demand-pull variety.

3. (a) Prices rise and real output falls. The horizontal portion of the AS curve shifts upward.
   (b) Y_F is sustained, but the price level rises. The AD curve shifts upward to the right. In addition, the horizontal portion of the AS curve shifts upward.
   (c) Wage cost-push inflation will cause price levels to rise and real output to fall. The horizontal portion of the aggregate supply curve shifts upward. However, if monetary policy validates this inflation the final result will be that prices rise but Y_F is sustained. The expansionary monetary policy causes the AD curve to shift upward to the right.
   (d) The AD curve will shift to the left and hence real output will fall but the price level will remain constant.
   (e) The kink in the AS curve will increase to the right. There will be no change in real output (in the absence of a shift in the AD curve) and prices will remain constant.
   (f) The money supply increase will cause the AD curve to shift upward but the price controls keep the price level at P_0. When the price control is lifted, prices will rise and the horizontal portion of the AS curve will shift upward. This post-control increase in prices is referred to as the "bubble" effect.

MULTIPLE-CHOICE QUESTIONS:

1. (d)   2. (b)   3. (a)   4. (d)   5. (d)   6. (d)   7. (c)   8. (a)   9. (b)
10. (d)   11. (b)   12. (a)
A.1. (c)   A.2. (a)   A.3. (c)

EXERCISES:

1. (a) K   (b) M   (c) M   (d) M   (e) K   (f) M   (g) M   (h) K
   (i) K   (j) K
2. (a) A deflationary gap of 1 ÷ 2 = $.5 billion. Also a GNP gap of $1 billion.
   (b) Yes; the increase in G will have an expansionary effect of $1 billion (.5 times 2).
   (c) Since in equilibrium 100 = .8(150) − 2i, i equals 10 percent.
   (d) The interest rate would rise to 10.4 percent. This is shown by the expression 100 = .8(151) − 2i.
   (e) Since the interest rate has increased by .4, it follows that investment expenditure falls by $500 million.
   (f) The interest rate increases by .4, but investment expenditure falls by only 4 x $25 million, or $.1 billion.
   (g) The crowding-out effect for part (e) is 100 percent or $.5 billion. The crowding-out effect for part (f) is $.1 billion. A strict monetarist is likely to advocate the result of part (e).

3. (a) Interest rate is currently 10 percent according to the equation.
   (b) The interest rate increases from 10 to 10.4 percent.
   (c) The money supply would have to increase from 60 to 60.8 in order to maintain an interest rate of 10 percent.

4. (a) The interest rate is 10 percent for both cases. The demand for money must be 400 in each case. Investment expenditure is 100 in each case.
   (b) Arc elasticity is −20/390 divided by 2/11 for Case A and −4/398 divided by 2/11 for Case B. Quite clearly, Case A has the highest interest elasticity and Case B the lowest. A monetarist is likely to advocate Case B.
   (c) Arc elasticity is −2/99 divided by 2/11 for Case A and −40/80 divided by 2/11 for Case B. Case A has the lowest interest elasticity of investment and would therefore reflect the view of a Keynesian.
   (d) The interest rate would fall to 9 percent in Case A and 5 percent in Case B.
   (e) If you were a monetarist you would use Case B for both the demand for money and investment expenditure. Hence, when the interest rate falls from 10 to 5 percent, investment expenditure rises from 100 to 200. This represents a very large increase in investment. If you were a Keynesian you would use Case A for both schedules. Hence, when the interest rate falls from 10 to 9 percent, investment expenditure rises from 100 to 101.

ANSWERS TO CHAPTER 43

MULTIPLE-CHOICE QUESTIONS:

1. (c)   2. (d)   3. (c)   4. (b)   5. (a)   6. (a)   7. (a)   8. (c)   9. (b)
10. (b)   11. (b)   12. (d)   13. (b)   14. (a)   15. (b)

EXERCISES:

1. (a) 4 percent = 2.5 percent + 1.75 percent − .25 percent
   (b) 4 percent − 1 percent = 3 percent
   (c) Using the "rule of 72," it will take 72/4 = 18 years.
   (d) 72/3 = 24 years

2. (a) decrease
   (b) increase current but decrease future
   (c) increase because the economy becomes more productive
   (d) decrease current but likely increase future
   (e) decrease current but likely increase future
   (f) decrease

ANSWERS TO CHAPTER 44

MULTIPLE-CHOICE QUESTIONS:

1. (d)   2. (b)   3. (d)   4. (b)   5. (c)   6. (d)   7. (d)   8. (d)

EXERCISES:

1.

	Country A	Country B	Difference
Year X	$2,000	$100	$1,900
Year X + 1	2,060	103	1,957
Year X + 23	4,000	200	3,800

2. (a) 18; 24; 72
   (b) 3 percent

3. (a) Opportunity costs are increasing in both countries. For example, in country
       A, to obtain an increase in 10 bushels of wheat from 20 to 30, the loss in
       production in peanuts is 3. However, to increase wheat from 30 to 40, a loss
       of 4 is required. For country B, an increase of wheat from 20 to 40 requires
       a loss of 10. An increase of wheat from 40 to 60 requires a loss of 11 pounds
       of peanuts.

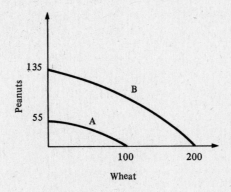

(b) A combination of 80 wheat and 16 peanuts represents X-inefficiency or a point inside the production-possibility frontier in country A. It is technically possible for country A to produce 80 and 19. However, country B is operating on its production-possibility frontier.

(c) GNP in country A is $2 x 80 plus $.5 x 16, which equals $168. GNP in country B is $2 x 160 plus $.5 x 35, which equals $337.5. Per capita GNP in country A is 168 divided by 8, which equals $21. Per capita GNP in country B is 337.5 divided by 10, which equals $33.75.

(d) Country B has avoided X-inefficiency. Although country A and country B have the same amount of resources, the resources in country B are used more efficiently. This may be due to differences in social and cultural attitudes, differences in market organization, or differences in labour skills and productivity. Land quality might also differ.

(e) Aid might come in many forms: retraining labour and improving land cultivation by various Canadian experts from agricultural schools in Canada; increasing the capital intensity of production by giving country A more tractors and other farm equipment; introducing better peanut and wheat seed. Hopefully, the production-possibility frontier would shift to the right in time.

Alternatively, living standards in country A could be improved by simply giving country A more wheat or peanuts as an outright gift. This would allow consumption to be greater than production, but it is hard to believe that this is an appropriate long-run solution to country A's problems.

82 83 84 85 9 8 7 6 5 4 3 2 1 ·